# 1,001
## Questions
### — *and* —
## Answers
## on Pesach

By the same author

Understanding the Synagogue Service (1974)
A Samaritan Chronicle (1982)
Festival Adventure (1982)
Understanding the High Holyday Services (1983)
Horizons of Jewish Prayer (1986)
Moments of Insight (1989)
Blessed Are You (1993)
Prayer and Penitence (1994)

# 1,001
## Questions
## — *and* —
## Answers
## on Pesach

Jeffrey M. Cohen

JASON ARONSON INC.
*Northvale, New Jersey*
*London*

11/9/10

The author gratefully acknowledges permission to quote from the following sources:

*Indian–Jewish Cooking* by Mavis Hyman, copyright © 1992 Hyman Publishers.
Used by permission.

"Pesach as a Child in Iran" by Parry Faigenblum, *At* magazine, March 1984.
Copyright © 1984 Emunah. Used by permission of *At* magazine.

Quotation from letter by Mavis Hyman used by permission.

This book was set in 10 pt. Times by AeroType, Inc., Amherst, NH.

**Library of Congress Cataloging-in-Publication Data**

Cohen, Jeffrey M.
   1001 Questions and answers on Pesach / by Jeffrey M. Cohen.
     p.  cm.
   Includes bibliographical references (p.    ) and index.
   ISBN 1-56821-523-1 (alk. paper)
   1. Passover—Customs and practices—Miscellanea.  I. Title.
BM695.P35C64  1996
296.4'37—dc20
                                     95-22903

BM
695
.P35
C64
1996

Manufactured in the United States of America. Jason Aronson Inc. offers books and
cassettes. For information and catalog write to Jason Aronson Inc., 230 Livingston Street, Northvale,
New Jersey 07647.

To Gloria,
with affection and gratitude

And to our children,
Harvey and Lorraine,
Suzanne and Keith,
Judith and Bobby, Lewis
and our grandchildren,
Joel, Phil, Alexander, Elliot, and Abigail

# Contents

# Foreword

No festival more powerfully embodies the Jewish experience than does Pesach. On it we recall the formative moment when the children of Israel became a people and first encountered the presence of God in epic events of history. We remember the slavery and oppression of our ancestors in Egypt and the great series of miracles that led to their redemption. We speak of large themes: servitude, freedom, exile, exodus, the "mighty hand" of God and the journey of a people across the wilderness in search of a physical and spiritual home. These have been the great motifs of the Jewish journey ever since, and it is on Pesach that we see them prefigured and given their most vivid expression.

More than this, it is on Pesach that we witness the miracle of Jewish continuity. It is the time, more than any other, when we hand on our story to our children, helping them to see that our journey is also theirs and that they are part of an immense drama that began more than three thousand years ago but that still continues and in which they have their part to play. We do not so much recall the ancient past as reenact it, eating *matzah* as Jews did long ago, tasting the bitter herbs of slavery and drinking four cups of the wine of freedom. There can be few more arresting moments than the one with which we begin the Seder service, lifting the *matzah* and saying, "This is the bread of affliction that our ancestors ate in the land of Egypt." With a single sentence we bridge the centuries, bringing past and present together and offering both to the future as our children's heritage. Not lightly did the rabbis say that "in every generation a person must see himself as if he personally went out of Egypt." More than it is about history, Pesach is about memory, that past that belongs to me, with which I identify and which makes me who I am. Pesach is about the handing on of Jewish memory across the generations.

From the very outset, the Torah speaks about the festival in terms of the asking of questions. "And when your children ask you, 'What does this ceremony mean to you?' then tell them, 'It is the Passover sacrifice to the Lord who passed over the houses of the Israelites in Egypt . . .'" (Exodus 12:26). Questions, not answers, are the beginning of understanding, and the genius of Pesach is the way it transforms the query "What is this?" into the more fundamental one of "Who am I?" It is by asking that we begin the long journey from curiosity to knowledge and ultimately to identity. Whether as children or as adults, on Pesach we are encouraged to ask. Traditionally on the Seder night we begin by asking four questions. But we also say about asking and answering, "The more one does so, the more one is to be praised."

At the hands of one of our master exponents, Rabbi Dr. Jeffrey Cohen, the four questions have become a thousand and one, and using Pesach's own distinctive pattern of query-and-reply, he has provided us in this book with a magnificent and encyclopedic survey of the festival, its laws and customs, meaning and history. The literature on Pesach is vast, and yet no reader can browse through this volume without coming time and again across new insights and explanations or scholarly investigations not encountered before. From the opening page, with its fascinating analysis of the etymology of *Mitzrayim,* the biblical name for Egypt, through to a closing survey of local Pesach customs throughout the world, we are led through a captivating tour of discovery, combining history, archaeology, philology, classic Jewish interpretation, original commentary, halakhah, and ethical reflection.

Rabbi Cohen has important things to say about the interplay between the natural and supernatural, miracle and history, and the relationship between the archaeological record and Jewish self-understanding. He guides us through the record of how Pesach has been celebrated from biblical times through to the present day, an important chapter of Jewish history in its own right, and lets us see how each era added its own contribution to the festival and its customs, even if sometimes, as during the "blood libels," this was etched with pain. His summary of the often complex laws of Pesach is clear and concise, and his history of the Haggadah, with its excursions into Samaritan and Karaite practice, is shot through with points of interest. Commenting on the Haggadah itself, Rabbi Cohen speculates on what the five rabbis may have talked about in their long night in Bnei Brak, why we are told to "blunt the teeth" of the "wicked" son and why we open the door when saying "Pour out Thy wrath."

But these are only highlights in a work of astonishing scope and erudition. There is hardly an aspect of this multifaceted subject that the author has not illuminated with his scholarship, as broad as it is deep, to which he has added his own creative insights in generous measure. Rabbi Cohen writes within a great tradition, bringing together Torah and *chokhmah,* Jewish wisdom and the broad panoply of human knowledge, and finding in their interplay a never-ending source of deepened understanding. He is both sage and man of faith, a lucid teacher and a source of inspiration, and no one will read this work without discovering that the festival they thought they knew so well has a depth and history that are enthralling. Scheherazade, so Arabic legend has it, had a thousand and one nights but only a single question, how to keep the sultan from falling asleep. On Pesach we have only one night (two in the Diaspora), but Rabbi Cohen has provided us with a thousand and one questions, and their effect is the same, keeping our interest alive in the inexhaustible dimensions of this festival of freedom and Jewish memory.

In his introduction, Rabbi Cohen reflects on the role of questions in Jewish spirituality. Famously, even notoriously, we are a people of questions. Some of the most famous utterances of the patriarchs and prophets were addressed as searching questions to God. In the Book of Job, God answers man's inquiries with a list of questions of His own. An early genre of the sermon, known as the *Yelamdenu,* began with a question asked of the rabbi by a member of the congregation. A major branch of rabbinic literature exists in the form of *She'elot uteshuvot,* questions and answers on points of Jewish law. In place of Descartes' "I think, therefore I am," Judaism would have substituted, "I ask, therefore I learn." Why do questions figure so prominently in the landscape of the Jewish mind?

Rabbi Cohen offers an intriguing suggestion of his own, which I leave the reader to discover. If I were to add one observation, it would be this: Pesach is the beginning of a journey, not its end. Since the days of Abraham and Sarah, Jews have known that they are called on to travel, sometimes physically, always spiritually, and faith itself— *emunah* — is the courage to undertake that journey, knowing that we will not complete it but that it has an ultimate destination that we call the Messianic age. A question is the beginning of a journey. It testifies to the faith that there is an answer even if, within this life, we do not reach it. Judaism acknowledges mysteries that lie beyond the finite limits of human understanding. But it has never contented itself with the resignation of indifference. The prophets, Sages, and philosophers searched, knowing perhaps that what they looked for lay beyond the horizon, but understanding that in partial answers and fragmentary insights lay a great adventure of the spirit, one of the greatest human civilization has known. Asking is the intellectual equivalent of traveling, and it begins, as does the Jewish journey, on Pesach itself.

The traditional way in which our queries start on Pesach is with the metaquestion, *Mah nishtanah halaylah hazeh,* Why is this night different from all other nights? The reply, taking us as it does through so much of Jewish history and faith, Jewish law and practice, does more than answer the question to which it was addressed. It tells us why this people is different from all others. Pesach is the Jewish story, and in it lies the secret of our singularity.

Rabbi Dr. Jonathan Sacks
Chief Rabbi of the United Hebrew Congregations
of the Commonwealth

# Preface

My purpose in writing this book is to provide, in one volume, as much information as possible on every aspect of the festival of Pesach. Pesach is a time when curiosity is aroused and interest rekindled regarding the multidimensional facets of our tradition. More time, effort, and money are invested in preparing for this festival than for any other; more and more people are returning to traditional religious practice, and, particularly as regards Pesach, they want "to get it right." More and more editions of the Haggadah appear each year; more and more people are eager to make their Seder nights interesting and informative; and more and more people are thirsting for explanations of the many rituals, laws, and customs that are associated with Pesach.

Of course, there are thousands of books on the background history of the festival, on its talmudic and halakhic sources and prescriptions, on its liturgy and commentaries on the Haggadah, on the practicalities of preparing for the festival, on the dos and don'ts of *Yom Tov* observance, and on the unique customs of exotic Jewish communities around the world. But one requires a lifetime to wade through them! My rash objective is to provide all that, in a readable manner, in one volume: in short, a veritable encyclopedia of Pesach.

Though written particularly for the Orthodox reader, who will be especially concerned for the minutiae of the halakhic dimensions, it is my hope that what is presented will inspire all my readers to greater observance by reawakening their interest in the fascinating traditions of the millenia, as well as through greater appreciation of the reasons for, and relevance of, everything that is prescribed. In presenting all the laws and customs, I have gone back to basic principles and described them in the context of their historical and sociological evolution. In some instances I have provided a *kitzur* (digest) of the *Kitzur Shulchan Arukh,* the official *Digest of the Code of Jewish Law.* In others, I have supplemented and gone beyond that compendium in citing present-day halakhic opinion and unique modern-day issues and situations.

A glance at the Table of Contents will reveal the broad scope of the book. Anyone seeking guidance as to how to prepare the home and kitchen for Pesach—newlyweds, students, converts, and so on—will welcome this volume, as will those more interested in the history of the festival and how it was celebrated down the ages. Those seeking to enrich and enliven their Seder with questions and answers on every detail of the festival, the ritual, and the Haggadah will, I trust, not be disappointed;

and anyone looking for questions to keep the youngsters' interest alive throughout the Seder, and during the succeeding days, will find them in this book.

I have tried to ensure that this is not a run-of-the-mill, superficial, question-and-answer manual. Every question is dealt with authoritatively, with reference to the sources. Where the answer could be given in a few sentences, a brief answer is employed. And where a few pages are required, they are provided. I have endeavored to marshal my information as lucidly as possible, so that both beginners as well as the religiously initiated and learned might profit from it. I have tried to write a book for college students and their parents, for teachers and homemakers, for rabbis and laymen.

The vehicle I have chosen—question and answer—is, of course, eminently appropriate for this festival, the details of which the Torah itself reveals in the context of questions that our children will ask in the future, and answers that we must have at the ready.

But "the question" has an even greater claim to primacy on this festival. There is a hackneyed, but relevant, Jewish witticism about a gentile who once asked a Jewish friend why Jews always answer one question with another. "Why not?" replied the Jew.

Questions spring naturally from the lips of our coreligionists, perhaps because our very existence has had the question mark placed against it down every page of our history. Indeed, the redemption from Egypt commenced with a question answered by a question. Moses' first words to his people, on leaving the royal palace and donning the mantle of champion and deliverer of his people, were framed as a question. When he saw one Hebrew striking another, he said to the former: "Why are you smiting your brother?" (Exodus 2:13). And the answer of that violent Israelite was to hurl back an insolent, rhetorical question in Moses' direction: "Who made you a ruler and judge over us?" (v. 14).

Again, at the Burning Bush, when Moses was given his mission to go down to Egypt and secure the freedom of Israel, his very first words to God were couched as a question: "Who am I that I should go to Pharaoh?" (Exodus 3:11).

Even Pharaoh's first recorded words to Moses were in question form: "Who is the Lord that I should listen to His voice?" (5:2); and the one and only time the collective voice of a Jewish demonstration against Pharaoh was heard, it also mouthed a pained question. Before Moses and Aaron managed to assume full representative authority, we are told that the Jewish overseers, who were appointed to ensure the full daily quota of bricks was produced, complained to Pharaoh, saying, "Why do you deal in such a way with your servants?" (5:15).

So, if anyone should ask why we ask so many questions on Pesach, we are entitled to answer, "Why not?" Questions are of the very essence of the spirit of this festival. And all the questions asked by all the Jews the world over can be distilled into one awesome question: Why did we merit the unique divine grace that has been extended to us in every generation?

Every theological question that the Jew asks is merely an attempt to unravel that one mystery. That is the question within all questions. And still God answers with a question. And still we have to provide the answers. And that is why I have chosen the "question and answer" genre for this book which, hopefully, will provide some extra insight into how we have viewed and celebrated our redemption from Egypt, and how we must acclaim the miracle of our redemption — *kol yemei chayyekha* — every day of our lives.

I would like to offer thanks and acknowledgement to several people who have been of great assistance in my research for this book. Primarily, I thank my beloved wife, Gloria, for her infinite patience and indulgence, enabling me to lock myself in my study, burn the midnight oil, ignore the numerous calls for meals, and generally be unsociable around the house, in order to complete this book within eight months. I thank her for being a wise sounding board and for many helpful suggestions.

I also thank friends and members of my Stanmore and Canons Park congregation in London for firsthand reminiscences of how Pesach was observed in the far-flung countries from which their families hailed, and from which some of them had themselves fled to find refuge and a more vibrant Jewish life in Britain. Those reminiscences have guaranteed the accuracy of our chapter on Pesach customs from around the world (Chapter 21).

An important facet of Jewish life over the past few decades, not only in Israel but also in the United States and Britain, has been the arrival of coreligionists from such far-flung countries as Iran, Iraq, Syria, Egypt, India, and Morocco. Marriage and acculturation into the Ashkenazi, or even Sephardi, host community could well spell the suppression and loss of many of their own distinctive, traditional Pesach customs. This would be most sad, not only for their families but also for the many who feel that such customs should at least be chronicled, if not observed.

One of the aims of Chapter 21, "Pesach Customs from around the World," is to ensure that those customs are not forgotten and to provide a nostalgic forum for their literary preservation. In this context, I thank Mrs. Tricia Brickman; Mr. Nicky Cohanim; Mrs. Parry Faigenblum; Mr. Percy Gourgey, M.B.E.; Mrs. Mavis Hyman; Rabbi Dr. Abraham Levy; my mechutanim, Mr. Ralph Levy and Mr. Max Moryoussef; Mr. David Moradoff; Mr. Victor Sassoon; Mr. Mendel Sudak; and Mrs. Ruth Synett.

I would also like to place on record my thanks to my dear nephew, Mr. Michael Cohen, for providing quiz questions for the younger generation (Chapter 22), to my dear son, Mr. Harvey Cohen, for reading and correcting the proofs, and to Mr. Ezra Kahn and his helpful staff, librarians of my alma mater, Jews' College, for their help in answering my various bibliographical inquiries.

I also acknowledge with thanks the permission granted to me by the editor of the *Emunah* ("At") magazine to quote freely from an article by Parry Faigenblum that appeared in its March 1984 edition, as well as by Mrs. Mavis Hyman for permission to quote from her book, *Indian–Jewish Cooking* (1992).

*Acharon acharon chaviv* — My sincere thanks to Chief Rabbi, Dr. Jonathan Sacks, for his encouragement and for gracing this book with his illuminating Foreword.

To all the above: *Tavo aleihem berakhah,* blessings and thanks.

# I

# Historical Background

## THE PROMISE TO ABRAHAM

**1. When God revealed to Abraham that his children would not inherit the Promised Land until they had first experienced servitude and affliction in a foreign land for four hundred years (Genesis 15:13), He also told Abraham that "The nation whom they serve I shall judge" (v. 14). We may ask why the Egyptians should have been punished at all if they were merely carrying out God's clear purpose!**

Moses Nachmanides, in his commentary on the verse, emphasizes the significance of the phrase "the nation whom they serve." God's plan was merely that the Israelites should experience "servitude." But this does not necessarily involve "affliction." There are many masters who treat their slaves kindly. God did indeed tell Abraham that "they will afflict them," but that constituted treatment that went beyond God's brief to the Egyptians. In the words of Nachmanides, "It goes without saying that casting the Israelite babes into the Nile goes far beyond the licence to make them serve, or even to afflict them. It is veritable genocide!" And for that the Egyptians deserved God's "judgment." Nachmanides goes on to draw the analogy of someone for whom it is decreed on Rosh Hashanah that he should die violently. The killer cannot offer the excuse that it was clearly God's decision that the man should die and that he was only acting as the divine agent. The reality is that he is still guilty of a murderous act, even though God was carrying out His own purpose by utilizing his violence as the means for punishing another sinner. Like that killer, the Egyptians still had to account for their evil actions.

**2. If God promised Abraham that his children would inherit the land of Canaan, why was there a delay of so many difficult centuries for the Israelites? Why not simply let Abraham's offspring remain in Canaan, multiply, and take over the land?**

The Torah itself provides an explanation when it relates that God told Abraham, "A fourth generation shall return hither, since the iniquity of the Amorites shall not be complete until that time" (Genesis 15:16). God, like any true judge, may not show partiality, even to His Chosen People, by taking away *without cause* land belonging to indigenous peoples. The land of Canaan is a uniquely spiritual land, "constantly

surveyed by the eyes of the Lord from the beginning to the end of each year"
(Deuteronomy 11:12). A basic level of moral and ethical behavior is expected of any
people (Israel included) that lives there.

God, therefore, disclosed to Abraham that a time would come, four generations in
the future, when the Amorite degeneracy would have reached such a cumulative level
that they would by then have forfeited their right to occupy God's favored land. Until
that time they were to be given ample opportunity to repent of their ways. Hence, the
children of Abraham had to be patient and wait until their moment of destiny arrived.

Perhaps another reason may also be that Abraham's offspring had to build up their
backbone and learn how to cope with adversity before they could expect to successfully occupy the land of Israel. To do so was no easy task. It was a land, not only
favored by God, but also coveted by many tribes and neighbouring states. It was the
land that straddled the "Fertile Crescent," the only trade route linking the two most
important cultural regions of antiquity: Mesopotamia and Egypt. Any other route
meant traveling through parched and inhospitable desert, the home of marauding
bedouin and wild animals. Whoever controlled Canaan enjoyed not only the lucrative
income from the imposition of transportation tolls and taxes on those traveling
through, but also the benefit of international maritime trade along its long Mediterranean shore. The experiences in Egypt, however harsh and tough, nevertheless
conditioned the Israelites to be able to protect themselves and deal with the many
problems of retaining their independence in the midst of a very violent and turbulent
environment. It also gave the Israelites an intimate knowledge of the power and
organization, as well as the psychology, of the Egyptian nation, which would always
remain one of the greatest threats to Israel's safety and stability.

## WHEN ISRAEL WAS IN EGYPT'S LAND

### 3.  What is the basic meaning of the Hebrew word for Egypt, *Mitzrayim*?

The biblical lexicons generally state that the origin of the name is "dubious." It is
composed of two elements: (i) the core form, *mzr,* and (ii) what looks like a dual
ending, *ayim.* The form *mzr* is most probably the equivalent of the Hebrew noun
*matzor,* "a fortress." The Aramaic word *mitzra* and the Akkadian form *mitzru* both
mean "boundary," and we may assume, therefore, that *Mitzrayim* denotes a fortified
or demarcated region.

### 4.  But what is the particular sense of the dual ending (ayim)? We understand its use in such nouns as yadayim ("two hands"), eynayim ("two eyes"), and raglayim ("two legs"), but it seems rather unusual and inapplicable for the name of a single country?

It is actually not so unusual. When the patriarch Jacob divided up his household
into two camps to confront his brother Esau, we are told that, "He called the name of
the place *machanayim,* 'Two Camps' " (Genesis 32:3). Other such place names are

*Bet Divlatayim* (Jeremiah 48:22), *Kiryatayim* (1 Chronicles 6:61), *Aram Naharayim* (Genesis 24:10), and, of course, *Yerushalayim* (Jerusalem).

Many and varied explanations have been offered, however, by scholars to explain the precise sense of the dual ending in the name *Mitzrayim*. It was most probably employed to emphasize inclusiveness, indicative of the fact that the country embraces the territory of both Upper and Lower Egypt. Those two regions originally constituted separate countries, but they were united by the earliest known Pharaoh of the first dynasty, Menes, who reigned around 4,000 B.C.E. His immediate successors, whose capital was in Memphis, in Upper Egypt, and their royal descendants, who reigned from Thebes, 600 kilometers to the south, in Lower Egypt, wore a double crown to emphasize the extent of their "dual" sovereignty, incorporating the "white crown" of Upper Egypt and the "red crown" of Lower Egypt. This was reinforced on the sides of their throne by the representation of two Nile gods intertwining the papyrus reed of the upper Nile Delta and the lotus of the lower Nile valley, which was symbolic of the union of the two states.

### 5. What precisely does the name Pharaoh mean?

This word, which is found 275 times in the Hebrew Bible, is a close Hebrew approximation of the Egyptian title, *Pr-'o,* meaning "Great House." Originally it would have been the simple designation of his palace. The title was then transferred to the government, after which it was reserved as the exclusive title of the monarch, who represented the embodiment of governance.

While there are biblical references to two Egyptian monarchs by their personal names, Pharaoh Hofra (Jeremiah 44:30) and Pharaoh Necho (Jeremiah 46:2; 2 Kings 23:29, 33–35), throughout the Bible it is by the title "Pharaoh" alone that reference to the Egyptian king is made. The employment of the monarch's title rather than his proper name was probably influenced by Egyptian etiquette, which avoided reference to the first name of one whom they revered as a divine being. Another reason may well have been simple convenience, since "royal names were composed of several symbolic expressions, and, in addition, hierarchic etiquette demanded that, before and after the mention of the name, a whole series of conventional laudatory terms should be pronounced" (A. S. Yahuda, *The Language of the Pentateuch in Its Relation to Egyptian,* London: Oxford University Press, 1933, p. 45). Thus, to avoid a most cumbersome reference, people simply referred to their king as the *Pr-'o,* "The Great House," and hence the biblical "Pharaoh."

### 6. Was there any contact between Israelites and Egyptians prior to the arrival of Joseph to Egypt?

There was. One must bear in mind that, according to Genesis 10:6, the founding fathers of Canaan (where the Hebrews lived) and Egypt were brothers, sons of Ham and grandsons of Noah. That kinship inevitably created a common bond at that early period of history, and helps to explain why Canaanites were made welcome whenever they sought refuge in Egypt from the droughts that regularly afflicted their own country.

Egypt was blessed with an abundance of water due to the regular overflowing of the banks of the Nile. The Egyptian farmers dug irrigation channels to carry the precious water throughout the country, thereby making it a source of great fertility: hence the biblical description of Egypt as "the garden of the Lord" (Genesis 13:10), and hence the regular migration of tribes, including the Israelites, into Egypt, where there was always a lush and plentiful supply of well-watered pasturage for their flocks.

But that did not mean that Egyptian hospitality was not without its hazards, especially for those who, like Abraham, did not hail from the common Hamitic stock. Abraham descended from Ham's brother Shem, whose moral and spiritual values were infinitely greater than those of his brother. Accordingly, before one such flight to Egypt, Abraham begged his wife, Sarai, to declare, if the Egyptians questioned her, that he was not her husband but her brother. He was certain that if they thought he was her husband, they would have no qualms in slaying him and seizing his exceedingly beautiful wife. His apprehensions were well-founded, for Sarai was indeed taken to the harem of the Pharaoh, while her "brother," Abraham, was plied with gifts. It was only when God visited a fearsome plague upon Pharaoh's household that, attributing it to his seizure of a married woman, he released her, but not without first chastizing Abraham for his deception (Genesis ch. 12).

### 7. How did the Israelites come to be enslaved in Egypt?

It is a long story, and one in which the hand of divine providence is visible at every stage. The outline of the story is that Joseph, the son of his father, Jacob's, old age, antagonizes his eleven older brothers by disclosing to them, rather rashly, the recurring contents of his dreams. There were two themes: the first, that the sun, moon, and eleven stars (representing his father, mother, and eleven brothers) came and did homage to him; the second, suggestive of the identical destiny, that the sheaves of corn belonging to his eleven brothers surrounded his sheaves, and bowed low to them in homage. These dreams convinced his brothers that he was suffering from delusions of grandeur and was determined to seize the position of leadership of the Israelite clan.

They take the opportunity, one day, of kidnapping Joseph and selling him to a passing cavalcade of traders, who, in turn, sell him into Egypt as a slave in the household of Potiphar, one of Pharaoh's highest military officers. Joseph distinguishes himself but soon finds himself in jail on a trumped-up charge of seducing Potiphar's wife. While in jail, he correctly interprets the troublesome dreams of Pharaoh's butler and baker, and, some two years later, the butler brings Joseph to the attention of Pharaoh, who is also seeking an interpretation of his troubled dreams.

Joseph not only expounds the dreams as foreshadowing the arrival of seven years of plenty followed by seven years of unprecedented famine, but he also provides Pharaoh with a unique blueprint for the avoidance of the otherwise disastrous consequences of the famine. Pharaoh is so impressed that he appoints Joseph to the rank of Viceroy of Egypt and entrusts to him supreme authority. Joseph oversees the building of store-cities to contain all the grain that is to be stored during the seven years of plenty, in readiness for the years of famine.

Before long, a famine stalks Canaan, and Joseph's brothers are sent to buy grain. This is also a long, and drama-packed, episode (Genesis chs. 42–46),* culminating in a reconciliation between Joseph and his brothers and his persuading them to come, with their now-aged father, Jacob, to settle in Egypt in the province of Goshen, under his protection and without fear for the looming Egyptian famine: hence the Israelite presence in Egypt, inaugurating a happy period of residence for the Israelites—and, at the same time, witnessing the fulfillment of Joseph's dreams! (See questions 871–880 for a fuller account of this episode.)

It was a few generations later, when a new Egyptian dynasty was established in Egypt, that fear of the extent of Israelite influence and power took root and a gradual process of deprivation of rights was introduced, ultimately leading to total enslavement.

## ARCHAEOLOGICAL EVIDENCE

**8. Bearing in mind that no Egyptian records refer to any of the events of the Israelite period as recorded in the Bible, are we not forced to conclude that the implausible story of (the Semite) Joseph's meteoric rise to power in an alien country is nothing more than a fascinating legend?**

There is no necessity for such a conclusion, especially as archaeology has helped us to reconstruct the historical events and circumstances of that period in a way that plausibly explains how a Semite might have come to occupy such a prestigious position in Egypt at that period. Nahum Sarna reminds us:

> From the time of the famous king Akhnaton (ca. 1370–1353 B.C.E.) we know of a Semite named Yanhamu who was Egyptian commissioner for Palestine and Syria. Under Merneptah (ca. 1224–1214 B.C.E.) a certain Ben-Ozen, who came from a place situated east of Lake Tiberius, rose to become the royal herald or marshal at the court, and received two Egyptian names from the king. . . . It was not at all extraordinary for foreigners, and Semites in particular, to be welcomed by the court and to rise to positions of responsibility and power in the government. (N. Sarna, *Understanding Genesis* [New York: Schocken Books, 1970], p. 221)

**9. But surely the appointment of Joseph goes far beyond the circumstances just described, for he becomes the veritable ruler of the entire country, determining policy with dictatorial power. Can archaeology justify such a situation?**

Indeed it can. Scholars have made a clear connection between the descent of Joseph and his family to Egypt and the invasion of that country by the Hyksos, meaning "foreign rulers," around 1700 B.C.E. They were an amalgam of ethnic groups, of which the predominant element were northwestern Semites, who marched on Egypt via the land of Canaan. One such mixed nomadic group is widely referred to in documents of the period by the name *Habiru* or *Hapiru,* and made their appearance around the year 2000 B.C.E., the period of the patriarchs. Scholars identify those

*Habiru* with the biblical Hebrews. Thus, the period and circumstances of the Hyksos invasion corresponds perfectly with that of the settlement of the Hebrews in Egypt; and the abrupt exodus of the Israelites from Egypt may also be explained in the light of the expulsion of the Hyksos around the year 1550 B.C.E. The "mixed multitude," referred to in the Torah (Exodus 12:38) as having joined the Hebrews at their exodus from Egypt, may well refer, therefore, to their fellow, non-Semitic coinvaders, who were banished with them.

**10.  But does not this way of describing the Exodus, namely as a circumstance of a counterrevolution by the native Egyptians, and their banishment of the Hyksos, suggest that the Torah's account is in some way inaccurate?**

No it does not. We have to realize that Torah is what its name suggests, namely "instruction," rather than bald history. Ancient historians were interested merely in recording events, and their effect upon the country concerned. Torah, on the other hand, seeks to reveal the hand of God underlying those events, particularly as they affected the Chosen People.

God does not generally choose to intervene in history in a sudden, dramatic, and miraculous manner. If He revealed Himself in such a way, it would destroy free will and render faith irrelevant, since everyone would have God's existence totally proved, and they would be frightened into submission to His will. Instead, God guides destinies in a hidden and inscrutable manner. His hand is certainly behind certain victories or defeats, but the people concerned believe that the result was obtained through the normal convergence of fortune and historical circumstance. Thus, there is no conflict between the notion of the Almighty God playing His part in visiting plagues upon Egypt in concert with the military exertions of the Egyptians in their effort to rid their country of the hated Hyksos conquerors.

The Torah, as a document of "instruction," was only concerned with the revelation of God's power being wielded on behalf of His people, not with the recording of the interplay of the more general political and military forces at work to secure the banishment of the Hyksos, even though Israel's release was inextricably interwoven with those wider events.

**11.  But does the Torah's record of the Joseph story betray any evidence that might lend support to the Hyksos theory?**

One particularly significant pointer to the Hyksos period is the fact that Joseph settles his family in Goshen in order that they might live close to him (Genesis 45:10). This suggests that the capital and royal palace must have been located in the northern, Delta region, near the border with Canaan, since it was to Goshen that Joseph traveled to meet his father, who was coming from Canaan. This situation clearly reflects the early Hyksos period, when the invaders established the northern city of Avaris (otherwise known as Tanis, or in Hebrew, Zoan) as their capital, in 1725 B.C.E.

**12. It has been suggested earlier that the turn for the worse in Israelite fortunes in Egypt took place after the Hyksos lost their control of the country and began to be persecuted, before finally being banished. Is there any hint of that historical situation underlying the biblical description of Israel's subsequent enslavement?**

The reference to the Israelites having to build the store-cities of Pithom and Raamses for Pharaoh is most significant. It was during the reign of Rameses II (1290–1224 B.C.E.) that the oppression of the Israelites and other former invaders reached intolerable proportions. Rameses had a passion for building, and archaeology has unearthed an inventory, listing Pi-Tum and Pi-Raamses as cities built by Rameses II. His monogram was discovered on an unprecedented number of temples and public buildings—all testimony to the truth of the biblical account.

**13. Does the fact that not a single document or royal record exists from ancient Egypt referring specifically to the Israelites or to Moses and the Exodus not make us wonder about the historicity of the entire biblical story?**

Not at all. Scholars of ancient Near Eastern history have long regarded it as axiomatic that the ancient monarchs never lost battles! When they did, they either instructed their royal chroniclers to record the battle as a resounding victory or simply omitted any record of it. Ancient potentates were most vainglorious and exceedingly concerned for how posterity would remember them and recount their exploits. Thus, it occasions no surprise that there is not a single reference in those same Egyptian chronicles to the lengthy period when their land was ruled by the invader Hyksos.

For Jews, the biblical account of our slavery in Egypt and the Exodus is of primary religious importance, forming the rationale of many of our ethical principles and the predominant themes of our festivals, ritual, and liturgy. For the Egyptians, on the other hand, it was an event of little or no consequence.

**14. Must we accept the biblical account of the Ten Plagues at face value, as punishments inflicted directly by the hand of God? After all, have not biblical scholars explained most of them as natural disasters?**

Jewish tradition does not make too clear a demarcation line between the "natural" and the "miraculous" character of events that have significantly affected the destiny of our nation. A phenomenon is no less so because some of its components or contributory elements are capable of rationalization. It is not necessarily the *method*, but the *fact* that all those various "occurrences"—rational or irrational—combined just at the moment of crisis and necessity to enable the Hebrews to realize their objective that constitutes the "miracle." It is the effect, and not necessarily the cause, that we hail as "miraculous." God is unique in being able to create the miraculous out of natural, basic elements.

## THE PASCHAL LAMB

### 15. Why were the Israelites commanded to take a Paschal lamb and keep it tied up in their homes?

The lamb was the Egyptian's symbol of divinity. Thus, by seizing it in that way, each and every family was demonstrating their unswerving belief in the folly of idolatry, their belief in the One God, and their determination to follow implicitly His every directive, even those demanding the greatest courage and self-sacrifice.

### 16. What was the purpose of the instruction to keep the lamb for just four days?

The Torah does not state the precise reason for the four days' delay. We may conjecture, however, that it had a very practical reason. Exodus 12:48 states that no uncircumcised person could participate in the ritual of the eating of the roasted lamb. Now circumcision had been neglected by most of the Israelites, including Moses himself, who had to undertake an unexpected and rather primitive operation (using a flint) on his son at an inn along the way to Egypt (Exodus 4:24–26). The result of that law – if not its purpose – was that the fulfillment of both *mitzvot,* circumcision and slaughtering of the Paschal lamb, should follow in the closest proximity, in order for Israel to gain a double merit. This may be proved from the fact that Joshua also waited to circumcise the new generation, born in the desert, until just before the celebration of the festival of Passover (Joshua 5:7–10).

Indeed, the Haggadah itself quotes the verse from Ezekiel 16:8: "And I saw you wallowing in your blood (*bedamayikh*)." The talmudic Sages, noting the plural form of the Hebrew word employed here for "blood," state that it refers to two types of blood – that of the circumcision and that of the Paschal lamb – with which the Israelites were preoccupied ("wallowing") at the time of the Exodus.

Now it was generally acknowledged that three full days were required in order to recuperate after circumcision (Talmud *Bava Metziah* 86b; Rashi on Genesis 18:1). The Israelite families could not, therefore, have been expected to undertake the physically demanding process of selection (that is, finding a lamb of requisite size for the exact number of participants), examination (to ensure that it was without blemish), slaughtering, roasting, and carving while they were still weak from circumcision.

It follows, therefore, that, in order to have the lamb ready for roasting on the fourteenth of Nisan, immediately after their recovery from the three days of their indisposition, it would have had to be selected, waiting and ready, on the day before the circumcision was to take place, that is, *four* days before, on the tenth day of the month. (For a fuller treatment of this question, see Jeffrey M. Cohen, *Moments of Insight,* London: Vallentine, Mitchell & Co., 1989, pp. 44–47.)

### 17. Did the Israelites observe the ritual of eating the Paschal lamb every year of their forty years of wandering in the desert?

Most surprisingly, they only celebrated the ritual once again, a year later, on the first anniversary (see Numbers 9:1–5). The Midrash (*Sifrei Beha'alotkha,* 67) deprecates this fact, though from the wording of Exodus 13:5 ("When the Lord brings you into the land of the Canaanites . . . you shall keep this service") it would seem that this was, indeed, the divine intention.

The single attempt to repeat the *Korban Pesach* ritual, a year later, may well have proved most uninspiring, and hence its nonrepetition. How, indeed, could they have hoped to successfully recreate the atmosphere and tension of that unique event which was still so vivid in their memories? Furthermore, during their travels in the desert there was not the same necessity to reinforce the message of the ritual of the lamb, since the presence of the pillar of cloud by day and fire by night was a most vivid and tangible sign of God's manifest covenant with the Hebrew nation.

### 18. Besides the explanation that the taking of the lamb constituted a test of the Israelites' faith, is there any other meaning in its symbolism?

In truth, the Torah nowhere states that its purpose was in order to test the courage and faith of the Israelites. That is an assumption. We have already accounted for the fact that it had to be kept in their homes for four days as simply a practical measure, so that they would have it ready for slaughter immediately after their three-day recovery period from circumcision. Perhaps for this reason, Moses Maimonides offers quite a different explanation, namely, that the slaughtering of the lamb was to serve as a sin-offering for the nation's previous idolatry.

We find difficulty with this suggestion for two reasons. First, the concept of an offering as an atonement for sin did not exist before the giving of the Torah, three months after they had left Egypt. Secondly, Moses' initial excuse to Pharaoh for insisting that the the Israelites leave Egypt was that they needed to celebrate "a festival unto the Lord" (Exodus 10:9). The implication was clearly that they could not offer their sacrifices in an idolatrous and unclean land. That being the case, it is difficult to justify Maimonides' interpretation of the lamb as a ritual sin-offering.

We prefer to view it as a solemn meal, in celebration of the covenanted national entity that was being created as they prepared to step forward into history as the Chosen People. In the Middle East, already in biblical times, the essential climax to the ratification of any treaty or covenant was the celebratory and confirmatory meal, which was participated in by all parties to it (see Genesis 26:30–31; 27:4, 7, 25, 31; 31:46, 54; Exodus 24:7, 11; see also *Ramban* on Leviticus 19:16. For a full treatment of this subject, see Cohen, *Moments of Insight,* pp. 37–64).

### 19. How was the Paschal lamb to be eaten?

The Torah prescribes that each household should consume a whole lamb unless there were too few in the family, whereupon they could join together with a neighbor. Its blood was to be used to smear over the doorposts and lintel of their homes, as a symbolic sign of faith that the angel of death would "pass over." They were to roast it whole in fire, in a state of readiness for the journey, with their shoes on, their staffs in their hands, and their flowing robes hitched up with a belt, so that they would not be impeded when they were given the signal to leave Egypt "in haste." Indeed, they were told that they would even have to eat the lamb hastily (Exodus 12:11), because the Egyptian tumult that would erupt at midnight at the death of their firstborn would hardly allow the Israelites to continue uninterruptedly with their meal.

### 20. Was anything else prescribed to be eaten with the lamb?

They were told to eat it together with *matzot* (unleavened bread) and *merorim* (bitter herbs). The *matzot* were symbolic of two diametrically opposite states: the "bread of affliction" (Deuteronomy 16:3), namely, the coarse, unleavened wafers that they subsisted on during the period of their oppression, and, at the same time, a happy reminder of the haste with which they were leaving Egypt and putting that oppression behind them, to the extent that they had insufficient time to allow their dough to rise into bread (Exodus 12:39).

The symbolism of the *merorim,* or *maror* as it is more commonly referred to, is not spelt out in the Torah, although it does not require much imagination to infer its significance, especially when we recall the identical word, "And they embittered (*va-yemararu*) their lives" (Exodus 1:14).

### 21. On what grounds may one defer one's Paschal lamb observance until *Pesach Sheni*?

The Torah is quite specific: "And the Lord spoke to Moses, saying: Speak to the children of Israel, saying: If any man of you or of your generation shall be unclean through contact with a dead body, or be on a journey far off . . . he shall keep the passover unto the Lord; in the second month on the fourteenth day at dusk. . . . They shall eat it with unleavened bread and bitter herbs" (Numbers 9:10–12).

### 22. Could outsiders, such as non-Israelite servants or friends, be invited as a guest when a family was celebrating the Paschal lamb ritual?

They could not. This was not just a barbecue. It was a meal of covenanted fellowship, cementing the bonds of Israelite nationhood. So, although not a secret act of initiation, it was inappropriate for outsiders to eat of the lamb and participate in an intimate ritual so supercharged with national and religious significance for Israel alone. Hence, the Torah prohibits participation to strangers, hired hands, and uncircumcised people (who have not been initiated into the covenant of Israel, and therefore cannot properly reinforce it through this meal of fellowship). Any bought servant, however, who enters the family circle of an Israelite for life, may, if he so desires, join the faith by submitting to circumcision, after which he is eligible to eat of the Paschal lamb.

### 23. Were there any other regulations governing the Paschal lamb ritual?

Other than those we have mentioned, the Torah prescribes that none of its flesh may be taken outside of the home. Every sacrifice in the Sanctuary, and later in the Temple, had its special direction and place where it had to be offered and the ritual performed.

As the location for the offering of the *Korban Pesach,* every home became transformed into a mini-Sanctuary, and so, as with the Sanctuary offerings, none of the flesh of this one could be consumed outside. At another level, this also helped to underscore the concept of the Jewish home as invested with the sanctity of a sanctuary.

Another regulation was that special care had to be taken that no bone of the lamb should be broken while eating (Exodus 12:46). Maimonides explains this as a precaution to ensure that it was eaten in haste, as required by biblical law. If it was permitted to break bones, people would do so in order to extract the bone marrow, which was regarded as a delicacy. This is a time-consuming operation which would cause delay in the proceedings and impair the prerequisite of promoting the idea of haste, in order to recall the haste with which the Israelites left Egypt.

## THE EXODUS

### 24. What did they take with them when they left Egypt?

We are not told. All that is mentioned is the fact that they carried "their kneading-troughs wrapped within their cloaks, slung over their shoulders" (Exodus 12:34). We are also told that they took all the silver and gold jewels and garments that they had asked their Egyptian neighbors to provide them with. The Torah says that "they despoiled the Egyptians" (12:35), so we may imagine that they came out pretty well laden with valuables. We are also told that "they went up armed out of Egypt" (Exodus 13:18), which suggests extra bulk.

At the Song of the Red Sea, we are told that Miriam led the women in a dance accompanied with timbrels. We must assume, therefore, that most people also packed their musical instruments. They were also able to contribute some quite exotic materials (such as sealskin) for the making of the Sanctuary; so again we have the picture of both people and animals laden to the hilt with as much as they could carry.

### 25. How can we justify the seizure of the Egyptian valuables?

We may assume that, if God commanded them to make such "requests" of the Egyptians, it must have been ethically justifiable. The explanation generally offered is that it constituted basic compensation for over two hundred years of slaving for the Egyptians without payment and under conditions that were intolerable. One may conjecture that every Egyptian lorded it over the Israelites and took advantage of their defenceless position to press them into labor for themselves, in addition to what Pharaoh demanded of them. The Israelites were taking but a fraction of what was really owed to them.

### 26. Why did it take the Israelites as long as forty years to arrive at the Promised Land?

In truth, the journey to Canaan, traveling in a Northeasterly direction, should have taken no longer than eleven days. However, we are told that "God did not take them that route, via the land of the Philistines, although that was near, since God said, 'Perhaps the people will have second thoughts when they see war, and seek to return to Egypt' " (Exodus 13:17).

The warlike Philistines captured from the Canaanites, and occupied, five cities— Gath, Gaza, Ekron, Ashkelon, and Ashdod—all along the coastal plain. Some sources suggest that they may have had support from the Egyptians for their conquest. If that was the case, then it may well explain why the Israelites would have had to avoid that route, where they would certainly have been engaged in battle by the Philistines on account of their being allies of the Egyptians. This is probably the meaning of the otherwise awkward biblical phrase, "when they see war."

The *Targum* preserves another explanation of why they took a circuitous route. It relates that 200,000 fully armed warriors of the tribe of Ephraim defied the will of God and fled Egypt thirty years before the time decreed for the Exodus. They attacked the Philistines at Gath, and were annihilated. The *Targum* identifies them with the dry bones that Ezekiel brought to life (ch. 37). Thus, the Torah was referring to them when it said that God did not want the people "to see war." He did not want them to see the disastrous *effects of a previous war,* in which their brethren were slain. That would have instilled total fear and despair into their hearts.

**27.  But even if they had to take the roundabout route, surely it did not necessitate a journey of forty years!**

Correct. The reason for that delay in the desert was that the people were punished for believing the evil report of the spies sent out by Moses to scout the land. The spies were away for forty days, and God punished them accordingly with "a year['s delay] for each day" (Numbers 14:34).

## SPIRITUALIZING THE EXODUS

**28.  The answer to question 13 refers to to the biblical account of our slavery in Egypt and the Exodus as "of primary religious importance, forming the rationale of so many of our ethical principles, and the predominant themes of our festivals, ritual and liturgy." How is this expressed?**

The experience in Egypt was meant to condition our people to a unique degree of ethical sensitivity. The Torah tells us not only not to discriminate against strangers, but to love them, "for you were strangers in the land of Egypt." We are to learn tolerance from having been at the receiving end of intolerance. We were also to learn morality from having been exposed to the gross immoralities practiced in Egypt (Leviticus 18:3).

An example of the influence of Egypt on our ritual is the Torah's emphasis on *tum'ah,* the impurity of the dead body, and the essential process of *tahara,* purification from such a state.

The Egyptians were obsessed with death and its aftermath. Their Bible is called "The Book of the Dead" and is a manual of guidance for the ultimate existence in the hereafter. This had significant ramifications for Judaism, which reacted sharply and virtually eschewed any consideration of life in the hereafter. There is not a single reference to it in the whole of the Torah. Jews are meant to affirm life, and only to confront death when it strikes. The dead body is, therefore, declared to be the ultimate source of impurity, rendering anyone who touches it defiled to such an extent that he or she even transmits that defilement to anything they, in turn, touch. A priest, to this day, may not touch, or even stand under the same roof as, a dead body.

Another influence of the Egyptian experience upon our ritual is seen in the ceremony of *Pidyon Ha-Ben,* the redemption of the firstborn son. Because God saved the Israelite firstborns, when He slew those of the Egyptians in the tenth plague, Jewish firstborns were henceforth in a special relationship of protection and sanctity. They had been the recipients of God's special grace; and that set them apart as the ideal spiritual representatives of their families and of the nation: "Sanctify unto Me all the firstborn, whatever openeth the womb among the children of Israel, both of man and of beast, it is Mine" (Exodus 13:2). So, technically, every firstborn *belongs to God* and should devote his life to service at the Sanctuary. Similarly, every firstborn beast of the Israelites was saved when those of the Egyptians were slain. Hence, the firstborn beast is also sacred to God. In order to shed the sacred status so that the firstborn child may lead a normal life and pursue his or her own objectives, and in order that ordinary benefit may be enjoyed from the firstborn beast, they have to be "redeemed," and their value in money donated to a sacred purpose. This act of "redemption" is called *Pidyon.*

Another direct influence of the Egyptian experience upon our daily ritual is the prescription to wear *tefillin.* The boxes, containing biblical verses, that are bound by straps to the head and upon the arm and hand, are described in the Torah as "a sign upon your hand and a memorial between your eyes . . . that with a strong hand the Lord brought you forth out of Egypt" (Exodus 13:9).

It is also possible to explain both the regulation to Israel to rest on the Sabbath, as well as the extension of that privilege of resting to one's man-servants and maid-servants, as a token of empathy with, and commemoration of, the lot of those who were given no such opportunity to rest in Egypt. This would account for the fact that, although the institution of the *Shabbat* is already introduced at Genesis 2:1, yet the reference there is exclusively to *God* having rested from all His work. There is no hint of it as a day of rest for man. Only in the Ten Commandments, given but three months after they had emerged from slavery, does *Shabbat* become a day of rest for the weary Israelite slaves, and, in turn, for any who are employed to serve them.

In the liturgy, the Exodus constitutes a predominant theme. We thank God each day "for not having made me a slave." We recite the *Shirat Ha-Yam,* "The Song of [Deliverance at] the Red Sea." In the third paragraph of the *Shema,* we quote God's words describing Himself as the One "who brought you out of the land of Egypt to be your God." This is followed by the *Geulah* (redemption) blessing, preceeding the *Amidah,* which praises God for His manifold acts of redemption of our people from Egypt. In the Grace after Meals, in the second (Thanksgiving) blessing, we thank God "for having brought us forth out of the land of Egypt and freed us from the house of bondage." During the *Shabbat* and *Yom Tov* morning services we recite Psalm 136, called *Hallel Ha-Gadol* ("The long praise"). This lists, and thanks God for, all the single acts of redemption from Egypt, after each of which comes the refrain, *"kiy le'olam chasdo"* ("For His loving-kindness is forever"). Again, the Friday evening and Sabbath morning versions of *Kiddush* refer to the Sabbath as *Zeikher litzi'at mitzrayim,* "a memorial of the Exodus from Egypt." This reinforces our interpretation, above, of the institution of Sabbath rest as a commemoration of the Egyptian experience when such rest was cruelly withheld. Also on festivals, in the special *Vatiker lanu* prayer, after highlighting the name of the specific festival we are celebrating, we continue immediately with the phrase, *Zeikher litzi'at mitzrayim.*

Egypt remains the Jewish symbol of oppression in all its guises. And these daily references to, and recollections of, that ancient experience are intended to stir us and galvanize us into humanitarian activity whenever our brethren, or indeed any members of the human family, are suffering a similar plight. Egypt taught us that freedom is the inalienable right of all humanity.

**26. Is this essential message of the Egyptian experience highlighted within the celebration of the festival itself?**

Undoubtedly. The rich Seder ritual, taking in and symbolizing every aspect of it, is a measure of its primary importance, as well as the threefold biblical repetition of the theme of children asking questions about it in the future and the most appropriate way of dealing with such questions. Another proof of its importance lies in the regulation that if one was unable to participate in the Paschal lamb ritual, one was given another opportunity to celebrate a *Pesach Sheni* (Second Passover) a month later on the same day of the month. This is a concession that the Torah does not make in the case of any other festival or major ritual.

## CELEBRATING THE FESTIVAL IN TEMPLE TIMES

**30. Did the festival undergo any major changes, once the Israelites had conquered their land and built the First Temple?**

The most significant change was, naturally, that once the Temple was built (around 970 B.C.E.), Passover became a pilgrim festival, when, in accordance with biblical law (Deuteronomy 16:16), Jews were enjoined to visit Jerusalem for the celebration of the three main festivals, for there alone was it permitted to sacrifice their Paschal lamb at "the place which the Lord chooses to cause His Name to reside" (v. 6). That transition, from small, family rituals to a national reunion and gala celebration in the hills around Jerusalem, must have drastically altered the whole character of the festivity, changing it, for many, from a holy day into a holiday.

We do not know the extent to which people were able to make the pilgrimage on such a frequent basis, particularly those who lived in the far-off, hilly, and inaccessible northern parts of the country. Reading the biblical description of the extent of idolatry during the first Temple period, it is highly unlikely that the Torah's prescriptions, especially if they involved travel and the expense of accommodations, would have captured the loyalty of the majority.

In this context, it is significant that both King Hezekiah (ca. 725 B.C.E.) and King Josiah (639 B.C.E.), on the occasion of their having completed a drastic purge of all the idolatrous influences in the kingdom and having inaugurated large-scale reforms based on the laws of the Torah, marked the reconsecration of the nation by a special celebration of Passover at Jerusalem (2 Kings 23:21; 2 Chronicles 30:1–5, 13–27). A similar thought was in the minds of the exiles who had returned from Babylonian captivity in 538 B.C.E. They limited participation in their first public Passover festivity to those "who had separated themselves from the pollutions of the peoples of the land, to worship the Lord, God of Israel" (Ezra 6:21). They clearly understood the celebration of this festival as a covenantal act of national reconciliation and spiritual union.

A highlight of the festival in Temple times was the formal offering of an *Omer* of barley from the newly ripening crop. *Omer* was simply the name of a dry measure; and no farmer was permitted to use his new harvest until that ceremony of "waiving the Omer," as a token of thanksgiving to God, had taken place in the Temple (see Leviticus 23:15–21).

## 31. Can we determine precisely the extent to which Jews did visit Jerusalem to observe the main festivals during the Second Temple period?

Politically and socially, the Second Temple period (537 B.C.E.–70 C.E.) was most turbulent. Until the arrival of Ezra (458 B.C.E.) and Nehemiah (445 B.C.E.) there was total national lethargy among those who had returned from Babylon. The Temple was in disrepair, and social polarization between the comfortably-off nobles, higher officials, and priestly families, on the one hand, and the peasants and small land-owners, on the other, was marked. Jerusalem of that era would hardly have attracted pilgrims, even for the celebration of Passover.

Things improved dramatically with the implementation of Ezra and Nehemiah's reforms, but the Persian Empire was engaged over the next century with staving off a succession of revolts in and around Palestine. We may conjecture that travel around the country was hazardous, and that pilgrimages to Jerusalem were not made on any large scale. In 334 B.C.E., Alexander the Great defeated the Persians, and, over the next century and a half, every aspect of life in Palestine was transformed by Hellenism. Torah and the public observance of festivals were positively discouraged, if not outlawed, and young Jews were attracted more to hippodromes and gymnasia than to the Temple and the synagogue. Again, the pilgrim festival of Passover must have suffered immeasurably, and the ritual at the Temple and the open-air eating of the Paschal lamb at sunset probably attracted, in the main, only the citizens of the city itself.

At the hippodromes, the horse-and-chariot races generally ended with a ceremony of praise to the gods, which was anathema to the Jewish religious leadership, even if the young Jewish spectators were themselves quite indifferent to that aspect of the proceedings. The encouragement of physical fitness and prowess at the gymnasia was, likewise, regarded by the religious leaders as totally at variance with the life-style of the "people of the book," whose ideal should rather have been the study of

Torah and the quest for spirituality. There was also the great fear of intermarriage and assimilation that such fraternization with the gentiles would inevitably engender.

In the period following the glorious victory of the Maccabees (165 B.C.E.) and the coming of the Romans (63 B.C.E.), religious life intensified greatly, with the growing influence of the Pharisees, *hasidim,* and Torah Sages. We may assume that it was during that century that the pilgrim festivals attracted their greatest number of visitors from all over the country and beyond. The magnificent and varied building projects—in the Temple and throughout the city—undertaken by Herod (37–34 B.C.E.) would have also been a major attraction.

During the last sixty years before the destruction of the Temple, the Jews of Palestine were ruled by Roman governors, with but one brief interlude when the government was entrusted to a Jewish king, Agrippa, who reigned from 41 to 44 C.E. The Talmud relates that, curious to know precisely how many pilgrims thronged Jerusalem, Agrippa requested that a census be taken. As Jewish law forbade the counting of heads, the problem was overcome by ordering the High Priest to count the number of kidneys offered on the altar from the Paschal lambs. The result was astounding: it was reported that 600,000 lambs had been slaughtered, each lamb on behalf of a group of diners numbering no less than ten (Talmud *Pesachim* 64b)! If that is not an exaggeration, then we may assume that it was a unique occasion and that the numerous pilgrims had been drawn there for a special reason: perhaps to take an oath of loyalty to their new king or to avail themselves of the relaxed conditions and safety of travel under a Jewish king, which had kept them from making the festival pilgrimage for many years.

**32. Have we any confirmation of that talmudic tradition from any independent historical source that also refers to such inconceivably vast numbers of celebrants at Jerusalem?**

We do. The Jewish military commander and historian, Flavius Josephus, who defected to the Romans during the great rebellion of 66–70 C.E. and later retired to Rome on a state pension, wrote his account of the Jewish War. He certainly had no cause to embellish his description of life at Jerusalem, so we may regard his description as accurate. He states in his book *Wars of the Jews* (bk. 6, ch. 9) that the emperor Cestius instructed the priests to conduct a census of those trapped in the city at Passover at the time of the Roman invasion. (See *The Works of Flavius Joseph,* vol. 2, trans. William Whiston [London, 1845], p. 465.) The leaders of every Paschal lamb fraternity were seized, and the number amounted to 256,500. Josephus points out that we have to allow for an average of at least ten participants at each fraternity, giving a minimum total of over 2.5 million people. He adds the rider that if we allow for those who were excluded from participation—through leprosy, gonorrhea, menstruation, or other types of impurity—we arrive at a far greater total! Three million people present at that most dangerous time, as the clouds of war were mushrooming, renders plausible the talmudic reference to 6 million at a peaceful and auspicious time.

### 33. What sort of sacrificial ritual took place prior to the roasting of the Paschal lamb?

Throughout the year, the priests were divided into twenty-four Mishmarot (administrative duty-rosters), each charged with officiating at the Temple for one week, twice a year. For the three main festivals, however, all priests were encouraged to attend in order to service the influx of pilgrims, receive and slaughter their lambs, and attend to the sprinkling of the blood and the prescribed rituals.

The festival began at nightfall, and the whole of the preceeding day would be spent in busy preparation. Everyone knew in advance which *chavurah* (Paschal lamb eating–fellowship) he was invited to join. The leader of his *chavurah* had the responsibility of transporting the lamb to the Temple and engaging a priest to do the honors. Three silver trumpets were sounded to announce the time for the commencement of the sacrificing, which was early in the afternoon. Twelve priestly ushers, holding silver maces, stood at the entrance of the Temple courtyard to ensure that the people queued in an orderly manner. Another twelve priests, holding golden clubs, were on duty inside. Their task was to close the courtyard gates when there was no more room inside, and also to ensure that there was easy access and exit.

A priestly conveyor belt stretched from the slaughtering-place to the altar, with each priest carrying either a silver or golden tray. The blood from the sacrifices was placed in bowls, which were then passed, with lightning speed, from priest to priest before being sprinkled on the altar by the last priest at the end of the row. The empty bowls were then returned along the row in similar manner. While all this was going on, a priestly choir sang *Hallel*-psalms to an orchestral accompaniment. The lamb was then returned to the *chavurah* leader, for him to commence preparation for its roasting.

### 34. Did the inhabitants of Jerusalem also roast their lambs on the hillsides of the city?

There was no necessity for them to do so. They probably preferred to celebrate in their wider family groups at home, perhaps also inviting some pilgrim friends to join them.

### 35. How did the Seder ritual develop in Roman times?

Until the Roman period, the order of service was fairly undeveloped, and probably took the form of the roasting of the lamb, followed by the recitation of appropriate biblical passages and the singing of *Hallel*-psalms, punctuated by the recollection of folk traditions embellishing the story of the Egyptian slavery and the miracles associated with the Exodus.

With the onset of the Roman period, Jews took the opportunity of borrowing some of Rome's aristocratic banqueting practices in order to convey the notion of *freedom.* The Roman nobility reclined full-length, on cushions, at their *triclinia,* low, three-sided couches skirting their buffet tables. The Jews did likewise, leaning back in a carefree manner. It subsequently became obligatory to lean at the Seder, and the last of the "Four Questions" draws special attention to that predominant aspect of the celebration.

It was also the practice of the upper classes to provide entertainment at their banquets. This took the form of appropriate readings, songs, and dramatic presentations from their classical literature. This particular genre is referred to as *Symposia Literature;* and this practice undoubtedly influenced the development of the Haggadah, an eclectic compilation of biblical passages, psalms, poems, blessings, and early rabbinic homilies and midrashim (see S. Stein, "The Influence of Symposia Literature on the Literary Form of the Pesach Haggadah," *Journal of Jewish Studies* 8 (1956):13–45.

In Roman times it was the practice to commence each meal with an appetizer, which took the form of dipping a piece of parsley or other vegetable into brine or spicy sauce. This custom of "dipping" was borrowed for the Seder ritual. But the Jews went one better: instead of dipping in once, they dipped twice! Hence, we have the *karpas* dip into saltwater, which is simply an aping of the custom of the free citizens of Rome, and the *maror* dip into *charoset,* which has a symbolic meaning more directly related to the theme of the festival.

There was also some rather negative borrowing from Greco-Roman traditions. Though there is some dispute about the meaning of the word *Afikoman,* scholarly consensus has it that it is a Hebraized form of a Greek word, *epikomon.* The *epikomoi* were riotous and licentious revelries in honor of Bacchus, god of wine. In this way we understand the rabbinic injunction, referred to in the Haggadah as one of the charges to the wise son (presumably to influence his peer group), "not to conclude, after the Paschal lamb ritual, by going on a Roman-style *epikomon.*" We may assume that there were strong grounds for introducing that caution into the formal part of the Haggadah recitation.

The introduction of the four cups of wine also came about during the last few centuries before the Common Era. We cannot be sure why wine came to be invested with such a measure of sanctity in Judaism that it accompanies such sacred ceremonies as *Kiddush, Havdalah,* Grace after Meals (in an assembly of three or more males), weddings, and circumcisions. The popular explanation takes account of two assertions by the psalmist: the first, that "wine gladdens the heart of man"; the second, that we should "serve God with joy." Taken together, these verses point to the benefit of wine, when used in our "service" of God, as promoting that requisite joyful mood. The fact that wine was prescribed in the Torah to be poured over the altar as a libation, accompanying the daily sacrifices (see Numbers 28:7, 14), naturally indicates its propriety in religious ritual.

It was probably during the late Persian and early Greek period, when the efforts of the Men of the Great Assembly (ca. 400–330 B.C.E.) to create blessings for all occasions bore fruit within circles of pious *hasidim,* that wine came to be regarded as an essential accompaniment, especially for *Kiddush* and *Havdalah.*

### 36. We referred above to the bringing of the *Omer* to the Temple. Was there any special ceremonial involved with this ritual?

Indeed. The *Omer* ritual, the harbinger of a new agricultural year, was supercharged with dramatic ceremonial. Prior to the festival, inspectors of the Sanhedrin would tour the fields of the outlying estates of Jerusalem to discover the barley crop that had ripened most. There was great prestige and honor for the farmer whose crop was chosen as representative of the nation's presentation to the Temple. Normally, one of the fields of the Valley of Kidron, north of the city, was the chosen venue. The inspectors then tied a cord around an *Omer*-sheaf, in order that there would be no delay when the proceedings commenced at the conclusion of the first day of Passover.

Word would spread quickly, and thousands would converge on the site. A specially worded dialogue was prescribed, in which the appointed reaper would exhibit his implements to the spectators and obtain their permission to begin the reaping, since he was representing the nation at large in this symbolic act of thanksgiving.

The sheaves were cut and placed into baskets, which were triumphantly borne aloft, in procession, to the Temple Court. There they were parched, winnowed, milled into flour, and sieved. A meal-offering was then prepared, which was compounded with oil and sweet-smelling incense. (For a fuller description of this ritual, see questions 456–466.)

### 37. Were any efforts made to involve children in the rituals?

Can one really imagine Jewish children taking a backseat? The Mishnah (*Pesachim* 8:3) records that it was the custom of families living in the villages around Jerusalem to organize races into the city for their older children. The child who reached Jerusalem first was appointed "supervisor," and the size of the portion of the Paschal lamb served to his siblings was determined "by his pleasure"! The Talmud interestingly refers to one year when the girls won the race to Jerusalem, thereby displaying greater zeal than the boys. In our day, this would not be considered so unusual as to merit special mention!

### 38. With the destruction of the Temple, did the Paschal lamb ritual immediately come to an end?

With the loss of the Temple, in the year 70 c.e., the entire sacrificial system was brought to an abrupt end. The Torah makes it abundantly clear that offerings are only to be made "in the place where the Lord causes His Name to be mentioned." The ritual eating of the meat of the Thanksgiving (*Korban Todah*) and Free-Will (*Shelamim*) Offerings, by the donors together with the priests, is referred to as "eating at the table of the Most High" (Exodus 20:21). Where God's House was in ruins, there was clearly no possibility of dining with Him, and sacrifices would, of necessity, have had to cease.

However, some romantics refused to accept that the old order had been nullified, and they attempted to preserve some aspects of the Temple ritual in the lands of their dispersal. Hence, according to the Talmud (*Pesachim* 53a), a certain Todos, spiritual leader of the Roman Jewish community, attempted to popularize the practice of roasting a lamb on Passover eve (as do the Samaritans to the present day). The Rabbis sent him a very strongly worded message, with an implied threat of excommunication, reminding him of the gravity of causing Jews to eat consecrated meat outside Jerusalem.

### 39. What other changes came about with the destruction of the Temple?

Since prayer then had to take the place of sacrifice, determined efforts were made during the following few centuries to standardize all the laws, ritual practices, customs, and prayers associated with the festival. This period corresponded with the general standardization of Jewish law, as incorporated into the Mishnah. The Seder service became more clearly delineated, and the Haggadah began to take the form that we still follow, with general consensus emerging regarding the biblical passages and midrashic homilies most appropriate for inclusion and most likely to stimulate further discussion about the Exodus, and, indeed, about the desperately longed-for future deliverance.

The latter sentiment prompted the addition of a fifth cup of wine, to be placed on the table during the Seder proceedings. This is popularly called "The Cup of the Prophet Elijah." According to the Book of Malachi (3:23), Elijah will herald the messianic redemption and the in-gathering of the exiles of our people. The Rabbis bolstered this toast to Elijah with the teaching that "in the month of Nisan our people were redeemed [from Egypt], and in Nisan they will experience the future redemption" (Talmud *Rosh Hashanah* 11b). Hence, on Passover, which occurs in Nisan, the month of redemption, we make a toast to the prophet Elijah and pray that he will soon appear to inaugurate our future salvation.

### 40. So in Roman times the atmosphere in Jerusalem during the festival must have been incredibly joyful and full of religious fervor?

Yes and no: there certainly was a unique atmosphere at such times, though it is doubtful whether "religious fervor" was the dominant feature. Many came merely to enjoy the social revelry and to have a holiday, a fact that much irritated the religious authorities. Others had their eyes on commercial enterprise, for which reason the festival was chosen as the most suitable time for staging an international fair, drawing merchants and their wares from Syria, Egypt, Babylonia, Cyprus, Greece, and Rome. As in modern Israel, there were always the ubiquitous souvenir vendors. To their clearly more affluent customers, they would offer for sale, "Golden Jerusalems," in the form of a ladies' headband of solid gold, upon which were engraved views of the holy city. So, "religious fervor" had to compete with other, far more practical and commercial, concerns!

As far as "joy" is concerned, it has to be said that it is doubtful whether the atmosphere in Jerusalem, at any time in Jewish history, has been pure, unadulterated joy! Because of its position as a source of political tension and a focus of religious bickering and international intrigue, there has always been trouble of some kind bursting out in and around Jerusalem. And Passover was generally the occasion for which this was especially reserved, as the many factions exploited the presence of the teeming masses of residents and pilgrims to make their demonstrations, to gain high profile for their views, and to enlist recruits for their factions.

For more constructive reasons, the great classical prophets, as well as the preachers of nascent Christianity, would utilize the occasion to go around preaching in loud voices to the people about the wickedness of their ways, calling them to repentance, and promising them that the kingdom of God was nigh, with the implicit message not to put their trust in any foreign powers—especially Rome.

Among the Zealot groups of Jewish freedom fighters, in the decades leading up to the great revolt of 67 C.E., were a group called *sicari* ("dagger men"), on account of the small daggers they would carry under their robes. They would sidle up to Jews whom they suspected of collaboration with the hated Roman administration and dispatch them with a lightning jab of their small weapon, before disappearing in an instant.

On many occasions, disturbances in the city over Passover gave the Roman governors excuses for sending in their tribunes and cohorts to apprehend those they suspected of being guilty of treason and the organization of riots. On one occasion, Archelaus, ruler of the central region of Judaea, did precisely that, but his cohorts were pelted with stones, and the majority were either killed or wounded. While the Jews were at their Paschal lamb festivities that evening, Archelaus let loose his entire infantry and cavalry on the city. He slaughtered about three thousand defenseless people and banished the rest of the inhabitants of the city to the hills (Josephus, *Wars of the Jews* 2:10–13).

The rise of Christianity and the ministry of its founder made its own contribution to the turmoil of Passover celebration. With the growth of his reputation as a Galilean politicoreligious leader and Messiah-in-waiting, he unwisely chose to make his first (and last) official, and most well-publicized, visit to Jerusalem just before Passover, accompanied by an entourage of several armed disciples. According to one source, he was accompanied by more than nine hundred highway robbers and armed followers (see M. Grant, *The Jews in the Roman World* [London: Weidenfeld and Nicolson, 1973], pp. 109, 302 n. 46). Not surprisingly, he constituted a threat both to the Roman occupation power as well as to the Jewish leaders who were trying to forge some modus operandi at a very volatile period.

Passover in Jerusalem in Roman times was far from pure spirituality and pleasure!

## 41. But how was that vast influx of pilgrims accommodated within the city?

Among the many miracles associated with the ancient Temple and the city of Jerusalem was the manner in which so many people were accommodated. Imagine them all surging into the Temple Courts! Yet the Mishnah observes that no one was ever heard to say, *"Tzar liy ha-makom,"* "It's too crowded for me to move!" (Mishnah *Avot* 5:5).

First, there was the legendary hospitality of the Jerusalemites. As they would never accept payment for their hospitality, it was customary for the pilgrims to give their hosts gifts of the hides of the animals they had sacrificed in the Temple (Talmud *Yoma* 12a). There were also the many inns of the city, and, when they were full, people simply erected tents in the open places in and around Jerusalem.

The teeming masses must have provided many a headache for the road-safety authorities, yet only one year was a fatality recorded, when an old man was crushed. So unusual was that occurrence that it was forever referred to as "the Passover of the Crushers!"

## MEDIEVAL BLOOD LIBELS

**42. In medieval Europe we hear of monstrous "blood libels." What form did this take?**

This was a ruse used by anti-Semites to whip up an irrational fear of Jews and to justify their wholesale slaughter.

It came to the fore in 1171, when the entire Jewish community of Blois, in France, was massacred on the pretext that it had collectively crucified a Christian child before Passover, in order to use its blood to sprinkle over the *matzot.*

This event probably inspired the pen of one Thomas of Monmouth, a monk of the Benedictine monastery of Norwich, England, who, two years later, publicized the libel that Jews require the blood of Christian children for that Passover ritual. He claimed that the thirty-year-old, unsolved murder of a twelve-year-old Christian lad by the name of William had been perpetrated by the Jews, "in scorn of the Lord's passion," that is, to mock the crucifixion. Evidence, at the time of his death, that he suffered from epilepsy and probably died as a result of a fit, was preemptively discounted by that monk in his single-minded and wicked attempt to harness latent anti-Jewish feeling, especially around Easter time when Christian feelings ran very high against those who were responsible (in their eyes) for the crucifixion of their lord.

The arrival of Passover was greeted, therefore, with considerable apprehension by medieval European Jewry.

**43. But presumably these blood libels soon came to be seen as pure myths?**

To the shame of medieval Christendom, those were not, in fact, isolated examples of the libels being ventilated and the alleged Jewish guilt avenged. In spite of frequent papal pronouncements vindicating Jewish innocence of the charge, the masses preferred to regard the libel as true, with the result that, during the ensuing six centuries, tens of thousands of Jews were done to death and a similar number imprisoned on that preposterous charge of ritual murder. The most blatant and violent manifestation of the blood libel canard took place in Damascus in 1840, when a Capuchin monk vanished without a trace. His fellow monks spread the rumor that the Jews had perpetrated the crime in order to use his blood for the baking of their *matzot,* a charge fostered, for diplomatic reasons, by the French consul in Damascus. Eleven Jews were arrested on the charge and cruelly tortured. Under duress, one confessed and pointed out some of his colleagues as the planners of the murder. He subsequently converted to Catholicism, and two of the Jews were hanged.

The "Damascus Affair" roused Sir Moses Montefiore to organize international agitation at such naked anti-Semitism, and the world's press took up the matter as a major issue. The *Times* of London went so far as to publish the entire text of the Haggadah, in its issue of August 17, 1840, in order to demonstrate beyond doubt that there was not a shred of evidence that the Jews required blood for any aspect of the Passover eve ritual.

The affair galvanized Jewish European solidarity as never before, and the positive aspect of that bitter episode was that it served as a stimulus for the establishment of Jewish representative organizations that, over the next century, boasted unprecedented achievements on behalf of Jewish civil rights, as well as for the realization of the millenial Jewish national and Zionist aspirations.

In the twentieth century, the libel was reincarnated by the Nazi propaganda ministry, and in May 1963, the Board of Deputies of British Jews discussed a reported blood libel that took place at Georgia and Vilnius in the former Soviet Union.

### 44. What answer may be given to rebut such a libel?

It is difficult to imagine that any anti-Semite who is prepared to allege such a calumny would be influenced by reasoned argument. However, Max Dimont's comment on the subject puts the Jewish position succinctly and accurately: "The fact that human sacrifice was something the Jews had fought against since the days of Abraham, while the Druids in England and Germany still practised it in the first century, or the fact that Jews never eat the blood of animals, which is prohibited in the Old Testament, while the Christians did, and still do, even to this day, never crossed the Medieval Christian mind" (M. Dimont, *Jews, God and History,* London: W. H. Allen, 1964, p. 238).

### 45. What precautions, if any, were the Jews prompted to take in order to frustrate such false allegations?

There was little the hapless and defenseless Jewish communities could do in the face of such virulent anti-Semitism, fanned by a clergy who had only contempt for the rejectionist religion of Judaism. The few precautions taken by Jews were rather pathetic and inevitably ineffectual. Thus, a seventeenth-century authority, writing about the four cups of wine drunk at the Seder states, "Nowadays Jews refrain from using red wine because of the allegations of the nations!" (*Turei Zahav* on *Orach Chayyim* 472:11).

The present writer believes that the practice of opening the door before the recitation of *Shefokh chamatkha* ("Pour out Thy wrath") – a most uncharacteristically revengeful Jewish sentiment – also arose as a similar precaution. Because there were plenty of apostate Jews who were deputed to inform on what the Jews were up to and report any anti-Christian activity or sentiment to the authorities, particularly when these were known to be part of the evening's proceedings, it became a natural precautionary measure for families to conduct a check first, to ensure that no one was eavesdropping outside their front door, before reciting such inflammatory verses (see also question 423).

# II

# Rabbinic Expositions on the Slavery, the Plagues, and the Exodus

## THE KING WHO KNEW NOT JOSEPH

**46. The sudden change for the worse in the fortunes of the Israelites is attributed to the ascension of a new king, "who knew not Joseph" (Exodus 1:8), to the throne of Egypt. Why, though, did the new king adopt such a radically different attitude to Egypt's erstwhile loyal Israelite subjects?**

After the death of Joseph, his family abandoned the covenant of *brit milah* (circumcision), wishing to become, in every way, like the Egyptians. God thereupon replaced the warm feelings and respect that the Egyptians had hitherto shown towards them with feelings of suspicion and hostility (*Shemot Rabbah* ch. 1).

The message is as true then as it is today: as long as a clear demarcation line between the Jew and his neighbor existed, they could coexist amicably and justify their separate ways of life. Once Jews try to abandon their unique religious and ancestral practices, however, and assimilate to the customs of their hosts, then the respect of the latter evaporates and they view the Jews merely as interlopers and threats to their own livelihood and stability.

**47. From the Torah's description, which referred to the old, friendly king as "Pharaoh" and to the new king by the identical title, would it seem that there was, in fact, no change of monarch, but merely a change of attitude on the part of the old Pharaoh?**

Indeed, this textual situation generated a dispute between two talmudists Rav and Shemuel. While Rav believed that it was a totally new king who ascended the throne, Shemuel maintained that the Torah sometimes employs the phrase "a new king [arose]" when the reference is merely to a king who has radically changed his policies.

Another midrashic tradition charts a midway path between those two views. This relates that when the Egyptian ministers suggested the introduction of oppressive measures to contain the growth and prosperity of the Israelites, Pharaoh rejected the suggestion, pointing out the great blessings the Israelites had brought to the country. When the ministers saw that the king refused to follow their recommendation, they forced his abdication from the throne. After three months he agreed to accede to their demand if they restored him to his throne. This is why the Torah refers to him as "a new king," in the sense of newly restored. And this is why he bears the identical title, "Pharaoh," both before and after that episode (Talmud *Sotah* 11a).

**48. The Torah states that "all the work that the Egyptians imposed upon the Israelites was done *befarekh* [with rigor]" (Exodus 1:13). What is the precise implication of that term?**

It suggests work to which they were wholly unsuited. They imposed heavy physical labor upon the women and tasks calling for women's domestic and culinary experience upon the men. The taskmasters cruelly whipped both men and women if they did not perform perfectly their respective tasks.

**49. But how was it possible for the Egyptians to enslave such a numerous people as easily as they did?**

This may also be explained according to a popular interpretation of the phrase referred to above, that they prevailed upon the Israelites to work—*befarekh*. This word is explained as a composite of the two words, *befeh rakh,* "with a soft mouth," that is, with subtle enticement. The implication is that the Egyptians first enticed the Hebrews into the building sites of Pharaoh, inviting them to join them in a common national enterprise in Pharaoh's honor. The Israelites could hardly refuse. Once they had become accustomed to that work, the Israelites were offered incentives to continue working while the Egyptians pulled out. Finally, the incentives were withdrawn, and the Israelites found themselves pressurized into continuing as slaves (Talmud *Sotah* 11b).

Modern history has also shown how, with subtle psychology, people can be deluded into believing what they dearly wish to believe. Jews willingly boarded the trains to Auschwitz, believing that they were merely going to work programs. Even when they arrived, their naive belief was reinforced by the slogan *Arbeit macht freie* ("Work makes one free"), over the gate. And even as they entered the showers, they were convinced that they would emerge clean and refreshed!

**50. The names of the two chief Israelite midwives, to whom Pharaoh issued the command to throw all male babes into the Nile, are given as *Shifrah* and *Puah* (Exodus 1:15). Why are these names never repeated in any of the geneological lists, so that we do not know their tribal or family origins?**

The reason is that those are not their real names, but rather a professional designation of the particular tasks they performed while assisting the Hebrew women to give birth. In the light of the report they gave Pharaoh, that "Hebrew women are not like Egyptians, but much livelier; for before we arrive at their homes they have already given birth," we know that their services were not required, therefore, at the actual birth. Their names reflect the exclusive tasks they were called upon to perform subsequently. *Shifrah* is from the Hebrew root *leshaper,* "to make nice, to beautify," and her task was to clean the baby and swaddle him after birth. *Puah* means "to pacify a crying child," which clearly describes her task.

As far as the identity of these midwives is concerned, *Shifrah* was none other that Yocheved, the mother of Moses, and *Puah* was Miriam, his sister.

### 51. In respect of what particular merit were the Hebrews redeemed from Egypt?

The redemption was mainly on account of the faith displayed by the righteous women of that period. Whereas the men gave in to despair and ceased cohabiting with their wives for fear that Pharaoh's decree would be implemented and their offspring doomed to death, the women believed that, with God's help, they could frustrate the king's evil design. They would gather up water in jars from the Nile, and within the water there were found very small fish with aphrodisiacal properties. They would bring to their husbands in the fields jars of boiled water to refresh them and fish to arouse them, and they would make love between the sheepfolds. When the time for giving birth arrived, they would go out into the fields and lie under the shade of apple trees to have their babies (Talmud *Sotah* 11b).

### 52. The Torah states that when the king of Egypt died, "The children of Israel sighed in anguish from their toil" (Exodus 2:23). Surely, the oppressive king's death should have brought a measure of hope that their burden might be lightened. Why were they even more fearful?

Although the Torah states that the previous king had "died," the midrashic view was that this is not to be taken literally. He had actually been struck down with leprosy, and "a leper is like a dead person" (*Nedarim* 64b; *Sanhedrin* 47a). His physicians had told him that the only remedy was to bathe in the blood of 150 Israelite babes, morning and evening. Hence, when the Israelites heard that decree, they "sighed in anguish."

## THE "CALL" OF MOSES

### 53. God had already designated Moses to be the chosen deliverer of His people. What special qualities marked Moses out for his future task?

When Moses was tending the sheep of his father-in-law, Jethro, in the desert, a kid escaped from the flock. Moses pursued it for hours until it stopped in a shady place and found a stream of water, where it began to drink. Moses caught up with it and addressed it tenderly, saying, "I am sorry. I didn't realize that you had run off because you were thirsty. You must be tired now." Moses then lifted the kid onto his shoulders and carried it back to the flock. God then said to Moses: "You, who exhibit so much concern for the flock of a human being, are the ideal shepherd for Israel, My flock" (Midrash *Shemot Rabbah,* ch. 2).

**54. Moses' "Call" took place by a Burning Bush. Why did God choose such a location?**

God wished to intimate to Moses that He was also suffering with Israel the pain of her oppression. Hence He called to Moses from amid a thorn bush (Midrash *Shemot Rabbah,* ch. 2).

Another explanation views it as symbolic of Israel's experiences. Because the thorns face inwards, no damage is suffered as one inserts one's hand into the thornbush. It is only when attempting to extricate one's hand that it is torn by the thorns. Similarly, when Israel came down to Egypt, the people were welcomed, and settled down easily. It was only when they wished to leave the land that they suffered all the wounds and afflictions (*Mekhilta deRabbi Shimon bar Yochai* on Exodus 3:1).

**55. What are we to understand by the fact that the Torah stresses that the Burning Bush "was not consumed"?**

It was a sign to Moses that, notwithstanding all the attempts of the Egyptians to destroy his people, Israel will never be "totally consumed." A remnant will always survive, and from that remnant a new generation and a revitalized nation will be created (Midrash *Shemot Rabbah,* ch. 2).

**56. When Moses asked God by what name He wished to be referred to when the Israelites asked about Him, God replied: *Ehyeh asher Ehyeh* ("I shall be as I shall be"). What is the sense of this Name?**

It may be construed as a promise: I shall be with them in all future situations of servitude just as I shall be with them throughout this present servitude and redemption.

**57. Moses was given strict instructions to take his staff with him when he went for his audience before Pharaoh. Was there any particular significance in that staff?**

Indeed. That staff was created on the eve of the first Sabbath of Creation, ready for the manifold tasks it was destined to perform. It was given to Adam in the Garden of Eden. Adam handed it down to Enoch, who gave it to Shem, who gave it to Abraham. Abraham passed it down his line, to Isaac and Jacob. Jacob brought it with him to Egypt and entrusted it to his son, Joseph. When the latter died, all his property was appropriated by Pharaoh. Now Jethro, father-in-law of Moses, was a court adviser. He saw it one day in Pharaoh's palace, and, noticing the mystical symbols engraved upon it, he coveted it for himself. He smuggled it out of the palace, and implanted it into the soil in his garden. Many people tried, in vain, to extricate it, until Moses arrived at Midian and came across the staff in Jethro's garden. He read the wording on the staff and lifted it gently out of the soil. When Jethro saw that, he observed, "Here is the future savior of Israel" (*Pirkei D'Rabbi Eliezer* on Exodus 4:17; *Yalkut Shim'oni* ad loc). It was that which prompted him to give his daughter, Zipporah, to Moses as his wife.

## THE TEN PLAGUES

**58. Why was the first of the Ten Plagues directed against the Nile, so that its water turned to blood?**

This was because Pharaoh and the Egyptians worshiped the Nile as their deity (Midrash *Shemot Rabbah,* ch. 9). God wished to demonstrate His overarching power at the very outset, so that the Egyptians would all witness and acknowledge God's sovereignty and power and allow Israel to leave immediately. They would thus never be able to claim subsequently that had God really convinced them at the outset of His sole divinity, they would have immediately capitulated and been spared the terrible subsequent plagues.

**59. Was the blood restricted to the River Nile?**

No. The Torah states that it was found "in their rivers . . . and in all their collections of water" (Exodus 7:19), from which the Midrash (Exodus 7:19) derives that wherever their water was located—whether in jars in their homes or even as spittle in their mouths—it became blood!

**60. Why did Aaron, not Moses, preside over the bringing of the first plague?**

It would have been gross ingratitude on Moses' part, since his life was saved by the River Nile, when, as a newly born babe, it provided a hiding place for him from Pharaoh's officers who were searching for new babies in order to drown them in the Nile in accordance with Pharaoh's wicked decree (Exodus 7:19).

**61. At the beginning of the description of the plague of frogs, the Torah employs the singular, stating that "The *frog* came up (*vata'al ha-tzefardea*) and covered the land of Egypt" (Exodus 8:2). All subsequent references, however, are to the collective "frogs" (*ha-tzefardim*). How is this to be harmonized?**

Rabbi Akivah offered the suggestion that, indeed, it was one gigantic frog that came up and covered the entire land. His colleague Rabbi Eleazar chided him, saying, "Akivah, keep out of midrashic folklore, and restrict yourself to the abstruse halakhic tractates wherein you are the master! How then do we harmonize the two references? Simply that it all began with one which then summoned all its mates to invade the land" (Talmud *Sanhedrin* 67b).

Rabbi Akivah clearly preempted Steven Spielberg's movie, *Jurassic Park,* by almost two thousand years!

**62. Why were the second and third plagues—frogs and lice—also brought by Aaron, and not by Moses?**

For the same reason as mentioned above: because the source of the plague of frogs was "the rivers, canals and pools" (Exodus 8:1), and Moses had been saved by the

River Nile. Similarly, the plague of lice originated with the command to "strike the dust of the ground" (8:13), and Moses had cause to be grateful for the dust, since it concealed the Egyptian whom he smote.

### 63. Why did God permit the Egyptian magicians to copy the introductory sign of the changing of Moses' staff into a serpent (see Exodus 7:11), as well as the first two plagues (see 7:22, 8:3)?

If God had not secured their involvement in some of the plagues they might always have claimed that they simply had held aloof from performing the identical signs and plagues because it was beneath their dignity to enter into a contest with the Hebrews. Once they had shown that they had no such qualms, however, then it was obvious to all that their inability to match any of the subsequent plagues was patently because of the superior power of Moses and Aaron and the Power they represented.

### 64. Why were the magicians unable to reproduce the third plague of lice, thus prompting them to withdraw from the contest and acknowledge the "finger of [the true] God" in all the subsequent plagues?

The demons that the magicians conjured up as agents of their magic were unable to create anything smaller than the size of a barley grain. That was because demons are unclean spirits; and the smallest measure that is susceptible to impurity is the size of a barley grain. Any substance or creature smaller than that in volume cannot become impure, which means that the demons can have no power over it. The lice were smaller than a barley grain, and were thus outside the control of the demons and the magicians who manipulated them (*Yalkut Me'am Lo'ez* on Exodus 8:14).

### 65. The fourth plague is referred to in the Torah by the term *Arov*. What is the literal meaning of that term?

*Arov* means, literally, "a mixture" and is assumed to refer to an invasion of several species of wild animals, reptiles, and poisonous insects. These included lions, wolves and bears, snakes and scorpions, gnats, and bees.

### 66. Why is it that, until the sixth plague, whenever Pharaoh changes his mind, the terminology used is, "And the heart of Pharaoh was hardened" (Exodus 7:13, 22; 8:15), "He hardened his heart" (8:11, 28), or "And the heart of Pharaoh was stubborn" (9:7), whereas from the sixth plague on, the expression, "And the Lord hardened the heart of Pharaoh" (9:12; 10:20, 27; 11:10) is employed?

This is clearly to forestall the accusation that God removed any free choice from Pharaoh and therefore inflicted that succession of punishments upon him unfairly. We see from the Torah's very specific description that God gave Pharaoh five opportunities to exercise freely his moral choice. With each of the first five plagues, Pharaoh was able to see, and experience to his cost, the punishment that immediately followed the crime. He nevertheless rashly chose to ignore the cumulative consequences. Five chances to exercise one's free will are the most one may reasonably expect. After that, it became patently obvious in which direction his freely exercised will was pointing. From then on, in the spirit of the talmudic principle, "In the way a man wishes to go, God points him" (Talmud *Makkot* 10b), God felt justified in helping Pharaoh to ensure that his heart remained "hard." Hence, from the sixth plague onward, the phraseology changes to involve God in Pharaoh's decision making.

**67. Why, regarding the plague of boils, does the Torah specify that "the magicians could not stand before Moses because of the boils, since the boils were upon the magicians and upon all Egypt"? (9:11).**

The magicians were singled out, even though the plague was "upon all Egypt," to indicate that they suffered the most; for, whereas eventually, all the Egyptians were healed, the magicians were not, and were consequently never able to "stand before Moses." The boils developed into leprosy, from which they died.

The reason for their particularly harsh treatment was because they had discovered, through their divination, that a child was about to be born who would be the savior of Israel. They therefore advised Pharaoh to throw every Israelite male child into the Nile. And for that advice they were punished more than the rest of the Egyptians.

**68. In regard to the plague of hail, after Pharaoh expresses remorse and begs Moses to remove it from his land, Moses says to Pharaoh, "As soon as I have left the city, I shall spread forth my hands to the Lord . . . and there shall be no more hail" (9:29). Now why did Moses first have to leave the city before praying to God?**

The reason was that the Egyptians erected their idols on high hills and trees around their cities. During the plague of hail, however, they brought them inside the city, away from the exposed places where the hail would devastate them. Hence, because the capital city was so jam-packed with idols, Moses regarded it as a place of total impurity where prayer to God was unacceptable.

**69. In connection with the removal of the plague of locusts, why did the Torah see fit to state that not a single one remained, a point that is not so specifically pointed out in relation to the removal of any of the other plagues?**

The reason is because the Egyptians, when they were first threatened with this plague, facetiously expressed their eager anticipation of being able to boil the locusts and enjoy them as a delicacy. Hence, the Torah stresses that "God brought an exceedingly strong west wind, which took up the locusts and drove them into the Red Sea, so that not one locust remained in all the border of Egypt" (10:19).

**70. What was the purpose of the plague of darkness?**

There were two main purposes: first and foremost, to enable the Israelites, "who had light in their habitations" (10:23), to visit their Egyptian neighbors in order to discover what valuables they possessed, since the command was soon to come to ask of them vessels of silver and gold as payment for all the years they had slaved without pay. The Egyptians were unable to deny that they had anything to give the Israelites, since the latter could tell them the exact location of what they wanted to take away with them.

Secondly, there were quite a number of assimilated Israelites who were disloyal to their own people and were disinclined to leave Egypt with the rest, and who sought to protect the Egyptians from the plagues. God determined that they should die, but in doing so He was presented with a dilemma, for if He brought upon them a plague and destroyed them thereby, the Egyptians would claim that the Hebrew God could not discriminate, but destroyed everyone, even His own people. Hence, He brought a three-day plague of darkness so that the Israelites would be able to bury their own dead without the Egyptians noticing what had happened.

### 71. What was the reaction of Pharaoh's advisers and courtiers to all the plagues that were visited upon them?

There are indications that some of them were convinced of the preeminence and omnipotence of the Hebrew God: hence, the reference to "those who feared the word of God among the servants of Pharaoh" (9:20). On the other hand, there were others who, for expediency, wanted to get rid of the Hebrews, whom they perceived as the agents of all these woes that had descended upon Egypt, but who were not prepared to make the obvious connection and affirm the truth of the Israelite God. They also had the feeling that Moses was some sort of super-magician and that it was his special powers that were wreaking such havoc on Egypt. It is in this sense that we explain the verse: "Some servants of Pharaoh said to him: How long shall this man be a snare unto us? Let the men go that they may serve the Lord their God; do you not realize that Egypt is doomed?" (10:7). Note also that they were only counseling here that the Israelite men be allowed to leave. This was clearly a ploy, since they knew full well that Moses had consistently demanded the release of all the people, without distinction.

### 72. What was the reaction of the Egyptian populace to what Moses and the Israelites were inflicting upon them and their land?

There is a clear indication that the general feeling among the Egyptians was that their country's treatment of the Hebrews had been deplorable and that Pharaoh was compounding his wickedness by refusing to give them their freedom. Surprisingly, although it was through the agency of Moses that they were suffering so greatly, they held him in the highest esteem. This situation is expressed in the verse: "And the Lord gave the people favour in the sight of the Egyptians. Moreover the man Moses was very great in the sight of Pharaoh's servants, and in the sight of the people" (11:3). It was only from the sight of Pharaoh and his advisers that the greatness of God and that of Moses were obscured!

**73. What is the significance of the apparently unnecessary reference, in the case of so many of the plagues, to the fact that after Moses had foretold the coming of the particular plague, he and Aaron "turned and went out from before Pharaoh" (10:6), "went out from Pharaoh" (8:8, 26; 10:18), or "went out from before Pharaoh in hot anger" (12:8)?**

The implication is that, whereas it was accepted protocol that one blessed the king before asking permission to leave his presence, and when this was granted one walked backwards, bowing, out of sight, yet Moses and Aaron refused to grant Pharaoh those tokens of deference; instead, after giving their warning of what was to come, they simply "turned [their backs] and walked out" (Ramban on Exodus 10:6).

**74. Psalm 136, referred to as *Hallel Ha-Mitzri*, "Praise for the Egyptian [deliverance]," has an enigmatic phrase: *Lemakeh mitzrayim bivkhoreihem*, "He who smote the Egyptians *through their firstborn*." What is the meaning of this statement?**

According to midrashic tradition, when the Egyptian firstborn got to hear of the impending plague of *Makat Bekhorim*, the death of all the firstborn, they led a violent demonstration to Pharaoh's palace to persuade him to let the Israelites go and spare them such a terrible fate. Far from giving them a sympathetic hearing or even attempting to assure them that they had nothing to fear, Pharaoh ordered his palace guard to fall upon the demonstrators and punish them for their presumptuous conduct. When the firstborn saw that they had nothing to lose, they counterattacked and slew a vast number of Pharaoh's guards, courtiers, and servants. This is the sense of that phrase: "He slew the Egyptians by means of their own firstborn."

**75. What was the scope of the term "firstborn" when used to describe those who met their deaths in the last of the Ten Plagues?**

It was a most comprehensive term, embracing firstborn girls as well as boys and the firstborn of fathers as well as mothers. As the Egyptians led dissolute lives and went from one alliance to the next, it was not uncommon for one mother to have several firstborn children from her different male consorts. One can imagine, therefore, the extent of the tragic ramifications of this plague in every single household.

**76. Moses foretold to Pharaoh that "all firstborn in the land of Egypt shall die, from the firstborn of Pharaoh . . . even unto the firstborn of the maidservant that is behind the mill" (Exodus 11:5). Why were the servants, who surely could not have been guilty of inflicting any punishment upon the Israelites, made to suffer?**

They were also guilty of rejoicing at Israel's suffering and thereby giving encouragement to the actual perpetrators. They were consequently regarded by God as accessories to the crime, and therefore conjointly responsible.

The parallel in modern times would be the collective guilt of all members of a terrorist organization, whether or not they individually had perpetrated any atrocity. Similarly, all the German people, as members of the Third Reich, bore the guilt of the Nazi atrocities. Not only acts of evil commission, but also those of omission— such as nonprotestation in the early period of Nazi ascendancy, when the excesses of their violent and discriminatory policies might have been checked by strong public protest and dissent, as well as the refusal, on the part of most Germans and Poles, to demonstrate any personal act of mercy and compassion or extend any covert individual help and protection to those in danger—are examples of what Jewish law and ethics regard as a partnership in evil. This is the meaning of the verse, "Do not stand idly by the blood of your neighbor" (Leviticus 19:16).

### 77. The same verse continues, "And all the firstborn of your cattle." What possible reason could there have been for slaying the cattle?

The reason is that the Egyptians worshiped cattle, and the lamb in particular, as gods. The punishment of their gods was to demonstrate to the nation just how misguided were their religious beliefs and how impotent were their deities.

### 78. What was the impact of all those plagues upon the Israelites?

Nowhere is there any elation on the part of the Israelites recorded as a result of any of the plagues. It would seem that they were only too aware that, but for the grace of God, they would have been in an identical situation, because they had little merit of their own at that time, which was before they were given the two *mitzvot* of the Paschal lamb and circumcision. The Rabbis maintain that they had, indeed, slipped to the forty-ninth level of impurity and that, had God not redeemed them at that precise moment, they would have sunk into spiritual oblivion and forfeited any chance of redemption from Egypt forever. This is, in fact, the meaning of the otherwise obvious statement in the Haggadah, "And had not the Holy One, blessed be He, brought us out of Egypt then we, and our children, and our children's children would still have remained subservient to Pharaoh in Egypt" (Haggadah, *Avadim Hayyinu*) (*Yalkut Shim'oni* [Jerusalem: Levin-Epstein, 1967] on Hosea, sec. 533).

So they stood in constant trepidation that, at any time, they might also be stricken down with any one of the plagues. And even when they left Egypt, the trepidation remained—and justifiably, as it turned out—that the Egyptians might recover from their devastation and still summon up the strength to pursue after them and bring them back to Egypt as slaves once again. It was only after the drowning of all Pharaoh's army in the Red Sea that the Israelites really believed that their troubles were over. That is the force of the first word of the Song of the Red Sea: *Az (yashir Mosheh)*, "*Then* [and only then] did Moses and the Children of Israel sing" (Exodus 15:1). Moses, naturally, had perfect faith in the ultimate outcome, but it was not until that fateful moment that he could have got the Children of Israel to sing with him and share his confidence.

At the Song of the Red Sea it states, "And they believed in God and in Moses His servant" (Exodus 14:31). This suggests that until they actually witnessed the doom of the Egyptians, they had even entertained doubts about Moses' claim to be God's true representative, if not about the omnipotence of God Himself. That God should have extended His unbounded love and eternal grace to a people of such little faith remains a true mystery!

Their great trepidation, their lack of belief in themselves, and their self-conscious *galut* (exile) mentality, inspired the comment that it was more difficult for God to take Egypt out of the Hebrews than to take the Hebrews out of Egypt!

## SONG OF THE RED SEA

**79. But, we may well ask, where is it indicated that the Israelites did ultimately undergo a change of heart and a conversion to faith, to the extent that God's efforts on their behalf were indeed proved to have been vindicated?**

The source for this is the verse that states, "The Children of Israel walked upon dry land in the midst of the sea" (14:29). The Midrash (*Shemot Rabbah,* ch. 21) finds this verse enigmatic; for surely, if they were on dry land, they were not "in the midst of the sea," and if they were in the midst of the sea, they were not "on dry land"! The Midrash answers that "this teaches that God did not divide the sea until they were up to their noses in water. Only when God saw that they had developed the faith to proceed, come what may, did He part the water of the Red Sea and create dry land under their feet" (*Shemot Rabbah,* ch. 21). It is only when man has proceeded to the very limits of his abilities, exhausting every ounce of energy in his body, that God activates the miraculous forces on his behalf. From that situation, of *mesirut nefesh,* of self-surrender to God's providence, we may detect the point of transition in the spiritual growth of the people of Israel.

**80. Why was the Song of the Red Sea included in our daily morning prayers?**

Because our synagogue liturgy finds a place for any prayers or compositions that were originally part of the Temple service, and the *Shirat Ha-Yam,* the Song of the Red Sea, was recited every Sabbath afternoon in the Temple by the Levites, while the *Tamid Shel Bein Ha-Arbayim,* the Continual (daily) Offering, was being offered up. Because of its great significance, and with the expansion of the liturgy after the destruction of the Temple, it began to be recited each day in Palestine, a practice that was then followed in Babylon by many communities and finally became almost universal.

**81. Why, in most editions of the prayer book, is the Song of the Red Sea set out in an unusual layout, with a centered half-line positioned directly above two broken half lines, a formation continued throughout the composition?**

This is a scribal requirement for the way the passage (Exodus 15:1–19) has to be written in the *Sefer Torah.* It is meant to be suggestive of a wall, and the way one brick is cemented above the join of the two bricks immediately beneath it. This artistic wall motif is to recall the fact that "the water [of the Red Sea] was a wall unto them on their right side and on their left" (14:29), enabling them to walk through on dry land.

# III

# The Lead-in to Pesach: The Special Sabbaths

## *SHABBAT SHEKALIM*

### 82. What point can rightly be described as the launch of the Pesach preparations?

Pesach is preceded by five special Sabbaths, which relate to the theme of the festival or to preparations for it that were necessary in Temple times. These Sabbaths are distinguished by special *Maftir* (concluding portions of the Torah) and *Haftarot* (readings from the prophetic books).

So the launch of the pre-Pesach season occurs with *Shabbat Parashat Shekalim,* which takes place on the *Shabbat* preceding (or, in some years, corresponding with) the Rosh Chodesh (new moon) of Adar, some six weeks prior to the festival.

### 83. What is the significance of *Shabbat Shekalim*?

The Mishnah tells us that in Temple times they would make public announcements to remind the communities, both of Israel and the Diaspora, that their half-shekel contributions toward the public daily sacrifices in the Temple should be sent in (to their local collection point) without delay, in order that it might reach the Temple treasurers in time for the new year, commencing on the first of Nisan.

### 84. What portion of the Torah and *Haftarah* is read on that *Shabbat*?

We read the first part of the *Sidra Ki Tissa* (Exodus 30:11–16), which refers to another half-shekel donation, the one required whenever a census of the Israelites was required. Rather than count heads (in an undignified way, like one counts sheep), every person was required to donate a single, half-shekel coin, which was counted instead.

The *Haftarah* (2 Kings 11:17–12:17) relates how, in the reign of King Joash, great renovations of the Temple were made, and, with the half-shekel precedent in his mind, the king introduced a special collection, to be administered by the priests, for the specific purpose of "repairing the breaches of the house [of God]." In this context we have the first reference to a charity collection box: "And Yehoiadah the priest took a chest, and bored a hole in the lid of it, and set it beside the altar, on the right side as one comes into the house of the Lord" (12:10).

## SHABBAT ZAKHOR

### 85. Which is the second of the five special pre-Pesach Sabbaths?

That is *Shabbat Parashat Zakhor*, "Sabbath of the portion of Remembrance," and occurs on the Sabbath preceding the festival of Purim. It derives its name from the opening word of the portion of the Torah prescribed to be read as *Maftir: Zakhor* — "*Remember* what Amalek did to you on the way as you went up out of Egypt" (Deuteronomy 25:17–19).

### 86. What is the significance of *Shabbat Zakhor*?

This biblical portion is, of course, related primarily to Pesach and the events of the Exodus from Egypt, when the Israelites were set upon by the murderous Amalekites, who, in cowardly fashion, did not engage the Israelite forces at the front of the people, but fell upon the elderly, weak, and defenseless stragglers bringing up the rear. It was prescribed for the Sabbath before Purim, however, because Haman, the arch villain of the Purim story, was a descendant of Agag, King of Amalek. Because he followed in the footsteps of his ancestors, we tar them both with the same brush by reading the biblical account of Amalek's dastardly act just a few days before Purim, when we recount the similar machinations of his evil descendant in the Persian era.

### 87. What is the relevance of the *Haftarah* prescribed for recitation on *Shabbat Zakhor*?

It is taken from 1 Samuel 15:1–34 and is directly related to the theme of that biblical Amalekite king, Agag. It describes how King Saul was commanded by the prophet Samuel to wreak just vengeance upon the Amalekites and wipe them out, with their cattle. Saul does not follow his instructions properly, instead preserving alive Agag, the king, as well as his choicest sheep and oxen and other possessions. This act of disobedience results in Saul's severe condemnation and the rejection of his royal line.

## SHABBAT PARAH

### 88. Which is the third of the special Sabbaths?

The third is *Shabbat Parashat Parah*, "the Sabbath of the Red Heifer." This always occurs on the Sabbath immediately preceding the fourth of the special Sabbaths, *Shabbat Parashat Ha-Chodesh*. It takes its name from the portion of the *Maftir* prescribed for the occasion (Numbers 19:1–22), which describes the purification rite undergone by those who had come into direct contact with the dead. The ashes of a perfectly red heifer were mixed with water, and this mixture had to be sprinkled upon them before they could enter the Sanctuary or, subsequently, the Temple precincts. Since no unclean person could offer the Paschal lamb without purification, this theme was especially appropriate to be read in the run-up to Pesach, to remind people who were impure to arrange their purifications in time for the festival.

### 89. What is the relevance of the *Haftarah* prescribed for the *Parashat Parah*?

It is drawn from the prophecies of Ezekiel (36:16–38), who uses another source of impurity—that of a menstrual woman—as a symbol of Israel's moral and ethical impurities which have estranged her from God, her husband, just as the menstruant has to keep away from close physical contact with her husband. Israel's punishment was exile from God's Promised Land, but the prophecy assures her that a time will come when the sin will be purged and Israel will be restored both to her land and to divine favor. At that time, "the cities shall be inhabited, the waste place rebuilt and the land that was desolate shall be tilled" (v. 33).

## SHABBAT HA-CHODESH

### 90. Which is the fourth of the special Sabbaths?

This is *Shabbat Parashat Ha-Chodesh,* which takes its name from the opening words of the special Torah reading (Exodus 12:1–20): *Ha-Chodesh ha-zeh lakhem,* "This month shall be for you the head of the months." It occurs on the *Shabbat* preceding the new moon of the month of Nisan.

The prescribed Torah portion records all the biblical laws of the Passover that Moses announced to the Children of Israel just before they were to leave Egypt. These related particularly to the preparation of the Paschal lamb and the eating of it, in family groups, as their ultimate covenantal and crowning meal of fellowship, to cement and celebrate their emergence as a nation.

### 91. What is the relevance of the *Haftarah* prescribed for recitation on this Sabbath?

This is another of Ezekiel's heartening prophecies of national restoration and the rebuilding of the Temple. He refers inter alia to the celebration of Passover at that Temple, though some of his description has baffled commentators, since it has no point of contact with the reality of the Temple traditions as recorded. Thus, he refers to a day of expiation or atonement to take place on the first day of the month of Nisan, which is unknown from any other source.

## SHABBAT HA-GADOL

### 92. Which is the fifth special Sabbath?

This is *Shabbat Ha-Gadol,* "The Great Sabbath," which is the name given to the *Shabbat* before Pesach. There is no specially prescribed *Maftir* for this *Shabbat,* only a *Haftarah* from the book of Malachi. This is especially relevant to Pesach, as it speaks of the future redemption that God will send after Israel has cleansed herself from her ethical shortcomings and spiritual waywardness. This theme, of *Pesach le-*

*atid,* "the future Passover," is taken up by the *paytanim,* composers of sacred poetry, whose compositions supplement the prayers of our festival machzor.

### 93. What is the origin of the name *Shabbat Ha-Gadol*?

We are not absolutely sure. The most popular explanation is that it is a name derived from the penultimate verse (repeated to serve, in addition, as the final verse) of the *Haftarah,* which refers to God sending the prophet Elijah "before the coming of the great and fearful day of the Lord [*yom ha-gadol*]."

### 94. Why is that penultimate verse repeated at the very end of the *Haftarah*?

Wherever possible, we never finish a portion of the Torah or *Haftarah* on a sad or unpleasant note. The final verse of Malachi's prophecy ends with the words, "lest I come and smite the land with utter destruction." Hence, to end on an optimistic note, the promise of sending Elijah, to announce and prepare the ground for the arrival of the future redeemer, is repeated.

### 95. Are there any other explanations of the name *Shabbat Ha-Gadol*?

There are several. One explanation is that it was so called on account of the great miracle that occurred on the Sabbath before the first Passover in Egypt. Talmudic tradition (Talmud *Shabbat* 87a) has it that the Israelites left Egypt on a Thursday. Thus, the tenth of Nisan, when they took the Paschal lamb in defiance of the Egyptians, occurred that year on *Shabbat.* The courage of the Israelites in taking the Egyptian god and disrespectfully tethering it to the legs of their beds, and the fact that the Egyptians became petrified and made no attempt to oppose the Hebrews, made it into a truly *Shabbat Ha-Gadol,* a Great Sabbath.

A thirteenth-century Italian scholar, Zedekiah ben Avraham Anav, offers another suggestion in his work *Shibbolei Ha-Leket* (S. Buber [Vilna, 1886, p. 205]). He believes that its proper nuance is that of "the long Sabbath" and is a reference to the fact that the congregants would be expected to spend many more hours than usual in Synagogue on that Sabbath, listening to the Rabbi giving a long and thorough exposition of all the detailed laws of the festival and answering the specific questions of the community.

A further explanation of the name takes account of the classical dispute between the Pharisees and Sadducees over the meaning of the biblical phrase, "On the morrow of the Sabbath" (Leviticus 23:15–16), from which day the counting of the *Omer* has to commence. The Pharisees maintained that the word "Sabbath," meaning, literally, "day of cessation from work," has an extended meaning, and may refer also to a festival day. In the verse quoted, then, its meaning is that we should commence counting the *Omer* on the morrow of the (first) *Yom Tov* day of Pesach, namely, on the sixteenth of Nisan. The Sadducees, who took the words of the Torah quite literally, insisted that "the morrow of the Sabbath" meant Sunday. They therefore commenced counting the *Omer* on the first Sunday of Passover, which meant that they always celebrated the festival of Shavuot, seven full weeks later, on a Sunday. Since the contention between those two factions was over the issue of whether or not the first Sabbath of Pesach was a significant Sabbath (for the *Omer* counting), the Pharisees, as a gesture of rejection of that claim, made great play of the Sabbath before, rather than after, Pesach, calling it the "Great Sabbath," the only one that has any significance at this period.

### 96. In what other ways is the importance of this Sabbath demonstrated?

It is customary to call up the Rabbi of the congregation to read the special *Haftarah*. Also, during the Afternoon (Minchah) Service, we read the first part of the Haggadah, and, between Minchah and Maariv, the Rabbi gives an extended *derashah,* a talmudic exposition on a theme related to the preparations for the festival.

### 97. How old is this practice of giving public expositions before the festivals?

The practice was referred to nearly two thousand years ago, in the Talmud (*Pesachim* 6a), which states, "One should raise issues (*shoalin*) and give expositions (*dorshin*) on the laws of Pesach from thirty days before the festival." This practice was not confined to Pesach, however, but was extended to the other festivals also. Another source (Talmud *Rosh Hashanah* 7a) credits Moses with having introduced the practice. Its proof-text for this attribution is the verse, "Assemble the people, the men and the women and the little ones . . . that they may hear and that they may learn . . . and observe to do all the words of this law" (Deuteronomy 31:12). In conformity with the talmudic dictum, it is customary to introduce *shiurim* (discourses) on the laws of Pesach starting immediately after the festival of Purim, which occurs about thirty days before Pesach.

# IV

## Cleaning, "Kashering," and Preparing the Kitchen

### PESACH SPRING CLEANING

**98. Why does the home have to be so thoroughly "spring-cleaned" for Pesach?**

It is all related to the prohibition of eating, even inadvertently, any leavened substance, even of the minutest quantity. The Rabbis tell us, "One is duty-bound to regard oneself as having personally come out of Egypt" (Talmud *Pesachim* 116b). By excluding every trace of leaven from our homes, we are existentially homing in on the experience of Exodus-man. As a slave, he ate hurriedly his *lechem oni*, "bread of affliction," in the form of broken pieces of quickly baked *matzot*, and as he left Egypt and emerged into freedom, he was told to bake the same. In freedom and comfort, we must never lose sight of our humble and troubled origins as fugitives and wanderers. For Jewish survival, throughout history, has been determined by our ability to accommodate to the most adverse of conditions and to emulate the resilience displayed by our ancestors in Egypt. For this reason, we are meticulous to banish all leaven from our homes and mouths at this time, and to ready ourselves thereby, on an annual basis, for whatever unexpected and adverse a fate we may have to confront.

**99. Is there a biblical source for such a thoroughgoing removal of all leaven from homes as well as mouths?**

Indeed: the Torah gives several separate prohibitions. The first states, "For seven days shall there be no leaven *found* in your homes" (Exodus 12:19). The second is, "You shall *eat* nothing leavened; in all your habitations shall you eat unleavened bread" (12:20). And finally, "And there shall be no leaven *seen* with you in all your borders seven days" (Deuteronomy 16:4). The absolute removal of every trace is, therefore, quite unequivocally demanded.

The explanation of the *Ran* (Commentary, beginning of Talmud *Pesachim*) is that in the case of leaven, a trebly strong precaution had to be issued, since not only is there nothing *treifa* (ritually unacceptable) about that food, but it also is the food that we are accustomed to eat throughout the year. We have to be especially on our guard when it comes to things that are second nature.

41

### 100. But where does the changing of cutlery and crockery for Pesach fit in?

Precisely in this context, and in the light of the symbolism of unleavened foods referred to above (question 98). Since the Torah is so clear on the absolute necessity of removing every trace of leaven from our mouths, we take every possible precaution, not only to avoid any contact with the forbidden substance, but also, psychologically, to remove any possible temptation to its inadvertent consumption. We therefore hide away, from sight and use, any implement or utensil that has any "association" with leaven, thereby totally excluding it from our minds for the duration of the festival.

The prohibition of using our everyday vessels for Passover is not only a question of the flavor of foods containing leaven ingredients being absorbed into those utensils, which would fall under the prohibition of "eating" leaven, it is also to prevent us from treating the prohibition lightly. If we were permitted to use leaven vessels, we would not treat the consumption of leaven as particularly serious.

### 101. When should this Pesach spring cleaning commence?

There is no prescribed moment, though the requirement of studying and revising the laws and regulations of the festival from thirty days before (see question 97), provides a general guide as regards home preparations as well. Clearly, it will depend upon the size of the house and the extent of its use.

## PREPARING THE KITCHEN

### 102. What level of cleaning is required?[1]

Pesach has become the Jewish equivalent of "spring cleaning," as practiced in most countries when the spring arrives and there is a disposition to remove every trace of the winter grime from windows, paintwork, curtains, and so on. It has to be said that this is not what is demanded, though obviously it is commendable to make the house spick and span in honor of the festival. But this applies to all festivals, and not exclusively to Pesach.

Generally, there is no leaven on window sills, windows, or curtains, so the like of these do not require any special treatment! Similarly, any rooms or areas of the home where one is certain that no leaven is brought in require no more than a vacuum, a dust, and a quick check that no one has inadvertently entered and left some leaven there. In families with children, however, nothing can be taken for granted! One should be careful to search the pockets of their clothing and any parts of the house, including cellars or attics, where they sometimes play.

Clearly, the rooms where food is prepared and eaten—kitchens, pantries, dining rooms, and family rooms—require being thoroughly cleaned. If food is taken into

---

1. The concise halakhic material contained in the rest of this section is intended only as a general guide. There are differing views as regards many aspects and details of the Passover laws of "kashering." In all matters of doubt, one should seek the guidance of a competent halakhic authority.

bedrooms they also need to be well cleaned; otherwise, a vacuum cleaning suffices. It is customary to change bed linen in honor of the occasion.

A thorough search should be made around fridges, freezers, and storage cupboards, and anywhere where spillage can result in food stains and residue. (See below for ways of cleaning cookers, fridges, etc., that are being used for Passover.)

### 103. How does one prepare one's kitchen for Passover?

One should keep an eye on the level of one's food stock from about four weeks before Pesach, and, if possible, use up as much as possible of that, rather than buying new packets of cereal and other leaven that will be impossible to finish in time.

The entire kitchen should be thoroughly cleaned. One should then earmark as many cupboards or shelves as will be required for storing exclusively Passover foodstuffs, pans, dishes, cutlery, and crockery. The shelves, drawers, and interior of those cupboards should be cleared out and washed down. Some individuals are particular to cover the surfaces with lining or grease-proof paper.

Cupboards that are to store the non-Passover utensils, as well as the remaining stock of foods that are unfit for use on Passover (see questions 127–128), should be kept locked. If this is impossible, a small colored sticker might be attached to the front of each cupboard door, so that these will not be opened and their contents used inadvertently during Pesach. Some individuals are particular to place paper over the contents on each shelf of these cupboards so that if they are opened inadvertently, it will be immediately apparent.

Obviously, until the day before Pesach it will be necessary to use the kitchen and some appliances for *chametz* (leaven) use. It will be easier, therefore, to have cooked well in advance the foods to be eaten during the last few days before the festival, so that the cooker can then be "kashered" (made fit) for the preparation of Pesach meals as early as is required. Cookers and stoves, as well as pans being "kashered" by means of fire or intense heat (see question 107), do *not* require twenty-four hours' wait before they are "kashered." This only applies to vessels being "kashered" by means of the boiling water, *hag'alah* method (see question 112). The householder will thus have to pace him- or herself, depending upon how much cooking is required to be done before the festival.

### 104. How are the surfaces of the kitchen "kashered" for Passover use?

Naturally, one cannot prepare Passover foods before one has ensured that all the surrounding area of the kitchen—the surfaces, storage cupboards, fridge, and freezer—are all previously prepared to receive the Passover foods. As regards the surfaces of the modern kitchen: generally, these are made of nonporous material, in addition to which hot foods are generally placed in containers (pans, plates, etc.), rather than directly onto the surfaces. This means that, apart from a thorough cleaning with a recommended cleaning product, no drastic act of *hag'alah,* "purging with boiling hot water," is required. It is recommended, however, that all surfaces be covered with plastic or similar material. If the surfaces are of stainless steel, boiling water should be poured onto them, after having administered a thorough cleaning.

### 105. How do we "kasher" the fridge and freezer?

Having removed all the *chametz* foodstuffs, we defrost the appliance, wash all inside surfaces, and thoroughly clean the trays whereon food may have spilt. We do not fear absorption of flavor, since only in conditions of heat is this a factor. Hence, no *hag'alah* purging (see question 112) is required.

### 106. How do we "kasher" the kitchen sink and draining boards?

Porcelain and enamel sinks cannot be "kashered." These should be thoroughly cleaned, especially around the faucets and spouts, and then covered with an insert or with aluminum foil. Stainless steel sinks and draining boards should be left for twenty-four hours, after use with hot *chametz,* after which water from a boiling kettle should be poured over them.

Bathroom sinks, which do not make contact with food, do not require any special "kashering."

### 107. How do we "kasher" gas or electric cookers?

It should be noted that grills and grill pans cannot be properly kashered. If they can be unscrewed, they should be cleaned and stored away. If not, they should be cleaned as thoroughly as possible with chemical cleaner and steel wool.

Wherever possible, one should obtain new movable parts of the cooker, to be kept especially for Pesach. This is particularly important for parts that come into direct contact with the pots and pans. There should be no difficulty in obtaining from the supplier new metal trays and pan supports. If this is not possible, then the following procedure should be followed: (i) remove all removable parts of the cooker top and clean thoroughly with a strong chemical cleaner (first, check manufacturers' instructions) and steel wool; (ii) clean all burners and grates with a recommended product; (iii) pay attention to the area around screws and bolts, and, if possible, unscrew them to clean more thoroughly; (iv) turn the burners up to full heat, ensuring, if possible, that the complete surface of the pan supports receives the heat. (Some employ a *blech,* a flat piece of thin metal or aluminum foil, placing it over the entire burner area; though this should only be done after taking expert advice.) Leave the heat on for approximately fifteen minutes in the case of gas cookers and about seven minutes in the case of electric burners; (v) if possible, cover the top of the cooker, the surface that absorbs all the rising vapours of the cooking, and the splashboard surface, with heavy duty aluminum foil, cutting out sections for the burners.

### 108. How do we "kasher" ceramic burners?

The ceramic surrounds should be thoroughly cleaned, and the burners should be left on full heat for about five minutes. The heating area should be covered with aluminum foil, if possible, with cutouts for the burner sections.

## 109. How do we "kasher" a self-cleaning oven?

Most authorities hold that it is sufficient to simply put it through an ordinary self-cleaning cycle. As regards the continuous self-cleaning oven, it is sufficient to set it to the highest temperature for about forty-five minutes.

## 110. How do we "kasher" a microwave oven?

If the inside is made of stainless steel, acrylic, or heavy-duty plastic, it should first be cleaned thoroughly and left for twenty-four hours. Then place a bowl filled with water inside the microwave. Switch on the microwave until the entire inside is filled with steam. It is then ready for Passover use. As regards microwaves with plastic or enamel interiors, some authorities believe that the above method is not sufficiently thorough and require all food to be placed inside some kind of plastic container before cooking.

## 111. How do we "kasher" a hot plate?

After thoroughly cleaning it, switch it on to maximum heat and leave on for about seven minutes.

## 112. How do we "kasher" cutlery, crockery, and silver or metal dishes?

Crockery made from china or earthenware cannot be rendered "kasher" for Pesach. Cutlery and metal dishes should be "kashered" by the *hag'alah* method of immersion in boiling water. The procedure is as follows: (i) clean thoroughly all items, preferably with a recommended cleaner. Ensure that they are free of cracks (which would necessitate removal with a blowtorch) or any joints wherein particles of food could penetrate. Bone-handled cutlery should not be "kashered." (ii) Ensure that twenty-four hours has elapsed since it was last used. (iii) Fill a large container—either a *chametz* or Pesach one is acceptable—to the brim with water, and boil until the water flows over the rim. (iv) Place the objects to be "kashered," a few at a time, inside a clean wicker basket or net container, wherein the water can amply penetrate, and lower carefully into the boiling water. (As a precaution, clean linen gloves may be worn.) Hold there for about seven seconds. Since all parts of every vessel or implement have to come into contact with the water, the container should be moved a little so that the contents will not rest on each other and thereby prevent some contact. (v) After removing from the boiling water, run cold water over the container bag and contents.

Once "kashered" for Pesach, cutlery becomes neutral, and one may therefore designate for meat the previously milk cutlery, and vice versa.

## 113. How do we "kasher" glassware?

Glassware is one of the thorny problems of halakhah. This is because there are two diametrically opposite attitudes towards it. One view is that its glazing prevents any absorption of flavor. Hence, throughout the year, glasses may be used for both milk and meat, as long as they are thoroughly rinsed between uses. There is another tradition that characterizes glass as akin to china and earthenware vessels, which may not be "kashered" at all. And it is the practice, for Pesach only, to take cognizance of the stricter view, and, if at all possible, not to "kasher" glassware.

If glassware—other than whiskey glasses, whose flavor even "kashering" cannot entirely remove—has to be used, then there is a special method prescribed for "kashering," called *millui ve-irui,* "filling and emptying out." A large, clean container should be filled with cold water. The glassware to be "kashered" should be placed inside and left for twenty-four hours. The water should then be poured away and the container refilled. This should be repeated every twenty-four hours, until the vessels have been immersed for three days.

There is a view that if china and earthenware vessels have only been used for cold foods, they may also be "kashered" by this method (see *Mishnah Berurah, Hilkhot Pesach* 451:21 [n. 117].). In this, and all other questionable situations, a competent rabbinic authority should be consulted.

### 114. How do we "kasher" ornaments?

Any object that does not come into direct contact with food does not require being "kashered." Silverware, ornaments, or vases used on one's dining table should simply be washed or cleaned thoroughly.

## HALAKHIC ASPECTS OF "KASHERING"

### 115. Where in the Torah is the principle of "kashering" vessels found?

It is found in Numbers 31:21–24, in the episode dealing with the aftermath of the battle against the Midianites, where a large number of utensils and other objects were taken as booty. The Israelites wished to use those impure vessels, and Moses gave them instructions as to the basic principles: "Everything that is brought onto the fire, you shall make to go through the fire, and it shall be clean. . . . All that is not brought onto the fire, you shall make to go through water" (v. 23). Thus, we have the established principle of "kashering," which is expressed by the Rabbis as *kebol'o kakh polto,* "in the like manner [of cooking] that a vessel absorbs a flavor, so it purges it." A vessel used on fire, like a frying pan, is made kasher through purging it with fire (a blowtorch); one used only with boiling liquids is made kasher by purging with boiling water.

### 116. What is the principle behind the act of "kashering"?

The halakhic principle is that "absorbed flavour is purged in the identical way in which it was absorbed" (Talmud *Pesachim* 30a). Thus, the absorption of flavor from a hot *chametz* fluid is neutralized by heating up that (metal) container, utensil, or article of cutlery by *hag'alah,* immersion in boiling water. If it was a pot, or a baking or frying pan, that absorbed *chametz* flavor through cooking over fire, without any water, it is "kashered" in similar manner. This process is called *libun*, "white heat," involving either heating in a gas or electric oven or by means of a blowtorch. The method required depends upon the level of heat attendant upon its use.

### 117. Is there any blessing to be made over the *mitzvah* of "kashering"?

No. Most authorities do not regard it as a positive *mitzvah*, for the very simple reason that it is not obligatory to perform the act of "kashering," if, for example, one can afford to buy new.

### 118. Are there any materials that cannot be made "kasher"?

Vessels made of synthetic materials, such as plastic or nylon, as well as Teflon, Pyrex, and Duralex vessels should not be "kashered." (Rabbi Ovadiah Yoseph does permit pyrex to be "kashered" by immersing it three times in boiling water. He does not, however, permit the "kashering" of glass. Sephardim may follow his rulings. See *Chazon Ovadiah*, p. 79.) Wooden, stone, and metal vessels may be "kashered" by immersion in boiling water *(hag'alah)*, though one should take care that there are no cracks or joins wherein the residue of food may have collected. One may also not "kasher" graters or grinders that have been used with pure *chametz* or with horse-radish (or any other sharp-flavored herb) that has been cut with a *chametz* knife. Such graters would require *libun* (direct heat application).

### 119. Can "kashering" only be performed by men?

Not at all, though whoever does it should familiarize him- or herself with the procedures and regulations. In some communities it was the practice for people to bring their pots, pans, and cutlery to the Shul kitchen where someone well-versed in Jewish law would "kasher" it for them (see question 825).

# V

# The Prohibition of *Chametz*

**120. Is there a minimum amount of *chametz* that, if found in the house, may be discounted on account of its minute measure?**

No. Unlike mixtures of milk and meat or traces of *treifa* food in a larger volume, where we assume the principle of *batel beshishim,* "it becomes annulled in sixty times its volume," this principle is not applied to *chametz,* where even the minutest amount (a *mashehu*) retains its significance and causes biblical law to be infringed. As regards eating, however, one only becomes liable to punishment, under biblical law, if he ate the equivalent volume of a *kezayit,* an olive.

**121. Where is this distinction referred to?**

The prohibition of the minutest amount was an extra stringency imposed by the Sages as a precautionary measure in order to protect a person from eating *chametz* food. This measure was felt necessary because of the fact that one is permitted *chametz* throughout the year (unlike *treifa* food), so that the instinctive tendency is to keep it in one's possession and put it into one's mouth (see *Tosafot* to Talmud *Pesachim* 2b).

The prohibition of the minutest amount is also popularly explained as indicated in the very Hebrew words *chametz* and *matzah.* The letters *mem* and *tzadi* are common to them both. The only distinction is in the third letter: *chametz* has the letter *chet,* and *matzah* has the letter *hey.* If you write down those two letters, the difference is a minute joining to meet the top horizontal bar, which occurs in the *chet* (ח) but not in the *hey* (ה). Hence, even such a minute amount of *chametz* is prohibited.

**122. By which time must the house be *Pesadik,* or ready for the festival?**

Apart from the corner of the kitchen or living room where the food for breakfast on the morning of Erev Pesach (the lead-in to Passover) should be kept, the entire home should be *chametz*-free by nightfall on the day prior to Passover. All *chametz* food that is being retained over the duration of the festival should have been stored (preferably locked) away by that time.

**123. How do we define *"chametz"*?**

*Chametz* only applies to foods or articles made from the five types of grain: wheat, spelt, barley, oats, and rye. For this reason, whiskey and bourbon are prohibited,

48

since they are made by distilling a fermented mash of cereal grains (usually malted barley), whereas brandy is permitted, since it is distilled from the fermented juice of grapes or other fruit, which are not, of course, *chametz*. Hence, we are permitted to use many liquors (cherry brandy and apricot brandy as well as chocolate and coffee liquors) that are brandy-based.

### 124. At what stage does grain become *chametz*?

According to talmudic tradition, grain cannot become *chametz* until it is milled into flour. At that stage, if it comes into contact with water for a period of eighteen minutes, the process of *chimutz* (leavening) is assumed to have begun. Only by constantly kneading that dough and working on it until the moment it is placed into the oven will the leavening be prevented. In the presence of heat, the dough may also start to leaven even before the eighteen minutes have elapsed.

### 125. But if grain can only become *chametz* once it is milled, why, then, do we require to have *Shemurah Matzah* made from grain that has been watched from the time it is cut?

In truth, talmudic law does not even refer to such an excessive level of supervision as *Shemurah mish'at ketzirah*, "supervised from the time of reaping." In much later times this became a pietistic requirement, and, other than in hasidic circles, is still only sought after for use during the Seder, for the three specially prescribed *matzot*. The basic supervisory requirement remains *Shemurah mish'at techinah*, "supervised from the time the corn is milled." From then on, it is to be stored in cool conditions and kept away from water or moisture until the time for baking into *matzah*.

### 126. What *chametz* foods may be stored away in one's home over Pesach?

Strictly speaking, no leaven or admixture of leaven may be kept over Pesach, even if the leaven is a hidden ingredient. However, any nonleaven food that has merely been baked or cooked in a *chametz* vessel before Pesach may be kept (though, naturally, not eaten) over the festival. It is forbidden also to keep in one's home any washed grain product, as well as any grain that has come into contact with water or other moisture or any product containing it. It is forbidden, therefore, to keep bread, cakes, or cereals.

Since the advent of the practice of selling the *chametz* to a non-Jew, the storage of even pure *chametz* would be permitted, technically, to those who have contracted such a sale, though many people still recoil from keeping bread and biscuits in their possession.

### 127. May one make use of such products that are no longer regarded as foodstuffs?

One may do so, and for that reason it is permitted to use inks, paints, cosmetics, and toiletries even though they contain alcohol or other leavening ingredients. Some authorities regard leaven that is unfit for an animal's consumption *(nifsal me'akhilat kelev)* as having totally lost its status as a food, to the extent that it may even be eaten on Pesach. Hence, ordinary toothpaste is permitted by them, though where a supervised product is available, one should naturally choose that.

### 128. Is one permitted, then, to take pills or medicines that contain leaven?

The authorities mentioned in question 127 would permit it for the same reason. Naturally, where it is a matter of a life-threatening condition or where a doctor insists that a course of treatment may not be interrupted, then there is no question that it may be consumed. Another consideration is that when we take pills, it is not a normal act of eating, since we do not relish them on our palate but rather devour them as quickly as possible. There may be problems with tablets or capsules that are coated with starch or with liquid medicines that may contain high percentages of grain alcohol. In all these instances, one should consult one's Rabbi.

## EGG *MATZOT*

### 129. Are egg *matzot* permitted to be eaten on Pesach?

This issue is a complicated one in Jewish law. It involves the principle of premature fermentation, which the combination of eggs and dough might stimulate. The Rabbis of the Talmud debated this issue in the context of the baking of dough together with fruit juices which, according to some authorities, is prohibited since it can cause the dough to rise even before it is placed inside the baking oven (see Talmud *Pesachim* 35b–36a). Indeed, practical observation confirmed that the process was too quick to retard in the usual way, by kneading and constantly agitating the mixture until it was brought to the oven. Consequently, since egg *matzot* were categorized together with *matzah* made from fruit juice, there were strong grounds for declaring them similarly forbidden.

However, some of the great medieval authorities (*Tosafot, Rosh,* etc.) gave a slightly different slant to the talmudic debate, claiming that the difference of opinion was not with regard to *matzah* made from pure fruit juice (called *matzah ashirah,* "enriched *matzah*"), which, they believed, did not stimulate premature fermentation, but only regarding fruit juice mixed with water. And this view, that dough mixed with fruit juice and water cannot be prevented from fermenting, was accepted by the *Shulchan Arukh* (and the gloss of Moses Isserles) as law.

This explains why many authorities are reticent to permit egg *matzot,* which are governed by those identical considerations. On the other hand, since there is a view that when there is exclusively fruit juice, with no added water, no such prohibition exists, some authorities permit egg *matzot* as falling within that category.

An exception may certainly be made, however, in the case of sick or elderly people who require a softer type of *matzah.* Again, where the egg is smeared on after the *matzot* have been baked and are still warm, then, of course, there is no question of any prohibition.

The *Arukh Ha-Shulchan* reminds us that, quite apart from the above considerations, such enriched *matzot* could never be permitted to be used for the three Seder *matzot* for quite another reason, namely, that those *matzot* are meant to remind us of *lechem oni*, the bread of affliction eaten by our hapless brethren. The meager fare of poor people at that time was nothing more than flour and water, while the enriched *matzah*, with fruit juices or eggs, was reserved for the free and wealthy classes.

## BAKING PRECAUTIONS AND QUALIFICATIONS

### 130. Were there any other precautions insisted upon by the halakhah to prevent the process of premature fermentation?

Indeed, the method of baking *matzot* was finely regulated to avoid the slightest possibility of the dough rising. The *Shulchan Arukh* (*Orach Chayyim,* 459 ad loc.) states that one may not bake in the open air since the warmth of the sun or the moisture in the air may cause premature fermentation. Moses Isserles adds the precaution of not carrying uncovered *matzot* outside on the way to be baked in the oven. From these concerns was derived the extra precaution of not baking, indoors, near to a window, which also concentrates extra warmth.

The water used in the baking also had to be as cold as possible. To ensure this, the halakhah insisted on *mayim shelanu,* "water that had been left overnight," preferably for twelve hours. Without the benefit of cold storage units, the coldness of the night was the only option.

As mentioned above, the dough had to be worked on without leaving it for a moment. The hands that knead the dough become warm, and they can also initiate immediate fermentation if the dough is left unattended. The entire process had to be completed within eighteen minutes or it had to be assumed that the mixture had become *chametz.* Great care had to be taken that the rolling pins and the boards on which the dough is rolled did not have any cracks or crevices wherein dough could be lodged, which could leaven unnoticed, and the baking process had to stop every eighteen minutes for them, and the bakers' hands, to be washed. Care had to be taken not to prepare more dough mixture than could be worked on at one and the same time, to avoid the remaining part of it becoming leavened; and the halakhah even warns against holding the dough *matzah* still, near the front of the oven, prior to inserting it, since the intense heat can also initiate the fermentation process. Care had also to be taken that the dough *matzot,* when placed in the oven, should not touch each other, since at the point of contact they may not be properly baked, and, when taken out, the soft dough may become leavened. For the same reason—especially with thick dough—one had to ensure that it was not doubled over, or puffed up, since unbaked dough, which will rise later, can become trapped inside the swelling.

### 131. Are there any qualifications required for the baking of *matzot*?

They should be baked by God-fearing people, who are aware of all the laws and procedures and will be meticulous to avoid the slightest possibility of any dough becoming leavened. For the special *matzah shemurah,* which is used at the Seder, the baking should only be done by intelligent adults who have reached the age of *Bar* or *Bat Mitzvah,* and who can be relied upon to keep at the forefront of their minds that they are baking these *lesheim mitzvah* for the purpose of enabling a *mitzvah* to be performed.

## MACHINE-BAKED *MATZAH*

### 132. But would that not disqualify machine-baked *matzah*?

Mechanization truly "put the cat among the pigeons"! The illustrious sage Rabbi Solomon Kluger of Brody (1785–1869) and other contemporaries expressly forbade the use of machine-baked *matzot.* Their reason was that fine pieces of dough, which could not easily be located and removed, would inevitably get lodged within the wheels of the machinery and become *chametz.* They also claimed that it infringed the requirement of an intelligent human agency for the baking.

A permissive ruling was given, however, by the great authority on practical halakhah, Rabbi Joseph Saul Nathanson (1810–1875), a Rabbi much given to lenient interpretations of Jewish law. He maintained that the fact that a human being was needed to control the machine was sufficient to satisfy that specific requirement. In his opinion, the machine was to be preferred on account of its cleanliness and the speed with which the process could be completed. He did not accept that dough caught in the machinery could not be adequately removed and the works cleaned.

### 133. So, with two opposing views, how long did it take for a consensus view to emerge accepting the use of machine-baked *matzot*?

Not long: the world authority, Rabbi Abraham Samuel Sofer (Schreiber), Rabbi and Rosh Yeshivah of Pressburg (1815–1871), very quickly gave his seal of approval to it, asserting that "times [have] changed, and the judge must assess each situation as it develops." (*She'eilot Uteshuvot Ketar Sofer,* Appendix Responsum 2. Quoted in *Shearim Metzuyanim Behalakhah,* 3, p. 25.)

### 134. So presumably there was no debate when electrically automated machinery was introduced?

Quite the contrary: the great authorities of the day were once again split on the issue, with some reiterating the earlier fears regarding the absence of a human agency in the process and the issue of residual dough clinging to the machinery. The matter was settled, however, when the two towering authorities, Rabbi Meir Simchah Ha-Kohen of Dvinsk (1843–1926) and Reb Chaim Ozer Grodzinski (1863–1940), permitted its use. Their reasoning was that the mere pressing of the button to initiate the flow of electricity and the beginning of the operation constitutes *koach adam,* "human power," in the eyes of the halakhah. Consideration is also taken of the fact that human involvement is necessary in the loading of the machinery. From the practical point of view, the impossibility of providing *matzot* for the entire Jewish world without utilizing such machinery was also accepted as a persuasive argument.

## DOUBTFUL, PROCESSED, AND UNSUPERVISED FOODS

### 135. May one soak *matzah* in water or soup on Pesach?

The only fear here is that some residual, unbaked flour may reside inside the *matzah;* and for this reason some do not soak *matzah* in warm or hot liquids, which stimulate fermentation. This is not, however, a common happening, especially with our present-day, wafer-thin matzot, and we do not generally issue preventive measures for rare occurrences.

The *Shulchan Arukh (Orach Chayyim* 461:4) states that, for the *mitzvah* of *matzah* at the Seder, "one fulfills one's obligation with *matzah* that has been soaked" *(Matzah Sheruyah).* The inference is, quite clearly, that there is no prohibition involved. The *Magen Avraham* quotes *Maharil,* however, who forbids the soaking of the Seder *matzot* in warm liquids or soup, and the widespread belief that one should not dip *matzah* into water or soup throughout Pesach may have arisen out of confusion with the law regarding the special Seder *matzah,* where the fear was that the proper taste of the *mitzvah matzah* would be obliterated by its immersion.

### 136. Why may Ashkenazim not eat rice and certain types of pulses?

This is also a gray area of halakhah! Sephardi Jews are permitted to eat rice and what are called *kitniyyot,* that is, peas, beans, or other podded vegetables (see question 137). This is, simply, because neither Maimonides nor Karo, author of the *Shulchan Arukh*—the two basic codes that are authoritative for Sephardim—record any such prohibitions in this respect. It was only among some Ashkenazi authorities that opposition to rice and *kitniyyot* grew.

That having been said, even Sephardim are advised to take care "to examine the rice carefully before using, to ensure that they do not contain minute grains of wheat, barley or other cereal" (R. Ovadiah Yoseph, *Chazon Ovadiah,* Jerusalem: Yeshivat Porat Joseph, 1979, p. 53). And this provides a clue as to the rationale of the prohibition, namely, that while growing in the field, seeds from grain crops of one field will inevitably be wafted across to other fields by the wind and may get trapped inside the pulse stalks.

The Mishnah *(Pesachim* 114a) states that, as part of the Seder proceedings, they used to "bring in two cooked dishes." The Talmud *(Pesachim* 114b) asks what particular dishes they would cook and provides the answer in the name of Rav Huna: *silka ve-aroza,* "beet and rice." Now, the Talmud continues, "But was not Rav Huna aware of Rav Yochanan ben Nuri's statement that rice is a grain product, to the extent that one is culpable for using it in a fermented state, and one may even fulfill the *mitzvah* of *matzah* with it?"

From this source, which suggests some doubt over the precise definition of rice in talmudic times, we may gain an insight into why later Ashkenazi authorities took the precautionary measure of prohibiting rice. Even for those who did not accept Rav Yochanan ben Nuri's definition of rice as a cereal crop, there was the fear that it might have attracted, amid its numerous grains, traces of cereal that were virtually impossible to locate and remove.

Yisrael Ta-Shema (*Minhag Ashkenaz Ha-Kadmon* [Jerusalem: Magnes Press, Hebrew University, 1992], p. 280–281) argues, however, that the prohibition of pulses was actually prompted by simple observation that a cooked pulse dish does swell up like dough, and pulses were consequently regarded as possessing fermentative properties. Hence, those who objected to the use of egg *matzot* for similar reasons (see above, question 129) also objected to the use of *kitniyyot*.

### 137. What is the precise scope of forbidden *kitniyyot*?

The term covers beans, peas, corn, maize (including popcorn), rice, and other pod vegetables. Bean sprouts are not regarded as *kitniyyot*, though some people are particular not to eat the sprout tip. It should be noted that unsupervised baked beans are prohibited not simply because they fall into this category of *kitniyyot* but primarily because their sauce is generally pure *chametz*.

The prohibition of *kitniyyot* also extends to any products made from its derivative, such as corn oil, corn flour, and margarine.

The abstention from garlic within some communities was not on account of it being classified as *kitniyyot* but rather out of fear that farmers may have soaked the garlic in beer to enhance its flavor. Where there is proper supervision, however, authorities do permit the consumption of garlic.

### 138. May an Ashkenazi eat a meal at a Sephardi home where rice and *kitniyyot* are eaten?

Obviously, he may not eat anything that is prohibited to Ashkenazim, but he need have no fear regarding eating other food cooked by his hosts in their Pesach utensils in which they have cooked and served rice and *kitniyyot* (*Chazon Ovadiah*, p. 55).

### 139. If an Ashkenazi woman marries a Sephardi, may she prepare for her husband, and also eat herself, rice, peas, and beans (*kitniyyot*)?

She may certainly prepare such foods for her husband, for, as we have indicated, there is nothing *chametz* per se about them. A woman in Judaism takes on the traditions of her husband, and this is to be encouraged because of the important objective of *shalom bayyit*, securing the harmony of the home. However, in a case like this, where it is a matter of dispensing with the more stringent halakhic practices of her parental home, there is a view that she should first approach an halakhic authority to grant her a formal release from what is categorized as a vow of commitment to her former traditions (see *Chazon Ovadiah*, p. 56).

### 140. May one eat dried fruits on Pesach?

Again we come to different traditions between Ashkenazim and Sephardim. Joseph Karo, the main authority for Sephardim, did not rule against the use of dried foods, probably because he had no grounds for suspecting that any grains or leaven extracts might be used in the drying process. Indeed, he states, "There is no basis for prohibiting honey produced by gentiles, and it may be eaten on Pesach" (*Orach Chayyim* 467:8).

Moses Isserles, in a gloss reflective of Ashkenazi traditions, states: "It is the custom of our communities not to eat honey unless it is brought direct from the hive for use in the drink called Mead. As regards dried figs and large or small dried grapes (called raisins), it depends upon the custom of the place. Some take a stringent view not to eat them, while others permit them. *However, the custom of our communities is not to eat any dried fruit unless it is known that their drying process does not involve any* chametz" (Orach Chayyim 467:8).

It is for this reason, because of the fact that frequently flour is spread over the fruit during the drying process, and also because the ovens and slabs used for the drying may have been used for *chametz* foods that Ashkenazim refrain from eating dried fruit unless processed under rabbinic supervision.

### 141. May one use unsupervised frozen foods on Pesach?

Frozen fruit and vegetables are permitted, providing there are no additives used.

### 142. Are there any prohibitions regarding fresh fruit?

None at all: some people take the added precaution of rinsing them well in case they were placed together with *chametz* during the various stages of their storage, packaging, and transportation from field to home.

### 143. May one buy *chametz* baby foods and feed them to babies on Pesach?

There are no grounds for permitting this unless the baby is ill and the doctor insists upon a vital *chametz* preparation. Baby cereals, rusks, and stomach-settling solutions are therefore not permitted. Substitute foods for Pesach have been found to be quite acceptable to babies. Instead of rusks, one can make oven baked sponge cakes; instead of cereal, one can mix *matzah* meal or potato flour with milk, adding egg or pure fruit juice for flavor. One can also puree one's own meat, fish, vegetable mixes, and fruit, in place of the ready-to-eat jars.

### 144. May one feed one's pets food containing *chametz*?

Again, the answer is no. The Torah made no exceptions to the prohibition of *chametz* in one's home. One needs to take advice, first from one's vet and then from one's Rabbi, regarding the ingredients of such foods and the availability of substitute products on the market.

### 145. Must food for Pesach be bought only from a Jewish shop?

Not necessarily. Certainly, tins, cans, jars, bottles, or cartons that are sealed, and that bear the *hechsher* (seal of approval) of a recognized rabbinic licensing authority may be purchased anywhere. As regards foods prepared by a local shop or deli, one would have to be sure that they were prepared with ingredients that were totally supervised by a recognized licensing authority, in ovens and kitchens that were specially prepared for Passover, and with machinery, cutlery, and crockery that were reserved especially for Passover. If one has any doubts, one should not patronize such an outlet for or during the festival.

# VI

# Searching for and Annulling the *Chametz*

## BEDIKAT CHAMETZ

**146. When does *Bedikat chametz*, the formal search for the *chametz*, take place?**

On the evening before the first Seder night, at nightfall.

**147. If the cleaning has been done, or overseen, by the homemaker, what is the point of conducting such a search?**

This is a common gripe! The search should not be construed, however, as casting doubt on the devotion to religious duty or thoroughness of application on the part of the person preparing the home for Pesach. It serves primarily to publicize the fact that the cleaning undertaken was not part of the usual domestic routine, but rather *lesheim mitzvah*, for the sake of fulfilling the sacred responsibility of clearing away all *chametz*. When the blessing is recited over this ritual search, it also hallows the hard work undertaken by the housewife and her helpers.

It should also be remembered that the search is made by the head of the household, because he (or she) is the one ultimately responsible to ensure that the home is *chametz*-free. Tours of inspection by the senior ranks are an accepted part of important military and quasi-military events. They do not imply in any way that such an inspection is necessary in order to discover any weaknesses of presentation or omissions that have been overlooked. This is merely the final, formal act of recognition of the great effort that has gone into the preparation of that particular exercise or enterprise.

**148. Why are pieces of bread hidden before the *Bedikat chametz* (search for leaven) commences?**

Bearing in mind what has just been said, it comes as no surprise that the basic assumption is that the cleaning has been so thorough that no *chametz* will, in fact, be discovered. This presents a problem, for we may not make a blessing unnecessarily (called a *berakhah she-eina tzerikhah*). Hence, we cannot make a blessing that refers to an obligation to search for something that we know will not be found! This explains the practice of wrapping up small pieces of bread and having someone, other than the ones searching, hide them in all the rooms of the house. This also ensures that the search is not conducted in a half-hearted manner.

The illustrious sixteenth-century mystic, Rabbi Isaac Luria, recommended that one should put out ten pieces of bread, claiming that there is a great mystic significance in that particular number. There is also an allusion to that situation in the Talmud: "If one put out ten and found nine" (*Pesachim* 10a).

## BLESSING OVER THE SEARCH

**149. Why is the blessing couched as *al biur chametz* ("has commanded us concerning the removal of *chametz*"), rather than, as expected, *al bedikat chametz* (concerning the search for *chametz*)?**

The act of "searching" is not the primary objective, which is rather the discovery and *removal* of *chametz*. Secondly, the biblical command is not to conduct a "search," but to remove and destroy *chametz*. Hence the blessing conforms with the proper biblical objective. Thirdly, the climax of the ritual is when we utter the *Kol chamirah* declaration, by which we mentally dissociate ourselves from any leaven in our possession, which should be regarded as ownerless, like the dust of the earth. That declaration is tantamount to an act of total removal and destruction of the *chametz*. Hence we allude to that act of total removal *(biur)* in the blessing we make at the outset.

**150. Why do we not say the *Shehecheyanu* blessing over this *mitzvah*, as we do over all other rituals and occasions that recur intermittently or on an annual basis?**

The search is not an end in itself, but a preparation for the festival. Thus, the *Shehecheyanu* that we recite over the festival covers all its sundry preparatory activities.

The fourteenth-century sage Rabbi David Abudraham gives another, interesting reason. He states that *Shehecheyanu* was prescribed as a thanksgiving exclusively over things that give humans pleasure, while in the act of clearing away and destroying *chametz*, a person will have a tinge of regret at the destruction and waste of his substance.

**151. Why do we repeat the same formula of *Kol chamirah* both after the search as well as, on the following morning, after burning the *chametz*?**

We don't! There is a subtle difference between the wording of the two formulae. There is a need, after the search, to make a formal mental annulment of all the *chametz* — "that which I have seen and that which I have not seen." There is also a requirement to make another such formal annulment after the burning. At that second occasion, the *Kol chamirah* adds the words, *debiartei udela biartei*, "that which I have destroyed and that which I have not destroyed," thereby dissociating the person totally from all the *chametz* in his possession. This could not have been recited the previous evening together with the *Kol chamirah* recited over the search, since at that time he is only annuling the *chametz* that he has collected and that which he has "not seen." *Chametz* is still being kept in the house, however, both that which is collected at the search as well as that which is required for breakfast the following morning. Hence, he could not complete at that time the declaration of total annulment.

## CONDUCT OF THE SEARCH

### 152. How is the search conducted?

We switch off the lights in the rooms we are searching and search by means of a single wax candle, which casts its rays into nooks and crannies. We use a brush and pan to sweep up the pieces of wrapped bread and any other suspicious traces. Tradition recommends the use of a feather, though this is not always easy to control. We are not supposed to speak about anything unrelated to the search until we have finished and recited the final declaration. We keep the pieces of bread together and burn them all the following morning, together with the remains of the *chametz* from breakfast.

### 153. May we not search, then, by the light of an electric lamp?

The distinguished halakhist Rav Aaron Kotler confirmed that there is no halakhic reason why it should not be permitted. For *Shabbat* lights, objections were raised against the employment of electric lights, since we require that the entire process of producing the light be initiated and completed by the Jew, whereas, in the case of electricity, the initial current is produced at the power station. In the case of the search for *chametz,* however, there are no such requirements, and it is merely a question of using a light that is most effective in reaching into corners and crevices. Nevertheless, the search for *chametz* is nostalgically undertaken by families in the traditional manner, using a candle.

### 154. Which rooms does one have to search?

The halakhah only requires the search to be made of rooms where *chametz* is at all likely to be taken. This includes cellars, attics, storerooms, garages, and even cars. It is not assumed that one takes food into the restroom.

### 155. Does one have to search through all the books in one's library?

This is not required. It is recommended, however, that books that one occasionally brings to one's table, such as *siddurim,* Grace after Meals booklets, or other Jewish books (e.g., *chumashim*) that one learns from occasionally—perhaps on a *Shabbat,* at one's table—should be checked out for crumbs.

**156. What if one is going away some time before Pesach and will remain away throughout the eight days of the festival: is the search for *chametz* and its removal still obligatory?**

One must still clean out one's home and should appoint someone to perform the search (with a blessing) on the appropriate evening, burn the *chametz,* and recite the two *Kol chamirah* annulment declarations. The householder, wherever he is, should also recite that formula of annulment.

If he is unable to find someone to conduct the search for him and he is leaving home after Purim, he must do it himself, in the usual way, on the night before he leaves his home, though without reciting the usual blessing. If he leaves home before Purim and will remain away over Pesach, no search is required, though he should recite the *Kol chamirah* nullification before Pesach, wherever he is (see also question 265).

The *chametz* left over from the search and from breakfast on the morning of Erev Pesach is burnt as soon as possible, and certainly not later than the end of the fifth hour of the day (around 11:00 A.M.).

# VII

# Selling of the *Chametz*

### 157. What does the selling of *chametz* involve?

During the week before Pesach, one visits one's synagogue Rabbi and formally sells him all the *chametz* in one's possession. It is a simple arrangement that takes no longer than a minute.

The Rabbi will have drawn up a special deed of sale, ready for his formal sale to a gentile of the *chametz* in the properties of all the signatories to the deed. He will hand you an object belonging to him—a pen, handkerchief, or book—and will clarify with you that, by this ancient method of appointing an agent, you thereby make him your representative to sell your *chametz* to the gentile. You hold the object for a second, return it, and then append your name and the address where the *chametz* is located. You will be asked its approximate value and, possibly, precisely where in your home you have stored the residual stocks. This is because, according to the technicalities of the halakhah, it is also necessary to let to the gentile the room or storage place where the *chametz* is located. Before leaving, it is customary to give a donation to the Rabbi's charity.

### 158. What type of arrangements are made between the Rabbi and the gentile?

As stated, the Rabbi has a formal deed of sale, which he and the gentile will sign. The gentile will be expected to truly purchase the *chametz,* paying the Rabbi, initially, a deposit on account for a sum, which should correspond to at least a token payment for each and every Jewish signatory. He is given the list with all the names and addresses and made to understand that the *chametz* in all those homes belongs to him from just before the specific time on the morning of Erev Pesach that *chametz* becomes prohibited. It will be gently suggested to him that if he has difficulty completing payment of the purchase price at the end of the festival, he will be at liberty to offer it back for sale at that time, when he will probably make a significant profit on the deal! When Pesach goes out, the Rabbi will remind his gentile friend that he still owes him the balance of the purchase price. Generally, there is no reticence on the part of the gentile to sell it back to the signatories!

### 159. But is it not a charade if the gentile has no rights of entry to collect his *chametz*?

To forestall this becoming a charade, the halakhah prescribes that the deed of sale should give the gentile free access, should he desire it, to retrieve any of the food. Not only that, but, as a rightful owner, he is also permitted to sell the *chametz* to another gentile, who will also have free access to the *chametz*.

### 160. Why is such a sale necessary if we are going to annul and destroy all our *chametz* anyway?

This has to be understood, not only halakhically, but also in the context of the historical development of the practice of removing *chametz*. Strictly speaking, even though one annuls one's *chametz*, as long as there remains in one's possession items of *chametz* that have accumulated over the year and that one cannot afford to destroy, such as tins and packets of foodstuffs, wines, and spirits, one infringes the biblical law that "leaven shall not be found in your home." Such leaven becomes *asur behanaah,* forbidden to be used or sold even after Pesach.

Now, before the sixteenth century, the only solution available was to actually sell it—obviously at reduced prices—to gentiles. Where Jews were on good terms with their gentile neighbors, the latter often agreed to purchase the goods on the understanding that they would sell them back, for a modest profit, after Pesach. There was no infringement of Jewish law, since the goods would be physically transferred to the gentile purchaser.

In many communities in Eastern Europe in the sixteenth to the seventeenth centuries, Jews were unable to find such trustworthy purchasers. Many Jews had inns or traded in food, wines, and spirits, and selling their total stock at reduced prices each year was economic suicide. Moreover, transferring it to the home of a possible anti-Semitic or unscrupulous—or both—gentile was not only impractical, but also most hazardous.

One of the most prominent halakhists of the age, Rabbi Joel Sirkes of Cracow (1561-1640), came to the rescue. Whereas Joseph Karo, in his *Bet Yoseph* and *Shulchan Arukh,* states specifically that the *chametz* has to be transferred out of one's house (see *Orach Chayyim* 448:3), Rabbi Sirkes declared a token sale to the gentile as sufficient to transfer ownership, even without removing the *chametz* to his home (see *Magen Avraham's* comment, *Orach Chayyim* 448:3).

So we now see that there is a halakhic precedent for selling the *chametz* stocks that are too bulky and costly to remove. This is especially necessary in our age, with the vast range of manufactured foodstuffs that we purchase, and in our modern homes, with the much greater storage space that we enjoy and the facility to stock fairly large quantities of food at the right temperature.

### 161. What if someone forgot to sell his *chametz*?

There are weighty authorities (e.g., Yechezkiel Landau, Vilna Gaon, Chatam Sofer) who inclined to the strict view that, whatever the circumstances, *chametz* that remained in the possession of a Jew over Pesach, whether willfully or because he forgot to sell it, is forbidden to be used after the festival, even if the person made the *Kol chamirah* declaration of annulment. However, the *Mishnah Berurah* states that, in the case of great financial loss, one may rely on the authorities who take a lenient view, particularly in cases where a person made the annulment and genuinely forgot to make the sale.

### 162. May one sell the *chametz* of another without being instructed?

From a comment of the *Magen Avraham* (*Orach Chayyim* 436:11) it may be inferred that the Rabbi may sell such a person's *chametz*. He argues that, if unsold, it is in the category of lost property, since the person would be forbidden to have any benefit from it after Pesach. Hence, the act of selling it on his behalf is tantamount to restoring a lost article, which naturally is a meritorious act. Another consideration is the halakhic principle that "one may take the initiative on another's behalf [without being instructed] if it is to his benefit" (Mishnah *Eruvin* 81b; *Gittin* 11b et al.) since it may be assumed that the person will be happy with the action taken.

### 163. May one instruct the Rabbi over the telephone to sell one's *chametz*?

It may be resorted to only in the case of an emergency, since really the kinyan method of properly appointing an agent by holding together a cloth or other object should be employed. A signed authorization should subsequently be delivered to the Rabbi.

### 164. May a woman sell *chametz*?

She may. If she resides in her father's home, he has the authority to sell any *chametz* belonging to her, as does her husband if she is married. She may visit the Rabbi as representative of her husband, to sell all the *chametz* in the home, or, if she lives alone or is a single parent, she may also instruct the Rabbi to sell on her behalf. She may also appoint another agent to sell the *chametz* on her behalf.

### 165. From what time does the sale have to take effect?

It must take effect from just before the time, on Erev Pesach, when any benefit from *chametz* becomes forbidden. That means, in effect, before the end of the fifth hour of the day (approximately eleven hours). The duration of each hour is not based upon clock time, but rather upon "halakhic hours," which are calculated by dividing up the daylight period of the day into twelve equal number of "hours." Thus one needs to consult a local Jewish newspaper, diary, or Shul mailing for the precise time when the sale takes effect.

### 166. What is the situation if one's *chametz* will be sold in one time zone though the person will be subject to time in another zone?

This question frequently arises in the case of people wishing to sell *chametz* prior to flying off to other parts of the United States or to Israel for Pesach, and who at the same time wish to sell the *chametz* they will have in their place of arrival.

It is important to realize that we are dealing with the concept of ownership, irrespective of where the person happens to be. Thus, he must be in a permitted relationship to that *chametz* in conformity with the times obtaining in both time zones. If, for example, he is selling his *chametz* in the United States, he cannot still own it at a time when the prohibition of *chametz* has already come into effect in Israel. He must therefore arrange for it to be sold in time for prohibition time in Israel. Similarly, the time for repurchase after Pesach has to be adjusted so that it does not become his until after Pesach ends at his home in the United States. Alternately, one may sell one's *chametz* in Israel (so that his *chametz* back home is prematurely sold) but instruct the Rabbi to insert in the contract that he is not repurchasing it after Pesach until such time as Pesach terminates in his home in the States.

### 167. Until what time on Erev Pesach may one eat one's remaining *chametz*?

Following the guidelines in the previous answer, we must finish eating all *chametz* by the end of the fourth hour of the day (approximately ten hours). As indicated, there remains one further hour during which to wash and store away the dishes remaining from the *chametz* breakfast and to complete the burning of the *chametz*.

# VIII

## Fast of the Firstborn

**168. What is the Hebrew name of this fast and when does it take place?**

It is referred to as *Taanit bekhorim* (fast of the firstborn), and it takes place on the eve of Pesach, that is, the day leading into the first Seder.

**169. What if that day is a *Shabbat,* when one may not fast (other than on Yom Kippur)?**

Then the fast is brought forward to the Thursday before.

**170. Why do firstborns have to fast?**

It is to commemorate the miracle of the deliverance of the Hebrew firstborn when God smote all the firstborn of Egypt. The Rabbis comment that the Israelites themselves had sunk to the lowest spiritual level (the forty-ninth level of impurity on a descending scale of one to fifty), so that their own firstborn were really undeserving of being spared. It was therefore a special act of divine grace which saved them; and this fast day commemorates that. Since God especially recalls, on this the day preceeding Pesach, His Egyptian firstborn children whom He was constrained to punish, our own firstborn are naturally in special focus on this day. The fast is, therefore, also to demonstrate, through fasting and prayer, their loyalty to Him so that He will maintain His covenant with Israel, however slender our merit.

**171. How old is this fast?**

It is first mentioned in *Masekhet Soferim,* one of the late (seventh-century) minor talmudic tractates, so that it probably began as a pietistic custom in some rabbinic circles a few centuries earlier and from there gained more widespread acceptance as a worthy practice. Some scholars believe that it was already observed in mishnaic times (second century) since there is reference to Rabbi Judah the Prince having fasted on the eve of Pesach (*Talmud Yerushalmi Pesachim* 10:1, 37b), though this is by no means certain, as his practice is explained by others in terms of his desire to create a great appetite for the *matzah* to be eaten that night at the Seder.

The fast may also have been introduced to fill the vacuum left by the abolition of the many sacrificial activities that had originally taken up most of that day in Temple times.

### 172.  How do we define a firstborn in this context?

This means a firstborn son, whether from the father or the mother. There was a view that the obligation also devolves upon firstborn women, but, if this indeed was the original practice, it did not win later rabbinic acceptance. A concession to the original practice may be detected in the statement of Rabbi Moses Isserles that, "the custom is that where the father is a firstborn [and fasting anyway], the mother fasts for her firstborn minor child; where the father is not a firstborn, he fasts for his son" (*Orach Chayyim* 470:2).

### 173.  How is it that the firstborn are enabled to avoid having to fast?

This being a nonbiblical fast, and, as we have said, one that originated purely as an optional pietist practice, early authorities already pointed out that it can be set aside for such important *mitzvot* as attending the festive meal that accompanies a circumcision (see *Magen Avraham, Orach Chayyim* 470:1). This led to the view that if the firstborn participated in a *siyyum,* the celebration of the conclusion of the study of a tractate of Talmud, then that was equivalent in importance to attending a circumcision feast. There were authorities, however, such as Rabbi Yechezkiel Landau (the *Nodah BiYehudah*) of Prague, who issued a proclamation expressly prohibiting firstborns from breaking their fast at such a *siyyum,* but that view did not prevail.

From this approach, the custom developed for the rabbi to time the conclusion of his study of a talmudic tractate for the morning before Pesach. The firstborn attend Synagogue, and listen to the final part of the tractate being learnt and to the *hadran* (the concluding prayer of thanksgiving for its successful conclusion, with a promise not to forget it, but to return one day to its study) being recited. They are then enabled to participate in the *lechayim* and refreshments served afterwards, and their duty of fasting for the rest of the day is thereby removed.

### 174.  Is it not unusual to permit a fast on the eve of a festival, which already partakes of the festive spirit, particularly on the afternoon of Erev Pesach when, in Temple times, the Paschal lamb was slaughtered, which was a festive event?

This is a very valid point. Indeed, we do not recite the *Tachanun* petitions during the Minchah service on the eve of either festivals or even minor holydays for precisely that very reason, namely that their abject petitionary and confessionary tones jar with the festive spirit that is already engendered in anticipation of the festival that evening. In the case of Pesach, the special *yom tov* spirit and atmosphere are so specific that the Mishnah (see *Pesachim* 50a) declared work to be prohibited on the afternoon preceding Pesach! It seems, however, that the Rabbis felt constrained to make an exception, because that was the time, in ancient Egypt, when the actual deliverance of the firstborn took place. Secondly, they had a talmudic precedent in the case of Rav Sheshet, who used to fast on Erev Pesach (Talmud *Pesachim* 108a).

It has been suggested that it is precisely because of the fact that Erev Pesach has the character of a festive occasion that it was permitted for firstborn to eat at a *siyyum* celebration.

**175. Is it only over the conclusion of an entire talmudic tractate that the *siyyum* can be made? What if he has insufficient time in advance of Pesach to complete the study of a full tractate?**

No, it is not made exclusively over a major volume of the Talmud. In fact the term *seudat mitzvah*, a "religious celebration"—capable of neutralizing this fast—is quite flexible. There is a whole range of halakhic opinion, therefore, ranging from those who, like Rabbi Yechezkiel Landau (mentioned above), do not recognize at all the validity of such a *siyyum* to neutralize an obligation to fast, to those who even regard a party hosted by an author to celebrate the completion of the writing of a Jewish religious book, or its launch, as satisfying the criteria of *seudat mitzvah!*

Between those extremes we have authorities who permit a *siyyum* to be celebrated over a single Seder (Order) of the Mishnah, while there are others who allow it for the study of the *Mishnayot* of a single talmudic tractate. Some permit it for the study of one of the short *Masekhtot Ketanot* (minor tractates) of the Talmud, while the most lenient view of all permits it over the completion of the study of one of the biblical books of the prophets! In the latter case, the only proviso is that it is the natural conclusion of an in-depth study course, and was not rushed through, a day or two before, for the express purpose of staging a *siyyum* to escape the obligation to fast. (For references to the above sources, see commentary of *Shearim Metzuyanim Behalakhah* to *Kitzur Shulchan Arukh*, vol. 3 [Jerusalem: Feldheim, 1978], p. 46 n. 10).

**176. If the firstborn was preceded by a stillbirth, does the duty of fasting still apply?**

Yes it does. We do not follow here the situation governing the requirement to perform *Pidyan Ha-Ben,* the redemption of the firstborn, which is restricted to firstborn that "open the womb," and consequently excludes a· situation where a stillbirth has previously occurred. The definition here is the firstborn who enjoys the special right of inheritance *(bekhor lenachalah)* according to biblical law, and this makes no distinction between the conditions of birth as long as the person occupies that firstborn status within the family.

**177. Since the *siyyum* only takes place at the conclusion of the morning service, when it is still, technically, a proper fast day, why does the chazan not recite the usual fast day *Aneinu* prayer in the repetition of the Minchah *Amidah*?**

It is not a "proper fast day" for the rest of the (nonfirstborn part of the) congregation. To recite *Aneinu* would unreasonably convert the day into a general public fast day.

**178. If, for some reason, a firstborn is unable to attend a *siyyum*, does he have to fast and recite *Aneinu*?**

He does, on both counts. The halakhah states that if a number of fasting firstborn attend a Minchah service, none of them should act as chazan, since that would necessitate the recitation of *Aneinu*, which, for the reason stated in our previous answer, is undesirable.

# IX

# Preparing the Seder for Adults and Children

### 179. What special food items are required for the Seder?

Here is a checklist: (1) a sufficient number of bottles of wine and, if required, grape juice; (2) Haggadot; (3) six unbroken pieces of *shemurah matzah*, three for each Seder evening; (4) sufficient boxes of *matzah* for the whole of Pesach; (5) horseradish or lettuce (for *maror*); (6) parsley, horseradish, or potato (for *Karpas*); (7) a hard-boiled egg, which should be roasted or scorched on an open flame; (8) a wing of a chicken or a shank bone that is similarly roasted; (9) for *charoset*, obtain apples, ground almonds (or other nuts), and cinnamon; (10) sufficient hard-boiled eggs to provide for the Seder *hors d'oeuvres* for each person for both nights (in addition to the many eggs required for general cooking and baking over Pesach); (11) salt (for the saltwater dip and for pouring over the egg *hors d'oeuvres* at the Seder), (12) cushions or pillows for reclining at Seder (some have the tradition that it is only the men who lean back on cushions); (13) gifts for the children who find the *Afikoman* and consolation prizes for those who don't!

### 180. What other items are required?

1. Naturally, a fairly large Seder plate will be needed. Any large dish will suffice, though it is a *mitzvah* to adorn the Seder table, and there is nothing like an artistically designed Seder plate to do that, to serve as a focal point— and a talking point!

2. Obviously, each person will require a *bechah* (silver goblet) or wine glass. It is recommended to have in stock a goodly selection of glasses and goblets of varying size. Some people wish to drink each glass in conformity with the volume requirement of the halakhah (see questions 185–186), whereas others can only manage a minute amount of wine. Those who opt for grape juice may prefer a medium-sized measure. Be prepared for all tastes!

3. Reserve your largest goblet for a place of honor on the table as the "Cup of Elijah."

4. Ensure that you have enough candles for all the days of *Yom Tov* and *Shabbat*, including extras for any visitors who may be joining you.

5. It might also be a good idea to have ready some small cloths, to put over your Seder cloth in the case of wine spillage.

6. For the occasion when the one leading the Seder (only) washes his hands, some prefer to have on the side a small jug, bowl, and towel for that purpose. This saves him having to leave the room for the kitchen, and also enables that particular act—an intrinsic part of the Seder ritual—to be performed in full view of the participants.

7. Have a few spare *kippot* (skullcaps) to hand, in case any of your guests forget to bring their own.

8. Where the one leading the Seder is accustomed to wearing a kittel (white robe, such as is worn in synagogue on Rosh Hashanah and Yom Kippur), this should be taken out in good time in case it needs cleaning.

## PROVIDING FOR CHILDREN

### 181. Is there anything that should be provided for children?

The Mishnah records that in ancient times the elders would provide nuts and other nibbles for the children in order to keep them awake. This remains a sensible practice. It is also advisable to ensure that, in order to keep their interest, they be provided with Haggadot that are geared to their particular age group.

Since Jewish law does not permit the Seder to commence before nightfall, few children will be able to survive until the meal is served rather late that evening. Their hunger generally means that there are pressures upon the one leading the Seder to carry it out quickly and to omit comment and discussion. This clearly conflicts with both the letter of the law and the spirit of the occasion. Children should therefore be served their supper at the usual time. (This is not permitted for adults, who must develop an appetite for the eating of the *matzah*.)

The halakhah is most concerned that children should remain awake during the Seder, and that everything should be done to keep them interested and involved. They should be encouraged, therefore, to have as good a nap as possible on the afternoons before the two Seder nights, so that they are as fresh as possible for the Seder experience.

Particular attention should be devoted to making part of the evening as interesting and meaningful as possible for the children. We suggest, therefore, an "activity hour," devoted to games, quizzes, and activities, all (naturally) related to general Jewish and Pesach themes.

### 182. Can you recommend any specific activities for children?

In Chapter 22 we have provided a Seder quiz and a selection of Seder activities for children. We would also recommend a visit to your local Jewish bookseller, who ought to stock books and materials calculated to interest children of all ages on Seder night.

## WINE FOR THE SEDER

### 183. Are there any restrictions on the type of wine one may use for the Seder?

Naturally, one should use only a kasher wine, bottled under rabbinic supervision and bearing the seal "kasher for Passover." Red wine is preferred for use at the Seder, though if one possesses a white wine that is superior to the red, then that may be used.

### 184. Why is red wine preferred?

Because it recalls the blood of the slaughtered Israelite children, which Pharaoh used for bathing in as a cure for his leprosy. Red wine was also regarded as a superior type, probably on account of the depth and richness of its color (see Proverbs 23:31).

### 185. We referred above to a specific minimum volume of wine that should be drunk for each of the four cups of wine. What is that minimum?

The halakhah prescribes that the cup should hold a *reviit*, that is, "one-quarter" of a *log*, which is the equivalent of the displacement of one and a half eggs.

### 186. How can one determine whether one's wine glasses are large enough to contain that volume?

Authorities differ as to the precise modern-day equivalent of the ancient *reviit*, some maintaining that it is about 112 grams, others assuming it to be only about 87 grams. It is possible, of course, to do a simple experiment to determine the displacement of one and a half eggs, though again authorities are not convinced that the present-day eggs are anything like the size of those in ancient times, so that we should really be drinking more than their volume.

To do the experiment: take two bowls, one larger than the other, and three eggs. Fill the smaller bowl with water. Then pour its contents into the larger bowl. Place the three eggs into the empty, smaller bowl, and then pour the water from the larger bowl into it. When the smaller bowl can take no more water, what remains in the larger bowl is the displacement of *three* eggs. Half of that liquid constitutes the *reviit*, the minimum amount that the wine glasses should contain.

### 187. How is the *charoset* prepared?

Take several tablespoons of ground almonds, or grate the equivalent volume in walnuts or hazelnuts (don't worry about making too much, as it won't be wasted—the children will see to that). Grate one or two apples, and mix in with nuts. Sprinkle in about one tablespoon of cinnamon, and pour in wine carefully, while mixing the mixture, so that it remains soft but not runny. Remember, it has to have the consistency of mortar (see also question 193).

# X

# Symbolism of the Seder Ritual

### 188. Why do we drink four cups of wine at the Seder?

Various interpretations are preserved in the Talmud (*Talmud Yerushalmi, Pesachim* 10:1). First, they represent a toast to the *four* expressions of redemption used by God when assuring Moses that He would bring Israel out of Egypt (Exodus 6:6–7). Secondly, they correspond to the four times the word "cup" is mentioned in the episode of Pharaoh's butler's dream (Genesis 40:11–13). Joseph's interpretation of that dream may be viewed as the starting point from which the presence of Jews in Egypt and the entire saga of their sad fate, followed by glorious redemption, all unfold. They may also be reminiscent of the four kingdoms that subjugated Israel, Assyrians, Persians, Greeks, and Romans, and of the four cups of retribution that God will ultimately give to drink to the nations who oppress Israel.

### 189. Are there any laws governing how the cups of wine have to be drunk?

As mentioned above, one should ideally drink red wine. For those who cannot tolerate red, white may be used. Alternatively, the red wine may be diluted with a little water, and for those who cannot drink any amount of wine, grape juice or raisin wine will suffice. The *mitzvah* of the four cups of wine is so important that, even if a person finds wine most disagreeable, he should, nevertheless, try to force himself to drink it at the Seder. The Talmud (*Nedarim* 49b) relates that Rabbi Judah bar Ilai was extremely allergic to wine. He nevertheless forced himself to drink the four cups each year, notwithstanding the fact that it necessitated him binding his temples with bandages from Pesach until Shavuot to assuage the pain!

We referred above (see question 180) to the requirement of drinking a fixed minimum amount of wine (a *reviit*) for each of the four cups. One should ideally drink the entire cup. If this is impossible, then he should endeavor to drink the greater part of it. It must not be sipped, but drunk in one swig.

## SHANKBONE, EGGS, AND *CHAROSET*

### 190. What is the reason for having a roasted shank bone or neck on the Seder plate?

This recalls the Paschal lamb that was roasted in fire in Temple times and partaken of in family groups. Since the destruction of the Temple (70 C.E.), Jews refrained from eating any roasted meat at the Seder (in order not to give the impression that they were maintaining the Paschal lamb practice), so that the roasted shank bone is merely a symbolic reminder and is not to be eaten. The shank bone was chosen as it symbolizes the "outstretched arm" with which God delivered the Israelites.

### 191. What is the reason for the roasted egg?

When the Temple was destroyed, the Sages introduced two commemorations of the Pesach ritual in Temple times, the roasted shank bone and the roasted egg. The bone recalls the Paschal lamb and the egg recalls the *Chagigah* (festival) offering that was offered on Erev Pesach. Two explanations are found in the sources for the choice of an egg: first, that its Aramaic name, *bei-ah* (Hebrew, *beitzah*), is reminiscent of the like-sounding word, *ba'ey*, "to be willing, desirous," which is suggestive of God's willingness to redeem Israel. Secondly, the egg is the ancient and common symbol of mourning. It is thus a most appropriate stimulus to the recalling of the destruction of the Temple.

### 192. Why do we have boiled eggs as an hors d'oeuvre at the Seder?

For precisely the reason we have just quoted. Because there are so many nostalgic references to the Temple in our Haggadah and because in Temple times the Paschal lamb constituted the meal proper, it was felt appropriate that at the meal itself we should have a symbolic token of mourning by eating hard-boiled eggs, the food given to mourners when they return from the funeral. Significantly, the first day of Pesach always occurs on the same day of the week as *Tisha B'Av*, when we fast for the destruction of the Temple: hence the appropriateness of a token of mourning at the Seder.

### 193. Is there any significance in the specific ingredients designated for the *charoset*?

Jewish custom preferred to choose ingredients that had a symbolic meaning or triggered off an association of relevant biblical verses, religious ideas, historical reminiscences, or personal or national petitions. This is also the case with the special foods that are prescribed for eating on Rosh Hashanah (see *Kitzur Shulchan Arukh* 129:9).

This explains the recommendation that, for the ingredients of the *charoset,* one should choose fruits "to which the children of Israel are likened" (*Kitzur Shulchan Arukh* 118:4). The choice of apples is associated with the verse, "Under the apple tree I awakened thee" (Song of Songs 8:5), which the Rabbis interpret symbolically as referring to the Israelite wives who went out into the orchards to give birth under the shade of the apple trees and to secure thereby the numerical strength of their people in defiance of Pharaoh's decrees.

The halakhah recommends that nuts should be used, on the basis of the biblical verse, "Into the nut garden I descended" (Song of Songs 6:11), which the Midrash interprets in a variety of ways as a symbol of Israel (see *Shir Ha-Shirim Rabbah* 6:17); for example, just as when a nut falls into dirt, one simply wipes the dirt off so that the nut's shell remains shining bright and the nut inside is still able to be enjoyed, so Israel, though she might descend into sin and impurity, yet, when she repents on Yom Kippur, she is forgiven and restored to grace.

Figs are also recommended, on the basis of the verse, "When the green figs will ripen on the fig trees" (Song of Songs 2:13), which the Midrash (*Shir Ha-Shirim Rabbah* 2:28) views as an allusion to the basket of firstfruits brought every Shavuot in the Temple.

In a similar spirit, the halakhah also recommends for *charoset* dates or pomegranates, as well as spices like cinnamon or ginger, which cannot be ground too finely and are therefore reminiscent of the straw that the Israelites had to go out and collect for use in the baking of their bricks. Wine is, naturally, multisymbolic: of the Israelite blood that was shed, of the Egyptian firstborn blood that was shed in the final plague, and of the wine libations that were poured over the altar in the Temple, whose destruction is so lamented at this time.

## SALT WATER, *KARPAS*, AND *MAROR*

### 194. Why do we have salt water?

Salt water is meant to recall the tears shed by the Israelites at the hurt inflicted upon them by the cruel Egyptian taskmasters. We dip the *karpas* into it and pour it over the hard-boiled eggs eaten before the meal.

### 195. What do we use for *karpas*, and what is its significance?

For the first "dipping" we use *karpas,* which is an Aramaic form of an original Greek word, *charpsaso,* an umbelliferous plant. The Palestinian Talmud (*Shevi'it* 9:1) queries which precise plant it is and defines it as *petrozel,* which is the *Petroselinum crispum* plant, known to us as parsley.

*Karpas* was regarded as an appetizer, to recall the custom of the nobility in Roman times who would take a relish to stimulate their appetites before a meal. Thus, it is taken on Seder night as a symbol of freedom. Because a variety of similar vegetables were used for such dips, much flexibility was exercised in the choice of vegetable for *karpas* (though not with the blessing of a number of religious authorities, such as Isaac Luria, followed by the Chatam Sofer, who insisted upon the authentic *karpas* plant, namely parsley). It frequently depended upon what was seasonal and available in the respective country: hence the various traditions of using lettuce, celery, radish, onion, or even potatoes for *karpas.*

Another interpretation of the significance of the *karpas* is that it is to recall the hyssop plant, which the Torah prescribed for the daubing of the blood on the doorposts of the Israelite homes (Exodus 12:22).

**196. Are there are particular regulations regarding how *karpas* is eaten?**

One must examine and wash the vegetable thoroughly, particularly in the case of parsley, before putting it on the Seder plate. One must eat less than the size of a *kezayit*, or olive (see question 199 for comment on the present-day equivalent of that measure). Authorities who interpret *karpas* as a symbol of slavery (rather than preparation for redemption) recommend that we do not lean—a symbol of freedom—while eating it. Either all participants recite their own blessing over it *(Borei periy ha-adamah)*, or the one leading the Seder may recite it on behalf of all.

**197. What is the significance of *maror*, and what do we use for it?**

*Maror* means "bitter herbs," and it is eaten in order to recall the bitter experiences of our ancestors in Egypt. The term "herb" is rather too narrow, for bitter vegetables will do just as well.

Here again we have diversity of opinion regarding the best species to use for this purpose. The Torah gives no guidance, referring merely to *merorim* (Exodus 12:8), and the *Shulchan Arukh* (*Orach Chayyim* 473:5) lists many herbs that are appropriate, either singly or in combination, and whether one eats their leaves (providing they are still moist) or their stalks. The roots, however, are not permitted for this purpose. They must be eaten in their natural state, not cooked, pickled, or boiled.

The most common herb used is horseradish, though romaine lettuce is recommended since while its initial taste is sweet, after a while it leaves a bitter aftertaste, which reflects the precise circumstances of the Egyptian experience, which began sweetly (in the period of Joseph and his brothers, who were welcomed by Pharaoh and the Egyptians) and then became bitter (with the onset of oppression and slavery).

**198. How is the *maror* eaten?**

If we use horseradish, it has to be cut up into pieces, and each person must eat a piece the equivalent of a *kezayit*, about the size of a large olive (see question 199). It is dipped into the *charoset*, and the temptation should be avoided to totally dilute the bitter taste by taking too much of the sweet-tasting *charoset*. Indeed, authorities recommend that one should shake off the *charoset* before eating the *maror*.

For the first *maror*, we use a single piece of horseradish or other herb. For Hillel's sandwich, we grate the *maror* and eat it between two pieces of *matzah* (see questions 399–407).

**199. We referred above (questions 196, 198) to *kezayit*, the size of an olive. But do not olives vary greatly in size and is not this too vague a measure?**

Indeed, halakhists point out that in the Israel of talmudic times the fruits and vegetables were much larger than in our own day. Hence, according to *Nodah Biyehudah* and *Chazon Ish*, our equivalent of the talmudic olive is half an egg, without its shell. That amount should be eaten both in the case of the *maror* and also, after making the special blessings (*Ha-motziy* and *Al achilat matzah*), when eating the *matzah*.

### 200. Why do we recite no blessing over the *charoset*?

According to the main view in the Mishnah (*Pesachim* 10:3), there is no *mitzvah* in partaking of *charoset*. It was introduced for purely therapeutic reasons, in order to palliate the harsh effects on the stomach of mites that are found in some bitter herbs. It is the dissenting view of Rabbi Eleazar bar Zadok that subsequently became popular, namely, that *charoset* is truly a *mitzvah*, reminiscent of the mortar that the Israelites had to make.

## THE THREE *MATZOT*

### 201. Why do we place three *matzot* on the Seder table?

Two are required to serve in place of the usual *Shabbat* and *Yom Tov challot* (loaves), and the third (the middle one that is broken into two) represents the *lechem oni*, "bread of affliction."

The *Da'at Zekeinim Mi-Ba'alei Ha-Tosafot* explains the three as a recollection of the three measures *(shalosh se'in)* of fine flour taken by Abraham in order to bake cakes for the three angels (Genesis 18:6), for according to tradition (see Rashi on Genesis 18:10), that day of their visit was Pesach. The middle *matzah* is broken into two, according to this source, in order to recall the splitting of the Red Sea.

The three *matzot* are also popularly explained with reference to the three divisions of the Jewish people, into Priests, Levites, and Israelites.

### 202. Is there a prohibition regarding the eating of *matzah* for some time before Pesach?

There is such a prohibition, though it only refers to the day of Erev Pesach itself. Its objective is that the *mitzvah* of eating *matzah* at the Seder should be fresh, and that we will have an appetite for it. There is a common practice, however, to extend the period of abstinence from *matzah* and not to eat it from Purim onwards.

## ARRANGING THE SEDER PLATE

### 203. Is there a recommended positioning of the symbolic foods on the Seder plate?

There are two basic traditions: the mystic tradition of Isaac Luria *(Ari)*, adopted as the hasidic way, and the more practical rationale, as codified by Rabbi Moses Isserles (Remah) in his gloss on the *Shulchan Arukh* (*Orach Chayyim* 473:4).

Luria views the various foods as representing the mystical characteristics of the ten primeval *Sefirot,* or divine emanations, which, at Creation, bridged the abyss between the pure spirituality of God and the physical world that came into being as an extension of His creativity. These ten *Sefirot* constituted ten mystical stages of progressive creativity, and at the same time corresponded to the ten aspects of the *Ein Sof*'s ("The Unending One") inherent and bestowed qualities. These sefirotic qualities are: *Keter* ("Crown"), *Chokhmah* ("Wisdom"), *Binah* ("Discernment"), *Chesed* ("Grace"), *Gevurah* ("Might"), *Tiferet* ("Beauty"), *Netzach* ("Victory"), *Hod* ("Majesty"), *Yesod* ("Foundation"), and the lowest and final emanation, *Malkhut* ("Kingdom"), which is a weakened synthesis of all the previous emanations in a form that can be concretized into the creation of a physical world.

Luria's concept of the Seder foods, as symbolizing those sefirotic qualities, prompts him to insist that they be placed in an order appropriate to their respective position in the mystical order of emanations. He therefore requires that the items that symbolize the higher order of qualities be placed at the highest position (furthest away from the Seder leader), and those representing lower levels of emanation be at the bottom, closest to hand. Thus, at the very top Luria has the three *matzot* (representing *Keter, Chokhmah,* and *Binah*). Beneath them are positioned, to the right, the shank bone *(Chesed),* and to the left, the egg *(Gevurah).* Beneath them, and centered, is placed the *Maror (Tiferet);* and beneath it we have, on the right, *charoset (Netzach)* and to the left, *karpas (Hod).* Beneath them, in the center, we have the *Chazeret* (the lettuce, recommended by Luria for use as *Maror* in Hillel's sandwich, and representative of the *Yesod* emanation). Luria viewed the Seder plate itself as symbolizing the final emanation of *Malkhut.*

The order preferred by Isserles follows the talmudic principle of *Ein maavirin al ha-mitzvot* (see Talmud *Yoma* 33b and *Tosafot,* D. H. *Avurei,* Talmud *Yoma* 33b), "We should not pass by *mitzvot,*" but attend to them in the order that they present themselves. Thus, the foods have to be arranged so that they come to hand in order, as they are required. Accordingly, the egg and shank bone are placed farthest away (the right and left side, respectively). Below, and centered, is the *maror.* Beneath that are placed *charoset* and *karpas* (right and left, respectively), and, closest to hand (bottom and centered), the horseradish. At the side of the dish, the saltwater should be nearer than the *matzot.* According to this arrangement, one does not need to pass one's hand over any of the foods that one will not be eating just yet.

# XI

# When Erev Pesach Falls on a *Shabbat*

**204. When were the last two occasions that Erev Pesach fell on a *Shabbat*, and when will the next two occurrences be?**

It last occurred in 1981 and 1994, and will next occur in 2001 and 2005.

**205. Is this a quirk of the modern, fixed calendar, and was it avoided in ancient Temple times when greater flexibility existed?**

It is true that in Temple times there was no fixed calendar, and the first day of each new month (Rosh Chodesh) was determined by witnesses coming to testify before the Sanhedrin that they had seen the first sign of the new moon the previous evening. However, once that testimony had been accepted and the day of the hearing declared "day one" of the new month (or, if no witnesses came, the following day), there was nothing that could be done to change the incidence of any festival during that coming month, however inconvenient the situation might be.

**206. Have we any evidence of Erev Pesach falling on a *Shabbat* during the talmudic period (first–sixth centuries)?**

Indeed, it was the occurrence of Erev Pesach on a *Shabbat* that catapulted Hillel to prominence, and ultimately to leadership (as elected *Nasi,* or Patriarch) of Palestinian Jewry, around the turn of the Common Era. The *Bnei Beteirah,* a patrician family who undeservedly wielded religious leadership, were unable to give a ruling one year when the eve of Pesach occurred on a *Shabbat.* They were asked whether the law prohibiting slaughtering on the Sabbath (apart, that is, from the Temple Continual Offering which tradition had established, superseded the sancity of the Sabbath day) applied also to the Paschal lamb. Hillel, who had already distinguished himself among the populace as a great teacher and a concerned protector of the poor and uneducated, gave a definitive ruling, buttressed with proofs from tradition as well as by logical inferences (see Talmud *Pesachim* 66a).

**207. What difficulties does this occurrence pose?**

Many: just wait and see! Put simply, it means that for Orthodox Jews, who abide by the restrictions of Sabbath law, none of the multifarious activities that tradition and necessity reserve for the eve of Pesach may be performed. These include searching for the *chametz* at nightfall (in this situation, that is Friday night, after the onset of *Shabbat*), burning it the following morning (one is not permitted to kindle a flame on the Sabbath), preparation of the Seder plate (even those activities involved in food preparation that are permitted on the Sabbath—such as laying the Seder table—may not be performed on this particular Sabbath because of the law that one may not prepare anything on Sabbath for after the Sabbath), cooking for the Seder, last-minute cleaning of the home, and so forth.

### 208. How do we overcome the problem?

Have everything prepared, and the entire home converted to Pesach mode, before *Shabbat* enters.

### 209. When is the Fast of the Firstborn observed?

The Fast and *siyyum* (see Chapter VIII) take place on the Thursday before because we do not normally like to fast on Fridays (Erev *Shabbat*), and may not do so on *Shabbat* itself.

### 210. But when do we make *Bedikat chametz*, "the search for the leaven"?

We make it on Thursday night.

### 211. When do we burn it?

We burn it on Friday morning at the same time as we would usually burn the *chametz* (see question 167).

### 212. And when do we recite the final *Kol chamirah* renunciation of all *chametz*?

We recite it on *Shabbat* morning, at the usual time, after disposing of all our *chametz*.

### 213. But is there not a problem here regarding the provision of two Sabbath challot?

There most definitely is a problem. We have stated above that one may not eat *matzah* on the eve of Pesach. Now, if the home has to have already been converted to Pesach mode by the time *Shabbat* enters, then we can neither eat bread nor *matzah*. How, then, can we eat the prescribed two challot on Friday night and at *Shabbat* lunch?

There is no problem with using two baby challot for Friday night, though we must keep them on a tray in a corner of the eating room that we reserve for this purpose. As regards *Shabbat* morning, we may only eat *chametz* until about ten hours, which means that in order to fulfill the *mitzvah* of having two challot at the *Shabbat* lunch, we have to eat our main *Shabbat* meal before that time. It is thus more a brunch than a lunch.

**214. But is there not a prohibition against eating a meal before prayer at synagogue?**

Good point: for that reason it is customary for Orthodox congregations to pray the Morning Service (some conclude, the entire service) before about nine hours, thereby enabling worshipers to return home, make *Kiddush,* wash, eat of the two prescribed *challot,* have the brunch, clear away the remainder of the meal and throw out the crumbs, recite the *Kol chamirah* renunciation of all *chametz,* and return to synagogue for the Reading of the Torah and the remainder of the service.

**215. What sort of food should be reserved for that brunch?**

Because of the prohibition of washing up and disposing of pure *chametz* and greasy *chametz* dishes, it is customary to eat only foods that are supervised for Pesach, such as cheese, herring, cake, and fruit.

**216. Is there not a bit of a problem in eating challah, albeit in a separate, circumscribed area, and then putting Pesach cutlery into one's mouth?**

This is a problem. There is also the fear, however remote, that crumbs may just be transferred from the side table to the Pesach crockery that one is using for one's meal (this may easily happen where there are children in the family). Indeed, for that reason some people use only disposable plates, cutlery and paper tablecloths for the Friday night meal and the *Shabbat* morning brunch.

**217. But how do we dispose of the remaining crumbs from these two meals, if we cannot burn the *chametz*?**

There is some controversy regarding the precise method to be employed. The easiest method is, naturally, to throw it into the outside trash can and await collection by the refuse department. Some permit this, since such an act is tantamount to *bittul,* "mental annulment." This attitude and status is, indeed, reinforced by the recitation of the *Kol chamirah* formula of official renunciation.

Other authorities are unhappy with this arrangement, maintaining that crumbs of bread and other *chametz* may not be kept on one's property, and therefore in one's possession, even if annulled, unless rendered unfit even for an animal's consumption (see question 127). They therefore insist that, before throwing it away, detergent be added to the *chametz* to convert it to that inedible state.

**218. Now what about the afternoon *Seudah Shelishit,* "The third meal," at which we are supposed to eat two challot?**

Here we really are in that impossible situation where we can eat neither *chametz* nor *matzah.* Some, who are zealous not to forgo a single *mitzvah,* overcome the problem by having that third meal almost immediately after the morning brunch, while challah may still be eaten. On returning from synagogue they eat the brunch.

They say *Birkat ha-Mazon* ("Grace after Meals"), have a brief interlude, perhaps by taking a little walk, and then return and have the "third meal," eating the prescribed challot together with some light accompaniment. It is a rush, to say the least! Several authorities state, however, that one may waive the "Third Meal" on this occasion "in order not to have to spend too much time at one's table" (*Nimmukei Yoseph,* end of Commentary to Talmud *Pesachim,* ch. 1). *Arukh Ha-Shulchan* reminds us that we set the obligations of these meals aside on Yom Kippur, because of the overarching biblical regulation governing the day, so we should not be surprised that the obligation of *Seudah Shelishit* may also be dispensed with on Erev Pesach.

### 219. May one set the Seder table during *Shabbat* for the evening's Seder?

While normally the principle of not preparing on one holy day for the next applies, and some authorities (*Pri Chadash, Pri Megadim,* etc.) insist that this is, similarly, the case here, yet there is on record the surprisingly lenient view (see *Hagahot Maharsham,* sec. 444) that, if such a fully set dining table also constitutes an adornment of the room during *Shabbat,* it may be set on that day in preparation for the evening. The analogy is the law that on *Shemini Atzeret,* the last day when we use the *sukkah,* one may remove the vessels and objects from it from late afternoon into the house (see *Shulchan Arukh,* sec. 666). Now that law also applies if that day coincides with *Shabbat.* But if one may not prepare from one day to the next, why, then, is this permitted?

*Chayyei Adam* explains that it was declared permitted since one needs those vessels for the evening (the *Yom Tov* of *Simchat Torah*) and it is most difficult to clear away the vessels from the *sukkah* after dark. Furthermore, if one is not completing an activity it is not regarded as *hakhanah,* "preparing," for the next day. On that analogy, some authorities allow the Seder table to be set, to avoid much rush and effort when *Shabbat* goes out and delay in commencing the Seder.

# XII

## *Shabbat* and *Yom Tov* Prohibitions: Cooking from One Day to the Next—*Eiruv Tavshilin*

### WORK ON *SHABBAT* AND *YOM TOV*

**220. What is the philosophy underlying the prohibition of "work" on *Shabbat*?**

*Shabbat* is the holiest day of the Jewish religious calendar. The Torah states in thirteen separate passages that no work may be done on that day, and rabbinic tradition defines "work" as activities of a positive and creative nature—not necessarily activities that involve effort or exertion. Thus, we may well regard carrying chairs several times up and down stairs in one's home as "work," but that activity does not, in fact, conflict with Judaism's definition of the term. Again, striking a match, switching on a light, or igniting a car ignition are truly nonexertive, yet they are expressly prohibited in the Torah in the words: "You shall kindle no fire in all your habitations on the Sabbath day" (Exodus 35:3).

Such highly creative acts, designated as *nolad,* "bringing something into being," are prohibited in order to demonstrate on the Sabbath that there is only one source of creative energy, and that is God. He rested on the first Sabbath of Creation; and we must do likewise, as a demonstration of deference and awe before the creative Spirit, which keeps our universe in existence and which invests man's own limitless progress and creative endeavor. *Shabbat* ensures that we put our genius into perspective and constantly regard ourselves as men, not supermen.

**221. What is the difference in this respect between *Shabbat* and *Yom Tov* (festival holy days)?**

Unlike *Shabbat,* which highlights God's cessation from His original creative endeavor, the resting from work on the holy days of festivals is intended rather to provide the Jew with a measure of tranquillity of spirit, the more to celebrate and enjoy the festival. The Torah was enabled thereby to make concessions in the level of prohibitions that *Yom Tov* involved.

Thus, the Torah states: "No manner of work shall be done on them, except that which is necessary for what a man must eat, that alone may be done by you" (Exodus 12:16). And this constitutes the basic difference between *Shabbat* and *Yom Tov:* any act, such as cooking or baking, required to provide food for that particular festival holy day may be undertaken. Rabbinic Oral Law and tradition disclosed that that concession to the food requirement was always interpreted in the very broadest sense

81

to include any other activity required for human enjoyment and convenience, such as lighting, heating, pushing a baby carriage, washing dishes, or (not recommended!) smoking. Thus, while carrying out of doors is prohibited on *Shabbat,* on *Yom Tov* it is permitted to carry, with the proviso that they were objects permitted to be touched and used on that day. Hence, one may carry books, clothes, food, tallit, and similar objects, but not money, since business transactions are not permitted on *Yom Tov.*

### 222. So may one strike a match or switch on a light on *Yom Tov*?

No, one may not. Some distinction between the ordinary working day and the holy festival day had to be made, and it was in this area of *nolad,* or primary creativity, that this was demonstrated. While all cooking, baking, boiling, and so forth are permitted on *Yom Tov* (as long as the food is required for that particular day), nevertheless, the medium or instrument of ignition of the fire or cooker has to be an indirect or secondary source. In other words, we may not light a new fire, but, if we have a gas burner, pilot light, or candle that was kindled before *Yom Tov* and kept burning throughout, we may take a taper and utilize that source of ignition for *extending* the flame to other sources of heat.

## PERMITTED ACTIVITIES

### 223. Are absolutely all activities permitted, then, if they are in the cause of the preparation of food or for other forms of human enjoyment?

No, they are not. The halakhah prohibited certain activities, such as reaping, grinding, squeezing, and hunting, even if it was intended to employ them in the preparation of a meal. This was as a preventive measure, since people are accustomed to performing these activities on a daily basis—reaping their fields, grinding and milling the corn, squeezing the grapes of the vintage, hunting animals and fish—and the Rabbis felt that if they permitted these activities, albeit strictly for the purposes of food, on *Yom Tov,* people would be tempted to go into their fields and spend the holy day at work. To become fully acquainted with the detailed laws of *Shabbat* and *Yom Tov,* and whether and how one may utilize the fruits of modern technology, requires detailed study. A highly regarded work is Rabbi Yehoshua Y. Neuwirth's *Shemirath Shabbath Ke-hilkhatah.* (See English edition Jerusalem and New York: Feldheim, 1984.)

### 224. Why is the cooking concession only extended to food required for that particular day of *Yom Tov*?

Whereas in the Diaspora we observe two days of *Yom Tov,* the Torah only states that "the first day is a holy convocation unto you . . . and the seventh day is a holy convocation" (Leviticus 23:7–8). Thus, to spend time and effort on the first day of the festival preparing food for the second day, or to prepare on the seventh day for the last day (or on *Sheminiy Atzeret* for *Simchat Torah*)—notwithstanding the fact that in the

Diaspora the next day is also holy—was nevertheless regarded as a diminution of the sanctity of the day.

### 225. Are there any exceptions to that rule?

Yes. The halakhah prescribes that, providing one requires to eat some of the cooked food on the first day of *Yom Tov,* he or she may cook a larger volume of food than necessary for that first day in order to have plenty left over for the following day. The first intention is regarded as his primary intention.

### 226. But if exceptions like that can be accommodated, why should it not be allowed to cook on *Yom Tov* for a *Shabbat* that follows immediately after it?

The objection is also a precautionary one, for if we permit people to cook on *Yom Tov* for the following day, they might easily jump to the conclusion that it is always permitted to do such cooking for the following day, *even if it is a weekday.* However, by insisting that cooking on *Yom Tov* even for *Shabbat* is prohibited, the clear inference will be drawn that obviously one may not prepare on *Yom Tov* for an ordinary weekday.

### 227. So how do we get around the problem of enabling people to eat appropriate *Shabbat* meals?

While we have just explained that one may not cook or prepare on one day of *Yom Tov* for the next, even if it be a *Shabbat,* nevertheless, having regard to the paramount sanctity of *Shabbat* and the prophetic challenge of calling it "a delight," the halakhah took account of the great inconsistency in having well-cooked food over the two days of the *Yom Tov* (Thursday and Friday) and then having to eat frugally on *Shabbat,* because of the prohibition of preparing food on *Yom Tov* for the day after.

In that spirit, tradition introduced a method of circumventing the strict law for those prepared to make a tangible statement, by thought, word and action, affirming their total commitment to the sanctity of *Yom Tov* and their awareness that by cooking on *Yom Tov* for *Shabbat* they are not allowing themselves any concessions that may be extended to other situations, such as cooking on any future *Yom Tov* for a following weekday.

## *EIRUV TAVSHILIN*

### 228. What is that ritual and what is its rationale?

It is the *Eiruv Tavshilin,* literally, "mixture of cooked dishes." This involves a symbolic act of reducing the volume of cooking required to be done on the second day of *Yom Tov* for the *Shabbat,* by setting aside some food for *Shabbat* even before the festival has commenced. Conceptually, one is already giving priority of thought to that *Shabbat* day, and setting in motion its preparations, not *on Yom Tov,* but *before* it has commenced.

### 229. How is the *Eiruv Tavshilin* prepared?

The head of the household sets aside a small piece of a cooked or roasted food (the size of an olive in volume) that is normally eaten with bread, such as meat, fish, or a boiled egg, and places it on a dish together with a small bread roll (the size of an egg in volume), or, on Pesach, a piece of *matzah.* After the formal declaration, the food is set on one side. It should be kept in a carefully designated place until all the cooking and preparations for *Shabbat* have been completed on the Friday, since, if it becomes eaten or is lost, no further preparations may be made for the *Shabbat.* It is customary, however, to use the bread roll or *matzah* of the *Eiruv* as one of the two loaves required for *Seudah Shelishit,* the "third meal," eaten late *Shabbat* afternoon.

### 230. What is the *Eiruv Tavshilin* declaration?

The blessing is recited: *Barukh attah . . . asher kidshanu bemitzvotav vetzivanu al mitzvat Eiruv*–"Blessed are You . . . who has sanctified us by His commandments, and commanded us concerning the *Mitzvah* of making an *Eiruv.*"

This is followed by the declaration: "By means of this *eiruv* it shall be permitted for us to bake, cook, heat dishes, light the Sabbath lights, and prepare during the festival all we need for the Sabbath–for us and for all Jews who live in this town."

### 231. What if someone forgot to make the *Eiruv Tavshilin*?

It is the tradition for the Rabbi of the community to have in mind when he makes his *Eiruv Tavshilin* that he is also making it, not merely for himself and his own family, but also on behalf of any people of his town who might have been ignorant of the law requiring an *Eiruv* to be made or for any who genuinely forgot to attend to it or were prevented by circumstances beyond their control. They may rely on the Rabbi's *Eiruv,* and proceed to do all their cooking for the *Shabbat.*

The Rabbi's *Eiruv* does not, however, cover those who, through laziness or indifference, just did not bother to attend to it in time. Nor does it cover religious and learned people who, knowing that, under certain circumstances, the Rabbi's *Eiruv* may be relied upon, decided not to bother but instead to rely on the Rabbi.

# XIII

# History of the Published Haggadah

## ILLUMINATED HAGGADOT

### 232. What is the literal meaning and origin of the term *Haggadah*?

The word *Haggadah* means "telling," and it is derived from the verse, "And you shall tell [*vehigadta*] to your children on that day" (Exodus 13:8).

### 233. Why is it that the Haggadah was such a popular text for artistic illumination?

Of all texts, the Haggadah was probably the favorite for medieval graphic artists to demonstrate their expertise, and upon which to give free rein to their creativity. In the case of the other sacred texts (the *Siddur, Machzor, Chumash,* etc.), they were more constrained by synagogue usage to remain within bounds of accepted solemn propriety. The Haggadah, on the other hand, being a home manual and religious textbook rather than a prayer book, allowed for more unrestrained artistic originality. The scribe was also expected to take account of the overarching Seder night objective: to keep the children instructed and interested.

### 234. How did those illuminated Haggadot originate?

Between the thirteenth and fifteenth centuries, before the age of printing and mass production, illuminated Haggadot were generally commissioned by wealthy patrons, for either personal use or family distribution. The average poor family would have had to content itself with a single rough, hand-written copy of the main text, and many would not even have possessed that. Thus, when we speak of "the most well-known editions," we are not referring to any mass popularity attending the wide publication of certain editions, but rather to the survival of single manuscripts, mainly from the late medieval period, which are of artistic merit and historical curiosity and which reflect a particularly creative approach to the textual material. The unusual characteristics of a number of these have been described in twentieth-century catalogues, articles, and printed editions, and, in addition, some excellent facsimile editions have been produced in recent decades. Hence it is that a number of those illuminated Haggadot have now become household names.

### 235. What are the most well-known illuminated Haggadot?

It would be impossible, within the scope of the present book, to do more than refer to just a few of the Haggadot that have been made famous this century.

One of the oldest surviving illuminated Haggadot is the *Birds' Head Haggadah*, discovered in 1946 by Mordekhai Narkiss and presently housed in the Israel Museum. It was copied around the end of the thirteenth century, in southern Germany. Its unusual characteristic—whence its name—is the replacement of human heads with those of birds. The artist also adopts some other devices to conform with the prohibition of representing the human form. Thus, he obscures the faces of the Egyptian soldiers by depicting them with the visors of their helmets (clearly, and characteristically, reflecting the military equipment of his own age) lowered. Angels have blank faces and other humans are endowed with grossly exaggerated features, such as a boy with a great bulbous nose.

The fourteenth-century *Sarajevo Haggadah*, though housed in the Sarajevo National Museum, actually originated in Spain, and it bears three coats of arms of the Kingdom of Aragon. It came into the possession of the museum when, in 1894, a child from a Sephardi family brought it to school to be sold, since his father had just died, leaving the family destitute. Most pages are divided horizontally into two framed sections, which depict an astonishing variety of subjects, from biblical themes of Creation to scenes from the stories of Moses and Joshua. There are also illustrations of the Jerusalem Temple, themes depicting preparations for the festival of Passover, and a view of the interior of a Spanish synagogue.

The earliest extant Sephardi (Spanish) illuminated Haggadah is *The Golden Haggadah*, housed in the British Museum and dating back to the beginning of the fourteenth century. It was probably produced in Barcelona for a very wealthy patron, being a most lavish and exquisitely wrought volume. In addition to the text of the Haggadah, it also contains about one hundred liturgical poems and fifteen full-page miniatures on early biblical themes.

The *Ashkenazi Haggadah*, another British Museum possession, is characterized by its great size, the equivalent of a tractate of Talmud, which provided unprecedented scope for the calligrapher's art as well as for commentary and rubrics down the side of the page. Many of these comments, as well as, on occasion, specific verses highlighted from the main body of the text, are set within marginal doodles illustrative of the themes of the verses highlighted.

The name of the Haggadah derives from the term with which the scribe, Joel ben Simeon, describes himself. His period of activity spanned nearly forty years, from 1449 to 1485, and there is no other known artist, throughout the Middle Ages, whose name is associated with so many illuminated Hebrew manuscripts. That having been said, it seems that, after leaving Joel's hands, the work was given to a second artist who added his own distinct style of representational figure.

Joel includes a colophon (on page 48b) stating: "My heart prompts me to reply to him who might ask who painted these pages. I answer: 'I am the one, Feibusch, called Joel; [I have produced this work] for Jacob Mattathias, may he live long, son of MHRZ, a godly man.' " One of the most charming and homely aspects of this manuscript (see the 1985 facsimile edition edited by David Goldstein, [London: Thames and Hudson, 1985]), is the residual wine stains on many of the pages, which lend character and immediacy to the history of the extant manuscript.

### 236. Was there any kind of convention to which Haggadah illustrators were expected to conform?

Not really: since the illustrators made their living from the private patronage they received, it was obvious that their exclusive concern was to produce an edition that pleased, and conformed to the clear instructions of, their commissioners. We may assume, therefore, that whenever the artists took liberties or injected some ironic or humourous theme, they would have first ascertained that it met with the approval of their patrons.

Presumably the wife of the patron of the thirteenth-century John Rylands *Haggadah* had a good sense of humor. Otherwise, the artist would certainly have gotten into hot water through his illustration of a man holding the bitter herbs in his hand and looking towards his wife! After the words, "These bitter herbs we eat," there follows the comment, "In some localities the husband points the bitter herbs at his wife!"

## EARLY HAGGADOT

### 237. But before the thirteenth-century artistic productions, in what form was the Haggadah produced?

It was regarded as part and parcel of the festival section of the earliest prayer books produced by the great Geonim of the Babylonian academies (ninth–twelfth centuries). Those early compilations did not separate the daily and Sabbath prayers (*Siddur*) from the festival prayers (*Machzor*), viewing both terms as synonymous and comprehensive. Thus, the first major prayer book, produced by *Amram Gaon* (d. 875), is called *Seder (Siddur) Rav Amram;* the next, and greatest, liturgical work of the Middle Ages, produced by *Saadiah Gaon* (892–942), was entitled *Siddur Saadiah;* and Maimonides' (1135–1204) prayer book is headed *Seder Tephillot Kol Ha-Shanah.* However, a most popular prayer book of the school of Rashi (eleventh century) is called *Machzor Vitri,* though it also contains full text and commentary on the weekday and Sabbath prayers. Thus, the Haggadah was merely reproduced in these works as part of the comprehensive prayer book in vogue at the time.

### 238. Are the texts of all those medieval Haggadot uniform?

No they are not. All medieval manuscripts of specific works exhibit, to a greater or lesser degree, some variety. This was inevitable in prayer books and Haggadot that were not specifically based upon an accepted and authorized master version. Furthermore, the commissioner of the work usually felt entitled to give specific instructions to the calligrapher on the matter of the version of the text that he expected to be reproduced, reflective of his local or family *nusach,* or textual tradition.

Medieval Jewish families, having wandered for either shorter or longer periods from country to country and province to province, absorbed a great variety of different textual traditions. Sometimes they replaced earlier versions and customs with those of their current place of domicile; at other times they grafted the new phraseology onto the old, and occasionally they made an arbitrary synthesis of the two (or more) versions. The memory being imperfect, where they were not perfectly sure of the precise wording of a passage or phrase or of whether their inherited tradition recited it or not, they did not hesitate to make arbitrary decisions or to leave it to the scribe to do likewise.

Hence, we frequently find, in the medieval manuscripts, strange forms of vocalization that do not conform to any pronunciation with which we are familiar today, centuries after standardization and printing have helped establish uniform versions and texts. It is still possible today, though not to any significant degree, to find slight variations in phraseology, words, and occasionally paragraph order, as well as conflicting rubrics, from one Haggadah to the next, even within the same Ashkenazi or Sephardi tradition.

### 239. When were the earliest printed editions of the Haggadah issued?

The earliest separate edition of a printed Haggadah was published in Guadalajar, Spain, in 1482 – only ten years before the expulsion of Jewry from that country – and comprised a mere twelve pages of double-columned text. The sixteenth century saw the evolution of the art of the illustrated printed text, and this period may be said to have been launched by the magnificent *Prague Haggadah* of 1526, a number of facsimile editions of which have been reproduced over the past few decades.

The text of the Prague edition was reproduced, in facsimile form, as early as 1560 and again in 1568, in Mantua, with new illustrations and marginal decorations that were more in line with Italian taste and style.

By the beginning of the sixteenth century, Venice had become a great center of Jewish publishing, and several editions, all based upon the Mantua edition, were produced there.

The Amsterdam edition of 1695 (revised 1712) was influenced greatly by the Venice editions, though, unlike all the previous editions, which were printed from woodcuts, this one was engraved on copper, providing a vastly superior quality of illustration. Another unique characteristic was that hitherto, all the illustrators had remained anonymous, whereas in the Amsterdam edition, the name of the illustrator, Abram ben Jacob the proselyte, is mentioned.

The Amsterdam edition had unprecedented popularity in Ashkenazi communities. It was reprinted in 1702, 1781, and 1810 and formed the basis of countless subsequent editions printed in Germany and Poland up until World War II.

Perhaps one of the most unusual publications of the Haggadah occurred on August 17, 1840, when, in the wake of the notorious Damascus blood libel, *The Times* newspaper of London published the entire English translation of the Haggadah in order to expose the false allegation that blood figures as a ritual component in the Seder.

### 240. When was the original Hebrew text of the Haggadah composed?

The Haggadah is a composite work, containing material composed over a period of nearly three thousand years. It contains biblical verses; psalms; early expositions that were probably first delivered in the period of the Ptolemies and Seleucids (third–second centuries B.C.E.) (see question 356); midrashic homilies from the talmudic period (first–sixth century C.E.); two compositions by Palestinian Jewry's earliest Hebrew poets, Yannai and Kallir (ca. sixth century); one by a tenth-century French poet, R. Joseph ben Samuel Tov Elem; as well as the final medley of table songs and jingles, which is supposedly based on popular Franco-German nursery rhymes of the twelfth century.

Like an archaeological *Tel,* the later material was superimposed upon the earlier kernel of material that had gradually won popularity and general acceptance for recitation at the Seder. One cannot, therefore, speak in terms of a specific date when the Haggadah was composed. We have to analyze each strand and composition, and leave it to scholars (such as E. D. Goldschmidt, *The Passover Haggadah: Its Sources and History,* Jerusalem: Bialik Institute, 1960) to determine for us when each individual element was composed, when it gained general acceptance as part of the Seder, and when the Haggadah was ultimately edited and regarded as complete.

## PRINTED EDITIONS

### 241. How many printed editions of the Haggadah are there?

Considering that currently about one hundred different editions (and reprints) appear each year, it is not easy to answer this question with any degree of accuracy. In 1960, Abraham Yaari issued his *Bibliography of the Passover Haggadah* (Jerusalem: Bamberger and Wahrman, 1960) listing 2,713 printed editions that had been published since printing began. This list was supplemented that year by some other scholars who took the number of printed editions to 3,404. Based on that information, we may conjecture that, to date, some 5,000 editions have made their appearance. It is expected that, in our desktop publishing era, the number may well double before the end of the millenium.

### 242. Why are so many new editions required?

The Haggadah is not only an account of our people's first period of oppression and subsequent redemption to become a nation, but it represents an annual catalyst for a Jewish national stocktaking. This presents a recurring opportunity to find, reflected in the Haggadah, parallels for our contemporary situation, and, hopefully, faith, strength, and inspiration to confront and solve our present problems against the backcloth of past experience. Thus, creative writers have always sought to update the old–new story, chronicling its newest twists through artistry and interpreting them through commentary.

Editions of the Haggadah have also provided, in recent decades, an opportunity for certain interest groups to read into it, and promote, their own ideologies and philosophies. Thus, we have nontraditional editions produced by the Karaites; the Samaritans; and movements for Progressive Judaism in America, Britain, and Israel; as well as editions issued by the secular Kibbutz movement, and by feminist groups, homosexual and lesbian associations, and humanists.

Editions have been issued as well by schools, Jewish university student societies, seminaries such as Yeshivah University, Zionist youth movements, and adult societies. Promotional editions have also been produced and distributed by educational, charitable, and welfare agencies in order to raise funds, as well as editions for "Third Seder" celebrations, which used to be a popular method of raising funds for Israel. The Sholem Aleichem College in Melbourne, Australia, produces a Third Seder Yiddish Haggadah on account of the largely Eastern European immigrant community that comprises its membership.

El Al, Maxwell House, Rakusens Matzot, and many other manufacturers of household brands of Passover foods have also jumped on the Jewish promotional bandwagon in recent years.

### 243. How far back can we trace the publication of Haggadot for fund-raising purposes?

Charitable organizations and yeshivot were probably the first to produce inexpensive editions, towards the end of the nineteenth century. In 1899, one was issued by the Yeshivah of Rabbi Chaim Berlin in Jerusalem. It contains a dedicatory subheading: "To all our friends and members, and to all Jews who are interested in Jewish education."

### 244. What are the main types of Haggadah currently being produced?

In addition to those just mentioned, editions for children of all ages now constitute a very important section of the market. *The Children's Haggadah,* first published in 1933 (ed. A. M. Silbermann; London: Shapiro Vallentine), deserves special mention as a trailblazer in this respect. Its attractive layout, large characters, simple and free translation, rhymes and ditties, and particularly the imaginative, richly colored, and informative and moving illustrations have ensured its passage through many editions and reprints and its position as possibly the most favored children's edition until the present day.

For adults, there are editions to suit absolutely every taste. Translated editions of the classical commentaries have appeared, as well as Haggadot that approach the text, the Exodus, and the evolution of the festival from a historical, archaeological, or mystical point of view. Other beautiful editions concentrate on artistic presentation. In this category, mention must be made of Arthur Szyk, described by Cecil Roth as "the greatest illuminator since the sixteenth century" (see *The Haggadah,* executed by Arthur Szyk, edited by Cecil Roth, Jerusalem and Tel Aviv: "Massadah" and "Alumoth," 1960, introduction, pt. 5). Szyk's Haggadah illustrations, much like Roman Vishniac's photography, brings to life all the characters of the vanished world of the Eastern European ghettos, as well as the young pioneers of the fledgling Jewish State.

New trends in Israeli religious art are also well represented in modern editions, which reflect, and cater to, the numerous cultures that comprise *Medinat Yisrael,* as well as a host of inexpensive translated editions for the communities that have been transplanted from the vast regions of the old Soviet Union, from Ethiopia, and from Arabic-speaking countries. In 1943 a Haggadah was published in Paarl, near Capetown, and in 1968 there appeared a second edition in Afrikaans.

## UNIQUE EDITIONS

### 245. Were any editions issued under conditions of war?

Indeed, special editions were published during World War I for the benefit of Jewish soldiers serving on both sides! They were printed in the United States, Great Britain, Germany, and Austria.

In World War II, Jews only fought on the Allied side, and the Jewish Welfare Board of America issued 145,000 Haggadot in 1943, and a similar number the following year, for Jewish soldiers in the army and the marines.

An edition published in North Africa in 1942 for the Palestine Jewish Brigade contains the following poignant Introduction: "As the festival of freedom begins on this night, the night of the 14th Nisan 1942, we sit together, soldiers of the Hebrew Drivers' Unit No. 5, with our hearts filled with emotion and celebration. The heart rages because 'Egypt' has not ended for Israel. For us, the entire world has become 'Egypt.' " Quoted in A. Yaari, *Bibliografiah shel Hagadot Pesach* (Jerusalem: Bamberger-Wahrman, 1961).

A Haggadah was produced by the Religious Services Department of the Hagganah in 1948 for the men under siege in Jerusalem, and, since the establishment of the State of Israel, several special editions have been produced by the Israel General Staff through the Chief Army Chaplain.

### 246. Were any editions issued in Europe during the Nazi era?

Several editions were produced, under clandestine conditions, in countries under Nazi domination, such as France, Hungary, and Romania. Two Haggadot were produced in Southern France, then under Vichy rule, for use by Jews in the concentration camps. There were even editions printed by the inmates of the camps themselves, in Germany and Holland, with poignant comments on their hapless situation.

A mimeographed handwritten Haggadah was produced by Rabbi Leo Ansbacher for the inmates of the Vichy internment camp at Gurs, near the Pyrenees (see Y. H. Yerushalmi, *Haggadah and History* [Philadelphia: Jewish Publication Society of America, 1975] plate no. 158), and S. R. Kapel, former rabbi of Muelhausen in Alsace, produced a Haggadah in 1941 for concentration camp inmates at Toulouse.

After the traditional toast—*Leshanah ha-ba'ah bi Yerushalayim*—he adds the poignant plea, *Die Hagodeh zol zayn die letzte in golus*—"May this Haggadah be the final one produced in exile" (ibid., plate 159).

At the liberation, special editions were produced by charitable organizations in the United States, Israel, and Britain, celebrating the exodus from that slavery, and expressing the fervent prayers of Jews and gentiles the world over for the rehabilitation and successful future of the survivors. Many editions published after the liberation of the camps contained dedications to the heroism of the inmates and memorials to the six million who perished.

# XIV

## Commentary on the Seder and the Haggadah

### INAUGURATING THE SEDER

**247. Why is it the custom, when lighting the *Shabbat* and *Yom Tov* candles, to cover one's eyes while reciting the blessing and then to look at the candles?**

In the case of all *mitzvot*, one has to recite the blessing *before* performing the act. The problem is, however, that as soon as the blessing "to kindle the Sabbath lights" has been made, it becomes *Shabbat* for that home. Once it is *Shabbat,* one can no longer strike the match and light the candle! We overcome this by lighting the candle without any sacred intention in our minds. We then cover our eyes, shutting out the light. We recite the blessing and then uncover our eyes, and the light suddenly flooding in before our eyes is regarded as tantamount to its being created at that instant. Hence, it is as if the blessing had indeed been recited before creating the flame.

The necessity to cover the eyes really only applies when lighting the *Shabbat,* and not the *Yom Tov,* candles. One may, of course, handle fire on *Yom Tov,* so that it is technically quite possible to recite the blessing first, and then to bring a taper and light the *Yom Tov* candles, thereby complying with the requirement of reciting the blessing before performing the act, with none of the complications that are created by doing so on *Shabbat.*

**248. Why do some have the custom of donning a kittel for the Seder?**

Some authorities explain its purpose in relation to the *Urechatz* section of the Seder, when the leader (only) washes his hands before commencing the formal eating of the ritual foods. This is reminiscent of the priests who had to wash their hands before commencing the *Avodah,* the Temple service.

On this analogy, the wearing of the white kittel robe is suggestive of the identical garment worn by Moses during the seven days of initiating Aaron and his sons into their priestly ministry (see Talmud *Avodah Zarah* 34a; Rashi on Leviticus 8:28). Since, according to some authorities, the eating of the *matzah* at the Seder is in the same category as the eating of the holy sacrificial food, the kittel provides, therefore, a graphic symbolic and nostalgic reminder of a bygone Temple tradition.

**249. Why should we have to wait until nightfall before commencing the Seder?**

The question is especially pertinent since on *Shabbat* and *Yom Tov* it is permitted to make *Kiddush* and to eat while it is still day, during that period which we add from the working day to the Sabbath by bringing *Shabbat* in before nightfall.

On Pesach we may not do so, however, since the *mitzvah* of eating *matzah* is only operative at night, akin to that of the Paschal lamb. In the latter case the Torah expressly states, "And they shall eat the flesh on this *night*" (Exodus 12:8). Since the same law is applied to the four cups (reminiscent of the four expressions of the redemption, which was also wrought only after nightfall), and *Kiddush* constitutes the first of the four cups, it follows, therefore, that we cannot make *Kiddush* and commence the Seder until nightfall.

## A BLESSING OVER THE HAGGADAH?

**250. Why was there no special blessing (quite apart from the general blessing over wine) prescribed over the *mitzvah* of drinking four cups of wine at the Seder?**

Several authorities explain this according to the above-mentioned principle that blessings were only precribed over *mitzvot* that are performed immediately and that are not protracted. The drinking of the four cups, on the other hand, is spaced out over the entire duration of the Seder and interrupted by the meal, when other drinks, including wine, may be drunk. This also explains why there is no blessing over the rabbinic *mitzvah* of eating three meals on the Sabbath.

Rabbi Ovadiah Yoseph (see *Chazon Ovadiah,* Jerusalem: Yeshivat Porat Yoseph, 1979, p. 117) explains it in the light of the principle that we do not recite a blessing over an activity the character of which leaves it unclear that it is being done as a *mitzvah* in honor of the Creator. Hence, there is no blessing over the meal taken on the eve of the fast of Yom Kippur, even though the Rabbis declare that meal a *mitzvah*. For the same reason, there is no blessing over natural obligations that our reason dictates are required of us, such as honoring parents and rising up before the aged. Similarly, the drinking of the four cups can be construed as mere social drinking. There is nothing intrinsically and obviously spiritual about its performance.

## *KADDESH URECHATZ*

**251. Why do we recite at the outset the list of the fifteen ritual components of the Seder (*Kaddesh Urechatz,* etc.)?**

The Haggadah (literally, "the telling,") is a kind of religious chronicle or history book. Like any book, therefore, we would expect to find a list of contents at the very outset, so that we may gain a clear idea of its scope. This is especially necessary in the case of this particular book, since it is a companion to the *Seder,* a name derived from the fact that it follows a specific "order" of proceedings.

**252. Why is the second component of the Seder described as *urechatz* ("and wash"), when none of the other headings has that prefixed *vav* ("and")?**

It is probably intended to convey the idea of haste, as if to say, *Kaddesh urechatz,* "Make *Kiddush* and wash *quickly.*" The Seder leader is being reminded at the outset that there is an urgency to reach the stage where the children ask their Four Questions, to ensure that, through their participation, they will not fall asleep.

## HINNENI

**253. Why is it that, in some Haggadot, before each of the four cups, and even before the eating of the various ritual foods, there is included a kind of meditation, beginning, *Hinneni mukhan umezuman lekayyem* . . . ?**

Such meditations were introduced into the rituals of medieval Jewish mystics as a means of generating *kavvanah,* special religious fervor and concentration. For such mystics, each *mitzvah* was not merely a "religious act," but a veritable means of uniting this world to the heavenly spheres, as well as of uniting elements of the *Shekhinah*'s (Divine Presence) composition that have become dispersed as a result of the evil that is rampant in the world and requires redemption.

Such meditations are called *kavvanot* ("stimuli to religious concentration"), and are not exclusive to the Pesach Haggadah. They were composed for recitation before almost all the biblical rituals, such as the Blowing of the *Shofar,* the Shaking of the *Lulav,* the counting of the *Omer,* and so on.

## KIDDUSH

**254. What is the significance of the *Kiddush* ceremony?**

*Kiddush* means "sanctification," and its purpose is to declare the sanctity of the *Shabbat* or *Yom Tov* and to express our joy in having been chosen by God to be the recipients of a uniquely joyful religious heritage. The joy is expressed in the phrase, *Ki vanu vacharta ve-otanu kidashta,* "For us You have chosen, and us You have sanctified."

The Talmud sees the ceremony of *Kiddush* as reflected in the wording of the fourth Commandment, "Remember the Sabbath day to *declare* it holy" *(lekadsho).* The Rabbis (Talmud *Pesachim* 106a) understand this as an instruction to cause the sanctity of the Sabbath—and the other festival rest days—to be constantly remembered by a weekly affirmation of its sanctity in the joyful context of a toasting of the Sabbath over a goblet of wine.

On Seder night, *Kiddush* represents the first of the four cups of wine (see question 249).

**255. When *Yom Tov* coincides with *Shabbat*, we commence *Kiddush* by reciting the paragraph commencing, *Vayehi erev vayehi voker yom ha-shishiy* ("And it was evening and it was morning the sixth day"); *Vayechulu ha-shamayim veha-aretz* ("And the heaven and the earth were completed"). Why do we merge these two verses into one, when in the Torah, they are not only two distinct verses, but are separated into two chapters (Genesis 1:31, 2:1)?**

The objective of appending to *Vayechulu* that first verse, which technically has no reference to *Shabbat* since it refers to the completion of the sixth day *(yom ha-shishiy)*, was in order to be able to weave into the *Kiddush* the initial letters of the divine name: *Yom Hashishy Vayechulu Hashamayim*. However, because the Talmud (*Megillah* 22a) forbids the utilization of just the second half of a biblical verse, it was necessary to employ also the first few words— *Vayehi erev vayehi voker* —though not relevant to the theme of *Shabbat*. Indeed, for that reason one should recite the latter phrase in an undertone, and one should pause between the phrase *Yom ha-shishiy* and *Vayechulu,* since we may not create a single verse out of two separate biblical verses.

**256. In the following paragraph, the main section of the *Yom Tov Kiddush*, we say, *Asher bachar banu mikkol am,* "Who has chosen us from all other peoples and sanctified us with His commandments." Does not this smack of a racially superior sentiment?**

It was certainly never intended to suggest that Jews were naturally superior to any other people. It was, however, an affirmation of our sense of privilege at having been entrusted with a heritage that did truly offer the opportunity for living at a higher and purer level than was possible elsewhere, given the idolatrous and immoral nature of the ancient world.

We have to put prayers into their historical context and appreciate the conditions that existed at the time such prayers and sentiments were first introduced. If the Jews had closed their ranks to any pagans or gentiles, then such sentiments may, with justification, have been interpreted as self-glorification and racial superiority. However, Judaism offered a warm welcome to any who earnestly wished to share in her spiritual heritage (that is, until the Romans made conversion to Judaism a capital crime), so that no allegations of racial exclusivism are valid here.

There is absolutely no denying that God did "choose" Israel, to bestow upon her His Torah. But that "choice" was not for privilege, but for responsibility and for the challenge of being a "light unto the nations," so that all peoples might be won over to His service. That blessed state, in which all mankind will share, is prayed for in the *Aleinu* prayer, at the conclusion of each service, when we quote the verse: "May they all accept the yoke of Thy sovereignty, and may You reign over them soon for ever and ever."

There is much truth in the doggerel:

How odd of God
To choose the Jews;
But not so odd—
The Jews chose God!

The fact that Israel has passed down her heritage to daughter religions, and has thus helped to civilize mankind, gives her the right, on occasions, to express pride in that mission, as we do in the *Kiddush* ceremonies that inaugurate our Sabbaths and festival days.

### 257. Why, when *Yom Tov* falls on a *Shabbat*, do we add the words *be-ahavah* ("with love") and *beratzon* ("with favor") to the text of the *Kiddush*?

These two words allude to the fact that the gift of *Shabbat* was a demonstration of special divine love for Israel. *Yom Tov* alone does not possess that quality of totally unadulterated love, since the three major festivals have a dimension of toil or (historical) suffering attached to their origins.

Pesach recalls the Exodus, but that was preceded by over two centuries of oppression. Shavuot recalls the bringing of the firstfruits to the Temple and the offering of the first-ripening sheaves from the wheat harvest. But that thanksgiving is but a one-day interlude in a period of feverish, round-the-clock, back-breaking effort in the fields, with still many more weeks to go until the entire crops are harvested. The same is true for Sukkot, festival of the ingathering of all the late-ripening fruits. It also recalls the booths in which the Israelites lived during their arduous forty years of wandering in the desert, a period replete with problems, tensions, and rebellions.

Only the Sabbath may be said to be garlanded exclusively with love and favor. It was created after God's creative efforts, not man's, and it comes each week, whether that week has been one of toil or relaxation, effort or pleasure.

Another, ingenious explanation has been offered by Rabbi Barukh Ha-Levi Epstein in his celebrated commentary, *Torah Temimah* (see on Exodus 25, n.36). When the Israelites encamped at Marah (see Exodus 15:23–27), the Torah states, "There he established for them a statute and an ordinance" (v. 25). The Talmud (*Sanhedrin* 56b) relates that to the institution of *Shabbat*, which God gave to Israel at that time, even before it was promulgated at Mount Sinai and enshrined in the Fourth Commandment.

Now there is a famous tradition that, at Sinai, God actually gave Israel no option but to accept the Torah. In a rabbinic flight of fancy, God is depicted as having raised Mount Sinai menacingly over the heads of the Israelites, saying, "If you accept the Torah, well and good; but if you do not, then here will be your burial ground!" (Talmud *Shabbat* 88a; *Avodah Zorah* 2b).

So, in the case of all the other Torah laws, we must accept the element of compulsion. However, in the case of *Shabbat*, that was not so, since that "statute and ordinance" was given before the Sinai encounter, at a time when the lawgiver was still in a much more indulgent relationship with Israel. We allude to this in the *Kiddush*, by characterizing the bestowal of *Shabbat* as an act of *ahavah veratzon,* "love and favor."

**258. Are we meant to stand for *Kiddush*?**

The halakhic authorities are divided on this point. The Talmud (*Pesachim* 101a) states that *Kiddush* is inextricable from the meal, serving to sanctify it and mark it out as a special *Shabbat* meal. As such, it is obviously more appropriate, therefore, to recite it while seated at the table. The first section *(Vayechulu)* was regarded by some authorities as an exception, however, since it constitutes an act of "testimony" to God's having created the world in six days and rested on the seventh. As regards testimony, the Torah already required that it be delivered in a standing position (Deuteronomy 19:17).

Rabbi Moses Isserles, the Ashkenazi glossator to the *Shulchan Arukh,* (see on *Orach Chayyim* 271:10) states that, "One may stand for *Kiddush,* but it is better to sit; and it is the custom to sit, even during the recitation of *Vayechulu.* However, when reciting the first few words, one should raise oneself a little into a standing position in honor of the divine name represented as an acronym by the initial letters of the opening words." Many still prefer to remain standing for the entire *Kiddush,* and one should follow one's family custom.

## *HAVDALAH*

**259. We see that the *Havdalah* ceremony is tacked on to the end of *Kiddush* if *Yom Tov* occurs on a *Motzei Shabbat* (Saturday night). Why do we recite a blessing over fire?**

The Talmud (*Pesachim* 54a) has a tradition that God invested Adam with his higher intelligence and creative talent precisely on the first *Motzei Shabbat* of Creation. Adam's first act was to take two stones and strike them against each other, creating a spark, with which he made a fire. God delayed this revelation to Adam throughout the Sabbath day, foreshadowing the prohibition of creating fire on *Shabbat;* and hence we mark the departure of that holy day by lighting a candle and reciting the blessing *Barukh attah . . . Borei me-orey ha-eish,* "Blessed are You . . . who created the lights of the fire." Since on *Yom Tov* we cannot strike a match and light the special *Havdalah* candle, nor extinguish it, we simply raise our hands to the already-lit *Yom Tov* candles before reciting the blessing.

**260. Why do we bend our fingers over into the center of our palms in front of the light, and then release them, turning our hands over with our nails towards the light?**

It is because of two principles, one of which we have already encountered above, namely, that one must recite a blessing before performing the *mitzvah.* The other is that we may not recite a blessing over light until we have derived a benefit from it. Now, the definition of "deriving a benefit," is seeing the reflection of the light. And the shiny and reflective surface of the nails provides a ready opportunity for activating this "benefit."

Hence, we commence by burying our fingernails inside our palms, so that we can recite the blessing first, and then we turn our nails to the flame, so that the "benefit" of its reflection can justify the blessing we have recited, and emerge only after its recitation.

### 261. Why do we recite a blessing over spices?

There is a mystical belief that, on *Shabbat*, we are endowed with a *neshamah yeteirah*, "an extra soul" (Talmud *Betzah* 16a), which gives us a special sense of tranquillity and spirituality on that day. The purpose of inhaling the spices is to restore our flagging spirit and relieve the withdrawal symptoms when that extra soul suddenly departs at the termination of the *Shabbat* (*Tosafot* on Talmud *Pesachim* 102b, D. H. Rav).

## SHEHECHEYANU

### 262. What is the purpose of the *Shehecheyanu* blessing?

The name given to this blessing in the Talmud is *Birkat Ha-Zeman*, "Blessing for the Season," which highlights its main purpose as a thanksgiving blessing for having being spared and enabled to celebrate another religious festivity of the religious calendar.

The three main festivals, Pesach, Shavuot, and Sukkot, are naturally joyous events that one looks forward to and would feel a natural wish to celebrate: hence the recitation of *Shehecheyanu* in the *Kiddush* and when lighting the festival candles. Because Rosh Hashanah and Yom Kippur stimulate more sober emotions, there was some discussion in the Talmud on whether *Shehecheyanu* should be recited. The prevailing view was that because they are also designated in the Torah as *Mikra-ey kodesh*, "holy convocations," the blessing should be extended also to them.

At the inauguration of *Yom Tov* on the seventh day of Pesach, however, we do not include *Shehecheyanu*, notwithstanding the fact that we do recite it on the eve of the eighth day of Sukkot *(Shemini Atzeret)*. The reason for this is that the seventh day of Pesach is not a separate festival, but merely the first of the two concluding days, whereas *Shemini Atzeret* is a totally independent festival which happens to follow on from the last day of Sukkot. Hence we inaugurate it with the *Shehecheyanu* blessing.

### 263. If *Shehecheyanu* is to mark the joy of holy celebrations, why is it not recited every *Shabbat* and on Rosh Chodesh?

It was perceived as a blessing recited to mark the *periodic arrival* of major festivals: hence the principle that it is not recited on holy days—such as *Shabbat*—that occur more frequently than every thirty days. Rosh Chodesh (new month) was consequently a gray area in this respect, and the view is imputed to the talmudic authority Rav (see *Encyclopedia Talmudit* 4:432, n.11) that one should recite it on that occasion. This was not the accepted view, however, as Rosh Chodesh was regarded as a minor festival, and is, for most people nowadays, an ordinary working day.

### 264. On what other occasions should *Shehecheyanu* be recited?

It should be recited over *mitzvot* that occur only periodically, such as *Sukkah, Lulav, Megillah,* and Chanukah lights; over *mitzvot* that devolve as a result of personal acquisitions, such as *tzitzit, tefillin,* and *mezuzah;* and on other *mitzvot* that do not recur calendrically and are infrequent, such as over a *Brit* (circumcision) and *Pidyon Ha-Ben* (Redemption of the Firstborn).

### 265. If *Shehecheyanu* is recited over *mitzot* that recur infrequently, why then do we not recite it over the search for the *chametz*?

There are several reasons for this: (i) It does not have a fixed date for the entire community of Israel to perform that *mitzvah,* since if someone is leaving their home, even a long while before Pesach, for a long trip, and intending to return just before the festival, they are obliged to search before they go away, in case they are delayed and do not arrive back in time to make the search. Similarly, people who are going away within thirty days of Pesach—even if they will be away for the duration of the festival—are obliged to make the search (without the blessing). (ii) The search is for the purpose of the proper celebration of the festival, and, since we must not duplicate blessings (containing the divine name) unnecessarily, we therefore regard the *Shehecheyanu* blessing recited over the festival at *Kiddush* as encompassing also the search for the *chametz*. (iii) We only recite *Shehecheyanu* over rituals that constitute, in themselves, the completion of the *mitzvah*. It is not the "search," however, but the "burning" of the *chametz,* that constitutes the completion. (iv) *Shehecheyanu* is an expression of the anticipation of the joy of positive religious celebration. It is not appropriate, therefore, to an activity that is merely to prevent one from infringing a prohibition. (v) One only recites it over something from which one gains benefit, whereas the search for *chametz* actually deprives one of the benefit of eating the *chametz* in his possession.

### 266. Why, then, do we not recite *Shehecheyanu* over the eating of *matzah* and *maror* and the drinking of the four cups, since they recur only once a year and they do provide benefit?

Because we have already fulfilled the duty in respect of those foods by the *Shehecheyanu* blessing we recite at the outset, in the *Kiddush*. That blessing covers all the *mitzvot* performed throughout the Seder.

### 267. Do those around the table interject with the response, *Barukh hu uvarukh shemo,* when the *kiddush* is being recited for them by the Seder leader?

No they do not, since that response is considered an independent praise, which, in this context, halakhically constitutes an interruption. The hearers are being wholly represented, in the duty of reciting *Kiddush*, by the Seder leader, and just as he does not include that response, neither must they. They do, however, respond with *Amen* ("affirmed!") at the conclusion, as that single word relates directly to the formula being recited.

### 268. How does one drink the first cup of *Kiddush* wine?

Seated and leaning on one's left side as a sign of freedom. As observed previously, one should endeavor to drink the greater part of one's goblet.

### 269. Why do we choose to lean specifically on the left side?

Believe it or not, we do so simply for health reasons. It was believed that in that position there was less chance of the wine (or food) being taken into the windpipe instead of the gullet and causing one to choke!

## *URECHATZ*

### 270. Why is it necessary for the Seder leader to wash his hands *(Urechatz)* at this stage?

In truth, this washing is a pious flourish that we observe on Seder night, though technically it has no special relevance to the Seder or to Pesach. The ancient halakhah governing the transmission of impurity *(tum'ah)* states that one should wash one's hands when handling anything that is moistened with certain commonly used liquids—such as the (salt)water that we dip the *karpas* into—since impurity is transmitted readily through the mediation of liquids. To forestall that we ensure that our hands are clean for the dipping.

Because that particular law of *tum'ah* is no longer applicable, the *Taz* (see on *Shulchan Arukh, Orach Chayyim* 473:6) asks ironically, *mah nishtanah halayla hazeh*—why we are so scrupulous only on Seder night that that special precaution should be observed?

One view is that it is introduced on Seder night simply so that the children's attention will be attracted by another strange ritual, and they will be tempted to ask about it, thereby fulfilling the Torah's challenge, "When your children will ask you, saying, What is all this service?" (Exodus 13:14).

### 271. Why is there such a halakhically unprecedented situation of only the Seder leader washing his hands when everyone else present is also handling the moist foodstuff, and why is no blessing recited over this washing?

It is truly anomalous. Indeed, Amram Gaon and the *Machzor Vitri*, representing the traditions of Babylon and Franco-Germany, respectively, require all present to wash their hands at this point. According to some authorities (see Goldschmidt, *The Passover Haggadah*, pp. 7, 19) it was in the seventeenth century, or, according to others, in the fifteenth century, that our custom developed, in Germany, of restricting the washing to the Seder leader.

It should be said that an impressive array of authorities, such as the Rif, Rambam, Tur, *Machzor Vitri,* and the Vilna Gaon, do require the recitation of the blessing. However, we follow the view that, since it is a doubtful matter, we do not make a potentially unnecessary blessing *(safek berakhah)*. The doubt arises from the fact that there is no specific *mitzvah* involved here, since, as we have explained, the washing is a mere precautionary measure to avoid the transmission of impurity when handling liquids. In our day we are no longer subject to such regulations, and, in any case, we do not recite blessings over mere precautionary measures.

### 272. How is this washing to be executed?

It is done in precisely the same way as for *Netilat yadayim,* the washing before a meal. He takes a cup of clean, cold water in his left hand and pours a sufficient amount to cover the hand over his right hand. He then transfers the cup to the right hand, and pours an equal amount of water over his left hand. Some repeat this twice or three times. Because of the principle, *teikhef lintilah berakhah,* "The blessing must follow immediately after the washing," with no interruption to divert one's attention, he should not speak until he has distributed the *karpas,* made the blessing, and eaten the *karpas.* (It is for the same reason that we must not speak after washing for a meal until we have made the blessing over the bread and eaten a little.

## *KARPAS*

### 273. What vegetables may be used for *karpas,* and what is its symbolic significance?

See questions 195–196.

### 274. How much *karpas* are we meant to eat?

Less than a *kezayit* (olive size). For the present-day equivalent, see question 199.

### 275. Why are we not permitted to eat as much as a *kezayit*?

The stated reason is so that no halakhic moot point arises as to whether or not we are obligated to recite (after a basic measure of vegetable) the concluding *Borei nefashot* blessing.

### 276. But why should any concluding blessing be necessary at this stage, since we are going to eat vegetables later during the meal, and the Grace after Meals surely serves as the concluding blessing for everything we have eaten?

That is, indeed, the view of Rosh and Rashbam. However, there is another view that the recitation of the Haggadah and the Hallel, two separate *mitzvot,* constitute an interruption between the *karpas,* eaten at this early stage, and the meal taken later, thereby necessitating the concluding blessing.

### 277. Do we lean while eating the *karpas*?

This is the subject of dispute between halakhic authorities. The majority opinion seems to be that we do not lean, since the *karpas* is a symbol of slavery, rather than freedom. In support of that view, they point to the popular interpretation of the word *karpas,* whose letters, in reverse, read *s(amekh)-Perakh.* *Samekh* has the numerical value of sixty, which stands for the 600,000 Israelites, and *perakh* means "to suffer rigor" (see Exodus 1:13).

Rabbi David Abudraham expressed the opposite view, asserting that we should, in fact, lean since the *karpas* is eaten primarily so that the children should ask questions. It has, therefore, a contemporary significance and purpose, and should not be construed as a symbol of slavery. Indeed, we and our children eat it in a spirit of freedom and free enquiry. The *Kitzur Shulchan Arukh* decides according to this view.

### 278. Is there any special intention that we should have when we recite the blessing over the *karpas*?

Yes. The blessing we make *(Borey periy ha-adamah)* is also intended to cover the *maror* that we eat later. As a result, we are enabled to omit that customary blessing (we do not recite unnecessary blessings) and recite merely the *al akhilat maror* blessing, to bring its role as a specific ritual food (rather than an ordinary vegetable) into sharper focus.

## *AFIKOMAN*

### 279. What is the meaning of the next section of the Seder: *Yachatz*?

*Yachatz* is derived from the Hebrew root *chatzah,* "to divide into two": hence, the noun *chetzi,* "one half." It refers to the division of the middle *matzah* into two unequal pieces by the Seder-leader. He hides away in a safe place the larger piece, in order that it should not be eaten by mistake, but will be available, and designated, for the *Afikoman.* Hence, this act is referred to as "hiding the *Afikoman.*"

### 280. Are there any specific regulations regarding what to do with the larger piece, designated for the *Afikoman*?

The *Shulchan Arukh* states that, "he [the Seder-leader] hands it to one of those present, who places it under the table cloth by his place" (*Orach Chayyim* 473:6). *Magen Avraham* adds that "some have the custom to place the *Afikoman* on their shoulders, symbolic of the Exodus from Egypt (when, according to Exodus 12:34, they carried their baking equipment on their shoulders).

### 281. But why does the *Shulchan Arukh* recommend that it be placed under a tablecloth, rather than remaining visible on the table, together with all the other symbolic foods?

It is to recall the way the Israelites carried their kneading troughs and the *matzot* they had baked, for we are told that "they were *bound up* in their clothes upon their shoulders" (Exodus 12:34). Another custom, based upon this verse, is to wrap the *Afikoman* in a table napkin.

**282. So from where did the custom develop of hiding the *Afikoman* away so that the children might look for it and demand a prize for returning it?**

What a question! Since when have Jewish children ever been slow to seize entrepreneurial opportunities? That having been said, some relate this custom to an obscure statement in the Talmud: *Chotfin matzah beleiley pesachim bishvil tinokot shelo yishnu*—"We make haste to get to the *matzah* [that is, to the meal] on Passover evenings for the sake of the children, that they should not fall asleep" (*Pesachim* 109a).

It is the opening word, *chotfin,* that creates the problem; for this verb, *chataf,* means not only "to make haste," but also, "to snatch." Hence, based on that interpretation of *chotfin matzah,* we arrive at an instruction to "snatch the *matzah*" on this night, as a diversion, "for the sake of the children, so that they should not fall asleep."

**283. But that source does not actually make it clear who does the snatching?**

Precisely: and that is why we described it above as "an obscure statement." Maimonides states, "We snatch this *matzah,* each person from the hand of the next" (*Mishneh Torah, Hilkhot Chametz Umatzah* 7:3). This strange adult behavior would be certain to elicit wonderment and questioning on the part of the youngsters, and thus keep them from falling asleep.

It is probably from that interpretation and practice that the custom arose to leave it to the children to seize the *Afikoman,* hide it, and refuse to return it until promised an adequate compensation.

**284. But why do some have a variant tradition, whereby the Seder leader hides it and the children go out to search for it?**

It might well have arisen out of an uneasy feeling that children should not be encouraged to seize things, even in fun, without permission. Indeed the commentary of the *Rashbam,* on the phrase *Chotfin matzah,* states: *Gozlin*—"They steal the *matzah.*" So, because there was clearly some unease about promoting such behavior, the practice was toned down, so that it was the Seder-leader who hides it away and invites the children to go looking for it.

**285. But would anyone really suggest that there is any issue of theft involved in the "stealing" of the *matzah* by children as an act of fun?**

Believe it or not, it is suggested by such authorities as Joseph Karo (*Shulchan Arukh, Choshen Mishpat* 348:1) and Maimonides. The latter states, "It is forbidden to steal even the most insignificant item by Torah law. It is also forbidden to steal *by way of jest,* or with the intention of replacing it or paying for it. All this is prohibited so that one should not become accustomed to taking other people's possessions" (Rambam, *Hilkhot Geneivah* 1:2).

It was probably for this reason that the original practice of "snatching" was modified to a more acceptable ritual whereby the Seder-leader hides the *matzah* and actually challenges the children to see if they can find it.

## *MAGGID*

**286. Since blessings are generally prescribed over rabbinic ordinances (see Talmud *Shabbat* 23a), such as Sabbath and Chanukah lights, the reading of the Megillot, and so on, why did they not prescribe a special blessing over the *mitzvah* of reading the Haggadah, which is biblically mandated?**

Indeed, a blessing such as *Barukh . . . asher kidshanu bemitzvotav vetzivanu lesapper biyetziat mitzrayim* ("Blessed are You . . . Who has commanded us concerning the relating of the Exodus") would have been most appropriate over the Haggadah. A number of reasons may be suggested why such a blessing was not prescribed. First, because blessings are recited only over *mitzvot* that are performed uninterruptedly and at once, whereas the relating of the Haggadah is spread over the entire evening and is interrupted by the meal and other activities and diversions that are not always directly related to the subject of the Haggadah.

The Rashba (Rabbi Solomon ben Adret, Spanish talmudic commentator and halakhist, 1235–1310) suggested that the reason is that a blessing is only recited over *mitzvot* that one fulfills, and is capable of fulfilling, entirely for oneself, not over one that is dependent in some measure upon someone else, as is the "discussion" at the Seder about the Exodus from Egypt. For that same reason, he states, there is no blessing made over the *mitzvah* of giving charity, since one's ability to donate is dependent upon there being a recipient.

This explanation is contested by Rabbi ShemTov Gaguine (see *Keter Shem Tov,* London: author, 1948, pp. 110–111), who points out that when the priests bless the congregation, they recite a blessing, even though they require a recipient to receive their blessing. (Indeed, they require a minyan of recipients in order to be able to bless the people!).

Rashba, perhaps conscious of the weakness of his first answer, suggests an alternative reason, namely, that reading the Haggadah and relating about the Exodus is a *mitzvah she-ein la kitzvah,* an ill-defined *mitzvah,* over which one does not recite a blessing. It is ill-defined because there is no objective definition of *sippur,* the obligation to relate. Does one fulfill it by merely alluding to it? Is it necessary to discuss with others around the table? How long and how deep has such a discussion to be? Is it necessary to recite the entire Haggadah or do Rabban Gamliel's three paragraphs suffice—as the phraseology there implies? It is all too uncertain for a blessing to be recited, says Rashba.

Isaac Abarbanel offers another reason, namely that, with the recitation of *Kiddush* at the very outset of the Seder, we have already embarked upon the fulfillment of the *mitzvah* of relating the Exodus. This is underscored by the reference in *Kiddush* to *Zekher liytzi'at mitzrayim* ("in commemoration of the Exodus from Egypt"). Thus, at that time we are effectively reciting a blessing (namely, *Kiddush*) over the Haggadah as well as over the festival. For that reason, there is no necessity to recite any further blessing over the Haggadah.

### 287. We now come to Maggid, the "relating" of the story of the Exodus. Is this *mitzvah* only incumbent upon men, or are women also obliged to recite it?

Women are also obliged to recite the Haggadah. As in the case of men, if they are unable to read it for themselves they should listen intently to the Seder leader, and they fulfill thereby their *mitzvah*. This is based upon the principle, *shome'a ke'oneh,* "listening [to a blessing] is tantamount to recitation." If they do not understand the Hebrew, the Seder leader must translate, or give a précis, of what is being said.

There is some difference regarding whether women are included in this *mitzvah* according to biblical law or only by rabbinic ordinance. Because of the doubt, some authorities do not countenance women reading on behalf of men (whose obligation is definitely under biblical law).

## HA LACHMA

### 288. What is the significance of the *Ha lachma anya* composition?

It seems to be a composite statement. There are two traditions regarding what to do when reciting it: one rubric has it that we lift up the Seder plate; another that we lift up the broken piece of *matzah* that remains after the hiding of the *Afikoman*. The latter seems a more logical rubric, for, having temporarily disposed of the *Afikoman,* we are left holding a pathetically small piece of *matzah*. The significance of this piece now has to be explained to the gathering; and the *Ha lachma anya* ("This is symbolic of the bread of affliction that our fathers ate in Egypt") provides the clearest of explanations.

### 289. But surely the *matzah* symbolizes the hasty bread that they baked when they came out of Egypt, the bread of freedom, and not the bread of affliction that they ate in Egypt!

Absolutely right: however, *matzah* also figured prominently during their period of oppression; for the Egyptian taskmasters doled out to them hard and minute pieces of *matzah* as their daily fare while they were toiling for Pharaoh (R. Elijah ben Solomon Zalman, *Commentary on the Haggadah* [Horodra: Menachem Mendel of Shklor, 1805], p. 16). Hence, *matzah* symbolizes two, mutually contrasting, states: freedom and slavery. Because we are now left holding a small, broken piece of *matzah,* this brings into sharper focus its slavery dimension, as expressed in the first sentence of the *Ha lachma* composition.

### 290. What are the other components of this "composite" passage?

The following sentence invites all who are hungry to join the family and participate. The third component is a statement that, although this year we are in exile, next year we will be restored to our land; and, although this year we remain deprived of our national sovereignty ("now we are slaves"), next year we will have our freedom restored.

### 291. Why is the *Ha lachma* written in Aramaic?

The reason is that this invitation to visitors to join the family at table dates back to a very early period in Palestine (second century B.C.E.) when pure Hebrew had been replaced by Aramaic as the lingua franca of the masses. It was only the rabbinic scholars who retained Hebrew, and even they spoke a mixture of Hebrew and Aramaic, which was later perpetuated in the writings of the Talmud.

Such an invitation, to anyone who required hospitality, inevitably had to be couched, therefore, in the language of the populace.

### 292. According to the rubrics in most Haggadot, we are told that, while reciting the words *Ha lachma anya*, we should remove the cover on the *matzot* and lift up the Seder plate. We can understand why we remove the cover of the *matzah*, since we are directly referring to it in this composition. Why, though, should we have to lift up the Seder plate?

The rubric is based upon an instruction found in one of our earliest Codes of law, the *Tur* of Jacob ben Asher (1270–1340). Joseph Karo wrote a monumental commentary on that work, entitled *Bet Yosef*. It was on that commentary that his early fame rested. His subsequent work, the *Shulchan Arukh*, was a mere digest of the law; and yet, ironically, it is with the latter work that his name is immortalized.

In his *Bet Yosef* (*Tur, Orach Chayyim,* 473), Karo explains the rubric in question by relating it to an early tradition, referred to in the Talmud (*Pesachim* 115b), of removing the entire table at this point, just before the *Ha lachma anya*. In those days they reclined at Seder, and their meals were brought in on small tables, akin to our coffee tables. The Seder plate was similarly placed upon such a table, together with the three *matzot*. The original, talmudic practice was to remove the entire table from the room just before reciting *Ha lachma anya*—again in order that the children should query such strange behavior of removing the *matzah* and other foods before one has even commenced one's meal. This is another example of the many gimmicks that were introduced in ancient times to ensure that the children—the primary actors in the relating of the Exodus story on this night—stayed awake.

Karo's note continues, "Nowadays, because our tables are so large, and it would be such an effort to remove them, we simply remove the Seder plate, upon which are the *matzot,* to the end of the table, as if to indicate that we have no wish to eat further." Karo proceeds to criticize those who merely lift up the plate, on the grounds that "that will not strike the child as unusual, and stimulate him to ask" (ibid.).

So we see in this rubric how changing dining habits have necessitated the abandonment of a dramatic ritual, and how even the adjusted practice has undergone a further dilution, to the extent that we merely allude to the original practice by a token lifting up of the Seder plate and uncovering of the *matzot*. We may conjecture that the abandonment of the practice, referred to by Karo, of removing "the Seder plate, upon which are the *matzot,* to the end of the table," was simply because of lack of space, especially in the post-Karo era of printing, when extra space had to be found for the Haggadah that everyone was now able to be provided with.

### 293. So how early is this composition?

Its earliest strand, the phrase *kol ditzrikh yeisey veyifsach,* "Let all who are in need [of an invitation] come and join us in the eating of the Paschal lamb," certainly predates the destruction of the Temple (after which the eating of the lamb ceased), and may be dated around the turn of the Common Era. However, the ending ("Now we are here, next year may we be in Israel; now we are slaves") is clearly set in the period of exile, after the loss of Jewish independence (70 C.E.).

### 294. Why is there some unnecessary repetition: *Kol dikhfin yeisey veyeikhol,* "Let all who are hungry come and eat," immediately followed by *Kol ditzrikh yeisey veyifsach,* "Let all who require it come and join in the Passover meal"?

This, indeed, underlines our statement that this is a composite passage. The earliest strand, as we have just explained, is certainly the invitation to "join in the Passover meal." Because of the law that *Ha-pesach eino ne-ekhal ela limnuyav,* "The Paschal lamb may only be eaten by those already pre-invited and counted-in" (Mishnah *Zevachim* 5:8), the invitation had to have been issued quite some time before the Seder. In Temple times, one could not, therefore, invite guests at the last minute. Hence, to be sure that no one visiting Jerusalem on their own was left without a family to join for the important *mitzvah* of eating the Paschal lamb, they would very likely walk around the Temple precincts, or send their children, proclaiming aloud the simple invitation, *Kol ditzrikh yeisey veyifsach,* "Let all who require it come and join in the Passover meal."

Jewish practices are rarely allowed to die without trace, especially those that were such an intrinsic part of the rich Temple festival celebration. Thus, after the destruction, although there was no longer a Paschal lamb ritual to which to invite visitors, yet the custom of issuing a public invitation to visitors in one's village or town to join the family at the Pesach table remained, and a revised formula, *Kol dikhfin yeisey veyeikhol,* "Let all who are hungry, come and eat"—omitting any reference to the Paschal lamb—was introduced.

Hence, we see that it is not unnecessary repetition. It is simply that our passage has preserved for us two alternative formulae, side by side: one used before, and the other after, the destruction of the Temple.

### 295. How is it that there is a variation between Haggadot in the opening word of *Ha lachma anya,* some reading *Ha;* others, *Keha*?

*Ha (lachma anya)* means, "This *is* the bread of affliction that our forefathers ate"; *Keha* means, "This is *similar to* the bread. . . ." The difference is not too significant, but merely reflects alternate versions that have survived and have been arbitrarily used according to the preference, or tradition, of different scribes and the printers who based their first editions upon those manuscripts.

The text of *The Ashkenazi Haggadah* has *Keha* (see facsimile edition, published by Thames and Hudson, London, 1985, folio 6a), whereas the commentary of Rabbi Eleazar ben Yehudah of Worms (d. 1230), accompanying the text, has, rather inconsistently, *Ha* as its introductory word. However, it provides us with an explanation of why some preferred the formula *Keha*. It is only on account of its size that it is designated, "bread of affliction," a poor man's fare. As regards its ingredients, however, it certainly does not merit such a disparaging description, since our present-day *matzot* are made of the finest flour. Thus, it is preferable to be honest, and state that "This is [only] like *[keha]* the bread of affliction"—in a restricted sense.

### 296. Are there any other versions of this formula?

From our sources it seems that some authorities were troubled by the point we have just raised, and they accordingly experimented with other syntactical ways of expressing the point that "this is like the bread of affliction." Thus, the *Magen Avraham* (Comment on *Orach Chayyim* 473:6 (24)) states, "One should not confuse the formula by saying *Keha lachma* [literally, 'Like this bread of affliction'], or *Ha kelachma* (literally, 'This is like bread of affliction')."

S. Ganzfried's *Kitzur Shulchan Arukh* (119:3) states, "Those who say *Keha lachma,* should not add the word *diy.*" He clearly believes that one may only translate *Keha lachma* as, "Like this bread of affliction." Hence, he asserts, one cannot continue with the relative pronoun, "which [our forefathers ate]," since this would leave the phrase without a proper continuation. On the other hand, the reading, *Keha lachma anya akhalu avhatana,* "Like this bread of affliction our forefathers ate," makes excellent sense.

A glance at *The Ashkenazi Haggadah,* however, proves Ganzfried to be overpedantic here. Its text clearly has *Keha lachma anya de-akhalu avhatana,* and there is really no reason to quibble with its syntactical sense of, "It is like this bread of affliction that our forefathers ate in Egypt"! Indeed, the same reading (including the word *diy*) occurs in another recently produced facsimile edition of an eighteenth-century Haggadah (see *Four Haggadot,* Heb. Ms. 8 5573, produced by W. Turnowsky Ltd., Tel Aviv, (n.d.). The *Maharal* of Prague states categorically, however (*Haggadah Shel Pesach LeMaharal,* London: L. Honig and Sons, 1960, p. 52) that the proper reading is *Ha lachma anya.* His proof is rebutted by *Magen Avraham,* however, who allows for any of the variations we have referred to (Comment on *Orach Chayyim* 473:6 [24]).

### 297. But what is the connection between the formulae of invitation to guests and the rest of the passage, which expresses the hope that our redemption will soon come?

The Vilna Gaon suggests that it is to put at ease the poor guests who have to accept hospitality at this time. Accompanying the invitation is an assurance that "we are all in the same boat." We are all slaves, exiles in a foreign land, dependent upon the mercy of the host country, and upon our faith in God the Redeemer. Implicit in this invitation, therefore, is a message to the guest that he should not think that his hosts are any more secure and fortunate than he. He should know that he will be joining equals, partners in distress, and should not, therefore, be reticent or embarrassed to accept the hospitality offered.

**298. It has been mentioned above that this composition is in Aramaic. So that the difference between that dialect and Hebrew will become clear, can we please have a Hebrew rendering of it?**

Glad to oblige! Indeed, we'll make it even clearer by placing them in parallel columns:

| Aramaic | Hebrew |
| --- | --- |
| Ha lachma anya diy akhalu | Zeh lechem ha-oni asher okhlu |
| Avhatana be-ara demitzrayim. | Avoteinu b'eretz mitzrayim. |
| Kol dikhfin yeisey veyeikhol, | Kol ha-r'eivim yavo-u veyokhlu, |
| Kol ditzrikh yeisey veyifsach. | Kol ha-nitzrachim yavo-u le'khol et ha-Pesach. |
| Hashata hakha; leshanah haba'ah | Hashanah poh; leshanah haba'ah |
| Be'ara deyisrael. Hashata | Be'eretz yisrael. Hashanah |
| Avdey; leshanah haba'ah | Avadim; leshanah haba'ah |
| Bnei chorin. | Anashim chofshi'im. |

## MAH NISHTANAH

**299. We now come to the *Mah Nishtanah*, the "Four Questions." Presumably, the fact that we give this to the youngest child to recite means that it is a less important part of the Haggadah?**

Quite the contrary: This is, in fact, such an important part of the Haggadah that the *Shulchan Arukh* (*Orach Chayyim* 473:7) states that even if an exclusive group of distinguished Sages are sitting together, they must still articulate these Four Questions—which provide a kind of outline agenda for what follows—and provide the answer through the recitation of *Avadim Hayyinu*. And even if one such Sage is sitting alone at Seder, he must still ask these questions aloud and provide the answers.

**300. But if they are so important, why give them to the child, the least important person present, to recite?**

First, this is done in order to reconstruct the biblical scenario, whereby in three separate passages (Exodus 12:26, 13:14–15; Deuteronomy 6:20–23) the Torah speaks of children, at some time in the future, asking their parents about the significance of these rituals. And, secondly, this is done for the simple reason that, because we want everyone present to listen to the Four Questions, we put them into the mouth of the youngest child, so that everyone will listen in rapt and admiring attention, hanging upon his or her every word.

### 301. What happens if a bright child asks his own questions about the Seder, making the recitation of *Mah Nishtanah* rather unnecessary? Is its recitation still obligatory?

The original purpose was to stimulate the child to ask spontaneous questions of his own, enabling the father to move smoothly to a telling of the Exodus story. The Mishnah (*Pesachim* 10:4) actually states, "But if the child has no spirit of enquiry, then his father should teach him, and lead him on, by saying, *Mah nishtanah halayla hazeh*—'Look how different this night is,' etc."

We see from here that the *Mah Nishtanah* is intended merely as a stimulus for those who do not ask their own questions. Indeed, there is a story in the Talmud of the young Abbaye, who asked his foster father (and uncle), Rabbah bar Nachmani, a question at the beginning of the Seder, to which the latter replied, "You have just relieved us of the necessity to recite *Mah Nishtanah!*" (*Pesachim* 115b).

### 302. But that means that *Mah Nishtanah* was not composed for the child at all, but rather for the father, as a means of pointing out the unique aspects of the Seder to his son?

We can't argue with that! What we have come to assume are the "kid's questions," were actually, originally, dad's! In fact, none of the great earlier authorities—neither the Geonim of Babylon, Maimonides, nor Rashi—know of any custom for the child to recite the *Mah Nishtanah!* It seems to have begun in Ashkenazi circles (Goldschmidt, *The Passover Haggadah,* p. 11). Moses Isserles (sixteenth century) is not aware of such a custom, so we assume that it came into being towards the end of the seventeenth century.

### 303. So, if they are not meant as "questions," but as parental stimuli, why are they couched as questions?

We cannot be so sure that they are couched as questions, since the Hebrew phrase, *Mah nishtanah,* can also mean, "How different is [this night . . .]." The subsequent "questions" would then simply be illustrative statements of the ways in which this night is so different.

But even if we accept the usual translation of *Mah Nishtanah* as a question, there is no difficulty here. For it is the usual rabbinic method to convey knowledge in question and answer form. Just like the book you are now reading: the respondent is also the one who creates the questions, to control the direction he wishes his work to take.

### 304. Why do we pour the second cup of wine before *Mah Nishtanah* if we do not intend to drink it for quite some time?

Once again, simply so that the child will keep asking questions about the "strange goings-on" around the table on this night. He will have observed that it is the custom (or, at least, it was so in talmudic times) for adults to sip one glass of wine, as an aperitif, before the meal. He will never have seen *two* glasses downed, however, and is likely to ask about the reason for this.

### 305. Is our version of the *Mah Nishtanah* the original one?

No: our version is the edited version, adapted for post-Temple circumstances. The original version is found in the Mishnah (*Pesachim* 10:4). The first two questions — about *matzah* and *maror* — are the same. The third is different. It reads: "On all other nights we may eat meat that is roasted, boiled or cooked, but on this night, we may eat only roasted." And the fourth question is the same as our third question: "On all other nights we do not dip even once. On this night, we dip twice."

Thus, there was originally no question on the subject of leaning (our fourth question); its place being taken (in a different position) by one about the roasted meat of the Paschal lamb. After the destruction of the Temple, and the prohibition of the roasted meat of the Pashal lamb, that question was replaced by the one about leaning. Since leaning is hardly in the category of the other biblically prescribed rituals, it did not attain the vacant position of third question, but was relegated to become the subject of the final question.

### 306. But surely, Judah the Prince, compiler of the Mishnah around 200 C.E., was writing long after the destruction of the Temple (70 C.E.). Why, then, did he leave in an anachronistic reference to eating roast meat which was, indeed, prohibited in his day?

This, indeed, is such a difficult problem that one scholar, Gedaliah Alon, has suggested that the Mishnah must be taken at face value, as reflecting the practice of its day. In other words, we must infer that, notwithstanding our present-day halakhic attitude to eating roasted meat, they actually prescribed its consumption, during the centuries following the destruction of the Temple, as a reminder of the Paschal lamb. Indeed, the Mishnah (*Pesachim* 4:4) states plainly that, "in places where it is the custom to eat roast meat on Passover eve, one may do so; in places where it is not the custom, one may not." Thus, the third question found in the Mishnah, about eating "only roast meat" may well reflect the custom of Judah Ha-Nasi's period in Palestine. We cannot be sure when the custom of avoiding roast meat became universal, but it was probably not until Geonic times (ninth–tenth centuries).

### 307. What is our present-day custom regarding eating roasted meat?

We do not allow the eating of roast meat at the Seder. This applies not only to roast lamb, but also to other meat, including chicken. Grilled fish is permitted, however, as fish is outside the criterion here of species that are subject to the laws of *shechitah* (the religious method of slaughtering).

### 308. Why, "on this night," do we "dip twice"?

Abarbanel suggests that it corresponds to the "immersion," into waters of purification, of the two main categories of people who may be initiated into the Paschal lamb meal of fellowship, according to the Torah law. They are the homeborn *(yelidei bayit)* and those purchased as servants *(miknat kesef)*, both of whom had to be circumcised (see Genesis 17:12), and both of whom had to undergo an initiation rite of immersion before the Exodus.

The difficulty with this explanation is that the Torah actually refers to a third category who may join the Paschal lamb gathering, and who would also require circumcision and immersion, namely the *gerim*, "converts" (Exodus 12:48). Perhaps it is for this reason that Abarbanel offers an alternative suggestion for the two dippings: that it corresponds to the two places where the blood of the lamb had to be daubed: once on the doorposts and once on the lintels (Exodus 12:7).

## *AVADIM HAYYINU*

### 309. What is the status of the *Avadim Hayyinu* within the Haggadah?

It is actually the true commencement of the Haggadah. We have already seen that the *Ha lachma* is merely a preliminary invitation, and *Mah Nishtanah* is a stimulus for the son to start asking questions.

The Mishnah (*Pesachim* 10:4) states, *Matchil bignut umesayeim beshevach*, "We begin the story of the Haggadah on a deprecatory note, and end with praise." We begin by tracing our national origins to a tribe of slaves, and we end by praising the God who raised us up, nationally and spiritually, to be His beacon of moral light to an uncivilized world.

We could so easily have begun this recounting of our national origins by referring to Abraham, whom God "blessed with all things" (Genesis 24:1), and who was hailed as "a prince of God in our midst" (Genesis 23:6) by Ephron, the Hittite ruler. We could, rightly, have traced our aristocratic geneology to Shem, the firstborn of Noah's three sons, and therefore senior in rank of the primogenitors of the three main civilizations of the ancient world—Hamitic, Semitic, and Indo-European.

But, instead, we are instructed to "commence the Haggadah on a self-deprecatory note." To paraphrase a famous maxim: those who forget their lowly origins are doomed to return to them! The Jew is cautioned never to make that mistake. The mishnaic Sages of the 1st century, who required us to refer to our slave origins at the outset of the Haggadah, could never have known that our subsequent history would be punctuated by nearly two thousand years of enslavement. They certainly put their finger on the most appropriate theme for the introduction to the story of our people.

### 310. In what way is the *Avadim hayyinu* an "answer" to the Four Questions?

It is not an "answer," in the sense of addressing the specifics referred to in the Four Questions. We have already stated that they were not originally intended as "questions," but rather as stimuli, to enable the father/Seder leader to gain the child's attention for a retelling of the story of the Exodus. So it does not matter if the specifics are not fully addressed. Nevertheless, the child does eventually get answers to three of the (original) questions (as listed in the mishnaic version of the *Mah Nishtanah*). These are dealt with in the passage where Rabban Gamaliel expounds the significance of Pesach, *matzah,* and *maror.*

There are commentators, however, like the Vilna Gaon, who attempt to locate, within the *Avadim Hayyinu,* the answers to the specific questions raised: (1) "We were slaves"—explains why we eat only bitter herbs, because of the bitterness of servitude; (2) "to Pharaoh in Egypt"—a harsh king in a harsh land, explains why we recline at having broken loose from those double fetters; (3) "But the Lord our God brought us out"—explains why we eat only *matzah,* because of the rushed manner of our departure; (4) "with a strong hand and an outstretched arm"—a double expression of deliverance, which accounts for the two dippings.

### 311. Does it not descend to the obvious when it states that had God not brought us out then we and all our offspring would still have remained subservient to Pharaoh in Egypt?

Rabbi Z. H. Ferber (*Kerem Ha-tzvi,* London: Jonathan Winegarten, 1983, p. 16) states that there is no doubt being expressed here that our redemption from Egypt would not have happened when it did. The only question is whether God might not have considered putting into Pharaoh's heart the willingness to release Israel without having had to beat him into submission through the Ten Plagues.

The sense of the statement in the *Avadim Hayyinu* is that if God had not taken us out—against Pharaoh's will—but had made it appear as if Pharaoh was demonstrating his own mercy and generosity of spirit, "then we and all our offspring would forever be *indebted [meshubadim]* to Pharaoh in Egypt." According to this valid sense of *meshubadim,* the meaning is not that we would have remained "subservient"—which would indeed be resorting to the obvious—but that our people would forever have remained "indebted" to that tyrant and committed to singing his praises for having granted us our freedom.

### 312. The last sentence of the *Avadim Hayyinu* states that "Even if we were all *chakhamim* (Sages), all *nevonim* (men of understanding), all *zekeinim* (elders), all *yod'im et ha-Torah* (knowledgeable in the Law) . . ." What is the point of listing these four synonyms?

The four categories are not, in fact, totally synonymous. *Chakham* is the "scholar." The word is an abbreviation of *talmid chakham,* which can mean either "disciple of a sage" or "wise student (of the Torah). It denotes one who has studied Torah full time, to an advanced level. The *navon* is understood to refer to a qualitative level that is higher than that attained by the *chakham. Navon* is a noun derived from the verb *lehavin,* "to understand," and suggests a scholar who is not only knowledgeable but also creative in his ability to apply the law to changing circumstances. The third category, *zekeinim* (elders), denotes a scholar who occupies a communal position, either as head of a Yeshivah or judge of a Bet Din. The final category, *yod'im et ha-Torah,* is, therefore, the summit of religious scholarship, and refers to that very small group, of the most illustrious authorities of the age, who attain total mastery of the entire Torah.

### 313. But how can that last category be inferred from the description *yod'im et ha-Torah,* which surely means no more than "those who know the Torah"?

The Hebrew language is multifaceted, and some verbal roots have more than one nuance. Granted, the verb *yada'* – which lies at the basis of the word we are querying *(yod'im)* – generally means, simply, "to know," but in early Hebrew, that verb connoted much more than knowledge of facts and people. The verb is used in the Torah to describe people who possess unique skills. Hence, Esau is described as *yode'a tzayid,* "a skilled hunter" (Genesis 25:27); and when King Hiram of Tyre undertook maritime expeditions, together with King Solomon, he is said to have sent along *yod'ei ha-yam,* "expert navigators" (1 Kings 9:27). Professional mourners are referred to as *yod'ei nehi* (Amos 5:16), and skilled musicians are referred to as *yod'ea nagein* (1 Samuel 16:18).

This nuance of the verb *yada'* explains why this verb is commonly used as a euphemism for marital intercourse, that most intimate experience of *knowledge* of another human being: *Veha-adam yada' et chavah ishto,* "And Adam *knew* Eve, his wife" (Genesis 4:1).

Now we may appreciate the sense in which *yod'im et ha-Torah,* "those who know the Torah," is being employed in this passage, to denote the climactic stage of attainment to total oneness with the Torah. We are being told here then, that even those on the ultimate four rungs of rabbinic scholarship, who have the traditions of the Exodus all in their heads, yet, on Seder night, they still have to articulate those traditions, and share them fully in the context of a dialogue with all those around their table.

### 314. Is not the final statement ("And all who speak at length about the Exodus are to be praised") at variance with the statement that precedes it ("It is a *mitzvah* [obligation] upon us to relate the Exodus from Egypt")? For, surely, if it is an obligatory *mitzvah,* then it can hardly be merely "praiseworthy."

We have already partially answered this point, when we referred to the view of Rashba that no blessing is recited over the Haggadah precisely because its scope is ill-defined (see question 286). Every person's level of ability to discuss the Exodus is different. For some, the simple reading of the Haggadah constitutes the limit of their *"mitzvah."* Others, of a more philosophical or creative bent, can provide their own "midrash" to the text and the history. Hence the two statements provide guidance for both levels. It is obligatory simply "to relate" the Haggadah. It is "praiseworthy" to expand upon it with personal insights, commentary, and discussion.

Rabbi Meir Simchah of Dvinsk states that the statement has to be understood in light of the view of Rabbi Eliezer ben Azariah that the *mitzvah* of [eating the *matzah* and] reciting the Haggadah has to be completed by midnight. Any further discussion on the Exodus that takes place after that time is not, therefore, obligatory (i.e., a *mitzvah*), but simply "praiseworthy" (see Meir Simchah Ha-Kohein, *Meshekh Chokhmah* [first edition, Riga, 1927]; Commentary to Exodus 13:14–16).

### 315. If someone converts to Judaism, how can they possibly recite the *Avadim hayyinu,* when clearly it is not true that their "forefathers" were slaves to Pharaoh in Egypt?

That is an interesting point. Indeed, the same problem arises with the *Ha lachma anya* composition, which refers to the bread of affliction which "*our* forefathers ate in the land of Egypt."

There is strong support for the view that they should not recite these passages from the Mishnah *Bikkurim* (1:4), which states that, at the ceremony of the bringing of the firstfruits on Shavuot, a convert should not accompany his gift with the recitation of the prescribed biblical passage (Deuteronomy 26:3–10), since it contains a reference to "the land which the Lord swore to *our forefathers* to give to us," when clearly his forefathers were not then of Israelite stock.

Maimonides states, however (*Yad, Hilkhot Bikkurim* 4:3), that the practical halakhah does not accord with that Mishnah, and that a convert may, in fact, declaim those sentiments, referring to the promise to his forefathers. The reason for this is that the land was given to Abraham, who was declared to be the father not only of Israel, but also of all converts. This was the implication of his change of name from *Avram* ("Exalted father") to *Avraham,* which is explained to mean, *Av hamon goyim,* "Father of a multitude of peoples" (Genesis 17:4).

*Rabbi Shem Tov Gaguine (Keter Shem Tov,* p. 109) supports this view with an incisive proof from the very next paragraph of the Haggadah, which refers to the five Sages at Bnei Berak relating the Exodus until the early hours. One of those Sages was Rabbi Akivah, whose genealogy midrashic tradition traces back to the non-Israelite Canaanite general, Sisera (Judges 4:2). Now if a convert was unable to participate fully in the recitation of the Exodus story, it would have been inconceivable for his colleagues to have allowed him not only to participate in their Seder, but even to host it. It is clear, therefore, that a convert does not need to measure the sentiments he or she expresses. They are all, in equal status with born Israelites, children of Abraham, the first convert.

## THE FIVE SAGES

### 316. What is the link between the *Avadim Hayyinu* and the section on the five Sages that follows?

In the *Avadim Hayyinu* we stated that all who speak at length about the Exodus are to be praised." We also stated that even if we are distinguished scholars the obligation to do so remains. Hence, it is appropriate, in the very next paragraph, to give a classical example of an occasion when the greatest Sages of the talmudic period–

and, indeed, of any age – fulfilled both those requirements: to discuss the Exodus even though they knew all the traditions about it, and, furthermore, to "speak at length" about it, to the extent that they completely lost all track of time.

### 317. What were those five Sages doing, celebrating Seder away from their own hometowns, together with Rabbi Akivah, at his home at Bnei Berak?

A popular theory has it that they were spending Seder at the home of Akivah because that Sage was the arch supporter of Bar Kochba, who led a revolt against Rome in the year 135 C.E. The theory has it that those five leading Sages of the age were invited there by Akivah to be briefed on the current situation, to approve Bar Kochba's final plans for the uprising, and to receive their own instructions regarding the lead they would be expected to take in galvanizing the nation to flock to the banner of revolt.

### 318. Is there any basis in the text for such a theory?

There is nothing explicit, or even implicit. There is a problem, however, with the reference to the disciples having to remind their masters that the time for the recitation of the morning *Shema* had arrived. The theory has it that this can hardly be taken literally, since those Sages – accustomed regularly to rising long before dawn, in order to learn – would have been zealous, of their own accord, to look out for the dawn in order to fulfill the biblical *mitzvah* of reciting *Shema* "when you rise up," that is, immediately when ordinary folk start getting up.

The protagonists of the theory state, therefore, that those words of their disciples were nothing less than a secret code to their five leaders, locked in secret discussion. The disciples were lookouts for any Roman soldiers who might be about. If any seemed to be approaching Akivah's home, they would shout "Our masters, it is time to recite the morning *Shema!*" That would be the signal for the Sages to lower their voices and to hide away any maps or plans that they may have been studying.

### 319. Is this theory totally plausible?

For several reasons, the present writer does not believe that it is. First, the Talmud tells us that even among the Rabbis and students there were informers to the Romans. It would thus have been highly reckless of Akivah to disclose to anyone at all, even to his most trusted disciples, the purpose of his "Seder" with his colleagues. Two famous rabbis, Ishmael and Shimon ben Netanel, were executed for being involved in plotting a rebellion (see Talmud *Sanhedrin* 97b). Akivah would not have taken any chances at all.

Secondly, the Romans had a highly sophisticated spy network, and the unusual presence of a gathering of the leading Sages of Palestine, at the home of a nationalist leader like Akivah, would have aroused the immediate suspicions of the Romans, who would have posted guards all around Akivah's home, and who would have had their own cruel methods of extracting full details of the meeting from the disciples.

Thirdly, the Sages who finally edited the Talmud, some four centuries after the period of the five Sages, would have had no reason, or pressure, to withhold the true purpose of that famous Seder, had its purpose been political and military. The fact that no such information is recorded suggests that there was nothing dramatic or sensitive about it.

Fourthly, Akivah's colleagues did not, in fact, share his confidence in Bar Kochba, and were positively opposed to such a dangerous adventure. They told Akivah, "Grass will be growing through your jaws, and the redeemer will still not have come" (Talmud Yerushalmi *Taanit,* ch. 4, 68d). They would hardly have agreed to spend Seder night, therefore, discussing an adventure that was patently unacceptable to them.

This leads us to our fifth objection, which is that, given their known objection, Akivah could not have chosen a worse time to try and convince them to join the revolt. For surely Seder night inspires the conviction that it is to God's mercy, and His strong hand and outstretched arm, that we should be appealing, to repeat the miraculous deliverance of the Exodus, not to a military adventurer like Bar Kochba! That, indeed, is the reason why even Moses' name only appears once in the Haggadah, and then indirectly in a quotation. That is also the point of the Midrash that stresses, *Ani velo mal'akh,* "I, God, brought you out, and not by the hand of any angel." Akivah would have known better than to torpedo from the outset his carefully laid plan to win them over to support the agency of a human deliverer!

Our sixth reason is that, on purely halakhic grounds, it could hardly have been appropriate to hold military and political discussions on a night when there is a biblical *mitzvah* to relate the events of the Exodus. We have just read that "whoever speaks at great length about the Exodus is to be praised" *(Avadim Hayyinu).* It would hardly have been seemly for the editor of the Haggadah to juxtapose to that a reference to the greatest Sages who totally flouted that principle by spending the night discussing plans for a rebellion against Rome! Clearly, the editors of the Haggadah had no such tradition regarding any sinister dimension to that Bnei Berak Seder, since they would hardly have included such a reference immediately after the plea for total preoccupation with the details of the Exodus.

### 320. From a chronological point of view, is there any problem with placing that Bnei Berak Seder in the period of the Bar Kochba revolt?

There is. Those Sages could hardly have been engaged in the preparation for Bar Kochba's revolt, for the simple reason that, as will be presently demonstrated, that meeting at Bnei Berak could only have taken place some thirty years before the revolt!

It has been noted that there was one notable absence from the group: the patriarch Rabban Gamaliel, leader of Palestinian Jewry, without whose support and involvement no such revolt could have been contemplated. From many references in the Talmud we know that he always led the many delegations to Rome, in the company of those leading Sages. Yet here he is mysteriously absent.

Gamaliel's absence — as well as the continuation passage in our Haggadah — points to the tragic period during his patriarchate when he was deposed by his colleagues on account of his unacceptable dictatorial style of leadership. They replaced him with the young and inexperienced Rabbi Eleazar ben Azariah. This explains why the latter appears as number three in the list of Sages, that is in the center of the group, the position always reserved for the senior colleague.

Now, talmudic historians tell us that Gamaliel died even before the revolt against the Emperor Trajan, in 116 C.E. We have to allow, before that, for the period during which Gamaliel was deposed, and also subsequently, for the years when he was brought back to share the leadership role with Eleazar (Talmud *Berakhot* 27b–28a). So the event of that Seder in Bnei Berak, reflecting the period when Eleazar clearly reigned alone, must have been at least ten years before Gamaliel's death, namely circa 106 C.E., which was nearly thirty years before the Bar Kochba revolt of 135 C.E.

### 321. So, if they were not planning the Bar Kochba revolt, what were they doing away from their own homes that Seder night?

They were doing one of two things: either they were coordinating their plans to have the patriarch Rabban Gamaliel removed from office, and exerting pressure on the young Rabbi Eleazer to be ready to stand in the breach; or, quite simply, they were enjoying Akivah's hospitality.

As to any objection that they would hardly leave their wives and children to spend a Seder away from home, there is no clear evidence that they did, in fact, leave their families! They may well have all been present at Bnei Berak with the Sages. The fact that they are not referred to in the passage is hardly significant, for they would certainly have turned in to bed long before their husbands' night-long discussion vigil, as described in the Haggadah.

In fact, from a similar passage in the Tosefta (*Pesachim* 10:12), it seems that the Sages did actually host their colleagues on a rotating basis: "Now Rabban Gamaliel and the elders were reclining at the table of Boethus ben Zonin at Lydda, and were occupying themselves with the laws of Passover the whole night, until cock crow."

There was probably nothing sinister, therefore, about that Seder of the five Sages, notwithstanding the scholarly imagination that has run riot over it!

### 322. What precise point about his age is Rabbi Eleazar ben Azariah making when he says, "I am like a man of seventy years and yet I could not persuade my colleagues to recite the passage containing the reference to the Exodus at night"?

As we mentioned above, Eleazar was still a teenager when he was appointed *Nasi*, patriarch of Palestine, to replace the deposed Rabban Gamaliel. The Talmud (*Berakhot* 28a) states that, miraculously, overnight his face became wizened and his beard white, replacing his fresh-faced look and making it easier for his much older colleagues to treat him with respect and his views with the deference usually reserved for the aged.

However, he laments in this passage, although he looked "like a seventy year old," his colleagues did not always accord to him the absolute halakhic authority his office might have warranted. They did not acquiesce, in this instance, in his fervent belief that that particular passage of the *Shema* should be recited at night. He laments that, although the other leading colleagues appointed him to that supreme office, not one of them supported his view on this issue, and he was left isolated until Ben Zoma seconded his opinion and rallied the support required to implement that liturgical reform.

It sounds as if Eleazar is chiding the colleagues who persuaded him, against his own better judgment, to accept the post, for not supporting him, perhaps out of fear of allowing the young newcomer to introduce such a reform behind the back of the deposed patriarch, Gamaliel. Eleazar was implying that he could not possibly wield any authority if the shadow of Gamaliel still hung over the leading talmudic academicians.

### 323. But what exactly was the bone of contention on this particular liturgical matter?

While a full explanation is beyond the scope of this work (see *Encyclopedia Talmudit, XII,* Jerusalem, 1967, 12:199–205), the dispute may be said to hinge upon the precise definition of the time of the Exodus. Some authorities explain that the Sages were opposed to reciting the third paragraph of the *Shema* (which contains the reference to the Exodus) at night, since the reality of the Exodus took place by day. Although permission to leave was granted at midnight, the Israelites did not move out until the next morning.

Hence the difference of opinion as to whether the elation of that eve of the redemption, and the technical freedom that was granted at midnight, makes the night an equally appropriate time to include a reference to the Exodus, in its evening service, or whether reality is to be measured exclusively by practical application, thus relating the Exodus exclusively to the morning service.

### 324. How exactly are those two opposing views justified with reference to that biblical verse: "In order that you may remember the day when you left Egypt all the days of [kol yemei] your life" (Deuteronomy 16:3).

The Rabbis believed that there was nothing superfluous in the Torah. Every word has a value; every letter a significance. The task of the Sage is to uncover the hidden meanings, and reveal the relevance of every nuance, in relation to the body of oral halakhic traditions handed down from Sinai.

Thus, for Ben Zoma, although the verse refers unequivocally to remembering the Exodus "all the *days* of your life," yet, if it had been the Torah's intention, by that phrase, to confine that rememberance to daytime only, then it could have simply written, "In order that you may remember . . . *during the days of* [*yemei chayyekha*] your life." For Ben Zoma, the addition of the word *kol (yemei chayyekha),* suggests the nuance of *"throughout* the days of your life," which also takes in the nights. He clearly believed that the Exodus proper commenced from the time when the permission to leave Egypt was granted, namely at night, and hence his support of Eleazar ben Azariah in his wish to include the reference to the Exodus in the evening *Shema.*

**325. But did Rabbi Eleazar have any other, halakhic reason for wanting to include the reference to the Exodus in the night Shema?**

He did. He regarded the night as a more appropriate time to recall the Exodus, since the period of the eating of the Paschal lamb, symbol of the Exodus, extended, in his view (see Talmud *Berakhot* 9a), only until midnight, and not over until the following morning. The Sages, on the other hand, took account of the view of Rabbi Akivah (Talmud *Berakhot* 9a), that the main redemption was the next morning, and that the meat of the Paschal lamb may be consumed until dawn. Thus, the obligation to recall the Exodus is related to the daytime rather than the night.

**326. But did that not leave the Sages with the task of finding an appropriate interpretation of that otherwise superfluous expression, kol (yemei chayyekha)?**

Indeed: their emphasis was entirely different, and rather in the realm of the mystical, an area of exploration in which Akivah was master. The phrase, *yemei chayyekha,* for the Sages, establishes the basic obligation of remembering the Exodus "in this world," that is, throughout Jewish history, even if its uniqueness is overshadowed by subsequent acts of greater redemptive power and mystery. The additional word, *kol* ("all"), suggests the sense of "throughout all your modes of existence." Hence the Sages' interpretation, "to include the period of the Messiah."

**327. Does that debate have any practical halakhic consequences?**

It does. There are some authorities who take the view that, because the *mitzvah* of remembering the Exodus, in the *Shema,* is applicable throughout the day and night—according to the exposition of Ben Zoma—it does not matter, therefore, if we recite the Maariv *Shema* before nightfall proper (as long as it is after sunset). This is based upon the fact that the key verse, "That you remember the Exodus from Egypt all the days of your life," makes no direct reference to *night,* and the obligation to recite it at night is only rabbinically inferred from the additional word, *kol.* On that basis, they take the view that one may rely on the recitation of the evening *Shema* in Synagogue, to fulfill the obligation of *keriat Shema,* even though the service takes place before nightfall.

## THE FOUR SONS

**328. The next composition commences, Barukh Ha-Makom. Makom, in Hebrew, means "place," so how does this phrase come to be used as a designation of God?**

*Makom* is an early rabbinic designation of God, used in the sense of place or space of the world (Midrash *Bereishit Rabbah* 68:9), and expressing the special nuance of God's ubiquity in the world. Best translated by "Omnipresent," it also comes to mean the One who is at hand to help in whatever crisis situation man finds himself: hence its employment in the greeting given to mourners, *Ha-Makom yenacheim etkhem,* "May the Omnipresent comfort you." May you rediscover His "Presence," even though your loss may cause you to feel alienated from It.

#### 329.  But what is its relevance to the continuation of the passage that refers to the Four Sons?

Again, its sense is that God is close at hand to every situation that man finds himself in. He is present, as author of the Torah which inspires the *chakham,* the wise son. He is there, throwing out lifelines to the *rasha,* the wicked, and creating opportunities for him to repent. He is there, as the *shomer petayim,* the One who "preserves the simple-minded" (Psalm 116:6), cushioning them from the pitfalls of life that they are ill-equipped to avoid. And He is there, as protector of the *eino yodea lishol,* "those who are too young to ask." God implants into the tender babes a unique instinct for self-preservation, so that, without having to articulate questions, they are enabled to communicate forcefully their needs, likes and dislikes. A baby's cry is the clearest and most powerful signal to its parent that it has an unfulfilled need; and a baby's contented gurgle or smile is a most generous expression of gratitude for needs fulfilled.

#### 330.  Why are the expressions *Barukh* and *Barukh hu* repeated so frequently in the opening line of the composition?

The word *Barukh* is actually repeated four times, which is clearly related to the Four Sons. It essentially reminds us of our obligation to "bless God" at all times, whether he bestows a righteous son upon us or an apparently wicked son; whether our child is permanently childlike, as a "simple-minded son," or merely a babe-in-arms proceeding through the fascinating and exciting stages of early development. As the Talmud expresses it, "Just as we bless God for the good things, so must we bless Him for the bad" (*Berakhot* 48b).

#### 331.  Is there any significance in the order of the Four Sons?

We would naturally expect the wise son to head the list, for the greatest and most spontaneous thanks are rendered for the gift of a wise son. We might have expected the simple-minded son to follow, or possibly the babe-in-arms for whom we have the greatest optimism that he will grow up to be wise. We would expect the wicked son to come last in the order.

Significantly, the wicked son is placed next to the wise son. Thus, wickedness may not be his essential, unredeemable characteristic. He may merely have been a victim of circumstances, a child who got into the wrong company and became overwhelmed by persuasive evil influences that he was not strong enough to resist. We have to counter that by putting him next to a wise son, placing him into a wholesome environment which might inspire him to choose more worthy role models.

The *rasha* thus takes precedent over the simple-minded son, because the former may well be won back to an emotional and intellectual attachment to his Judaism, something which is beyond the ability of the simple-minded.

The one who is too young to ask questions is placed last in the order, simply because, at this stage, the Seder is beyond his ken. Indeed, he may not even manage to keep awake for it! For certainly, it will not be long, however, when his moment of involvement will arrive.

**332. Much is made of the wicked son's use of phraseology that suggests that he excludes himself from those within the fraternity of observers. This is because he uses the term *lakhem:* "What does all this ritual mean to you [*lakhem*]." But surely, the wise son does precisely the same, when he says: "What are all the testimonies, statutes and judgments which the Lord our God has commanded *you* [*etkhem*]"?**

True, he uses that pronoun, but his use, at the same time, of the phrase, "the Lord *our* God," makes it quite clear that he includes himself. The thrust of his question is simply that he wishes to understand the psychology of his fellow believers. He asks his parents to share with him something of their perception of the relevance of all the Torah's laws to their life.

It is naive to imagine that every wise son is not without his doubts. It is to be noted that there is no "righteous son" at the Seder table. The author of the Haggadah assumes that righteousness is a comparative standard. We are concerned with enlightening normal kids, not saints. And if the son is "wise," if he is an intellectual, then he will not be satisfied with ritual alone. He will want to appreciate the existential and emotional pull of all Judaism's components. He will want to understand how the weight of all those multifarious laws, regulations, traditions, and customs of the Torah has enriched the lives of his parents. Unlike the wicked son's "jibe," the wise son asks an honest and personal question of his parents. Their emotional and spiritual responses are of the most profound importance to him as a guide when he makes his own religious decisions in life.

**333. Besides the employment of the reference to "the Lord, our God," is there any other indication, in the respective questions of the wise and wicked sons, to suggest that the former asks respectfully, while the latter speaks critically?**

Indeed. If we consult the biblical verses, attributed, respectively, to the wise and wicked sons, we will note that while the wise son "asks," the wicked son "tells." The verse attributed to the wise son is Deuteronomy 6:20, which commences, "When your son *shall ask* you in the time to come, saying, What are the testimonies, statutes. . . ." However, the verse attributed to the wicked son states, "When your children *shall say* to you: What does this service mean to you?" (Exodus 12:26). Furthermore, the wise son comes, respectfully, on his own ("when your son will ask . . ."), whereas the wicked come as a group ("when your children will say . . ."), a rabble to mock your observances.

**334. Is there any other telltale sign, in the way they formulate their question, that the wicked son is critical of tradition and the wise son respectful?**

There is. Note how the wise son describes Jewish tradition: in terms of "testimonies, statutes, and judgments." He wants to understand fully the distinction between each and every category of Jewish law. Then see how the wicked son alludes to Judaism: "What does all this *avodah* mean to you?" *Avodah* generally refers to work involving effort. Hence the noun derivative, *eved,* "a slave." For the wise son, the Torah is multifaceted and challenging; for the wicked son, it is a burden!

**335. What is the significance of the vague response that, it is suggested, we make to the wise son: "And, according to the law of the Paschal lamb, we do not have any dessert after partaking of the Paschal lamb"?**

This might well be a symbolic answer, which, if he is truly wise, he will fathom. The parent is, in effect, hinting that, just as we leave the Paschal lamb meal unfinished, so there is a whole area of religious responsiveness that one cannot just "lay on the table" and share, even with one's nearest and dearest. There are certain intimate experiences in life that are of a differing quality for each and every person, and which vary in intensity at different times and under different circumstances. It is, indeed, frequently impossible to explain how observance of detailed Torah laws benefits us personally, especially those which are abstruse "testimonies and statutes," which we perform without fully comprehending their purpose. It is certainly imposs- ible to explain the separate relevance of each individual precept.

We eat the main course; we know that Judaism as a whole is our authentic fare and our satisfying heritage. We can never hope to understand and even feel the total relevance of it in its entirety. It must remain an unfinished meal, like that of the Paschal lamb. The *chakham* may well wish to probe, to determine whether or not his parents have savored that glorious dessert. But the parent is also permitted to be candid, and hold out to his offspring the possibility that the son may well succeed in soaring even higher than him in religious perception.

Another, more literal, explanation of the answer proffered to the wise son is that it is merely an example of the minute detail into which parents of such gifted children must be prepared to go. In all areas of Judaism, one must be able to cover the very finest of points, such as, "in the case of the laws of the Paschal lamb, that one must not partake of any dessert after it."

The answer may also be symbolic, implying that the wise son should be so satisfied intellectually with the answers you give him and the education you provide for him, that he will not go off to rival cults for his "dessert," his search for intellectual stimulation and pleasure (see also question 411).

**336. What is the meaning of the instruction, *hakheh et shinav*, to "blunt the teeth" of the wicked son?**

It means, simply, to stop his offensive sentiments in mid flow. The instruction, contained in the *Shema*, to "teach one's children diligently," is *veshinantam le- vanekha*. The word for "tooth" in Hebrew is *shen*. So *veshinantam* means, literally, "you shall sharpen their teeth." The objective of teaching is thus to stimulate children to be responsive in a "sharp" and incisive manner. "Blunting the teeth" means making oneself deaf to an ill-informed, unacceptable, and offensive response. A parallel to this imagery underlies the English verb "rebut," meaning, to assail a person with verbal violence, in order to refute his argument.

**337. Is there not a problem with the grammar in the instruction regarding the answer to the fourth son, who asks no questions? It states, *at petach lo***

("You shall open him up to questioning"), using the feminine personal pronoun *at,* whereas the accompanying verb, *petach,* is in the masculine!

There is, in fact, a grammatical incompatibility here, although there are three passages in the Bible where the same situation occurs, of the feminine form, *at,* being used for the masculine (see Numbers 11:15, Deuteronomy 5:24, and Ezekiel 28:14). The feminine form is employed, according to some commentators, in order to indicate that a soft, sympathetic approach is required here, as opposed to the harsh rebuttal that is recommended in the case of the wicked son.

### 338. Are there any other ways in which the "Four Sons" motif may be construed?

The traditional commentaries offer several interpretations of the specific types alluded to in the passage of the Four Sons. A slightly different approach might be to view them as representing the "four ages," and stages, of a Jew's encounter with his Torah heritage, and his quest for knowledge and spirituality.

The word *banim* usually occurs in the sense of "sons" or "children," as derived from the Hebrew root *banah,* "to build, beget." But Hebraists will know that it may also have the totally different meaning of "those seeking to understand." In this sense its origin is the root *bun,* a variant of *bin,* from which are derived the words for "understanding," *tevunah* and *binah.*

It occurs in the Bible in this sense, in the phrase *ovdah eitzah mi-banim* (Jeremiah 49:7). Thus, the Jewish Publication Society translation renders, "Is counsel perished from *the prudent?*" And the rendering of the New English Bible Translation is, "Have *her Sages* no skill in counsel?"

Accordingly, *arba'ah vanim* may justifiably mean "four [types of] seekers after understanding," or "four levels of understanding," which we view as four stages, and progressive ages, of interaction with Torah.

The child is invariably a *chakham,* a wise, curious soul, with a thirst for knowledge and a profound capacity for its assimilation.

Regretfully, in the teenage years, rebelliousness sets in, and he espouses scepticism and nonobservance, joining forces with those whose attitude has to be characterized as that of the *rasha,* the *wicked son.*

In later life, however, maturity and experience frequently bring a reevaluation of his relationship with Judaism. Much of the rebelliousness evaporates with the growing realization that his earlier, antireligious "certainties" are no longer so certain. In its place comes an awareness that the solid moral and spiritual foundation that Torah gives to the lives and homes of its adherents is so much more satisfying and enriching than the superficial crutches upon which he has hitherto relied. This brings with it a heightened respect. He no longer challenges his tradition arrogantly, as a *rasha.* He now enters the reverential stage of *tam,* which we view as that of the honest and humble searcher after enlightenment. Esau is described in the Torah as an aggressive hunter; by contrast, Jacob is called an *ish tam,* "a straightforward, guileless man" (Genesis 25:27). Middle age frequently brings with it the transition from *rasha* to *tam,* from rebel to earnest seeker after ultimate truths. He now deferentially inquires, *Mah zot,* "What is my tradition all about?"—The tradition I have long neglected, but often needed so desperately during the many crises of my life.

Some are fortunate and can manage to change the direction of their lives in time, taking on the philosophies and observances of the *chakham* while they still have their faculties and the capacity to live out their remaining years in spiritual joy and tranquillity of spirit. Others, regretfully, leave it too late, and, with old age, enter the stage of *eino yode'a lishol*, "those who can no longer ask." Such people are forced to face the unpalatable reality that they simply no longer have the strength of will and the concentration of mind to change direction. The bad habits of a lifetime are their bedfellows until their dying day.

It is not that they are without questions. They have plenty: "What have I done with my life? How did I come to squander the talents I once possessed? Why did I pursue vain diversions? Why did I alienate myself from my heritage? Why did I lead such a selfish existence? Will I be called to account for my sins of omission and commission?"

But now it is too late:

I should have asked those questions decades ago! I should have grabbed the opportunity to join the Synagogue fraternity, to experience the spirit of Jewish observances. I should have been a role model to my children and grand-children, a bearer and transmitter of the heritage of my grandparents. I had my chance to ask, and to receive instructive and beneficial responses. I had my chance to live properly, Jewishly.

His own teachers have long since passed on. He certainly cannot relate to the young Rabbis, even if he had the strength to go to their lectures, even if his hearing wasn't so bad, even if his power of concentration was not so limited, even if he could stop himself from falling asleep in the warm, stuffy atmosphere of the schoolroom where the shiurim are conducted. No, he is now definitely an *eino yode'a lishol*, one whose questioning days are over. His only hope is that a merciful divine Father and Teacher will, one day, answer all those questions, and allay his fears and anxieties. Perhaps then he will be assured that, surprisingly, it is still not too late to learn.

*Arba'ah vanim*—these are the four ways of relating to Jewish knowledge and religious experience.

## YAKHOL MEIROSH CHODESH

**339. The next passage states, *Yakhol meirosh chodesh*, that "I might have assumed that the obligation of relating the Exodus to our children commences from the first day of the month [of Nisan]," rather than only on the first evening of the festival, on the fifteenth of the month. On what basis would we have made such an assumption?**

The assumption would have been based upon the analogy with Purim, where the entire month takes on a festive character, in anticipation of the joyous day that occurs in the middle of the month. Indeed, the Talmud (*Talmud Yerushalmi, Megillah* 1b) states that "the entire month is really appropriate for the reading of the Megillah, since it states, 'And the *month* which was transformed from grieving to joy (Esther 9:22).' " Hence, although the festival may only be celebrated on its appropriate day, nevertheless the *mitzvah* of recalling the historical events becomes operative from the beginning of the month. And it is that recollection that underpins the recommendation that, "from the day the month of Adar commences, one should increase in celebration" (Talmud *Taanit* 29a).

It is, therefore, on that analogy, and bearing in mind that the Torah states "Observe *the month* of Spring, and keep the Passover" (Deuteronomy 16:1), that we may well have assumed that, in the case of Pesach also, the obligation to speak of the Exodus, and read the Haggadah, commences with the very beginning of the month.

Another reason for that assumption is that, according to the view of Rabban Shimon ben Gamaliel, one should study the laws of Pesach from two weeks before the festival, that is from the beginning of the month of Nisan, since Moses stood before Israel on that day and taught them the laws of the festival (see Exodus 12:1).

### 340. Why, then, is the Haggadah not prescribed to be read from the first day of Nisan?

This question is answered precisely in the passage under review. It is because the Torah specifically enjoined us to confine the telling of the story of the Exodus to one specific day of the month (and, in the Diaspora communities, to two). Hence the statement "And you shall relate it to your children *(bayom ha-hu)* on that day" (Exodus 13:8).

### 341. On what basis is the next assumption made, namely that we might have been expected to recite the *Haggadah mib'od yom*, "while it is still daytime," on the eve of the festival?

The assumption might have been made on the basis of the Paschal lamb, which is slaughtered while it is still day, on the eve of the festival. I might have thought, therefore, that the Haggadah should likewise be read at that time.

## OUR FOREFATHERS WERE IDOLATERS

### 342. What is the significance of the next passage, *Mitchilah ovdei avodah zarah*, "Originally our forefathers were idolators"?

The Talmud (*Pesachim* 116a) states, *"Matchilin bignut umesayem beshevach,"* that we must commence the Haggadah with a disparaging reference to our spiritually barren origins, and end with praise of God. According to the view of Rav, the disparaging reference refers to the present passage, which he sought to place at the beginning of the Haggadah, whereas his colleague, Shemuel, refers it to the *Avadim Hayyinu* composition.

We may assume that their difference of opinion reflects the situation during the period of the second Temple, and before there was any consensus regarding the precise texts to recite, or the order in which to recite them. This situation is presupposed in the Mishnah (*Pesachim* 10:4) which states, "One is obliged to expound the biblical verses (Deuteronomy 26:5-9) from *Arami oved avi* ('My father was a wandering Aramean') until the end of the passage." It is a remarkable instruction, given that one would have had to be a Torah scholar to give such expositions at the Seder! We must assume, therefore, that there were in existence a number of popular expositions of the verses referring to the Exodus, as well as to the concise survey of patriarchal history as contained in the *Arami oved avi* passage, and that these were known by heart by the masses.

We have retained in our Haggadah three compositions—the *Avadim hayyinu,* the *Mitchilah ovdei avodah zarah,* and the *Arami oved avi*—all of which conform to the principle of "commencing with a disparaging element" ("We were slaves to Pharaoh," "Our fathers were idolators," "My father was a wandering Aramean") "and ending on a praiseworthy note" ("But God brought us out from there," "And now God has brought us close to his service," and "He became there a great nation").

Thus, before the Haggadah text, as we have it, was formalized, people made their own arbitrary choices of any one or more of those passages, all conforming to the required principle. However, once the talmudic debate got under way, to decide which particular passage should take priority of place as the opening exposition, we find Rav and Shemuel expressing their different preferences.

### 343. For what particular reason was it considered important to commence on a note of national disparagement?

The early talmudic Sages believed that the only way to melt God's heart was to throw ourselves on his mercy, and to abase ourselves before the bar of divine judgement. The statement, "Originally our forefathers were idolators" serves, on the other hand, to remind God of the quantum leap of faith and spiritual discovery made by our people since the days of our founding fathers. The implication is that, notwithstanding our own religious shortcomings, God should, in the words of the High Holyday composition, "remember the covenant and not our evil inclination *(labrit ha-beit ve-al tefen layeitzer)."*

The identical petitionary philosophy is also at work near the beginning of our daily prayer book, where we commence on a desperate note: "Master of the worlds! It is not because of our righteous deeds that we lay our supplications before You, but because of Your abundant mercies. What are we? What is our life? What is our piety, our righteousness, our helpfulness? . . . Man has no superiority over the beast, for all is vanity."

Having abased ourselves, the prayer book then makes a sudden shift of direction, to espouse the second half of the Haggadah principle that we end on a praiseworthy note: "Nevertheless we are Your people, sons of Your covenant, the children of Abraham, Your friend . . . the offspring of his only son, Isaac, who was bound on the altar; the congregation of Jacob, Your firstborn son."

Against that background, we see that the principle of moving from national self-deprecation to praise of our patriarchal origins is a well-established liturgical means of intercession. In the present passage of the Haggadah, the merit of the patriarchs, and the blessings conferred upon them, make that same marked contrast with the idolatrous situation of our prepatriarchal ancestors.

**344. Why, in the Mitchilah composition, is there mention of Esau, son of Isaac, and his tribal possession, but not of Ishmael, son of Abraham?**

R. David Kimchi explains that Esau remained an inhabitant of Canaan, and therefore merited a tribal inheritance, whereas Ishmael was banished from the holy land, with the unequivocal promise that "the son of this handmaid shall not inherit together with . . . Isaac" (Genesis 21:10).

## BLESSED BE THE ONE WHO KEPT HIS PROMISE

**345. In the passage commencing, *Barukh shomer havtachato* ("Blessed be the One who kept His promise to Israel"), there are two problems: First, would we have expected otherwise than that God should have kept His promise? Second, it states that "the Holy One, blessed be He, calculated the end [of the exile]." What sort of "calculation" was necessary, bearing in mind that He told Abraham quite clearly that his children would be strangers in a foreign land "for four hundred years"? (Genesis 15:13).**

The commentators tell us that, instead of serving a full four hundred years in Egypt, as implied in God's promise to Abraham, God reckoned the period of enslavement as commencing from the birth of Isaac.

Isaac was 60 when Jacob was born; and when Jacob came down to Egypt he told Pharaoh that he was 130 years of age (Genesis 47:9). Together this makes a total of 190 years. Now, they remained in Egypt for a total of 210 years. So God "kept His promise to Israel," namely, that they would be under the threat of slavery for a total of four hundred years, while, at the same time, reducing the actual period of servitude in Egypt by 190 years. And it is in that sense that the Haggadah uses the term "calculating the end," and blesses God for having found a formula whereby He could keep His word, while, at the same time, grant a concession.

According to the Hebrew method of *gematria,* whereby each letter of the alphabet has a numerical value (*Alef* = 1; *Bet* = 2, etc.), the value of the word *keitz* (in the phrase, "God calculated the *[keitz]* end") is 190 (*Kuf* [100] + Tzadi [90]). Thus, God calculated a reduction of 190 years from the originally conceived period of oppression.

**346. Can we identify any event with the commencement of the real oppression in Egypt?**

It coincided with the birth of Miriam, sister of Moses. It was for that reason, the mounting oppression, that her parents called her by that name, with its association of bitterness, from the words *mar* and *maror.*

**347. What was that "great wealth" referred to in the verse quoted in this passage?**

The reference is to the silver and gold vessels and garments that they took from the Egyptians as wages for the 210 years of unpaid slavery. The Talmud (*Berakhot* 9a) states that it was vital for them to take away that wealth, as otherwise Abraham would have had a claim against God that, while He was true to the first part of His promise to him—that his children would be slaves in a foreign land—yet He did not keep the second part of His promise, that they "would come out with great wealth."

## *VEHIY SHE'AMDA*

**348. The first word of the *Vehiy she'amda* ("And it is *that* which has sustained our fathers and ourselves") is rather vague. What precisely does "that" refer to?**

Commentators refer it to the promise contained in the verse just quoted, from the "Covenant between the Pieces" sealed between God and Abraham (Genesis, ch. 15), when God revealed that Abraham's offspring would be slaves for 400 years, but that, ultimately, "Also the nation which they serve shall I judge" (v. 14). It is that promise that has sustained our people, throughout the long years and millenia of exile, and assured them that their subservience must one day come to an end, and that, in the words of Maimonides, "Though he [the Messiah] may tarry, yet shall I wait patiently for him." The Hebrew word for "promise" *(havtachah)* is feminine, and hence the pronoun used to refer to it—*vehiy* ("And it")—is in the feminine.

**349. Is it not rather paranoid to assert that "for not only one nation [Egypt] rose up against us, but in every generation they rise up to destroy us"?**

No, it is a cold fact of history. There is not a single century when Jewry has had an interlude of release from anti-Semitism. If one reads any Jewish history book, one will be faced with an unremitting catalogue of national and religious discrimination, Crusade, bloodshed, exile, blood libel, pogrom, anti-Semitic propaganda, holocaust, attempted destruction of the Jewish homeland, terrorism against Jews and Jewish communal organizations. The list is endless. The Haggadah foresaw all this as the inevitable fate of the Jew. And it records its tragic and prophetic assessment of the Jewish situation with total accuracy.

**350. But how can the passage conclude by saying that God "delivers us from their hands," when so many of our brethren were not "delivered"?**

The Haggadah is clearly speaking in the plural, reflecting the general fate of the nation. God has, truly, delivered *Israel* from their hands, even though, tragically, it has been at enormous cost in Jewish blood. The State of Israel is the most obvious proof of the accuracy of the Haggadah's assertion. Our people, snatched from the flames of the Nazi crematoria, nevertheless survived, and within three years of the end of World War II, a sovereign Jewish state was proclaimed.

The Haggadah would hardly have been so naive as to suggest that in every generation God totally frustrates our enemy's attempts to inflict devastation upon Jews and Jewish communities. He specifically uses the word *lekhaloteinu,* which means their attempts "to totally destroy us."

That design, God has truly frustrated. A remnant has survived. It is now our challenge to ensure that the growth rate, which increased so dramatically during the period when our ancestors were in Egypt (Exodus 1:7), is similarly augmented in our day. Tragically, we are now creating our own enemies to decimate our communities, in the form of intermarriage and assimilation. God hates suicide. National suicide is an abomination. When we read this passage, each year, we should reaffirm our personal determination to remain loyal, and at the same time to foster our communal and national cohesion.

## TZEI ULEMAD

### 351. What is the purpose of the *Tzei ulemad* composition and its association with the previous passage?

The *Tzei ulemad* seeks to expand upon the point previously made that "in every generation they sought to destroy us." We are now given a classical example, from the story of Laban's evil designs against Jacob, of just how early in our history that antipathy towards us began.

It is found in Deuteronomy (26:5), where it is prescribed to be recited by the Jewish farmer as he presents his *Bikkurim,* "first fruits," to the priest. The farmer utters this potted history of Israel, from the time of Jacob, a fugitive from the holy land, until his own day when he can glory in his settled life in Israel, and in the luxuriant blessings of its blessed soil.

### 352. But is it true that "Laban wished entirely to uproot" Jacob? Where is the evidence of that from the account in the book of Genesis?

The Vilna Gaon points out that this is an example of where the Torah conceals something in one context, and reveals it in another. It is true that there is no clear statement of any murderous intention on Laban's part in the description of their relationship in Genesis (chs. 29–31). However, we must supplement the earlier description by the reference in Deuteronomy to *Aramiy oveid avi,* "The Aramean [Laban] seeking to destroy my father," a sentiment expanded upon in this *Tzei ulemad* passage, where we are given an insight into the true feelings and intentions of Laban.

From one phrase used by Laban, we may infer that he did indeed harbor violent intentions towards Jacob. After Jacob had fled, and Laban had pursued after him, Laban says, "I had it in my power to do you harm" (Genesis 31:29).

Miraculously, God frustrated those intentions, enabling Jacob to escape with his family. However, no sooner had he left Laban, when he received the news that Esau was on the way to attack him (Genesis 32:7). Thus, the life of Jacob–Israel encapsulates within it the future experiences of his offspring that, "in every generation they rise against us to destroy us."

### 353.  Is that meaning of the phrase *Aramiy oveid avi* beyond any shadow of doubt?

It is interesting that you should mention that, because the great Bible commentator, Abraham ibn Ezra (see his comment on Deuteronomy 26:5), discounts that interpretation entirely, on the grounds that *oveid* is not a transitive verb (i.e., it cannot take a direct object). He rightly states that:

> If Laban was the subject of the phrase, then the Hebrew would have to be rendered *Aramiy ma'avid* or *me'abeid avi*. Furthermore, what is the sense in saying that my father went down to Egypt because of the fact that Laban wished to destroy him, when that was patently not the reason why Jacob settled in that country.
>
> I incline to the view, therefore, that the "Aramean" referred to is actually Jacob, in the sense of "the one who sojourned in Aram [Mesopotamia]," and that the phrase *Aramiy oveid avi* means, actually, "an impoverished Aramean was my father."

Ibn Ezra views the continuation "and he went down to Egypt," not as an immediate consequence of what Laban did to Jacob, but as referring to a much later period when that "impoverished Aramean" settled there to join his son, Joseph.

It is on the basis of Ibn Ezra's interpretation that many translators prefer to render the phrase *Aramiy oveid avi* as "A wandering Aramean was my father."

### 354.  But, if Ibn Ezra is, strictly, correct, and the meaning is, simply, "a wandering Aramean," then where does our Haggadah get its tradition from, that "Laban wished to uproot Jacob"? Surely that is based on understanding the biblical verse *Aramiy oveid* as, "The Aramean [Laban] wished to destroy my father"?

This is a crucial point, which goes to the heart of the midrashic approach. We are now able to see that Ibn Ezra follows the literal sense of the biblical verse, whereas the midrashic approach, contained in our Haggadah, allows itself to become liberated from the grammatical and syntactical constraints, and to give interpretations based merely upon applied meanings and root-associations of phrases and words.

### 355.  But, surely, even according to the midrashic interpretation, there is no basis in the text for understanding *"oveid"* in the sense of "wishing" to destroy.

Rashi, who follows the midrashic rendering, deals with this problem, and comments: "Because it was in Laban's mind to destroy Jacob, God accounted it as if he had actually perpetrated the deed; for God reckons even the evil intentions of the heathens as if they had actually carried out their plans."

Hence the text has *Aramiy oveid avi,* which the Midrash renders as, "The Aramean destroyed my father," even though, in reality, it remained an unfulfilled desire.

**356. But, at the risk of laboring the point even further, is it not strange, to say the least, that on Seder night, when we should be focusing on Pharaoh as the villain of the piece, we are actually painting Laban in even blacker colors, saying that, by comparison with Laban, who wished to destroy everyone, Pharoah was really not so bad: after all, he "only" wished to destroy the males!**

It indeed seems totally incomprehensible, unless, that is, we view it as a typical example of midrashic propaganda. We have to realise that the early talmudic Sages frequently employed Midrash as a vehicle to disseminate their views on political issues of the day. Hence, they often superimpose onto the biblical canvas ideas and issues that could in no way be regarded as authentic "history," but that enabled them to reinterpret the biblical events as reflecting the concerns of their own talmudic era, with its stresses and strains.

Professor Louis Finkelstein has brilliantly demonstrated the political background which formed the backcloth and rationale for the creation of this Midrash, which apparently extols Pharaoh over and above Laban (L. Finkelstein, "The Oldest Midrash: Pre-Rabbinic Ideals and Teachings in the Passover Haggadah," *Harvard Theological Review* 31, 1938: 291).

He traces it back to the period following the death of Alexander the Great (323 B.C.E.), and the division of his Middle Eastern conquests between his generals, Ptolemy and Seleucus. The Ptolemaic dynasty ruled Egypt; the Seleucids established themselves in Syria and Mesopotamia. Both sides had designs upon Palestine, the strategic buffer state between them. Palestine changed hands several times, bringing the devastation of war and poverty each time to its hapless population. In 301 B.C.E. it finally fell to Ptolemy I of Egypt, and his descendants managed to repulse several Seleucid attempts, over the next hundred years, to wrest control of it from the Ptolemies.

Finkelstein attributes the *Tzei ulemad* composition to that period of Ptolemaic, Egyptian rule of Judaea. The author of the composition wished to ingratiate the Jews with their conquerors, and to demonstrate their loyalty to Egypt and their antipathy to the enemies of the Egyptian Ptolemies, namely the Syrian (Aramean) Seleucids. The way he chose to do that was to tone down the wickedness of the Egyptians, implying that Jewry could readily come to terms with Egypt, a situation that could never happen in relation to our ultimate enemy, the Seleucid Syrians, symbolized by Laban.

The author of this polemical Midrash clearly had to reinterpret the simple, grammatical meaning of the phrase, *Aramiy oveid avi* ("A wandering Aramean was my father") since that would have identified Jacob as an Aramean, that is, a Seleucid Syrian. He had to attribute the reference to Laban, and was therefore constrained to render the phrase in the sense of "The Aramean [Laban] *sought to destroy* my father."

**357. Can any other parts of the *Tzei ulemad* passage be related to that period?**

Finkelstein sees the reference to Jacob being "coerced by divine direction" *(annus al piy ha-dibbur)* to go down to Egypt as also representing a political Midrash. Its motivation, he believes, was to discourage the Jews of the third and second centuries

B.C.E. from leaving Judaea to settle in Egypt, where the standard of living and the prospects of work were so much greater. Hence the Midrash stresses that father Jacob would never have taken up residence in Egypt had it not been for divine intervention and coercion in a unique crisis situation. Even then, says the Midrash, "Jacob did not go down to Egypt with the intention of *settling* there, but merely to sojourn there for a short period," until the famine in Canaan had passed. The implication was clearly that fellow Judaeans should follow Jacob's example and only leave if truly coerced to do so.

## *BIMTEI ME'AT:* "FEW IN NUMBER"

**358. Does the continuation of the exposition, *Bimtei me'at,* also have a political motivation?**

According to Finkelstein, it does. The statement, "The Israelites were distinct *[metzuyyanim]* there" is a plea for the Jews who had settled in Ptolemaic Egypt, not to assimilate, but to follow the example of their ancestors, who strove to keep their religious identity at all times.

## *METZUYYANIM:* "DISTINCT"

**359. In what way were the Israelites "distinct" in Egypt?**

The Rabbis had a tradition that the Israelites were distinct in four ways: they did not exchange their Hebrew names for Egyptian names, they did not exchange their Hebrew language for Egyptian, they did not abandon their religious traditions, and they did not change their distinctive clothing for Egyptian fashion. One may assume that the last factor probably reflected the talmudic Sages' opposition to Roman apparel, which may have started to become fashionable among the young Jews of their day.

## *VARAV:* "AND NUMEROUS"

**360. What is the meaning of that abstruse and rather erotic verse from Ezekiel (16:7), which is quoted in order to explain the meaning of the word *Varav* ("and numerous") in the *Aramiy oveid avi* verse?**

The author of this exposition interprets the sense of *Varav* not in its usual sense, as "numerous," but rather as "fertile." The root of the word rav is *ravav,* "to grow, to increase," so the notion of fertility is, indeed, well founded.

Now, that Ezekiel passage describes Israel's rapid rate of growth, from small beginnings, in terms of the dense "vegetation of the field." The meaning of that illustration is that just as a plant's growth is fostered by pruning, so the Egyptian attempt to cut Israel down, and prune her numerically, had the diametrically opposite effect.

Mixing his metaphors, Ezekiel then proceeds to use the imagery of the female form, in its postpubescent stage, as a symbol of the virility and beauty that characterized Israel's early development in Egypt: "And you came to full womanhood; your breasts became firm and your hair grew, but still you were naked and exposed." The motif of nakedness is probably an echo of the state of Adam and Eve at the dawn of Creation. Israel was also vulnerable in Egypt to the allure of the forbidden fruits of an alien culture and civilisation.

She was also without Torah and merit. So God gave her two *mitzvot* to perform, in order to earn her redemption: the ritual of *milah* (circumcision) and the *Korban Pesach* (Paschal lamb). Both necessitated the release of blood; and that is alluded to in the continuation of the Ezekiel verse, which refers to two types of life-giving blood: "And I came by, and saw you wallowing in your blood, and I said unto you: In your blood, live; Yea I said unto you: In your blood, live" (v. 6).

## *BEFAREKH:* "WITH RIGOR"

**361. On the exposition of the phrase, *Va-yaanunu* (Deuteronomy 26:6), "And they afflicted us," the Haggadah quotes the prooftext, "All the work which the Egyptians imposed upon the Israelites was done *befarekh* [with rigor]" (Exodus 1:13). What is the precise implication of that term?**

Some commentators understand that the implication of this "rigorous work" was that, although Israel's enslavement in Egypt was reduced to 210 years (the 400 being calculated from the birth of Isaac), nevertheless, the severity of that enslavement was equivalent to 400 years of general subservience to a foreign power (see also question 48).

## *VA-YAR ET ONYEINU:* "AND HE SAW OUR AFFLICTION"

**362. In the continuation of this lengthy Midrash, the Haggadah draws parallels between the potted history of the Egyptian saga, as described in the *Arami oveid avi* formulation, and the actual verses in Exodus (ch. 2). Most of the parallels are straightforward, but some are abstruse. How does the Haggadah derive the Israelites' forced abstinence from marital intercourse from the verse, *Va-yar et onyeinu,* "And He saw our affliction" (Deuteronomy 26:7).**

Employing the common midrashic device of "like-word linking," the Haggadist links the word *va-yar* here with the identical word in Exodus 2:25, "And God saw [*Va-yar Elokim*] the children of Israel, and God knew [*va-yeidah Elokim*]." The Haggadist understands the latter phrase to mean that God noted an oppression that only "God knew," namely, one that was of a concealed and intimate nature. In biblical Hebrew, the verb "to know" is also employed as a euphemism for marital intercourse (see Genesis 4:1). So the Haggadist is also interpreting the phrase *va-yeidah Elokim* as "God noted the [prevention of] intercourse."

## VE-ET AMALEINU: "AND OUR TOIL"

**363.  How does the Haggadist derive the meaning of "These are the children [*eilu ha-banim*]" from the phrase, *ve-et amaleinu* ["And our toil"]?**

This is clearly related to his explanation of the previous phrase *(et onyeinu)* as denoting forced abstinence from marital intercourse. He now explains how this was achieved, namely by the imposition of unremitting toil *(amaleinu)*, which meant that the Israelites came home totally exhausted, and too weak to engage in marital relations. This serious reduction in the birthrate as a result of their toil is what the Haggadah means here. Again, we should understand *eilu ha-banim,* as in the previous interpretation, in the sense of "These are the *[absence of]* children."

## LO AL YEDEI MAL'AKH: "NOT BY MEANS OF AN ANGEL"

**364.  How can the Haggadist possibly interpret the verse, "And God brought us out of Egypt" to mean, "Not by means of an angel or a Seraph or a representative, but the Holy One, blessed be He, Himself, in His glory," when the Torah itself states that "God sent an angel and brought us out of Egypt" (Numbers 20:16), and when just such an intermediary is referred to as "going before the Israelites when they went out of Egypt" (Exodus 14:19)?**

Indeed, there is no denying that God employed His intermediaries during the period of the actual Exodus. The point that is being made here is that the "signs and wonders," and the actual plagues inflicted upon the Egyptians, were all initiated and carried out exclusively by God Himself. This reached its apogee with the climactic plague of the death of the firstborn; and hence the verse describing that plague is quoted here *(Ve-avartiy be'eretz mitzrayim)* to indicate the emphasis it contains on God's direct activity: "I [Myself] passed over the land of Egypt on that night, and I [Myself] smote every firstborn . . . and against every god of Egypt I [Myself] executed justice, I [alone] am the Lord" (Exodus 12:12).

The overemphasis here on God's direct activity seems to be a conscious piece of polemic, on the part of the Haggadist, against the preoccupation with angelology that characterized the early pharisaic period. Already in the late biblical books of Zechariah and Daniel, and, in more developed form, in the postbiblical books of the Apocrypha, angels appear as independent beings, with their own personal names and distinguishable traits. With the rise of Jewish sects, such as the Qumran Covenanters, a developed system of angelology undergirds their apocalyptic vision.

The popular obsession with such ideas would well have alarmed the Orthodox, pharisaic authorities of the period, struggling hard to promote pure monotheism among uneducated masses for whom angelic intermediaries exercized great fascination, and represented a less awesome and most convenient and accessible agency of intercession. Seder night was an occasion not to be missed in the mainstream fight against such sectarian ideas.

## SPILLING OUT THE WINE

**365. Do we tip out some wine when we recite the words, *Dam va-eish vetimrat ashan*?**

We tip out wine three times at this stage, once for each of the three words of that biblical verse (Joel 3:3). Some Sephardim are most superstitious about this wine, that, according to the interpretation of the verse, refers primarily to the "wonder" of the first of the Ten Plagues, the plague of blood. Since we are not permitted to partake of blood, they are particular that this wine, together with the other wine poured out for the recitation of the Ten Plagues, should be collected in a bowl and properly disposed of. They then fill up the wine glasses, ready for the second cup.

**366. Is there any special way in which this wine should be spilt out?**

Moses Isserles, in his *Darkei Mosheh* (473:18), states that, "because it represents the finger of God, one should use one's forefinger, and not, as some sources recommend, the little finger." Isaac Luria, founder of the mystical circle at Safed in the sixteenth century, was particular that one should not use any finger, but spill out the wine from the glass onto a saucer.

**367. We mentioned above that some were superstitious about the wine spilt from the glass. Did any superstition extend also to the wine remaining in the cup?**

We do have sources that refer to some superstitions in relation to the remaining wine. Rabbi Jacob ben Judah, the author of the *Etz Chayyim*, a twelfth-century liturgical work, reflecting the French and pre-Expulsion English traditions, states that his father-in-law, after spilling out the wine for the plagues, would pour away the remaining wine. He would then wash out the wine goblet, and fill it up with fresh wine.

**368. What is the reason for the custom of pouring away the wine three times: at *Dam va-eish*, for the Ten Plagues, and for Rabbi Judah's mnemonic?**

We can see from the foregoing that it was generally understood to symbolize the freely flowing blood of the Egyptians.

Indeed, Rabbi Shemtob Gaguine (see *Keter Shem Tov,* London: author, 1948, pp. 130–131) unequivocally attributes the practice of pouring out the wine to the superstitious belief in the *Ayin ha-ra* (evil eye), namely, that the mere act of refering to such destructive forces could have the effect of reactivating and unleashing them.

It was for this reason that Jews universally uttered formulae calculated to deflect the evil eye whenever reference was made to unpleasant matters or tragic occurrences. Hence the Yiddish interjections, *Gott zol ophitten* ("God should protect us!"), *Nisht af dir gezukt* ("It should never be said of you!") or *Zol nit traffen ba dir* ("It should never happen to you!").

Since the references to the devastating plagues have been uttered over the goblets of wine, there was a superstitious fear that a destructive germ might have been released into that wine. Hence some of it is skimmed off, or, as we have mentioned, in some communities, the entire goblet is emptied and cleansed. The pouring out also indicates that the destruction should befall our enemies, but not, God forbid, those around the table.

In the course of time, however, perhaps to wean people away from the type of superstition we have described, a new interpretation is popularized, namely that it is simply a gesture of sympathy with the suffering Egyptians, indicative of the fact that our own cup of salvation is depleted at the thought of the punishments they had to suffer. This is in keeping with the words of the Book of Proverbs, "When your enemy falls do not rejoice, and when he stumbles let not your heart exult" (24:17).

## RABBI JUDAH'S ACRONYM

**369. What was the purpose of Rabbi Judah giving his generation an acronym (*simanim*) to help them remember the order of the plagues? Surely any child can recite them in their proper order.**

There are several popular explanations to account for Rabbi Judah's particular division of the Ten Plagues into just those three particular groups: three, three, and four. For we do, in fact, find that the plagues within those three groups are marked by specific characteristics.

The first three plagues were administered by Aaron, utilizing his staff. The subsequent three plagues were initiated by Moses, but without using his staff; whereas the last four were brought by Moses by means of his staff. Another difference is that, before the first two plagues in each of Rabbi Judah's three groups, Pharaoh was given a clear warning of their impending arrival, which was not the case with the third plagues of each group.

**370. But if that was the main point of Rabbi Judah's, why then did he not spell out that reason for his tripartite subdivision? The simple introductory statement, "Rabbi Judah would give an acronym for them," surely suggests no more than that he was providing an easy way of remembering the order of the plagues for people who could not remember them! Surely, then, the necessity for the provision of such a basic acronym must lie in that area of popular ignorance of Torah?**

A plausible explanation along those very lines is, in fact, offered by Solomon Zeitlin (see S. Zeitlin, "The liturgy of the First Night of Passover," *Jewish Quarterly Review* [n.s.] 38 [1948]: 455), inspired by an idea quoted in the name of Rabbi Judah He-Chasid, the leader of the twelfth century German pietistic movement.

He reminds us that the conditions of our own day, with every congregant being supplied with a *chumash* (Pentateuch), at Hebrew classes and synagogue, and probably possessing one at home, was not the case in antiquity. Before the age of printing (fifteenth century) only the very wealthy would have been able to afford a handwritten manuscript. Without books, the masses were largely illiterate.

Furthermore, we must not forget that in ancient Israel the custom was to follow a triennial cycle for the Reading of the Law in synagogue each week. As the reading of the Torah had to be stretched over three years, unlike our annual cycle, it followed that their weekly reading of the *Sidra* was much shorter than ours. Thus, the average person, forgetful of what he had learnt in his youth at Hebrew school, would only hear the account of the Ten Plagues read in synagogue once every three years. Even then, he would not have possessed a printed *chumash* to read it through in the original, and to have all the details of the episode reinforced. We must not make the assumption, therefore, that they would automatically have known the correct order of the plagues.

Since long before the standardization of the Haggadah, Rabbi Judah regarded it as important that people should recite the Ten Plagues, it was essential for him to remind them of the proper order in which they occurred.

**371. But could there really have been any confusion regarding the order of the plagues? Surely someone around the table could have been expected to have known the proper order?**

In truth, this could not have been assumed, for the very good reason that variant orders, and even numbers, of the plagues abounded, even in such authoritative sources as the book of Psalms, with which the masses were more familiar, since they recited them more widely than is our practice in their synagogue liturgy.

This can be illustrated with reference to Psalm 78, which describes the plagues inflicted against the Egyptians, but which omits as many as three of the plagues, namely, lice, boils, and darkness. This is compensated for by the enumeration of a further eight plagues (caterpillars, frost, fiery bolts, fierce divine anger, wrath, indignation, trouble, and messengers of evil), making a total of fifteen plagues.

The same confusion occurs in Psalm 105, where only eight of the plagues are mentioned, with no reference to pestilence or boils. The first-century Jewish renegade and historian, Josephus Flavius, in his *Antiquities of the Jews* (ch. 14), enumerates only nine of the plagues, omitting the fifth; and the extracanonical *Book of Jubilees* (48:5) places boils before pestilence.

We can now see how easy it was for the uneducated masses of the early talmudic period of Rabbi Judah to have been either totally ignorant of the biblical account of the plagues, or to have been totally confused by the varying literary sources and traditions being quoted by all and sundry regarding their precise number and order: hence the importance of Rabbi Judah's *simanim*.

## HOW MANY PLAGUES?

**372. The next few sections comprise attempts, by Rabbi Jose the Galilean, Rabbi Eliezer, and Rabbi Akivah, to prove that the ten biblical plagues represent only**

the kernel of a much greater torrent of plagues visited upon the Egyptians. What is the basis and purpose of this type of exposition?

It was the realization that the miracle of the drowning of the Egyptians by the Red Sea was also an important facet—indeed the climactic stage—of the Exodus. Those Sages believed, therefore, that we should not focus exclusively on the Ten Plagues, but should also take account of the other miracles performed at the Red Sea.

After the drowning of the Egyptians, the Torah states that, "The Israelites saw the great hand which God wielded *against the Egyptians [bemitzrayim],* and the people feared the Lord, and believed in the Lord and in Moses His servant" (Exodus 15:31). Now, the Hebrew *bemitzrayim* may also mean "in Egypt." The meaning would then be that, only after their ultimate redemption, by the Red Sea, did the Israelites attain to true faith. Even during the period of the Ten Plagues, they were apprehensive and had doubts about whether or not Moses could lead them to freedom. So the Ten Plagues and the miracles by the sea were as much a test of the Israelites' faith as they were a punishment of the Egyptians. For that reason, those three Sages felt that all the signs, wonders, and plagues, in Egypt and by the Red Sea, have to be considered as an integrated unit; and for that reason they felt it was important to have a clear idea of how many divine manifestations it took to convince our ancestors that they could have implicit faith in God and in Moses as His servant.

**373. But does there not seem to be an element of gloating here over the volume of plagues inflicted upon our enemies, which would be in direct conflict with the verse we quoted above, "When your enemy falls do not rejoice"?**

This was never in the minds of those three Sages. One popular reason for attempting to discover more and more plagues was in order to turn it to the greatest advantage of Israel. This was because, but a few days after the drowning of the Egyptians in the Red Sea, God promised that, "None of the disasters that I imposed upon the Egyptians shall I put upon you" (Exodus 15:26). Hence, the more extensive the scope of the plagues, the greater the protection afforded to Israel. Hence the exercise indulged in by those three Sages was for national self-interest, rather than out of an antipathy towards Israel's enemies.

## DAYYEINU

**374. Is there any significance in the number of benefits that are listed in the *Dayyeinu* composition?**

According to the Vilna Gaon there are fifteen benefits referred to. The number fifteen is significant on the following grounds: it corresponds to (i) the mystical doctrine of fifteen gradations between heaven and earth—the seven heavens, the separating layers of atmosphere between each heaven, and the groundwork of earth; (ii) the fifteen *Shir Ha-Ma'alot,* Psalms (120–134) of Degrees; (iii) the fifteen steps of the Jerusalem Temple, separating the Court of the Women, on the lower level, from the Court of the Israelites; (iv) the fifteen generations from Abraham, who took his son to Mount Moriah, until Solomon, who built the Temple there.

We may add to that list, (v) the fifteen morning blessings of *Birkot Ha-Shachar*, recited at the beginning of our daily prayers; and, (vi) the fifteen successive epithets of praise found in the *Emet Veyatziv* blessing after the *Shema*.

**375. Every line in the *Dayyeinu* composition offers a couplet of benefits, and makes the point that, had only one been conferred, then *dayyeinu*, "it would have sufficed." There is one line, however, that cannot be understood properly in this sense, namely, "Had God brought us near to Mount Sinai but had not given us the Torah, it would have sufficed." How could it possibly have sufficed, when there would have been absolutely no point in bringing Israel near to that place if it was not to confer upon her the Torah?**

The present writer has attempted elsewhere (see J. M. Cohen, *Moments of Insight*, London: Vallentine, Mitchell & Co., 1989, pp. 64–68) to resolve this problem by understanding the Hebrew phrase – *illu keirvanu lifney har Sinai* ("Had God brought us near to Mount Sinai") – in a slightly different sense.

I have demonstrated, from several biblical and rabbinic sources, that the verb *karav*, normally rendered "to bring near," sometimes has the particular nuance of "unique and intimate proximity; self-disclosure." This proximity may be either physical or spiritual. In the physical sense, it explains why this verb is used as a euphemism for sexual intercourse, as in the verse, "And Abimelekh was not intimate [*lo karav*] with her" (Genesis 20:4), or again, "None of you shall indulge in intimacy [*lo tikrevu*] with any that is near of kin" (Leviticus 18:6).

In the spiritual sense, we have the noun *kirvah* used to denote the closest possible relationship with God, as in the verse, *kirvat Elokim liy tov*, "God's proximity is good unto me" (Psalm 73:28). Again, in Psalm 148:14 we have an ascending spiritual gradation:

> He has raised up a horn for His people *(le'amo)*,
> A praise for all His saints *(chasidav)*,
> For Israel, a people in the closest proximity *(am kerovo)*.

Thus, *karav*, denotes the very highest spiritual stage, even beyond that of *chasid*.

Elsewhere in the Haggadah itself we find that special nuance clearly reflected in the line, "Originally our forefathers were idolators, but now God has brought us close [*keirvanu*] to His service."

In the light of this special nuance of the verb *karav*, our problem verse in *Dayyeinu* takes on a new dimension which solves our problem. It may now be rendered, "Had God made us experience a close personal proximity before Mount Sinai [*Illu keirvanu lifnei har Sinai*], but without having given us a Torah, it would have sufficed." The presumption is that God could actually have raised Israel to the same lofty spiritual gradation without having given them a tangible, written Torah. He could have inspired them spiritually with His mere proximity. That revelatory experience alone could have galvanized a permanent bond of religious loyalty, as it did with the patriarchs.

The fact that God chose rather to give us a tangible Torah, to inspire and challenge us intellectually, to enable us to give free rein to our creation in His image, and to bring that image into sharper focus through the prism of His Torah, is a special boon deserving of our extra and eternal gratitude.

## RABBAN GAMALIEL *HAYAH OMEIR*

**376. What does Rabban Gamaliel mean by saying that, "Whosoever does not recite these three things on Pesach has not fulfilled his duty"? Which particular duty is he referring to?**

It is probable that the author of this statement was Rabban Gamaliel the Elder, grandson of Hillel, who lived in the most turbulent period, a few decades before the destruction of the Temple. He could certainly not have meant that unless one actually verbalizes the meaning why we eat the Paschal lamb, the *matzah* and the *maror,* then one does not fulfill the *mitzvah* of eating them, as that would not reflect the halakhic reality!

It would also be difficult to assume that he was making obligatory such an accompanying explanation of those three *mitzvot,* in order to heighten *kavanah,* religious concentration, since we do not find such a prerequisite in relation to any other *mitzvah* in the Torah! The reason for the *mitzvah* of dwelling in the *sukkah* is expressly stated in the Torah—"That your generations may know that in *sukkahs* I made the Children of Israel to dwell when I brought them out of the land of Egypt" (Leviticus 23:43)—and yet, there is absolutely no obligation to repeat that explanation of the *mitzvah* while performing it!

Some scholars view Rabban Gamaliel's statement as a polemical broadside, aimed at the early Christian sects of his day who were taking to eating those three foods in commemoration of Jesus's last supper (see Goldschmidt, *The Passover Haggadah,* p. 52). For those sects, the three foods were already taking on a symbolic meaning: The Paschal lamb represented the one who was taken to the crucifixion as the "lamb of God." The *matzah* wafers represented, as they still do in the Church's Communion, his body; and the *maror* symbolizes the bitterness of the suffering that he endured. Alarmed by such ideas, Rabban Gamaliel introduced an unprecedented measure, namely the necessity of explaining publicly the precise—and traditional—reason why we are obliged to eat these foods. This would have constituted a further measure to isolate the early Christian sectarians from the mainstream community which they were trying to infiltrate. They could hardly join a traditional Seder, knowing that they would have to suppress their own interpretation, and would be called upon to affirm the traditional explanation of these foods.

We know from talmudic sources that Rabban Gamaliel was most zealous to outlaw any sectarian or non-Orthodox propaganda, and hence he decreed that an unauthorized *Targum* on the book of Job should be buried under the Temple foundations (Talmud *Shabbat* 115a). It is consistent with such an approach, therefore, that he should have demanded that Seder leaders lay inordinate stress on the Orthodox explanation of Pesach, *matzah,* and *maror,* given its new sectarian slant.

The present writer inclines rather to the view that Rabban Gamaliel was addressing the politically turbulent situation of his day, when there would have been a dramatic falling off in the number of pilgrims, from around the country and the wider Diaspora, coming to celebrate Pesach at Jerusalem. The Talmud (*Rosh Hashanah* 11b) refers to Gamaliel dictating letters to his scribe Jochanan, to be sent to the communities of the upper and lower Galilee, to those of southern Palestine and to those in the Babylonian Diaspora. The necessity for such a method of communication suggests a period when the regular festival pilgrimage visits of community Sages and leaders had ceased, and direct verbal communication was no longer possible.

We may conjecture that Gamaliel was reacting to reports that many had abandoned the proper observance of Seder night, and that, remaining at home and unable to partake of the Pesach, they were also dispensing with the ritual of *matzah* and *maror,* since the Torah regards the three as a unity to be eaten together (Exodus 12:8). Hence Gamaliel, zealous to maintain the tradition of the Seder in Jewish homes, would announce each year (this is the special force of the words *hayah omeir*) that nonparticipation in the eating of the Paschal lamb ritual at Jerusalem is not an excuse for nonobservance at home.

Gamaliel would go even further, and state that, in the present emergency circumstances and in order to keep the flame of the Seder observance burning, "Those who do not celebrate a Seder, the minimum definition of which is the formal exposition of the significance of the three biblical foods, have not fulfilled their duty." The particular "duty" is precisely that "recitation," which Gamaliel would have derived from the verse, "And you *shall declare,* 'It is the Paschal sacrifice to the Lord who passed over the houses of the Children of Israel' " (Exodus 12:27).

**377. In Rabban Gamaliel's Pesach section, the verse just quoted, from Exodus 12:27, seems to contain an unnecessary repetition: "It is the Paschal sacrifice to the Lord who passed over the houses of the children of Israel . . . and saved our houses." Is there any explanation of the double reference?**

Some commentators explain this on the basis of the midrashic tradition that, before the last plague was due to strike, many Egyptians brought their firstborn children to the homes of the Israelites, hoping naively that they would gain refuge there and escape the plague. Hence the verse tells us that God passed over "the houses of the Children of Israel"—referring to houses where there were only Israelites present. "And He saved our houses" is a reference to those houses that contained both Egyptian as well as Israelite firstborn. The plague only struck the Egyptians sheltering therein, and "saved [the rest of] our houses."

**378. In Rabban Gamaliel's *matzah* section, there seem to be two different reasons being offered for eating *matzah.* How is this to be explained?**

That indeed seems to be the case. The first explanation alludes to the *matzah* baked *while still in Egypt,* and refers to the fact that "our forefathers' dough did not have time to become leaven before the Holy One . . . appeared and redeemed them." However, the subsequent prooftext speaks of the dough that they baked *subsequent to the Exodus:* "And they baked unleavened bread from the dough *which they had taken with them from Egypt,* for it was not leavened, because they were thrust out of Egypt and could not stay behind and prepare food for the journey."

The explanation of this is that we are being provided with a double rationale: the first, of why we have a *mitzvah* to eat *matzah* on Seder night, namely, because the Israelites did not have time to allow their dough to rise that night; and the second, a rationale of why we are bidden to eat *matzot* for the entire seven days (eight in the Diaspora) of the festival, namely, because of the *matzah* that they baked subsequently as fare for their journey.

**379. Are not the final two items of the "Pesach—*matzah*—*maror*" sequence in the wrong chronological order? If *matzah* symbolizes freedom and *maror*, the bitterness of the oppression, should we not then relate the significance of *maror* before that of *matzah*?**

It is perhaps for that reason that Maimonides (*Mishneh Torah, Hilkhot Chametz Umatzah* 8:4) reverses the order. However, Rav Ovadiah Yosef provides a plausible rationale of our order (see *Chazon Ovadiah,* p. 254). He states that *matzah* stands independently as a binding biblical *mitzvah* in our day, whereas *maror* is inextricably connected to the eating of the Paschal lamb, and in our day (when we have no Paschal lamb) it remains binding only by rabbinic law. Hence *matzah* takes priority in the order of recitation, as it does in the order in which we eat the two symbolic foods.

Rav Yosef quotes later authorities who explain the order psychologically. Although *matzah* represents redemption, yet there is what we presently call "the survivor syndrome," a delayed trauma from the opening up of the emotional scar tissue. Hence, even after tasting the *matzah* of liberation, there is likely to remain the vivid recollections and residual taste of the *maror.*

He concludes on the note that the redemption from Egypt was not destined to be the final and lasting redemption; and that is symbolized by the eating of *maror* after the *matzah.* However, the final symbolic act is to eat the *Afikoman matzah,* to indicate that there will ultimate come about a lasting, messianic redemption, after which there will be no further bitter experiences. Hence the regulation, *Ein maftirin achar ha-Pesach Afikoman,* that "there is nothing more to be eaten after the *Afikoman,* the [*matzah*] symbol of the ultimate redemption."

## *BEKHOL DOR VADOR:* "IN EVERY GENERATION"

**380. In the next section, *Bekhol dor vador,* we are told to regard ourselves as if we personally had come out of Egypt, and in the following passage, Lefikhakh, we are asked to praise "the One who performed, *both for our fathers and for us* all those miracles." But, if we are honest, can we truly say that we can feel an identity and empathy with a generation of our ancestors who lived over three thousand years ago?**

It is a difficult question, and its answer will vary according to the degree of sensitivity and emotional identity that Jews have with their history. There are some people, who, regretfully, feel little empathy or kinship with their own immediate, let alone wider, family. It depends upon complex emotional needs and other factors. One who is immersed in Jewish sources, and absorbed in the study of Jewish history, is far more likely to feel the emotional draw, and far more likely to view him or herself as a link in the meaningful chain of Jewish history, stretching back to the formative period of our ancestors in Egypt. One who observes the Torah – the same Torah as given to them at Sinai some three months after the Exodus – is far more likely to feel a sense of shared responsibility and spiritual destiny. So the answer must be: yes, under certain, rarefied circumstances.

An interesting illustration of this was provided shortly after the discovery, in Cornwall, England, in 1994, of the body of a man, preserved in ice for over five thousand years. A DNA search revealed that a young Cornish lady shared a direct genetic relationship. In an interview she stated: "One normally thinks only of one's parents and grandparents as members of one's family. I now feel that sense of identity with someone two hundred generations back!"

The Jewish people have a prouder boast, and a more compelling reason to feel an identity and relationship with ancestors who lived a few thousand years ago. For we have the surviving testimony of our forebears, in the form of the Bible, the Mishnah, the Talmud, and the medieval codes of law, the legacy that those men of the spirit left to their offspring. They did not leave us estates and lands, which can be taken away by marauders and invaders and benefit only their richer offspring. They left us a spiritual and ethical heritage, the account of their encounter with God and the fruits of their dialogue with His word. They left it to every Jew, as a precious gift and an incomparable challenge.

We are what we are as a people, only because we have drunk deeply of the wells they have dug. Our wealth is their literary and spiritual legacy. The lady from Cornwall did not know a single thing about the history, the religious observances, the nature of her ancient ancestor. We even know the names of ours: Moses, Aaron, Miriam, Joshua, Saul, David, Solomon, Isaiah, Jeremiah, Ezekiel, Ezra, Nehemiah, Judah the Maccabee, Hillel, Rabban Gamaliel, Rabbi Judah Ha-Nasi, and so on. We know, in many instances, the names of their wives, children, and brothers. We know, from the talmudic and midrashic records, their professions and the agonies and ecstasies of their lives.

It is truly not difficult emotionally to transport ourselves back in time, and to see reality "as if we ourselves had come out of Egypt," as if God had, indeed, performed the miracles for us also.

## LEFIKHAKH: "THEREFORE"

**381. But for those who cannot feel that empathy with bygone generations, can they make any response at all to a challenge like that contained in this *Lefikhakh* paragraph?**

The advice to such people would be to reinterpret it in the light of the recent history of our people in the land of Israel. The hand of God has been visible on the many occasions when our people were confronted, not just with an advancing Egyptian army, as in the case of the Israelites, but with the advancing—and numerically, vastly superior—forces of five Arab armies.

The teeming millions of enemies that surround Israel and the vast financial resources and stockpiles of military hardware at their disposal have still failed to give them any qualitative edge, or undermine her national confidence. They have also failed to impede her incredible achievement of *kibbutz galuyyot,* ingathering her exiled and oppressed children from the far-flung lands of their dispersal. No greater "miracle" has ever been achieved since the Exodus from Egypt. We, in our day, are witnesses to a second Exodus, no less wonderful or heroic than the first.

The Jew who can only identify with recent history can assuredly recite the sentiments of this passage, and bless the Lord, "Who performed all these miracles for our fathers *and for us.* He has brought us forth from bondage to liberty, from sorrow to joy, from mourning to festivity, from deep darkness to bright light, and from slavery to freedom. Therefore let us recite a new song before Him, Halleluyah!"

## HALLEL: "PSALMS OF PRAISE"

### 382. Where are the next two paragraphs taken from?

The paragraphs beginning *Halleluyah hallelu avdey* and *Betzeit yisrael mim-itzrayim* are the opening two psalms (113 and 114) of *Hallel,* the psalms of praise and thanksgiving that we recite on minor and major festivals of our religious calendar.

Its theme is most appropriate to Pesach. The opening phrase, *Hallelu avdey Ha-Shem,* "Praise, O you servants of God," suggests a people that has been redeemed from being servants of Pharaoh, and who have become liberated to become exclusively servants of God. The second paragraph contains an even more direct reference, "When Israel went out of Egypt. . . ."

One marked difference between the recitation of *Hallel* during prayer and its recitation on Seder night is that during the former we are obliged to stand, whereas on Seder night it is permitted to remain seated as a symbol of freedom. Another reason offered for this concession is because we are not reciting it fully and with its usual blessing, but are splitting it up, by reciting its first two psalms before the meal, and the rest after the Grace after Meals.

*Hallel* is recited over the second cup of wine, which is raised before the *Lefikhakh* paragraph which precedes it and serves as its introduction.

### 383. Why is *Hallel* divided up in this way?

It is not possible to answer this with any certainty. We know from the Mishnah (*Pesachim* 5:7) that *Hallel* was recited during the period of the second Temple as an accompaniment to the slaughtering of the Paschal lamb on the afternoon preceding

Pesach, and then again at night, during the eating of it. We may conjecture that the splitting up of the *Hallel* at the Seder is to recall the two recitations in Temple times, in the afternoon and at night.

Another practical reason for dividing it might have been the concern for the children, expressed in a number of ways on this night, that they should not fall asleep before enjoying the Paschal lamb, and, in the post-Temple period, the meal.

There is a scholarly view (see L. Finkelstein, "The Origin of the Hallel," *Hebrew Union College Annual* 23:2 [1950–1951]: 324) that the first two psalms of the Hallel were composed as a specific praise for this festival, whereas the rest (Psalms 115–118), reflecting the politics and theology of the later, Maccabean period (second century B.C.E.), were composed for the other festival days. This would explain why only those first two psalms are recited before the meal. That was their original position, as a prelude to the eating of the Paschal lamb. When further festival *Hallel*-psalms were added, they were naturally accorded a less important place, as general concluding psalms to the meal.

**384. Why is it that we recite a blessing over *Hallel* on all other occasions, but not here in the Haggadah?**

One reason is that when we recite a blessing, we are not to interrupt until the *mitzvah* has been completed. In the case of this particular recitation of *Hallel* we are interrupting the *Hallel* for the eating of the symbolic foods and for the meal.

Another reason is that there is a difference of opinion among authorities as to whether one reciting *Hallel* privately, and not as part of the synagogue *minyan*, should recite the blessings before and after *Hallel*. We follow the view of the *Rif* that such an individual does not recite the blessings; and this explains why at the Seder, construed as a private gathering even if ten males are present, we omit those blessings. Where there is any doubt among authorities as to whether or not a blessing should be recited, we always refrain from making a potentially unnecessary blessing.

From a historical point of view, the great Geonic and later authorities did not take the view that *Hallel* required the recitation of a blessing, and it was only in the late Middle Ages that a blessing over *Hallel* was introduced. Thus, the original Passover *Hallel* was not endowed with a blessing; and even when the synagogue incorporated it, it was felt inappropriate to interfere with the nostalgia of Seder night by altering the traditional practice.

## THE CONCLUDING BLESSING

**385. We have just observed that no concluding blessing of the *Hallel* is required. But surely we do recite such a blessing, namely, *Barukh . . . asher ge'alanu vega'al et avoteinu*?**

This is not a concluding blessing over the *Hallel*, as will be obvious if we compare its contents with those of our usual concluding blessing, which refers specifically to the theme of "singing praises to God's name," and which concludes with the words *melekh mehullal batishbachot,* "a king extolled [*mehullal*] with praises." Our concluding blessing, on the other hand, makes no reference to the theme of praises. It is simply a *Geulah,* a blessing for past redemption and a hope for the future redemption. It is, therefore, to be construed as a concluding blessing not specifically over *Hallel,* but to the entire first part of the Haggadah, which we have just completed.

**386. In some Haggadot the rubric states that if Seder night occurs after the termination of *Shabbat* we reverse the order of the words *min ha-zevachim umin ha-pesachim* ("and we shall eat of the festival offerings and of the Paschal lambs"). Why is such a reversal required under these circumstances?**

This section of the Haggadah is a quotation from the Mishnah (*Pesachim* 10:6), which has *min ha-zevachim umin ha-pesachim.* This order follows the chronology of the sacrifices, wherein the *zevachim* ("festival offerings" or *chagigah*) were eaten on the day before Pesach (14th Nisan), whereas the *pesachim* ("Paschal lambs") were not eaten until after nightfall. Indeed, the rule was that the Paschal lamb had to be eaten on a stomach that was already full, with people having already eaten of the *zevachim.*

However, if we consult the version of the Mishnah that is printed together with the talmudic text (*Pesachim* 116b), we find the reverse order: *min ha-pesachim umin ha-zevachim!* A marginal note there tells us that the proper reading, however, is *min ha-zevachim umin ha-pesachim,* as in the editions of the Mishnah, and for the reason stated above.

Now, the instruction that the order be changed around on Saturday night is clearly based on an error. Indeed, Rabbi Jacob Emden, in his *Siddur Bet Ya'akov* (Lemberg: 1904, p. 249) states categorically that, "It is not necessary to change the order at any time, since when Pesach is on Saturday night no *chagigah* [festival offering] is permitted to be offered at all during *Shabbat.* We should therefore follow the version that is applicable for most occasions."

**387. So, how did that erroneous rubric, interchanging the order of the sacrifices when Pesach occurs on *Motzei Shabbat,* come into being, since it is clearly not based upon any halakhic consideration?**

It has been suggested that it arose out of a simple misinterpretation of a scribe's marginal note. After the phrase, *min ha-zevachim umin ha-pesachim,* a pedantic scribe must have added the letters *mem shin* (מ"ש), which he meant as an abbreviation for the word *Mishnah,* indicating that that is the version found in the editions of the Mishnah, as opposed to the version found in the Mishnah as quoted in the talmudic tractate, *Pesachim.* For the sake of completeness, he then proceeded to append the latter version: *min ha-pesachim umin ha-zevachim.*

A subsequent copyist, wishing to present a text with no abbreviations, mistakenly assumed that the letters *mem shin* stood for *Motzei Shabbat.* He compounded his ignorance by attaching his *"Motzei Shabbat"* rubric to the following phrase, the alternate version. Thus, many subsequent printed editions were published, all based upon that erroneous rubric which gives the impression that on *Motzei Shabbat* we reverse the order of the sacrifices!

## DRINKING THE SECOND CUP

**388. Before drinking the second cup, we are required to recite the blessing, *Borey periy ha-gafen*. But, on the basis of the principle that we do not recite unnecessary blessings, why is it necessary to recite a further blessing after we have already drunk one cup of wine?**

This is a valid point, to the extent that the *Shulchan Arukh,* reflecting Sephardic practice, states quite categorically that, "We drink here the second cup, but do not recite a blessing over it" (*Orach Chayyim* 474:1). The Ashkenazi gloss of Moses Isserles adds the caveat: "But the custom among the Ashkenazim is to recite a blessing before each and every cup . . . and that is the view of most of the Geonim."

Taz explains the Ashkenazi custom on the basis that, although we do not regard the recitation of the Haggadah as an interruption, yet, we require a separate blessing for each cup of wine for quite another reason. It is to underscore the fact that the Sages, when they instituted four separate cups of wine, intended them to be regarded as four separate *mitzvot.* The recitation of separate blessings serves to emphasize that special status.

**389. Does one have to lean while drinking this cup of wine?**

Indeed. So much so, that according to Rav Ovadiah Yosef (see *Chazon Ovadiah,* p. 154) if he drank the wine without leaning, he has to drink another cup of wine in the required position (leaning on his left side).

## WASHING OF THE HANDS

**390. We now come to the washing of the hands. What is the purpose of performing this sacred ritual?**

First, it should be known that its purpose is not to render one's hands clean. It is assumed they are clean beforehand. Two reasons are given for this ritual washing: Israel is termed "a kingdom of priests." Since the table is regarded as an altar, which atones for our sins, we perform a symbolic washing, therefore, just like the Temple priests who had to wash their hands from a laver before performing their service, which included effecting atonement for sinners through the medium of the sacrificial act. Thus, every time we wash before eating, we are reminded of our sacred priestly mission.

The second reason is a variation of the first, namely, that the ritual washing is in order to recollect the priestly obligation of washing in this way before eating the tithes and sacrificial foods, which had to be eaten in a state of purity.

### 391. How is the washing to be performed?

We have to use a glass or other container that is complete, with no cracks or perforations, and that holds sufficient water to pour freely and liberally over each hand. Rings should first be removed, so that the water will reach to every single part of every finger.

After filling the glass, we take it in our left hand and pour the water over our right hand, to reach up to the wrist. We then take it in our right hand and pour the water over our left hand. One should repeat the process once more.

While wet, we rub the hands together, raising them slightly upwards. Some recite the verse, *Se'u yedeikhem kodesh uvarkhu et ha-Shem* ("Lift up your hands in holiness and bless the Lord," Psalm 134:2), before reciting the blessing, *Barukh . . . al netilat yadayim.* After reciting the blessing, they should be dried well.

### 392. If blessings have to be recited before performing the act, why do we not recite the blessing before pouring the water over our hands?

The reason for this is in case one's hands were not properly clean before performing this ritual washing. One cannot recite a blessing with dirty hands; therefore an exception was made, and it was declared preferable to have the hands washed before reciting the blessing.

However the principle of making the blessing first is still not really compromised, since the drying of the hands is also regarded as an essential part of the *mitzvah.* Thus, by making the blessing before drying the hands it is still regarded as a blessing which preceded the *mitzvah.*

## BLESSING OVER THE *MATZAH*

### 393. How do we make the blessings over the *matzah*?

We take the three *matzot* in our hands, in their correct order: the broken piece between the two whole pieces. We then recite the *Ha-motziy* blessing, before releasing the bottom *matzah* (for use presently in the making of Hillel's sandwich). We then recite *Al akhilat matzah* over the broken piece (though while still keeping the top *matzah* in our hand), and we distribute to all present two pieces, one from each of the top two *matzot,* and together equivalent to the size of *kezayit* ("approximately an olive's size") (see *Biur Halakhah* on Mishnah *Berurah* 475:1). Since talmudic olives were much larger in size than ours, we require that both pieces should, together, be the equivalent of about the size of an egg.

### 394. Why do we take all three *matzot*?

The two whole pieces represent the *Lechem Mishneh,* the two whole loaves that we use every *Shabbat* and *Yom Tov;* the broken piece is a reminder of the *Lechem oni,* "The bread of affliction."

### 395. Do we follow the normal practice of salting the *matzot*?

There is here a difference of opinion between Ashkenazim and Sephardim. The latter, basing themselves upon one of their main authorities, Joseph Karo (see *Shulchan Arukh* 475:1), do salt the matzot, whereas Ashkenazim, following the gloss of Moses Isserles, refrain from doing so.

The reason for the Ashkenazi practice is unclear; though a recent scholar, Y. M. Ta-Shema (*Minhag Ashkenaz Ha-Kadmon*, Jerusalem: Magnes Press, Hebrew University, 1992) has offered the interesting suggestion that it is meant as a demonstration of our total indifference on this night to the dangers that, it was universally and superstitiously believed, the demonic forces could inflict.

It seems to have been common practice in medieval Franco-Germany to refrain from salting the *matzah* throughout Pesach, though no authorities could offer a plausible explanation for it. The *Tur* (Laws of Passover, section 455) states, "There is no reason to prohibit it; but, because of the principle of *Do not forsake the Law of your mother* [Proverbs 1:8], one should not change this practice."

It is clear that the reason no explanation is given in the sources is because those authorities were aware of its superstitious basis, but felt powerless to oppose a very deeply held popular superstition. The belief was that salt should be brought to the table because of its efficacy in neutralizing the malevolent intentions of the demons, which are directed particularly against humans enjoying themselves at table.

They refrained, therefore, from using salt on Seder Night—and, by extension, throughout the festival—in order to demonstrate that on this *Leyl Shimmurim* ("divinely protected night") they felt totally protected and had no fears from the demons.

## MAROR

### 396. When dipping the *maror* into the *charoset,* how much *charoset* is one meant to add?

While *charoset* is generally regarded as something of a palliative to the eye-watering *maror,* and while children tend to devour it by the mouthful, we are reluctant to report that the halakhah actually states that, "after dipping the *maror* into the *charoset,* we should shake off the *charoset,* in order that it should not neutralize the taste of the bitter herbs" (*Shulchan Arukh* 475:1).

### 397. Do we lean while eating the *maror*?

No, we do not. Leaning is a sign of freedom, whereas the *maror* is a symbol of the bitterness of the oppression. The *Ba'er Heitev* states that "if one wishes to lean, however, he may do so" (*Ba'er Heitev* on *Shulchan Arukh, Orach Chayyim* 475:1 (7). This is probably because of the fact that we are celebrating the Seder with the hindsight of redemption, so that, notwithstanding the symbolism of the *maror,* the element of relief and liberation is still predominant. And this is underscored by the addition of the sweet *charoset.*

## HILLEL'S SANDWICH

**398. Why do we not recite the usual blessing, *Borei periy ha-adamah,* over the bitter herbs, together with the special *Al akhilat maror* blessing?**

Because we were meant to have the eating of the *maror* in mind, earlier in the proceedings, when we made that blessing over the *karpas.* Another reason is that the blessing we have just made, over the *matzah,* relieves us of the obligation of reciting the ordinary blessings over all food that we subsequently eat between then and the recitation of Grace after Meals.

**399. How do we perform the ritual of Hillel's sandwich?**

We take the bottom piece of *matzah,* and divide it up into small pieces, with each piece being about a quarter of an egg in volume. We then take two of the pieces for each person, to make the sandwich, and we fill it with grated horseradish.

**400. What if there are too many people to be served with a kezayit volume of *matzah* from that single piece of bottom *matzah*?**

We are permitted to have a supplementary stock of *matzah shemurah,* and to add it to the pieces of the special three *matzot* that we distribute during the Seder.

**401. Why do we have that special Hillel sandwich?**

Hillel was the most distinguished patriarch of the century preceding the destruction of the Temple. In our wish to preserve all the rituals of the Temple period, it was felt appropriate to eat *maror* a second time, in a way that symbolized the Temple tradition. That tradition followed the strict biblical injunction of eating the Paschal lamb, "together with *matzot* and *merorim*" (Exodus 12:8). Obviously, we cannot include in our sandwich the Paschal lamb, but we do as much as we can to recall the Temple "sandwich," by making up ours out of *matzah* and *maror.*

**402. But if it is the biblical method, of eating *matzah* and *maror* together, that we are recalling here, why do we attribute it to Hillel?**

The specific reference to Hillel, in this context, is, indeed, perplexing. It may be explained on the basis of the fact that, until his day, it was the custom to eat all three — the Paschal lamb, the *matzah,* and the *maror* — together, as indicated by the biblical verse. Hillel, however, introduced the practice of separating the Paschal lamb from the other two. This would also explain why there is no mention of the Paschal lamb in Hillel's list. The key point was that he made a sandwich of *matzah* and *maror separately,* which was a major departure from the traditional practice.

**403. Why did Hillel introduce this radical departure from traditional practice?**

Why he chose to do that is unclear, though the *Kanfei Yonah* commentary refers to the talmudic view (*Keritot* 13a) that the esophagus cannot take a volume of food larger than the size of an egg. Thus, it would have been regarded as dangerous to eat, at one and the same time, the Paschal lamb, *matzah* and *maror,* each to the volume of a (talmudic-sized) olive, together making up the equivalent of one of our eggs.

We may speculate that he had heard of cases of people choking on Seder night, and that this was a preventative measure.

**404. But how can we use that formula in relation to Hillel, saying that "he used to bind together *matzah* and *maror,*" when he, living at the time of the Temple, also used to include a *kezayit* (olive-sized piece) of the Paschal lamb?**

That is a very valid point. And for that reason, the *Mishnah Berurah* observes that, "Some authorities have written that it is necessary to say *Hayah koreikh **pesach matzah umaror,** "Hillel used to make a sandwich of the *Paschal lamb,* the *matzah* and the bitter herbs."

**405. Having learned above that one is not permitted to interrupt once one has recited a blessing, why does the *Zeikher lemikdash keHillel* formula not constitute an interruption?**

Indeed, the *Borei periy ha-adamah* blessing, which we recited over the *maror* dipped in *charoset,* does serve to cover the *maror* of Hillel's sandwich, for which reason it is reasonable to require that there be no interruption between the two consumptions. The Chafetz Chayyim (in his *Biur Halakhah* commentary) raises this question and states that we cannot explain it away on the basis that this declaration is an essential part of the eating (just as, after washing one's hands, one may ask for the salt to be passed before eating bread, and it is not considered an interruption), since the *Zeikher lemikdash keHillel* is merely a commentary and is not essentially related to the *mitzvah.*

The *Biur Halakhah* reveals that he has not found that formula, *Zeikher lemikdash keHillel,* prescribed for recitation in any sources outside the *Shulchan Arukh.* He goes on to say that where the *Shulchan Arukh* states, "And we recite [*Zeikher . . .*] and eat the *matzah* and *maror* leaning," it did not really mean that we should actually recite those words *before eating,* and that the text, which clearly suggests that, is imprecise.

**406. Do we have any corroborative evidence that the *Zekher lemikdash keHillel* formula should actually be recited after eating?**

We do. If we consult the Ashkenazi Haggadah (mid-fifteenth century), we find a bold rubric that states: "We make a sandwich, and eat it without any blessing. We then say, *Zekher lemikdash keHillel.*"

The rubric of the Copenhagen Haggadah of 1739 is even more enlightening. It states: "After that, he takes the third *matzah,* and eats some of it together with lettuce (a species of *maror*). He then recites, 'Thus Hillel used to do, etc.' " This Haggadah then follows with a note which states: "[This is eaten] without any dipping and without any blessing, and is in commemoration of the Temple, according to Hillel's custom [*Zekher lemikdash keHillel*]." Then follows the text proper of the Haggadah, commencing with *Kein asah Hillel.*

We see from this that the words *Zekher lemikdash keHillel* were not regarded as Haggadah text, but were simply part of the traditional rubric, to explain why we have the extra *maror* helping, inside a sandwich — in commemoration of how it was done in Temple times, when Hillel was living.

**407. So should we ignore the rubric in most of our Haggadot, and the custom of a lifetime, and recite the *Zekher lemikdash keHillel* only after eating Hillel's sandwich?**

No, this is not responsible advice, especially as there are a number of outstanding authorities (these are cited in *Chazon Ovadiah,* p. 174) who give clear directions to adhere to the existing custom. We must assume that, especially as we have already eaten *maror* once, these authorities were not too concerned about an interruption of this kind.

## THE MEAL

**408. We now come to the meal. Are we permitted to drink wine during the meal, or do we have to restrict ourselves to four cups of wine at the Seder?**

It is quite permissible to drink more wine or any other beverage during the meal. No blessings are required over such drinks, since everything that we normally eat and drink during our meals is covered by the blessing *Ha-motziy,* made over the *matzah,* as an introduction to the entire meal.

**409. Is it necessary to lean on the left while eating the meal?**

It is necessary to lean. We should bear in mind that it was the meal, in the form of the eating of the Paschal lamb, that constituted the main ritual of the evening in Temple times, and that it was the leaning at that meal that constituted the main demonstration of our liberation from Egypt.

**410. Why do some have the custom of performing a ritual washing of the hands at the end of the meal, before Grace, while others do not observe it?**

This ritual is called *mayim acharonim,* "The later water." It was not introduced for any reasons of purity and impurity, as in the case of the washing before meals (see question 390), but simply as a precautionary health measure. A talmudic Sage, Rabbi Hiyya bar Ashi, revealed (*Eruvin* 17b) that the practice was introduced out of fear of a certain, highly potent ingredient, mixed together with ordinary table salt, being transferred inadvertently to the eyes, and possibly causing blindness. This ingredient was known as *melach Sedomit,* "Sodomite salt."

Tosafot (*Eruvin* 17b), representing the Franco-German, Ashkenazi tradition, states that "nowadays we do not practice the custom of *mayim acharonim*, since we do not utilize Sodomite salt." Certainly today, with our more sophisticated table manners, with our salt kept in dispensers, and with the use of cutlery, so that our fingers do not usually come into contact with food or salt, we may certainly rely on Tosafot and regard the practice as optional.

The Sephardim did not apply such rational up-dating of practices, and they continue to perform the *mayim acharonim*. The Sephardi mystics of sixteenth-century Safed handed it down to the hasidic movement of the following century, and from Hasidism it has spread to other Ashkenazi enclaves, particularly within the ultra-Orthodox, *Charedi* orbit. In Israel it is possible to acquire exquisitely wrought *mayim acharonim* sets — further proof of the more widespread popularity of this ancient ritual.

## AFIKOMAN

**411. After the meal we eat the *Afikoman*. What exactly is the meaning of the word *Afikoman*, and what is it meant to symbolize?**

The word is certainly a loan-word from Greek, though its precise etymology is uncertain. It is suggested that it has the meaning of "aftermeal entertainment." This would shed light on the answer given to the wise son in the Four Questions: *Ein maftirin achar haPesach Afikoman,* which could be translated, therefore, "We may not conclude, after eating the Paschal lamb, with any form of aftermeal entertainment." This links up with another interpretation of *Afikoman,* which is that it is actually the name of a riotous and orgiastic carousel, the *epikoman,* in honor of Bacchus, god of wine. The wise young Jews are counseled, therefore, not to ape the Greek practice by following the Paschal lamb celebration with any such form of entertainment.

The Talmud (*Pesachim* 119b) is also unclear as to its etymology, and various suggestions are made, all, surprisingly, attempting to view it as having an Aramaic origin. Hence the view of *Rav,* that it stands for *epiku* ("Let's take out") *manaykhu* ("the crockery"). The Mishnah, by prohibiting such a suggestion, is attempting to stop the practice of doing a "Seder-crawl" and taking one's plate from Seder to Seder to partake of the lamb at various gatherings, converting the evening, thereby, into a merry-go-round of mere socializing.

Shemuel offers his own interpretation of the etymology of *Afikoman* (*Pesachim* 119b), in the sense of "bring out [*epiku*] the sweetmeats [*manei*]." He sees the prohibition as referring not to the joining of other gatherings, but to one's own Seder. It constitutes, therefore, a prohibition against partaking of a sweet dessert after the eating of the Paschal lamb, whose taste is supposed to be the last to remain on the palate that night.

Following the latter interpretation, the Yemenite Haggadah explains the etymology of *Afikoman* as a word comprising the initial letters of *egozim* (nuts), *peirot* (fruit), *yayin* (wine), *keliyyot* (parched grain), *u-vasar* (and meat), *mayim* (water), and *nerd* (spices).

**412. Are there any folk traditions centering on the *Afikoman*?**

Jews who hail from Iran, Afghanistan, Salonika, and Bukhara recall that the *Afikoman* was invested with special properties of warding away evil spirits: hence the practice in those countries of preserving a bit of it throughout the year for good luck. Women would carry a piece with them (together with salt and pieces of coral) during pregnancy, and even hold it in their hand during confinement. In Kurdistan it was the practice, at this point in the Seder, to bind it on the arm of one's oldest unmarried son and say, "May you so bind your ketubah to the arm of your bride."

**413. What is the *Afikoman* supposed to represent?**

It is meant to symbolize the Paschal lamb, after which nothing more was allowed to be eaten. Since the Paschal lamb had to be eaten by midnight, one has to ensure that the meal is completed and the *Afikoman* eaten by that time.

**414. How much *Afikoman* are we meant to eat?**

The volume of *kezayit* ("about an olive"), which, as we have observed, refers to talmudic olives, which were much larger than ours. We should therefore eat a little more than that, the equivalent of the volume of half an egg. Once again, it is likely that the single piece of *Afikoman*—already only half a piece—will not suffice. One may supplement it, therefore, with another piece of *matzah shemurah*. If the *Afikoman* piece is inadvertently eaten during the meal, or cannot be located, another piece of *matzah shemurah* may, similarly, be substituted.

**415. We have said that the taste of the *Afikoman* should remain in one's mouth. What if one is very thirsty after the Seder?**

Where possible, one should restrict oneself only to the drinking of the remaining two cups of wine after the *Afikoman*. If one is very thirsty, however, one may drink water. There are authorities, however, who permit the drinking of tea or coffee, especially if its purpose is to clear one's head, after the wine, to enable one to stay awake studying the laws of Pesach and the Haggadah into the early hours. Only intoxicating drinks are totally prohibited.

## *BIRKAT HA-MAZON:* "GRACE AFTER MEALS"

**416. Is there any custom regarding who should lead the *Birkat Ha-mazon* (Grace after Meals)?**

Normally, where there are at least three adult males dining together, it is customary to invite one of the guests to lead the Grace. On Seder night, however, that courtesy is suspended, and the host leads it.

The reason for this is that there is a principle, based upon a rabbinic paraphrase of Proverbs 22:9, that only "one who is generous hearted, shall be called upon to bless" (literally, "is declared blessed")." On Seder night it may be assumed that the host is most qualified for that designation, especially given his unqualified invitation at the beginning of the Seder, "Let all who are hungry come and join our table."

We fill the third cup of wine before Grace, as that cup is essentially the one over which Grace is recited. On Sabbaths and festivals, at wedding and *Bar Mitzvah* dinners, and at the celebration meals for a circumcision and *Pidyon Ha-ben* (Redemption of the Firstborn Son), it is similarly customary to recite Grace over a cup of wine. Here, at Seder, it is, of course, one of the statutory four cups of wine and is drunk at the conclusion of Grace.

### 417. Why do we recite *Shir Ha-Maalot* (Psalm 126) before the *Birkat Ha-mazon*?

This psalm refers to the overwhelming joy felt by those privileged to witness the restoration of the Holy Land after the end of the Babylonian exile (537 B.C.E.). It contains a plea that God should now bring back, "like streams in the dry Negev," all the dispersed of our nation, and it affirms that "those who sow in tears shall reap with songs of joy," and those who were burdened with sorrow when they went out to cast the seed, "will come in, laden with sheaves of corn at harvest time, and singing joyful songs."

These themes were regarded as most apposite to the Grace After Meals, which itself focuses upon precisely those blessings: the bounty conferred upon us by God and the gift of the land of Israel, "a desirable, goodly and ample land."

### 418. What is the origin of the responsive introduction to the Grace after Meals, recited when there are at least three adult males present?

This is called *Zimmun* ("invitation"), or, more popularly, with the Yiddish overtone, *Bentsching mezuman.* It consists of an invitation, by the one leading the Grace, to the others, to join him in the act of thanksgiving for the divine gift of food.

It is traced back (see Midrash *Bereishit Rabbah,* chs. 43, 49; Talmud *Sotah* 10a) to father Abraham, who would invite wayfarers to his table. After the meal, he would "invite" them to offer thanks to the one who had provided the food. When they proceeded to thank him, he would stop them, saying, "Thank the Lord of the Universe, Whose gifts we have enjoyed."

Our *Zimmun* is, therefore, a reenactment of that religious outreach undertaken by Abraham and a challenge to us to follow his example of hospitality, and his mission to observe and spread the word of God far and wide.

### 419. Who composed the blessings of the Grace after Meals?

Tradition attributes authorship of the first blessing *(Birkat Ha-zan),* which refers to God providing food for all his needy creatures, to Moses, who is said to have composed it as a thanksgiving for the provision of Manna for the hungry and apprehensive Israelites in the desert.

The second blessing *(Birkat Ha-aretz)* refers to the inheritance of the physically and spiritually rich land of Israel. It is attributed to Joshua, who composed it on entering the land and commencing its conquest. In addition to its primary theme, that of the abundance of the land, it also includes the themes of the Exodus, circumcision (a prerequisite for Exodus from Egypt), and the Torah, given to Israel a mere three months after the Exodus.

The third blessing *(Boneh Yerushalayim)* is a composite one, with themes added during the course of its evolution. The references to Zion and Jerusalem are attributed to King David, who acquired Jerusalem as his capital. The references to "the great and holy house" are attributed to Solomon, who built the first Temple in Jerusalem.

Having first been couched as a thanksgiving, once the Davidic throne was lost and the Temple destroyed, it was revised to express Israel's yearning for the restoration and as a blessing of consolation: hence the opening word, *Racheim,* "Have mercy!"

The fourth blessing *(Ha-tov veha-meitiv)* was a later addition to the statutory Grace After Meals, and hence the addition of the word *Amen* at the end of the closing blessing: *Boneh berachamav yerushalayim [Amen].* We never add the responsive *Amen* to our own blessing. It is included here merely to indicate the end of the original Grace, and to mark off the additional blessing.

The fourth blessing was introduced during the Hadrianic persecutions (135–138 C.E.) when thousands of Jews were massacred at the fortress of Bethar during the abortive Bar Kochba revolt. The Romans did not allow the Jews to bury their slain comrades, and the corpses remained unburied for years on the battlefields. This created a deep sense of outrage and horror among the Jews, for whom speedy and respectful burial of the dead is a cardinal religious priority.

When permission was finally granted for them to be buried, the sense of relief was so great that the religious leaders composed a special thanksgiving, in the form of this fourth blessing *Ha-tov veha-meitiv.* The sense of that key phrase is revealed in the Talmud *(Berakhot* 48a): "We bless God Who is good *[Ha-tov]"* – in that he prevented the corpses from decaying. "And Who bestows goodness *[veha-meitiv]"* – in that He ultimately extracted permission to have them buried.

Thus, in our Grace after Meals, while thanking God for the rich gifts of a most fertile land, we also remind ourselves of a tragic fact of Jewish history, namely, that it is a land that is also too well fertilized with the blood of Jewish martyrs.

**420. One statement in the last paragraph of the Grace after Meals is more than puzzling, namely, "I was young, and now I am old, but never have I seen [*velo ra'itiy*] a righteous man forsaken or his seed begging bread." The author must have led a very sheltered life!**

We do King David, author of this verse (Psalm 37:25), a gross injustice to imagine that a man as worldly as him was blissfully ignorant of the suffering of the righteous. He had a sufficient number of personal experiences of righteous people suffering, such as the priests of Nov, who were butchered for providing him and his men with help when they were on the run from Saul (1 Samuel 21).

It is clear that the Hebrew words, *velo ra'itiy,* are not to be translated here in the simple sense of, "I have not seen." The verb *ra'ah* is also found in the sense of "to watch," that is, to be a spectator, to see something happen without intervening, to feast eyes upon, to gloat over (see Judges 16:27, Micah 7:10, Ezekiel 28:17, Psalm 22:18, 54:9, etc.). And in that sense we may understand that King David is asserting that he was never a passive bystander when righteous people were in financial distress. He, who had himself been the recipient of aid in extremis situations, remained forever grateful, and rendered similar help to others whenever possible.

## ELIJAH'S CUP AND THE OPENING OF THE FRONT DOOR

### 421. Why do we fill a special cup for Elijah?

The usual explanation is that the custom owes its origin to the dispute in the Talmud (*Pesachim* 118a) regarding the precise number of cups that should be drunk: four or five. The problem is that the passage which contains the four expressions of deliverance (Exodus 6:6–7)—on which the four cups of wine are based—also contains what is construed by some as a fifth expression of deliverance, namely, "And I shall bring you up unto the land" *(Veheiveitiy)* (Exodus 6:8).

Hence, the filling of Elijah's cup, which is not drunk, satisfies the rabbinic preference for harmonizing, or at least finding a place for, all the views that are expressed by the distinguished authorities of the talmudic period on disputed questions of ritual and tradition.

In hasidic circles they mix the wine from Elijah's cup together with that of the fourth cup, and drink it down. Karliner *hasidim* drink it separately, immediately after downing the fourth cup, whereas the Lubavitch practice is to pour it back into the bottle after the recitation of *Leshanah haba'ah biYerushalayim,* to the accompaniment of a special melody.

### 422. Why, after Grace after Meals, do we open the door for the recitation of *Shefokh Chamatkha*?

These verses, taken from Psalms 79:6–7 and 69:25 and Lamentations 3:66, call down eternal wrath and damnation upon the heathen nations "who devour Jacob and lay waste his habitation." The popular explanation is that the door is opened to welcome Elijah, the harbinger of the Messianic redemption, in whose honor we fill a large goblet of wine before reciting these verses.

The precise purpose of his visit is also popularly related to that halakhic doubt over the number of cups to be drunk. In the talmudic academies, whenever a matter of debate remained unresolved, it was agreed that it be left in abeyance "until Elijah comes." This is indicated in the pages of the Talmud by inserting the word *teiku,* popularly explained as an acronym for the phrase, *Tishbi Yetaretz Kushiot Ve'abbayot,* "The Tishbite [Elijah] will come and resolve questions and problems." Hence, we open the doors, after pouring Elijah's doubtful fifth cup, in the hope that he will enter and resolve this particular problem of how many cups we are really obliged to drink.

### 423. Are there any problems with that "popular" explanation?

There are: notably, the significant fact that we make absolutely no reference to Elijah at this point! This alone is enough to cast doubt on whether there is really any connection at all between his cup and the recitation of *Shefokh Chamatkha*.

At circumcisions, we make special reference to Elijah as the "Angel of the Covenant" (of circumcision), and, at the same time, we formally designate a special "chair of Elijah." The absence of any such reference at this point of the Seder has convinced some scholars that we have to look elsewhere for an explanation of the custom of opening the front doors of our homes: hence the suggestion that it symbolizes the practice of opening of the gates of the Temple, late on Passover night, so that the pilgrims could take a stroll around its precincts to digest their heavy meal of festival offering and Paschal lamb. (This might well have been an enlightened measure, to provide a diversion for the younger generation, and a rendezvous, so as to deter them from organizing *epikomoi*, riotous and irreverent revelries.) Viewing the opening of the door as a Temple reminiscence might also explain the relevance of the recitation: "For they have devoured Jacob and laid waste *his habitation*," a clear reference to the Temple.

The present writer is of the opinion, however, that the opening of the front doors has a simpler and more practical explanation, related to the medieval blood libels and the tension that marked Jewish–Christian relations at that Passover-Easter period of the year. Feelings ran very high, as Christian clergy would preach fiery anti-Semitic sermons, denouncing the Jews as Christ killers. Frequently, Jewish communities were forced to attend church and to listen to such rabid ravings, which were invariably an invitation to the mob to set on the Jews, to loot, rape, and massacre. One could hardly blame the Jews for including the vindictive *Shefokh Chamatkha* verses, as a token release for their pent-up emotions.

The opening of the doors may now be understood in either of two ways. Either it was a precautionary measure, before uttering such inflammatory verses, to ensure that no gentile neighbors, or professional informers, were eavesdropping outside their houses in order to frustrate the recitation of such sentiments which, they must have known, were prescribed for the Jewish Seder. Alternately, the doors may have been opened as an act of defiance and confidence that, on this *Leyl Shimmurim*, "protected night," no enemy of Israel could inflict any harm no matter how great the provocation (see questions 42–45).

### 424. But if these *Shefokh Chamatkha* verses, and the opening of the doors, have nothing to do with Elijah, why then do we fill his cup just at this time?

We believe that the filling of his cup is related rather to the continuation of *Hallel*, to which it and the *Shefokh chamatkha* verses form an introduction. The *Hallel* expands upon the theme of God's redemption of Israel from the grasp of those who would devour her. Israel stands in stark contrast to "the nations that do not know You and the kingdoms who call not upon Your Name." The latter worship "idols of silver and gold," but Israel, by contrast, is "blessed of the Lord." They "devour Jacob and lay waste his habitation," but "Out of my distress I called upon the Lord . . . and He delivered my soul from death and my eye from tears."

We detect the real key to the connection between Elijah's cup and *Hallel* in the verse, "I lift up *the cup of salvation,* and call upon the Name of the Lord." Elijah's cup (of salvation) thus served the purpose of giving tangible form to that concept. Since Elijah will announce the coming of the Messiah, when all Israel's foes will be "destroyed from under the Lord's heavens," it was natural that the filling of his cup should have been (quite erroneously) linked to the *Shefokh chamatkha* verses and the opening of the doors that accompany them. And, once that link was established, it was but a short step from that to the creation of a popular myth that it is to welcome Elijah that the doors are opened. As in many of these situations, the myth is powerless, however, to explain why there is absolutely no reference to Elijah at this point, within the body of the Haggadah!

## CONTINUATION OF *HALLEL*

**425. Towards the end of the paragraph commencing *Lo lanu* (Psalm 115:9–11), three categories of Jews are mentioned: Yisrael (Israel), Bet Aharon (House of Aaron), and Yir'ei HaShem (God-fearers). They are all called upon to "trust in God." What is the distinction between these three categories, and why the repetition, in each case, of the words *betach ba-Shem* and *ezram umaginam hu* ("He is their help and their shield")?**

This tripartite division of Jewry and the repetition of the same words to each category can only be understood against the background of the origin of this psalm. The psalm itself is a composite, with the first part addressing itself to a situation of rampant idolatry.

The verses in question were clearly composed for use in the second Temple, and reflect the characteristic liturgical interaction between the priest and the other sections of the community gathered there for worship. The phrase *Yisrael betach ba-Shem* ("O Israel, trust in the Lord") would have been addressed by the officiating priests, in a ringing voice, to the entire gathering. As a response to the final word—God's Name—the entire congregation would shout: *Ezram umaginam hu.* The assembled throng would then throw back the identical spiritual challenge to the priests: *Bet Aharon bitchu ba-Shem* ("O sons of Aaron, you, also, trust in the Lord"). At the last word, God's Name—the priests would also make that identical response: *Ezram umaginam hu.*

The final call is addressed, once again by the priests, but this time to a more specific category of worshiper, who bore the title *Yir'ei Ha-Shem* ("God-fearers"), and in Greek, *sebomenoi.* They came from neighboring communities, particularly Idumeans, who had been forced to convert to Judaism by the Hasmonean invaders. They did not take on all Jewish observances, however, but, in the course of time, were highly regarded as friends and sympathizers. Their numbers swelled in the Diaspora as they were joined by those who were disaffected with Hellenistic polytheism, and by the first century it is calculated that they numbered several million. They are particularly venerated in midrashic literature for having willingly forfeited wealth, security, and status in order to embrace the Jewish way of life so scorned by the heathen world.

In tribute to them, this psalm incorporates them, as a core element of the Jewish religious community, into this responsive affirmation of faith. Once again, at mention of God's Name in the phrase *bitchu ba-Shem,* the converts this time respond with, *Ezram umaginam hu.*

### 426. Is there a connection between the next paragraph, *Ha-Shem zekharanu,* and the previous one?

Not only is there a connection, but, in the Bible, these two paragraphs are actually all one psalm, with the second paragraph constituting verses 12–18 of Psalm 115. The theme begun in verses 9–11 is continued here, with a blessing for each of the three categories of Jewry: the *Bet Yisrael,* the *Bet Aharon,* and the *Yir'ei Ha-Shem.*

### 427. Does not the verse, *Ha-shamayim shamayim la-Shem veha-aretz natan livnei adam* ("The heavens are the Lord's heavens, but the earth He gave to the son of man") (Psalm 115:16) conflict conceptually with another psalm verse: *La-Shem ha-aretz umeloah* ("To the Lord belongs the earth and the fullness thereof") (Psalm 24:1)?

First, it has to be said that, in a work as composite as the Book of Psalms, one cannot speak of conflicting philosophies any more than one can query the numerous variations of style, language, and mood. The psalms are the product of many centuries of poetic and liturgical creativity, the bulk of which is attributed to King David, but which also includes writers both before his time, such as Moses (Psalm 90), and the Sons of Korach (Psalms 42–49, 84–88), and after, such as Solomon (Psalm 72), Asaph (Psalms 73–83), Heiman (Psalm 88), and Eitan (Psalm 89). Inevitably, therefore, varying theological formulations will occur.

That having been said, the Talmud (*Berakhot* 35a) does take that apparent contradiction seriously, and provides a harmonization which, inter alia, constitutes a rationale of the wider problem of how mortal man can, in any way, "bless" God (for a full discussion of this, see Jeffrey M. Cohen, *Blessed Are You,* Northvale, NJ: Jason Aronson, 1993, pp. 104–106). The Talmud states that, where we are told that the earth and its fullness belongs to God, that refers to the state of the earth *before* man has recited a blessing, and merited thereby to eat at God's table. Where it states that He has given the earth to the son of man, it refers to the situation *after* man has gained title to it in that way.

By our blessings we are not conferring anything upon God. We are rather acknowledging that God is master of the universe and that we are enabled to enjoy His largess as a gracious concession, one that is to be appreciated and not abused.

### 428. What is the connection between the next paragraph (Psalm 116:1–11) and the theme of the preceding psalm?

In the preceding psalm, reference was made to the dead being unable to praise God (*Lo ha-meitim yehallelu Yah*). In the present psalm, this point is expanded upon, and the psalmist attempts to convey just how deeply he appreciates that privilege of praising God, since at one time he had not thought he would have survived to do so. He describes the many crises that he confronted in life: "The pains of death encircled me; the confines of the grave overtook me." He avers that it was only his deep faith that helped him through.

### 429. What does the psalmist mean by saying, "Yet I have said in my haste, 'All men are liars' "?

Rashi views this as the reminiscence of King David on the time when he was on the run from King Saul, and the men of Zif disclosed to the king where David was hiding (1 Samuel 23:15–28). With hindsight, he refers to his despairing assessment of the integrity of "all men"—on the basis of a single and circumscribed experience—as "hasty." As his life unfolded, and he made true and trusted friends, his faith in humankind was restored.

Don Isaac Abarbanel, an exile from Spain in 1492, interprets the phrase more generally as an expression of despair on the part of the Jews in exile, and their loss of faith in the promises of imminent redemption, as articulated by the great prophets of Israel.

### 430. In the paragraph commencing *Mah ashiv,* it states, "I am Your servant, son of Your handmaid." In what sense is this meant?

There are several explanations. Rashi understands it as an expression of the lowliest possible act of obeisance to God. A free man, who is forced into slavery, retains a rebellious spirit and a determination to unshackle himself at the earliest opportunity, and regain his freedom. However, one born to a "handmaid," who has known nothing but servitude, is more likely to accept his condition, and serve his master without reservation. Hence, the psalmist describes his total commitment, faith and loyalty to God in terms of one born to both parents enlisted in the service of God, and happy to remain for the rest of his life in that service.

It is of interest that, when reciting a prayer for someone who is ill, we refer to their Hebrew name and that of their mother, not, as is usually the case, their father. This is on the basis that King David stated, "I am Your servant, *son of Your handmaid*" when giving expression to the distress in which he found himself.

### 431. The psalmist states that "precious in the eyes of the Lord is the death of His pious ones [*chasidav*]." Does Judaism—a life-affirming religion—believe then that martyrdom is something to be desired?

Of course Judaism does not idealize the tragic conditions that might necessitate the option of martyrdom having to be exercized. Indeed, Maimonides penned a famous open letter to the community of Fez in Morocco, wherein he expresses great sympathy with the decision of that community to accept the vow of allegiance to Islam rather than to suffer martyrdom. This is known as *Iggeret Ha-Shemad* ("The Epistle on Martyrdom"). See Abraham Halkin and David Hartman, eds., *Crisis and Leadership: Epistles of Maimonides* (Philadelphia: The Jewish Publication Society of

America, 1985), pp. 13–90. He sharply condemns the view of another Sage who categorically informed them that even though their conversion was under duress and their vow to Islam a sham, nevertheless, they had divorced themselves thereby from Judaism and were no longer permitted to observe any of its *mitzvot* in secret.

Maimonides countered that view, proving that vows taken and actions performed under duress were not regarded as valid, and that the hapless victims of forced conversion are not regarded as apostates. Nevertheless, those who are in situations where martyrdom is halakhically mandated, and who do surrender their lives for their faith, are certainly regarded as having made a *kiddush ha-Shem* (Sanctification of the Name of God) of the highest order.

### 432. Under what circumstances did the psalmist utter such a strange sentiment that God desires the death of His pious ones?

Some scholars place that statement in the period of the Maccabean revolt (168–165 B.C.E.). The Book of Maccabees refers to a stratagem of the Syrians to attack the stronghold of the *hasidim,* ultrapietists, on the Sabbath day, knowing that they would not take up arms to defend themselves on that day, with the result that many thousands were slain. It is to that specific situation that they refer our psalm verse. The sentiment, "precious in the eyes of the Lord is the death of His *hasidim,*" was probably part of the eulogy delivered at their interment.

In response to that massacre, subsequent religious leaders realized that such martyrdom offered Israel's enemies a golden opportunity to wipe her off the face of history by attacking her religious enclaves on the Sabbath days. They therefore publicized the opposite view, that it was indeed incumbent to profane the Sabbath if survival was at stake. Better to profane one Sabbath, and live to observe many more Sabbaths in the future. And this remains the rationale for the law that we profane the Sabbath to do everything necessary to save a person who has collapsed, and whose life might be in danger.

### 433. How is it that the next psalm (117), commencing *Hallelu et Ha-Shem kol goyim* ("Praise the Lord all ye nations"), contains only two verses?

This is, indeed, the shortest psalm in the entire Book of Psalms, as well as the shortest chapter in the entire Bible. Some scholars believe that it may originally have been part of a much longer psalm, though this cannot be proved. It is a call to the other nations of the world to join in praise of God, and may have been introduced into the liturgy of the Temple whenever official visits of foreign leaders or delegations took place, or, at a later period, when offering sacrifices on behalf of the emperor.

### 434. What is its link with the previous psalm?

Its link with the previous psalm is based upon the employment of the identical opening word, *Hallelu,* as that with which the previous psalm closed (*Halleluyah!*). It is also inextricably linked to the following psalm (118), through the association of the phrase *kiy gavar aleinu chasdo* ("For *His kindness* has overwhelmed us") with the identical word, *(kiy leolam) chasdo* which occurs as the refrain of each line of thanksgiving in the next psalm.

### 435. How is it that, by contrast, the next psalm (*Hodu la-Shem*) is so long?

There is, indeed, no consistency in the length of psalms. Psalm 119 has 168 verses, whereas the following psalm has a mere 7! The length of the present psalm, which stretches almost to the end of the *Hallel,* may be explained on the grounds that it is clearly a composite of five thanksgiving songs, the first (*Hodu*), third (*Anna Ha-Shem*), and fifth (*Hodu*) of which are responsive.

### 436. What themes are contained in this final *Hallel*-psalm?

The first song (*Hodu*) takes up the theme commenced in Psalm 115:9–13 and calls upon the three classes of Temple worshipers—Israelites, priests, and God fearers—to "give thanks unto the Lord."

The second song (*Min ha-meitzar*) proclaims the deliverance of Israel from a situation of great national distress, and expresses her confidence in the God who has helped her to triumph over her enemies. The theme then changes in midstream, and we have a description of a worshiper entering the Temple precincts and calling to the priests to "open the gates" (*pitchu liy shaarei tzedek*). He receives the response that only the righteous may enter through "the Lord's gate" (*Zeh ha-shaar la-Shem, tzaddikim yavo'u voh*).

The third song (*Anna Ha-Shem hoshiah . . . hatzlichah*) seems to have originally been a battle cry: "Please, Lord, save us now! Please, Lord, bring us success now." It was probably introduced here to amplify the opening line of the psalm, "Out of my distress did I cry unto the Lord." The *Anna Ha-Shem* verses represent the cry uttered.

The fourth song, *Barukh ha-ba beshem Ha-Shem* ("Blessed be he that comes in the Name of the Lord") seems to refer back to the scenario of the petitioner seeking to have the Temple gates opened to him. The priests, having now ascertained that the pilgrim was, indeed, worthy, accede to the request and welcome the man with the greeting, *Barukh ha-ba,* which subsequently became the traditional Jewish form of greeting, especially to the house of God.

The final responsive song (*Hodu*) is merely a repetition of the lines recited at the outset of the psalm.

### 437. Is there any way of dating this last psalm?

It is not easy, especially as there are several strands in this composite psalm. However, the present writer detects two tell-tale hints. The priestly guard on the Temple gates and their reticence to admit only those whose credentials are impeccable suggests a period of religious turbulence when security was intensified. The precise period might be indicated by the repetition of an uncommon Hebrew form: *amilam.* From the context it is clear that this word is used in the sense of "to beat down, destroy," but it is impossible to connect this transitive meaning with the root from which it is derived. The roots *mll* and *aml* are both intransitive, conveying the sense of "to be weak, to languish."

It is clear that the psalmist is forcing the language in order to create an association with the root *mll*, "to circumcize." He is effectively saying that he will "circumcize" his enemies. We construe this as an ironical reference to the Syrians who, in the Maccabean period, prohibited circumcision. If this construction is correct, then we may date this section of the psalm around 168–165 B.C.E.

## YEHALLELUKHA

**438. Some Haggadot print the concluding blessing of *Hallel*, *Yehallelukha*, at this point, while others insert it a little later, after *Nishmat*, and just before the fourth cup. Why are there these varying traditions?**

Liturgical traditions were not created by some synod at one period of time. Different halakhic authorities, both in the Ashkenazi and Sephardic world, established their own independent liturgical principles and priorities, which probably went back to earlier differences between the traditions of Babylon and Palestine. Variations of liturgical custom arose even from town to town, though frequently a regional consensus ultimately emerged.

As regards the appropriate conclusion of the *Hallel*, different views emerged. The *Shulchan Arukh* (*Orach Chayyim*, sec. 480), as followed by the Sephardim, places *Yehallelukha* after *Nishmat* and *Yishtabach*. The logic in this is clearly that, since *Hallel* is immediately followed by Psalm 136, called "The long *Hallel*," it follows that the concluding blessing should be deferred until the end of that psalm. Since *Nishmat*, while not a biblical psalm, is, nevertheless, a lengthy and majestic praise of the Creator, it was felt that it should also be brought within the parameter of "praises," and that the concluding *Yehallelukha* blessing should climax the entire section.

Ashkenazi customs vary. Some recite *Yehallelukha* at this point, at the conclusion of *Hallel*, to mark its statutory conclusion, though without reciting the final blessing (*Barukh . . . melekh mehullal batishbachot*), and only at the end of *Nishmat* and *Yishtabach* do they recite the final blessing.

Other authorities, such as the Vilna Gaon, omit *Yishtabach* entirely at the Seder. The reason for this is that many communities have the custom of reciting *Hallel* in Synagogue, before the Seder, together with its concluding, *Yehallelukha*, blessing. It was therefore regarded as inappropriate to recite the same blessing twice in one evening.

## NISHMAT

**439. Why do we recite *Nishmat*, which properly belongs to the Sabbath and festival morning service?**

*Nishmat* includes, among its several themes, a reference to the Exodus: "You have redeemed us from Egypt . . . and rescued us from the house of slaves." Since we have the overriding principle that, "whosoever speaks at length about the Exodus is to be praised," it was certainly regarded as "praiseworthy" not to overlook such an ancient and much loved liturgical composition that deals with that precise theme.

Furthermore, its recitation is actually a Mishnaic prescription. The Mishnah (*Pesachim* 10:7) states that, "Over the fourth cup we conclude the *Hallel* and recite the *Birkat Ha-Shir* [Blessing over the Song of Praise]." In the subsequent talmudic discussion (*Pesachim* 118a) there is a dispute as to which composition is meant by that term. Rabbi Judah thought it referred to *Yehallelukha*, whereas Rabbi Yochanan referred it to *Nishmat*. Because of that uncertainty, it was decided to follow the usual course of satisfying both opinions and including both of those compositions (see Rashbam ad loc.; and *Tosafot* D. H. Hai).

## HA-GEFEN OR HA-GAFEN?

**440. Why do Sephardim pronounce the last word of the blessing for wine (*Borei periy*) ha-gefen, whereas Ashkenazim pronounce it ha-gafen?**

It has to be said that, according to the strict rules of Hebrew grammar, whenever segholate words (that is, words that comprise two syllables, each of which is endowed with the *eh*-vowel), like *gefen* (wine), *eved* (slave), and *even* (stone), occur at the end of a sentence, the first seghol sound *(eh)* is converted into a *kamatz (ah)*. There are some exceptions, but these are few and far between.

The explanation that is offered for the Sephardi practice is that it is based upon a talmudic law (*Berakhot* 47a) that, when reciting *Kiddush* over loaves, one may not break the bread until all present have recited *Amen*. The same will consequently apply, it is assumed, when reciting *Kiddush* over wine, namely that one may not drink the wine until all those listening have recited the *Amen* response. Hence, it is the word *Amen*, not *ha-gafen*, that is the final word of the *Kiddush*. And for that reason, the Sephardim pronounce it as *ha-gefen*, as they do not construe it, halakhically, as the end of the sentence.

## NIRTZAH

**441. After drinking the fourth cup and reciting *Berakah Acharonah*, the concluding blessing over wine, we arrive at the final section of the Haggadah, called *Nirtzah*. What is the precise meaning of this term, and how is it related to the poem *Chasal siddur Pesach*?**

*Nirtzah* means, simply, "may we be accepted," and denotes that we have now reached the end of the Seder proper, and that, through the merit of having observed it faithfully, we anticipate the grace of the Almighty.

The practice of reciting such a sentiment is common in rabbinic tradition, as anyone who has attended a *siyyum* (ceremony at the conclusion of the study of an entire talmudic tractate) will know. After reading the last words of the tractate, a prayer is said, which includes the plea that "Just as You, Lord, have enabled me to conclude the tractate *[such-and-such]*, so may You aid me to commence other tractates and books, and to conclude them. . . . And may the merit of all the talmudic Sages and the scholars stand to my credit, and that of my children, so that the words of this Torah will never depart from the lips of my offspring and my descendants forever."

There is a similar concluding plea recited on leaving the *sukkah* for the last time on the final day of the festival of Sukkot: "May it be Thy will . . . that just as I have fulfilled the *mitzvah* of sitting in this *sukkah,* so may I merit to sit in the *sukkah* of the Leviathan" (that is, at the banquet for the righteous in the hereafter). (This prayer probably originated among mystical circles in Safed in early seventeenth century.)

We see then that the *Nirtzah,* the plea for God's grace in response to our fulfillment of a religious ritual, is a well-established genre.

The form it takes here is slightly different. It is not expressed, like the two instances above, as a prosaic prayer, but rather as an adaptation of a medieval *piyyut* (sacred poem). The *Chasal siddur Pesach* was actually a very lengthy poem composed by the distinguished halakhist, Rabbi Joseph bar Samuel (eleventh century) for recitation on *Shabbat* Ha-Gadol, the Sabbath before Pesach. Into his poem he weaves many of the detailed laws of Pesach, and he concludes with the plea that, "Just as we have merited to *expound upon* its laws, so may we merit also to fulfill its precepts."

The last lines of his poem, commencing *Chasal siddur Pesach kehilchato* ("Ended herewith is the survey of the laws of Passover"), were lifted from that context, and brought into the Haggadah according to the German rite. At the same time, they altered the words "Just as we have merited to *expound upon* its laws," to read, *kaasher zakhinu lesader oto,* "Just as we have merited to celebrate it in Seder form. . . ."

## 442. If *Chasal siddur Pesach* was introduced in medieval Germany, does that mean that elsewhere, at that period, the Haggadah actually concluded with the final blessing over wine?

Precisely. It was only from the fourteenth century that Haggadot began to include the *Chasal siddur Pesach,* and in many manuscript editions it is not found. It is not recited in Sephardic communities, and in the *Chazon Ovadiah* edition of the former Sephardi Chief Rabbi, Ovadiah Yosef (p. 191), he merely highlights the word *Nirtzah,* and states: "May God favour the deeds [of the Seder participants], and may their reward be great."

## *UVEKHEIN VAYEHI BACHATZIY HA-LAYLAH*

## 443. Who wrote the poem *Uvekhein vayehiy bachatziy ha-laylah,* and why did it merit its place as the first of the hymns added to the Haggadah?

It was composed by one of the earliest Hebrew poets, Yannai (on Yannai, see J. Cohen, *Blessed Are You,* pp. 55–56, 77), who lived somewhere between the fourth and the sixth centuries. He wrote a number of *Kerovot,* poetic supplements to the blessings of the *Amidah;* and this particular poem was originally penned to be recited in the *Amidah* annually, on the Sabbath when the *sidra Bo,* which describes the final plagues leading up to Exodus, is recited.

Its pride of place in the Haggadah was certainly in recognition of its author's distinction as one of the earliest and greatest of our religious poets. "Yannai's poetry became so popular that its influence on subsequent Hebrew poetry was enormous. His style was imitated so faithfully that it is often difficult to separate the work of the master from that of his emulators" (J. Cohen, *Blessed Are You,* p. 57). Yannai's poem was transferred to the Haggadah from its original context around the early fifteenth century.

### 444. What is the subject matter of the poem *Uvekhein vayehiy bachatziy ha-laylah?*

It is an alphabetical acrostic poem and recounts a whole series of miracles (*rov nissim*) which, according to the Midrash, occurred on the night of Pesach. These include: Abraham's escape from the fiery furnace that King Nimrod made him enter; the punishment of Avimelech, the Philistine King of Gerar, for holding Sarah prisoner; the divine warning, conveyed in a dream (*be-emesh laylah*) to Laban not to do Jacob any harm; Jacob's vanquishing of the angel with whom he wrestled the entire night (of Pesach); the defeat of Sisera, general of Jabin, King of Canaan (see Judges 4–5); the revelation to Daniel of the meaning of Nebuchadnezzar's dream (see Daniel 2), and his deliverance from the lion's den; the death of Belshazzar who removed the holy vessels from the Temple; and the reading of his royal Book of Chronicles to Ahasuerus, which marked the ascendancy of Mordechai and the beginning of the downfall of Haman.

## *UVEKHEIN VAAMARTEM ZEVACH PESACH*

### 445. Who is the author of the next poem, *Uvekhein vaamartem zevach pesach,* and why did it merit to be recited first in the order of concluding hymns for the second Seder night?

It was written by Eleazar Kallir (on Kallir, see J. Cohen, *Blessed Are You,* pp. 55–57, 62), and its prime position in the order of poems for the second night is in recognition of his importance as the most prolific synagogue poet of the Ashkenazi rite. He takes second place to Yannai since he was the latter's disciple.

As in the case of the previous poem, it was also originally written as a poetic insertion into the *Amidah* – this time, the *Amidah* for the first day of Pesach – and was brought into the German Haggadah at the same time as the previous hymn.

### 446. What is the subject matter of the poem, *Uvekhein vaamartem zevach pesach?*

This alphabetical acrostic poem was composed as a supplement to the theme of the previous one, relating more of the wondrous events (*Ometz gevurotekha*) that coincided with the festival of Pesach. It begins by stating that God had already revealed to

Abraham all the glorious events of the Passover of the Exodus, and in recognition of that, Abraham celebrated the festival. Indeed, the visit of the three angels coincided with the date of Passover.

The Sodomites met their just desserts and Lot was saved on Pesach; Jericho was conquered by the Israelites during Pesach (Joshua 6); Gideon, the judge, defeated the Midianites (Judges 6–8) on that festival of Pesach; the Assyrian general Sennacherib's army was destroyed by angelic intervention on the night of Pesach (2 Kings 19:35); and it was on Pesach that the mysterious hand appeared, at Belshazzar's feast, and wrote upon the wall that Babylon would be destroyed; the three-day fast that Esther proclaimed coincided with Pesach; and, finally, Haman lost his head and was hanged on Pesach.

## KIY LO NA'EH

### 447. What is the connection between the next hymn, *Kiy lo na'eh,* and Pesach?

In truth, there is no reference to Pesach in this hymn. It is a general alphabetical table hymn that was recited, together with the other Seder hymns, in Germany and Italy, and it represents a general praise of God and a reinforced assertion that everything in the universe belongs to Him, and, in concert with Israel, His many powerful heavenly agencies constantly pay tribute to His kingdom and glory.

Isaac Abarbanel, on the other hand, views this hymn as having a direct relevance to Passover. It was at the Exodus that Israel had the clearest confirmation that all the kingdoms—Pharaoh, Canaan, and so on—were all powerless as compared with the One who was the truly omnipotent king of the universe. Hence, Abarbanel asserts, this hymn, with its reference to God's kingdom (*melukhah*) in the opening phrase of each stanza, is intended to convey the magnitude of Israel's awe and faith as inspired by the events of the Exodus.

Abarbanel views the sevenfold employment of the word *lekha* as denoting, variously, the seven heavens through which God descended to redeem Israel, the seven days of the week (representing God's constant supervision of Israel's destiny) and the seven chief constellations. There is no doubt, however, that the repetitive vocabulary and the number of times it is employed are derived from the seven biblical verses where the phrase, *kiy lekha,* or, simply, *lekha* is employed to introduce a main attribute of God: *Lekha Ha-Shem ha-gedulah* (1 Chronicles 29:11); *Kiy lekha ya'aah* (Jeremiah 10:7); *Lekha zeroa im gevurah* (Psalm 89:14); *Lekha yom* (Psalm 74:16); *Af lekha laylah* (Psalm 74:16); *Lekha shamayim* (Psalm 89:12); and *Af lekha eretz* (Psalm 89:12). All of these verses are recited as part of the collection of *Shome'a tephillah* verses, which introduce the penitential and fast day *Selichot* services.

### 448. Do we know the name of the author of *Kiy lo na'eh?*

We cannot be sure, though there is a suggestion that it may have been written by Rabbi Jacob Chazan of London, who wrote a liturgical work, entitled *Etz Chayyim,* which represents the northern French and pre-Expulsion English prayer rite.

He has a version of *Kiy lo na'eh* which contains quite a number of variations on ours, as well as an additional stanza that provides the name acrostic: *Ya'akov,* which some scholars assume is a reference to his own name.

## ADDIR HU

### 449. What is the subject matter of the next alphabetical poem, *Addir Hu,* and what is its association with Pesach?

It is a proclamation of the attributes of God (Mighty, exalted, famed, acclaimed, pious, etc.), accompanied by the plea that He might rebuild His House "soon, speedily, most speedily, soon, in our days." medieval Jewry's desperation to be relieved of its unremitting national misery is reflected in the urgency of its repetitious vocabulary.

Whereas the first two Temples were built by human hands, the future, third Temple, according to Jewish tradition, is to be built miraculously, by the hand of God. And it is for that blessed sign of messianic salvation that this hymn pleads.

Like the previous hymn, there is no obvious thematic connection with Pesach, but it belongs to a general genre of festive hymns. The liturgical historian, Leopold Zunz, tells us that in medieval Avignon it was sung on each festival as a table hymn. It entered the Haggadah of the German rite from the fourteenth century, and was so popular that it was also widely sung in the German vernacular. Some of the early printed editions of the Haggadah even include its German translation.

## ECHAD MIY YODE'A

### 450. What is the subject matter of the next song, *Echad miy yode'a,* and what is its association with Pesach?

Again, it has no specific connection with Pesach, and it appears for the first time in Ashkenazi Haggadot of the sixteenth century. This song was also sung in Avignon as a festival table hymn, and, in a book of hymns, published in Amsterdam in 1757, it appears as a song to be sung at the *Shabbat* table when celebrating a *Shevah Berakhot* (week of festivity for bride and groom).

The song consists of thirteen stanzas, each one beginning with the question, "Who knows one? . . . two? . . . three?" up to "Who knows thirteen?" In each case it offers the response, "I know one . . . two . . . three," and provides, for each number, the most significant thing associated with it. Thus *one* represents the One God; *two* represents the Two Tablets (of the Ten Commandments); *three* represents the patriarchs; *four,* the matriarchs; and so forth.

### 451. Are there any precedents for this type of song in Jewish tradition?

Questions and answers are, of course, very close to the Jewish heart, and form the basic structure of talmudic legal and literary presentation. However, this kind of song clearly owes its inspiration to the general, secular folk song genre of the medieval period, wherein simplistic songs of this kind were common. One particular German pastoral song, *Guter Freund Ich Frage Dich,* is pointed out as being uncomfortably similar, though, naturally, the pastoral elements have been replaced here with Jewish religious elements.

### 452.  Are there any other ways of construing this song?

Whether or not its origin is Jewish, the form in which it appears may also be construed as a polemical jibe at Israel's oppressors, particularly against the other faiths—especially the daughter religion of Christianity—which Jews have always regarded as having replaced and distorted the authentic and original tradition.

Viewed in this light, "I know One" represents Israel's commitment to pure monotheism, as against the belief of the Persians in dualism and Christianity in the Trinity.

"I know two" suggests that the two gods—Ahriman and Ahura Mazda—of Persian Zoroastrianism are as nought, and the only "two" that is of any consequence are the Two Tablets.

"I know three" is, similarly, directed against the Trinity. "I know four" suggests that we apply the noble title "mother" exclusively to the four matriarchs of Israel (Sarah, Rebecca, Rachel, and Leah), and not, as in Christianity, to women who lead a monastic life.

"I know five, . . . I know six," represents the Five Books of Moses and the Six Orders of the Oral Law, which we believe are an ever-binding covenant. The Written Law has not been replaced, as Christianity asserts, by any new dispensation; neither is the Oral Law a figment of the rabbinic imagination, as the Christians and some Jewish schismatic sects maintained.

"I know seven. Seven are the days of the *Shabbata,*" emphasizes that the Sabbath, for Israel, climaxes the seven days of the week. It is not, as in Christianity, the first day of the week.

"I know eight. Eight are the days of circumcision," emphasizes the Jewish sign of the covenant *within* our bodies, as opposed to the Christian rituals of Communion, which display external symbols of the body of their God.

"I know nine . . . the months of confinement" comes to make the point that we do not believe in any such doctrine as an immaculate conception. All births, we assert, have to go through the full, natural term.

His penultimate reference is to the Twelve Tribes, reiterating Israel's firm belief that the entire house of Israel, including the ten "lost" tribes (captured by the Assyrians in 721 B.C.E., and deported to Assyria, where they ultimately assimilated and were "lost"), will one day, in the Messianic Era, be reunited.

His final reference, "Who knows thirteen?" is to the thirteen principles of rabbinic interpretation of the Written Law. These are the cornerstone of Jewish Oral tradition, and the mechanism whereby the ancient text is interpreted in the light of any modern-day issue. This keeps Jewish law dynamic, and again gives the lie to the Christian charge that Jewry has an "Old" and outdated Testament, as well as to the Sadducean and Karaite critique that the rabbanite Oral Law has no authority.

## CHAD GADYA

### 453. What is the origin of the *Chad Gadya* poem and its relationship to Pesach?

Once again, we must report that this poem is also a variation of a popular German folk song, and a parallel is made to the well-known medieval German ditty, *Der Herr, der schickt den Jockel aus*. This, in turn, is supposed to have been based upon an Old French nursery song, though songs with a similar theme and construction occur also in Persian and Indian literature.

It differs from the previous poems in that it is written in Aramaic. We should not be deceived, however, into placing it, on that evidence, in a much earlier period, since its Aramaic is faulty, and is clearly in the "Aramaic style" rather than an authentic production. It was not introduced into the Ashkenazi ritual until the end of the sixteenth century.

Like most of the other songs in this section, it bears no obvious relation to any Pesach theme. It describes the law of the jungle, with the stronger species devouring the weaker, and ending with what is clearly the "Jewish" appendix, that ultimately it is "The Holy One, Blessed be He" who exacts the final revenge. This might be seen as an allegory on the fate of the Egyptians and on all who seek, like them, to devour those weaker than themselves, especially the Jewish people. In this respect, it echoes God's original promise to Abraham that "Also the nation that they [the Israelites] serve will I judge" (Genesis 15:14). There is a law of cause and effect; Israel may draw a little comfort from it, and the nations should take it to heart.

### 454. But does its place in the Haggadah not suggest that it is being viewed in specifically Jewish historical terms?

Jewish tradition has understood the song, primarily, as an allegory, with the list of animals representing the succession of nations that persecuted Israel, and who, in consequence, declined, lost their position of supremacy on the world stage, and ultimately vanished.

The "kid" symbolizes Israel, and the "father who bought it for two zuzim" stands for God who redeemed Israel from the Egyptians through the agency of his two representatives, Moses and Aaron. The "cat" is Assyria, who conquered the northern kingdom of Israel in 721 B.C.E., taking ten of the twelve tribes into captivity. The dog is Babylonia, which conquered the southern kingdom of Judah in 586 B.C.E. The "stick" stands for Persia, which replaced the Babylonians in 538 B.C.E. as super power of the Middle East. The "fire" symbolizes the Greeks, who vanquished the Persians in 334 B.C.E. The "water" stands for Rome, which invaded Palestine in 66 B.C.E. The "ox" is Islam, which displaced Roman rule in Palestine around 640 C.E. The "slaughterer" is the eleventh-century Crusaders, who attempted to rescue the Holy Land from the hands of the Muslims and who initiated their campaigns with the wholesale destruction of Rhineland Jewish communities. The "Angel of Death" represents the Turks who, at the time of composition, still occupied Israel's land. Ultimately the "Holy One" would displace the Turks and, vindicating the cause of the "one kid," would restore her to her rightful inheritance.

It is only in the twentieth century that the final act was played out. The Turks joined the Axis powers in World War I and lost their hold over Palestine as a result. It was handed over to Britain to administer as a mandate from the League of Nations, before being declared once again, after a break of nearly two thousand years, a sovereign Jewish State. *Chad Gadya* is not merely a simple rhyme; it is a veritable prophetic blueprint.

### 455. Are there any other interpretations of *Chad Gadya*?

Surprising as it may seem, there is a considerable literature of commentary and scholarship centering upon the *Chad Gadya* song. There are several variations of the allegorical explanation we have outlined above, and during the eighteenth century a number of Christian scholars actually produced learned tracts on it, treating it as a profound philosophical work, yielding many layers of hidden meaning. In the *New York Times Saturday Review* of February 9, 1901, there appeared a review of a small book that sought to identify *Chad Gadya* as the source of the popular nursery rhyme "The house that Jack built."

# XV

# The *Omer* and the *Sefirah*

**456. On the second evening we commence counting the *Omer*. What is the biblical source for this counting?**

The Torah states:

When you come into the land which I give unto you, and shall reap the harvest thereof, then ye shall bring the sheaf of the firstfruits of your harvest unto the priest. (Leviticus 23:10)
And ye shall count unto you from the morrow after the day of rest [*mim-mochorat ha-Shabbat*], from the day that ye brought the sheaf of the waving, seven complete weeks. (23:15-16).

The term *ha-Shabbat*, though normally used in the sense of "the Sabbath day," was understood traditionally in this context, in its literal sense as "the day of rest," and specifically understood to refer to the first day of Pesach, which, being *Yom Tov*, is aptly described as a day of rest (but see question 474). Hence, the counting of the *Omer* was intended to link the two festivals of Pesach and Shavuot.

**457. What is the underlying purpose of this counting?**

The Israelite farmer was never to forget that all the blessings of his fields were gifts from God, without which all his efforts and toil would be in vain. When his main harvests, the barley, the wheat, and the fruits, ripened, his first task was to present a sample at the Temple as a token of thanksgiving. On Pesach an *Omer* (a specific measure) of barley, the earliest ripening crop, was presented as a meal offering, and seven weeks later a similar presentation was made from the first batch of wheat to ripen. The Torah prescribes that we formally count each successive day and week of those seven weeks that span the two offerings, and that the wheat offering be made precisely on the fiftieth day, which is the festival of Shavuot.

**458. But is Shavuot only linked agriculturally to Pesach?**

No. There is also the spiritual link between the two festivals. The whole purpose of the Exodus was in order to bring Israel to Mount Sinai, and bestow upon her the Torah. This was already foretold to Moses at his first encounter with God at the

Burning Bush: "When you bring out the people from Egypt, you will all worship God upon this mountain" (Exodus 3:12).

Israel's liberation was not contrived merely to enable her to throw off the yoke of physical servitude to a foreign overlord; it was primarily with the objective of bringing her under the benign and inspirational yoke of the heavenly Lord. Hence, the *Omer* bridge between Pesach and Shavuot (the anniversary of the giving of the Torah) comprises two tracks: the agricultural and the spiritual. Indeed, the purpose of the tithes and gifts of the land which the ancient Israelite farmer brought to the Temple was to spiritualize his labor, and enhance his self-esteem as a privileged steward of the Lord's garden.

## THE *OMER* IN TEMPLE TIMES

### 459. In what sort of spirit was the ceremony of the bringing of the *Omer* performed in Temple times?

It was a joyous, public ceremony, with all participants full of happy anticipation of an imminent rich harvest to guarantee livelihood and prosperity for the coming year. The joy was compounded by the pleasurable experience of the Paschal lamb festivities of the previous evening, and by the general good feeling that the onset of the Spring month of Aviv brought with it.

### 460. How was it decided from where to select the *Omer* barley sheaves for the ceremony of reaping of the *Omer*?

Prior to the festival, inspectors of the Ecclesiastical Court would tour the fields of the suburbs of Jerusalem to discover the barley crop that had ripened the most. The prestige and honour that attached to the farmer whose *Omer* was chosen would have known no bounds. Normally, one of the fields in the valley of Kidron, north of the city, merited selection as the site for the annual ritual. The inspectors tied an identification cord around the *Omer* sheaves, so that there would be no delay the following night, at the termination of the first day of the festival, in commencing the formalities.

### 461. Do we have any sources that describe the *Omer* ceremony?

We do. The Mishnah (*Menachot* 10:3) describes it in full detail, and in a manner that suggests a rather exaggerated ritual:

At nightfall, he [the appointed reaper] would call to the spectators, saying, "Has the sun set?" And they would respond, "Yes." He would then repeat the question twice over, and they would answer accordingly. He would then ask, "Is this a scythe?" And they would reply, "It is." He would then repeat the question twice over, and they would answer accordingly. He would then ask, "Is this a basket?" And they would answer, "Yes." He would repeat the question twice over, and they would answer accordingly. . . . He would then ask, "Shall I reap?" And they would respond, "Yes, reap!" He would then repeat the question twice over, and they would answer accordingly.

### 462. What was the point of that exaggerated ritual?

The Mishnah (*Menachot* 10:3) goes on to ask that precise question, and answers: "Because of the Boethusians who asserted that the cutting of the *Omer* does not take place at the termination of [the first day of] *Yom Tov.*"

Reflected here is a famous dispute between the two main divisions of Palestinian Jewry in the third through first centuries B.C.E., the Pharisees and the Sadducees (of which the Boethusians were a subgroup). This particular dispute hinged on the question of the proper interpretation of the biblical source for the counting of the *Omer.*

The crux of the problem was the precise meaning of the phrase, *mimmochorat ha-Shabbat* (Leviticus 23:15). As we mentioned above, Pharisaic Judaism, which inherited the oral traditions of the Israelites who had stood at Sinai and handed them down to rabbinic Judaism, strenuously asserted that the word *Shabbat* in this context referred to *Yom Tov,* and meant, simply, "day of rest." They therefore cut the *Omer* sheaf, and commenced counting the seven weeks, immediately at the termination of the first day (and opening *Yom Tov*) of Pesach.

The Sadducees, on the other hand, were committed to a literalist understanding of the biblical text and denied the authority of any oral traditions. They therefore took the biblical phrase *mimmochorat ha-Shabbat* literally, as "the morrow of the Sabbath day." They, accordingly, held the ceremony, and began counting, on the first *Sunday* of the Passover week. Hence, for them, since the *Omer* of barley was always brought on a Sunday, it followed that Shavuot, when the *Omer* of wheat was brought, seven weeks later, also always occurred on a Sunday.

We may now answer our question regarding why Pharisaic Judaism created such an exaggerated ritual out of the cutting of the *Omer* on the "morrow of the day of rest." Their objective was to give the greatest publicity to their own tradition on this sensitive issue, and to stress that they had supreme confidence that they were fulfilling the biblical requirement to the letter, at the time that the Law Giver had had in mind when He employed the term, "morrow of the *Shabbat.*" The people were also drawn into this ritual, so that they might affirm their confidence in their Pharisaic heritage, and express a symbolic rejection of the Boethusian–Sadducean tradition.

### 463. But, did not the Sadducees have a point? For, if the Torah had wanted the *Omer* to be brought, and the counting commenced, immediately after the first day (and *Yom Tov*) of Pesach, why did it use that misleading word, *ha-Shabbat,* which, in most instances, does mean simply the Sabbath day?

Their argument was not so strong. They failed to appreciate the necessity for the Torah to avoid an even greater ambiguity. For, had the Torah stated that the *Omer* should be brought *mimmochorat ha-Pesach* ("on the morrow of the *Pesach*"), it might have been construed as referring to the (slaughtering of the) Paschal lamb. This would have suggested that the *Omer* should be brought on the first day of Pesach, since the lamb was slaughtered the previous day. Furthermore, use of that term might also have been erroneously interpreted to mean the day after the conclusion of the entire festival.

The Torah was not delivered to Israel without a full explanation of all problematic formulations; and the Israelites would have certainly sought clarification of a vague phrase like this. The Pharisaic reliance upon oral traditions was obviously necessary, therefore, and a guarantee of an authentic heritage.

**464. But surely the Sadducees could argue that the Torah should have made it abundantly clear by using a phrase such as, "From the morrow of the first day of the festival"! Can we point to any basic flaw in the Sadducean interpretation that it refers to the first Sunday ("morrow of the *Shabbat*") of the festival?**

There is a flaw because, according to their interpretation, the date of the commencement of the *Omer* always fluctuates, depending upon the occurrence of the first Sunday of the festival, it follows that the date of Shavuot (exactly fifty days later) will vary each year. That would make for an anomaly in the cycle of the festivals, for there is no other festival of the Jewish calendar whose date is not fixed for a specific day of a specific month. Of the two, it is only the Pharisaic tradition, therefore, that is consistent in this respect.

**465. To return to the ancient *Omer*-cutting ceremony: What happened after the exaggerated preliminaries referred to in the Mishnah?**

They then cut the prescribed *Omer* measure of barley and, placing the sheaves in the baskets, they carried them ceremoniously to the Temple court. There they were parched in fire, in accordance with the biblical requirement that the meal offering be made of "parched corn" (Leviticus 2:14). The barley grains were then spread out in the courtyard of the Temple, so that the wind might dry the moisture that exuded from the parching process. They then transferred the grains to a mill which ground them down to the required amount and consistency of barley flour. To this was added an ample amount of oil and incense, well mixed together to make the required meal offering, which was smeared at the southwest corner of the altar.

**466. Did the ceremony have any practical significance?**

It did. It was forbidden to use any grain from the newly ripened harvest before the meal-offering had been made at the Temple. There might have been a great temptation for people to do so, or to offer it to potential customers to sample, but it was strictly forbidden. It would probably have been regarded as bringing bad luck to enjoy the harvest before it was "blessed."

**467. What form does the counting of the *Omer* take these days?**

Since the destruction of the Temple (70 c.e.), no offerings or sacrifices could be made, but the obligation of counting the seven weeks of the *Omer,* between Pesach and Shavuot, remains. A blessing is recited, followed by the enumeration of the specific day and week of the *Omer*. Thus, on the eighth day the counting would take the following form: *Ha-yom shemonah yamim sheheim shavua echad veyom echad la'omer*—"This is the eighth day, which makes one week and one day of the *Omer*."

### 468. Why is it necessary to be so specific? Why not merely mention the particular day of the forty-nine-day unit?

The reason for this is to conform to the Torah's blueprint that actually refers to both the counting of days and the counting of weeks: "And ye shall count . . . seven complete *weeks* . . . you shall count fifty days" (Leviticus 23:15–16).

### 469. Why was a blessing prescribed over this particular counting, when there are other examples of biblically prescribed counting of days, such as for those afflicted with a contaminating bodily flux (*zav*) (Leviticus 15:13), or the suspected leper, who, on being given a clean bill of health, counts seven clean days before rejoining the community (Leviticus 13:4–5), or a woman after childbirth, who counts thirty-three days for a male offspring and sixty-six days for a female (Leviticus 12:1–5), yet no blessing was prescribed?

One of the most distinguished of the twelfth-century circle of German pietists (*Chakhmei Ashkenaz*), Rabbi Ephraim bar Yaakov of Bonn, states that it was for polemical reasons (to combat an unacceptable sectarian view) that this blessing over the *Omer* was prescribed.

He believes that it was introduced by the early Pharisees in the context of their bitter dispute with the Sadducees over the meaning of the phrase "on the morrow of the *Shabbat*" (see questions 456, 462). In order to demonstrate their supreme confidence in the truth of their interpretation, against that of the Sadducees—states Rabbi Ephraim—the Pharisaic Rabbis introduced a special *berakhah* over the *Omer*. The blessing boldly asserts that "*God* has commanded us to count the *Omer*" when Pharisaic-Rabbinic Judaism does so (R. Ephraim bar Yaakov, *Sha'ar Efrayim* [Sulzboch: R. Aryeh Loeb Ha-Kohen, 1689], p. 32). (On this and other examples of rabbinic polemic, See Jeffrey M. Cohen, *Blessed Are You*, pp. 46–48.)

### 470. Is there not some doubt as to whether we introduce the reference to the *Omer*, in each day's counting, by adding the preposition *la* (*la'Omer*) or *ba* (*ba'Omer*)?

There is some difference of opinion, though the almost universal employment of the term *Lag Ba'Omer* to describe the joyful thirty-third day of the period might indicate that the preposition *ba* must be correct. Indeed, this is the version recommended by the Vilna Gaon and followed by the *Minhag Perushim* ("custom of the ascetics"), the community of his disciples that was founded in Jerusalem in 1770.

Surprisingly, however, Joseph Karo, in his *Shulchan Arukh* (*Orach Chayyim* 493:1–2), employs the formula *Lag La'Omer*, which is also the tradition of the Yemenites.

Both versions are acceptable. The word *Omer* may be taken in two ways. Either it is an abbreviation for *Sephirat ha'Omer,* "the period of the counting of the *Omer,*" in which case it is grammatically correct that, each day, we should say that we are so-and-so-many days *Ba'Omer,* "into the *Omer.*" Alternately, it can also refer to the *Omer* offering of wheat brought on Shavuot. In that case, it is correct to say *la'Omer,* "so-and-so-many days towards [*la*] the *Omer* [offering]."

## THE *MITZVAH* OF COUNTING

**471. What if one forgot to count the *Omer* for a day or two, can he resume counting with the blessing?**

Since the *Omer* is, technically, a single forty-nine-day unit, the blessing presupposes that the *mitzvah* will be performed in its entirety. We do not make blessings over the partial fulfilment of *mitzvot.* Hence, if the chain is totally broken, by which we mean that one has let the entire following day pass, until nightfall, without recalling his omission and proceeding to count the current day of the *Omer,* he can no longer continue to recite the blessing, but should continue to count on subsequent nights without the blessing. However, if he remembered at any time during the course of the day following the previous night's omission, he should immediately count that particular day of the *Omer,* but without reciting the blessing. He may then resume, that and subsequent nights, to count with the blessing.

**472. Is there truly no remedy for someone to continue counting with a blessing if they have missed an entire day?**

Rav Joseph Baer Soloveitchik, in his *Beit Ha-Levi* (vol. 1, sec. 39), makes the novel suggestion that, since the Torah gives two separate prescriptions, to count forty-nine "days" and to count seven "weeks," it follows that someone who has omitted one of the days still has an obligation to count the weeks. Hence, on the night that a new week is reached, he may recite the blessing.

**473. Is that just a theoretical point, or are there those who in practice continue to recite the blessing even when an entire day has been missed?**

It is related that the disciples of the Baal Shem Tov, founder of Hasidism, did not follow the view of the *Shulchan Arukh,* but counted with a blessing even after missing an entire day. Their rationale was that it was the better of two evils, since, in previous generations, when people were more devoted to *mitzvot,* they would continue to count without reciting the blessing if they had missed a day. However, with the later generations there was a fear that if a person is instructed not to recite a blessing, he will conclude that he is not really fulfilling a *mitzvah* in counting without the blessing, and he will not bother to continue to count. Hence their view that one should not advise anyone not to recite a blessing. In any case, most of the *Rishonim,* the authorities who lived before Karo, were of the view that one may, indeed, continue to recite a blessing if one missed an entire day.

### 474. What if he could not recall whether or not he had counted the *Omer* the previous night?

He may still continue on subsequent nights to count with the blessing, even if he did not count again (without the blessing), to be on the safe side, during the course of that day.

### 475. What is the proper time for counting the *Omer*?

The correct time is as soon as possible after nightfall, to indicate eagerness to perform the *mitzvah*. However, it may be recited with the blessing until dawn next day.

On Friday nights and during the other days of the *Yom Tov* of Pesach, it is counted after *Kiddush,* in order to give precedence to the sanctification of the day, and at the termination of *Shabbat* and *Yom Tov* it is counted before *Havdalah,* in order to delay the end of the holy day.

### 476. If one observes the correct law of not counting until after nightfall, but one is present at a synagogue where they count the *Omer* while it is still day, at an early evening service, should one refrain from counting with the congregation?

The *Shulchan Arukh* (*Orach Chayyim* 489:3) recommends that one recite the day of the *Omer,* but not the blessing, with the congregation, in order not to "separate oneself from the congregation." If he remembers after nightfall he should then recite the blessing and count once again.

This view is strongly challenged, however by Rashba (see *Magen Avraham,* ad loc.), who states that "whoever counts while it is still day has done nothing. On the contrary, he is testifying to that which does not exist [yet], and if we permit him to count with the congregation he might well come to rely on that counting and forget to count at the proper time."

The Taz, perhaps with tongue in cheek, expresses surprise at the basic premise that there could be a congregation that might count the *Omer* while it is still day. "Are we legislating for wicked people?" he writes. He concludes that the sources that discuss this issue could not have been referring to counting while it is still day, but rather when it is twilight, namely, that quarter of an hour or so before nightfall, which is regarded as a period of halakhic doubt as to whether it is day or night.

### 477. Is there not a tradition that, if asked which day of the *Omer* it is, one should only state yesterday's day, and not the actual day?

There is a popular tradition to that effect, but it does not apply as broadly as is generally believed—if at all!

The *Shulchan Arukh* (*Orach Chayyim* 489:4) states, "If one's friend asks one *during* the *twilight period* which day of the *Omer* we shall be counting tonight, he should reply, 'Yesterday we counted such-and-such a day,' since if he replies with the formula: *Hayom* . . . ('Today is such-and-such a day'), he can no longer count again with a blessing [since he has already fulfilled his own obligation]. *However, before twilight, since it is not the proper time for counting, it makes no difference* [if he uses the proper Hebrew formulation]."

So the first thing to note is that we only consider adopting that pedantic approach when it is that doubtful period which we cannot define with certainty as either day or night. Secondly, it is clear from the *Shulchan Arukh* that it is only problematic if he were to reply using the traditional formula of counting (though the *Magen Avraham* states that omitting the final word — *Ba'Omer* — would in no way affect the situation, and he would still be regarded as having already fulfilled his own obligation to count).

From the discussion above, and especially from the comment of the Taz, it is clear that if he replied in English (for example, if he said, "It'll be the eighth day"), or even if, in Hebrew, he made the abbreviated response, *yom sheminiy* ("the eighth day"), without employing the prescribed introductory formula, *Hayom yom* . . . , or did employ the prescribed formula but did not have in mind that this answer should serve to fulfill his duty of counting for that evening — in all these circumstances there is no reason to be halakhically apprehensive, and he is still required to count properly, with a blessing, that night.

Taz concludes, therefore, that the *Shulchan Arukh* did not intend, in fact, to state a categorical prohibition of responding to one's friend with the forthcoming evening's *Omer* number, but rather to offer a recommendation that, in the first instance, and if one has the presence of mind, one should avoid doing so, and (if it is at twilight) should refer rather to yesterday's number.

### 478. What if he had counted with a blessing, and then discovered that he had counted the wrong day?

If he remembers immediately, then he may simply substitute the proper number. If, however, there had been some time delay, he must recite the blessing again with the proper number.

## FROM JOY TO SADNESS

### 479. The *Omer* period was clearly originally a period of great joy. What subsequently transformed it into a period of semimourning?

It was the deaths of thousands of the disciples of the great Rabbi Akivah that converted a joyous period into one of semimourning. The Talmud (*Yevamot* 62b) states that they died "from Pesach until Shavuot," which establishes the entire period as a time within which to mark that tragedy, though there is also a variant tradition which has it that the deaths only occurred for the first thirty-two days, and on the thirty-third day, *Lag Ba'Omer*, no deaths were recorded.

### 480. What was the cause of the deaths of so many of Akivah's disciples?

The Talmud (*Yevamot* 62b) states that it was "because they did not show respect to each other," which is clearly an attempt to conceal the real reason, and yet to do so in a blatantly transparent way that makes it obvious that there was a deeper, political cause that the Talmud was constrained to conceal.

Knowing that Rabbi Akivah was the arch-supporter of Bar Kochba, who led the revolt against the Romans in 132–135 C.E., it seems obvious that such a vast number of his disciples could not have met their deaths other than as martyrs on the field of battle. The talmudic Sages of the day were traumatized by the fate of their colleagues and students, and they probably concealed the real facts in order to spare having to state that Rabbi Akivah, one of the best loved and most illustrious Sages of the talmudic, and any other, era, had been so misguided in his politics, and so deluded in his messianic expectations (he, after all, hailed Bar Kochba as the Messiah), as to have caused the massacre of all those disciples he drafted into the hopeless revolt.

The later generations of talmudists, who lived in far less militant times, might also have feared to state the real circumstances in order not to lend encouragement to any of their young nationalistic disciples to attempt another vain insurrection against Rome.

### 481. But how could an event, however tragic, displace the entrenched joyful spirit of what was, after all, a biblically prescribed celebratory period?

We may assume that the semimourning could not have been introduced if the *Omer* period still partook of a joyful spirit at that time (second century C.E.). Most likely, with the loss of the Temple, which brought to an end the joyful ceremony of cutting the *Omer* sheaves and offering the meal-offering in the Temple, coupled with the devastation caused to Judaea as a result of the three abortive Jewish rebellions against Rome (in the years 70 C.E., against Titus; in 117 C.E., against Trajan, and in 132–135 C.E., against Hadrian), the nostalgic recollection of the halcyon Temple days struck sadness into the hearts of Jewry, so that the *Omer* period was automatically converted into a sad time. Its commemoration of the deaths of Akivah's disciples was, therefore, most appropriate to the already currently prevailing spirit.

### 482. Mention has been made (see question 479) of some doubt as to the precise period of Akivah's disciples' deaths; how did such doubt arise?

We have already mentioned that the Talmud was anxious to conceal the full facts of the tragedy. Hence, although it alludes to their deaths, it does not refer to any commemorative mourning. It is not until the eighth century that the Gaon Natronai discloses that the *Omer* had become transformed into a period of semi-mourning for that catastrophe. (Quoted in B. M. Levin, ed., *Otzar Ha-Geonim* to Talmud *Yevamot* 62b.)

Now, it is not until the *thirteenth century* (see Meiri, *Bet Ha-Bechirah* on *Yevamot* 62b) that there is reference to "a tradition of the Geonim (eighth–eleventh centuries) "that the deaths ceased on the thirty-third day of the *Omer* (*Lag Ba'Omer*). Even that tradition is unclear, however. One view understands it to mean that the mourning period is from Pesach to *Lag Ba'Omer;* another view is that it means that the catastrophe lasted for thirty-three days during the *Omer* period, but that it was not necessarily the first thirty-three days (see *Taz* on *Shulchan Arukh* 493:2 [2].)

### 483. Is it permitted to choose, therefore, which thirty-three days one will observe?

No, that would make for chaos within families and communities, with different people unable to participate in the festivities of their family, neighbors and friends, because they were all observing different periods of mourning.

In any case, even though the sources left it doubtful, nevertheless halakhic authorities had their own traditions, and these were binding upon their followers. Thus, the *Shulchan Arukh* (493:2) states that it is their (Sephardi) practice to keep the mourning observances from Pesach until (and including) the thirty-third day of the *Omer.* Moses Isserles (*Shulchan Arukh* 493:2), on the other hand, records an Ashkenazi custom of not commencing the thirty-three days until *Rosh Chodesh Iyyar.* This was in order that no mourning should be observed during the joyous month of Nisan. According to the latter practice, the thirty-three days of mourning stretch until Shavuot, though with the exception of *Lag Ba'Omer* which enjoyed the spirit of a day of release and muted celebration.

*Magen Avraham* records a variation of the latter practice in his communities, where it was felt inappropriate to observe mourning during the three days prior to Shavuot (*Shloshet yemei hagbalah*). Another three days of mourning had to be found, therefore, in compensation, and they therefore observed mourning also on the two days of *Rosh Chodesh Iyyar* and a token hour on the first of the *Shloshet yemei hagbalah.*

The Anglo-Jewish (United Synagogue) practice is to observe the mourning prohibitions from after *Rosh Chodesh Iyyar* until *Rosh Chodesh Sivan,* and, naturally, excluding *Lag Ba'Omer*. This gives a mere twenty-seven days of *Omer* observance!

### 484. What forms of semimourning are prescribed?

We do not permit marriages and we do not cut our hair. Some authorities (see *Ba'er Heitev* to *Shulchan Arukh* 493:1) do permit the solemnization of marriages under certain urgent conditions, such as where a man with small children is remarrying and he has no one to look after his children, or where someone is remarrying his divorced wife. One authority even suggests that the biblical *mitzvah* of procreation, for a previously unmarried person, overrides the mere rabbinic custom of observing this period of semimourning. However, this is not current Ashkenazi practice.

### 485. Does the prohibition make any distinction between the cutting of the hair of the head and the shaving of one's beard?

The question is dealt with in an article by Rabbi Aharon Halevi Pichenik ("*Tisporet ha-zakan biymei ha-sefirah,*" in *Shanah BeShanah* Yearbook, Jerusalem:

Heikhal Shelomo, 1974), pp. 220–223. He reminds us at the outset that these mourning observances have no basis in the Talmud, and are not codified by Maimonides. He also states that, on *Chol Ha-Moed* (the intermediate days of Pesach and Succot) where a similar prohibition applies, nevertheless many authorities acknowledge that the prohibition was only directed at the outset to the hair of the head, not the beard. Since the *Omer* prohibition is certainly less strict than that of *Chol Ha-Moed,* it follows that this distinction would certainly also apply.

Rabbi Pichenik proves from the Chatam Sofer and other authorities that the Sages never made any decree prohibiting shaving, which, for people who shave daily, would create an intolerable feeling of discomfort that, even for a mourner, constitutes grounds for relaxing the prohibition against shaving! He quotes Rav Mosheh Feinstein who stated that, "the days of the *Sefirah* [the *Omer* period] are more lenient, and we may relax the prohibition if someone's unkempt appearance causes him upset" Rabbi M. Feinstein, *Iggrot Mosheh* (*Orach Chayyim,* pt. 2) (New York: Moriah Press, 1964, sec. 96, "Shaving during *Sefirah* for those permitted to shave during *Chol Ha-Moed*", p. 299). Obviously, leaving one's hair uncut for four to five weeks does not cause the same problems.

### 486. Are there any exemptions to these prohibitions?

There are. At a circumcision, which partakes of the spirit of a *Yom Tov* for the family, the father of the child, the *Sandek* (who holds the baby) and the *Mohel* (who performs the circumcision) may have a haircut and shave towards evening on the day previous.

### 487. May one organize an engagement party during the *Omer* period?

One may celebrate an engagement, since the Rabbis appreciated the bridegroom's wish to secure the woman of his choice, and "not to lose her to another" (Talmud Yerushalmi *Taanit* [Krotochin ed.] 64d). It may be accompanied by a reception or even a proper meal. However, a full celebration, with music and dancing, is not permitted during this period.

## LAG BA'OMER

### 488. What form does the celebration of *Lag Ba'Omer* take?

Originally, it was merely marked in synagogue, as a semi-holiday recalling the cessation of the massacre of Akivah's disciples. It would have been marked merely by the nonrecitation of Tachanun, the mournful and petitionary verses omitted on all major and minor holidays.

The kabbalistic movement, which developed in Safed in the sixteenth century and made the *Zohar* the cornerstone of their mystical theology, transformed that day into a day of intense celebration associated with their great spiritual father, the second-century talmudist, Shimon bar Yochai, the (traditional) author of the *Zohar.* The thirty-third day of the *Omer* was, by tradition, significant as his *Yahrzeit,* (or, according to another tradition,) as the day he was ordained by Rabbi Akivah. Yet a further tradition has it that it commemorates the day when he emerged from the cave wherein he lived for twelve years, having fled there from the Romans.

Basing themselves upon the first of the above three explanations, the Safed kabbalists celebrated *Lag Ba'Omer* as the *Hillula D'Rashbi,* "the marriage celebration of Shimon bar Yochai," an allusion to the union of his holy soul with its Maker at death. For the mystic, the death of a righteous person is not to be lamented. Quite the contrary: it is to be celebrated as the ultimate state of holy bliss after a lifetime of separation from its divine source.

This concept was given practical expression on *Lag Ba'Omer,* in an annual religious pilgrimage to Meron, near Safed. There bonfires are lit, and the night is passed in singing, dancing, feasting and celebration. This celebration originated in the sixteenth to seventeenth century, and has gained momentum in modern Israel, with the burgeoning hasidic sects for whom mysticism is a venerated area of spiritual quest. In those and other *Charedi* (right-wing Orthodox) circles it has long been the practice not to cut a baby boy's hair for the first three years of his life. The annual visit to Meron provides the opportunity for making the first haircut an act of joyous religious significance, in an atmosphere already supercharged with mystic quality. It is related that the great Isaac Luria, sixteenth-century leader of the Safed mystics, already brought his son to Meron for his first haircut.

## BLESSINGS AND PRAYERS

### 489. Why is no *Shehecheyanu* blessing recited over the biblical *mitzvah* of counting the *Omer*?

First, it has to be said that, since the destruction of the Temple, when it was divorced from its moorings as a chain linking the bringing of the barley and wheat sheaves to the Temple, the counting of the *Omer* was relegated to the status of a rabbinic ordinance.

As a *Birkat Ha-zeman,* "blessing over holy times," it could certainly justify its recitation as marking a festival ritual that occurs infrequently. However several reasons are offered in the sources for not reciting the *Shehecheyanu.* Among them are the fact that, nowadays, the ritual provides no pleasure or benefit. Quite the contrary; it forcefully reminds us that our Temple is in ruins, and we can no longer perform the many ceremonies originally associated with this period. Secondly, as a blessing over the entire counting of forty-nine days, we fear that it might turn out to be a "blessing in vain" if one forgets to count an entire day during the *Omer,* and breaks thereby the unity of the entirely integrated numeration. Thirdly, because the counting is not an end in itself, but merely a method of accurately determining the date of the festival of Shavuot, it is only at the inauguration of that festival—when the *Omer* is concluded—that we recite *Shehecheyanu,* as a thanksgiving for having "reached this time."

**490. Why do we follow the counting of the *Omer* each night with *Yehiy ratzon* — a prayer for the restoration of the Temple?**

We mentioned above that, since the destruction of the Temple, the *Omer* is only mandated by rabbinic law. We therefore express this yearning for the rebuilding of the Temple, when its biblical status will be restored.

**491. Why do we then recite Psalm 67?**

This psalm was chosen for two distinct reasons. First, it contains the sentiment, "the earth has yielded her produce," which is, of course, apposite for the *Omer,* an agricultural counting ritual. Secondly, for the very prosaic reason that this psalm contains seven verses (excluding the psalm-heading), corresponding to the seven weeks of the *Omer,* and forty-nine words, corresponding to the number of its days.

**492. What is the background of the next passage, *Annah Bekhoach*?**

It is traditionally ascribed to Rabbi Nechunyah ben Ha-Kanah, a first-century Sage who was acclaimed for his humility, piety, and nobility of character. He was also a mystic, to whom a number of seminal works in that field, such as the *Sefer Ha-Bahir,* are attributed.

On the basis of that attribution (denied, however, by critical scholars, who view it as having emananted from a thirteenth-century school of Spanish kabbalists), the *Annah Bekhoach* was credited with great mystic potency as an expression of Israel's longing for spiritual and national redemption, and as a plea to God that penetrates all the normal barriers to prayer.

It comprises seven verses, each of six words, making a total of forty-two words, corresponding to the forty-two letter mystical name of God. In addition, the initial letters of each word combine to comprise that forty-two letter name. It is also said to combine other mystical combinations, the clearest of which is the acrostic *Kera Satan* ("tear Satan in pieces") in the second line.

In some prayer rites it is also recited together with the morning *Korbanot* (sacrificial passages), but it is more widely recited on Friday evenings, before *Lekhah Dodiy,* which emanated from a later kabbalistic circle, the sixteenth-century Safed mystics. Its plea (fourth line) that God should "purify" Israel (*tahareim*) made it an appropriate lead-in to the *Ribbono Shel Olam* prayer that follows, and which, at the outset, defines the rationale of the entire counting of the *Omer* as an opportunity "to purify us of our contaminations and impurities."

**493. What is the background of the *Ribbono Shel Olam* prayer and its mystic allusions?**

We have just observed that the mystic literature viewed the *Omer* period as an opportunity for spiritual purification and renewal. The symmetry of the *Omer,* with its seven weeks of seven days, representing the epitome of wholeness and perfection, suggested a time for self-perfection.

The process could not be rushed, and each day the mystic was challenged to rise one extra gradation of spirituality by contemplation of the mystic qualities and attributes of God, as developed in the kabbalistic literature. At another level, the forty-nine days of the *Omer* represented Israel's ascent through all the forty-nine gates of impurity, until they arrived, on Shavuot, at the requisite level of purity to enable them to receive the Torah.

The *Ribbono Shel Olam* meditation gives expression to that mystical explanation of the *Omer* as a means of "purifying us from our *kelippot* and impurities." The term *kelippot* means, literally, "shells," and is borrowed from the symbolism of the Zohar. It is an element of the doctrine of the *Sefirot*, the theory of "emanations," which sets out to explain how the physical world, with all its imperfections, could possibly have emerged as the handiwork of a God who is total perfection. The *Sefirot* are not of the essence of God, but created extensions, spiraling downward from the highest and purest form of existence, the *Ein Sof* (the Eternal One), through ten *sefirotic* extensions, each weaker and less perfect than the previous emanation.

The term *kelippot* denotes the shells or husks of evil, which are understood by some as the point of contact or transition between the penultimate emanation and the base world of physicality. From that context it is applied more generally as denoting the impulse towards sin within man. As a husk or shell, it deprives man of his instinctive freedom to break out and soar heavenward on a swirl of purity.

Another mystical reference in this prayer is the request that "through this *mitzvah* there may flow abundant bounties throughout the world." This is the idea of the cosmic effect of every act of purification. This is identical with the notion that every *mitzvah* redeems some of the primordial divine light—the very essence of the *Ein Sof*—that became spilt and diffused at the outset of the process of *sefirotic* emanation. The vessels of light, created to contain the potent substance of the first emanation, shattered, and rays of Higher Light were shed all over the universe. This makes God incomplete, according to this most daring mystical concept. That hiatus is referred to as the separation of the Holy One and His *Shekhinah;* and every *mitzvah*, every act of spiritual rectification, penitence and purification, is believed to have the effect of scooping up some of that spilt heavenly matter, and restoring it to its source: hence the reference here to the abundant bounties flowing "throughout the world."

# XVI

# The Festival Services

## MAARAVOT

**494. What are those special insertions into the blessings before and after the *Shema* that we recite in the *Maariv* service?**

They are poetic embellishments, composed by our earliest religious poets, some of whom, like Yannai and Kallir, we have already referred to. These poetic supplements into the *Maariv* service are referred to as *Maaravot,* and their purpose was to inject into the regular prayers the atmosphere of the particular festival being celebrated. Thus, on each of the three main festivals, of Pesach, Shavuot, and Sukkot, the *Maaravot* refer to specific themes from those festivals, generally making ample use of talmudic and midrashic allusions.

**495. Why, when the festival coincides with *Shabbat*, do we omit the *Maaravot*?**

In the preelectricity era, when people read by the light of oil lamps, it was feared that, because of the unfamiliarity of the festival *Maaravot,* someone might forget that it was the Sabbath, and if the lamp in front of him was not sufficiently bright, he might instinctively stretch out his hand and adjust the wick. On festivals there is no problem with doing that, but on *Shabbat* it is, of course, forbidden to touch the wick in case he inadvertently extinguishes the light.

**496. When the first night of a festival coincides with *Shabbat* (that is, Friday night), do we always recite the *Maaravot* of the first night on the second night, in place of those prescribed for the second night?**

This is normally the case on all other festival evenings. The one exception is Pesach, when, even if the first night of the festival is Friday night (when we omit *Maaravot*), we nevertheless still recite the *Maaravot* for the second evening on Saturday night.

**497. What is the reason for this exception?**

The reason is that the *Maaravot* for the second evening have as their theme the *Sefirat Ha-Omer,* Counting of the *Omer.* In the case of most of the *Maaravot,* those for the second day of each *Yom Tov* are merely duplications of the first day's themes. This is because the *Maaravot* were composed in Israel at a time when, as today, there was only one day (and evening) of *Yom Tov*. The poets did not, therefore, compose any special poetry for a second day. Diaspora Jewry had to resort to splitting up the original sacred poetry between the two evenings, notwithstanding the thematic repetition that this necessitated.

Now Pesach was the exception, since the Diaspora was able to draw on poetry that was composed especially for the theme of the Counting of the *Omer*, which commenced at *Maariv* on the eve of the second day of Pesach. Hence, because of its direct relevance to the second evening of Pesach, we read the *Maaravot* of that night, even if we omitted *Maaravot* the previous evening because it was Friday night.

## WHEN PESACH AND *SHABBAT* COINCIDE

**498. The Friday evening service throughout the year commences with *Lekhu nerannenah* (Psalms 95–99 and Psalm 29). Why, when Pesach (or any other festival) occurs on Friday night, is this omitted?**

The *Lekhu nerannenah* psalms were introduced by the mystics of Safed in the sixteenth century, who would go out into the surrounding fields, on late Friday afternoons (in good time before *Shabbat*), in order to welcome the Sabbath Queen to their town with the accompaniment of joyful songs of praise and the recitation of those six psalms. This ceremony was called *Kabbalat Shabbat,* literally, "welcoming in the Sabbath." The recitation of those psalms ultimately spread to most other communities.

The Safed pietists did not perform this ritual of going out to the fields and reciting those psalms when the Friday was a festival day, because of the prohibition of walking beyond 2,000 cubits outside the town. From that situation, those psalms came to be omitted whenever *Shabbat* and *Yom Tov* occurred in proximity to each other.

**499. Normally, on Friday evenings, we follow the *Amidah* with the recitation of *Magen Avot*. Is it recited when Pesach coincides with Friday night?**

Customs vary. The French custom, as reflected in *Siddur Rashi* and *Machzor Vitri*, as well as the Italian rite of the *Shibbolei Ha-Leket* and a number of West-European Ashkenazi communities, is to recite it as usual. Other authorities (quoted in the *Tur*, ch. 487) do not.

Both views take account of the fact that *Magen Avot* was originally introduced primarily in order to prolong the Friday night service. Most worshipers only managed to attend synagogue on Friday and Saturday nights because of their work commitments. The Friday night *Maariv*—especially before the *Kabbalat Shabbat* psalms were introduced more widely in the seventeenth to eighteenth centuries—was very brief indeed, and there was concern that late-comers to synagogue, staying on to finish their prayers, and having to walk home in the dark on their own, might be vulnerable to lurking dangers.

Those who prescribed it for recitation even on Pesach took account of that ever-present fear, whereas those who omitted it on Pesach night did so in recognition of the fact that this night is *Leyl shimmurim,* "the protected night," when no Jew need have fear of any danger, and there was consequently no need to prolong the service by its recitation.

## NO *KIDDUSH* IN SYNAGOGUE

**500. Why do we not recite *Kiddush* in synagogue on Seder nights as we do every other Friday night and festival eve?**

*Kiddush* should really be recited at home, as a prelude to the meal. It was only introduced into the synagogue service for the sake of the poor and any travelers joining them, who were provided with a communal meal served in an anteroom of the synagogue. The proximity of their table made *Kiddush* in synagogue an appropriate gesture, to give some added publicity to the important and sacred act of sanctifying the Sabbath and festival.

Now, on Seder night, it was arranged that everyone, even the destitute, should be entertained at a home, or at least provided with wine for the Four Cups. It was, therefore, not necessary to recite *Kiddush* on their behalf, since they would be either hearing it at the Seder or reciting it for themselves. That being the case, if *Kiddush* were to be made in synagogue, it would be tantamount to having five cups of wine, since whoever merely hears *Kiddush* can fulfill his religious duty thereby. For this reason, to avoid confusion, *Kiddush* was omitted in synagogue on the two nights of Seder.

## *HALLEL* IN SYNAGOGUE ON SEDER NIGHTS

**501. Do some have the custom of reciting full *Hallel* as part of the evening service on Seder night?**

Indeed, this ancient practice, which by the tenth century had already been abandoned, was subsequently reintroduced through the insistence of the great mystic of Safed, Isaac Luria (sixteenth century). It is recorded in the *Shulchan Arukh* (*Orach Chayyim* 487:4), though the Ashkenazi glossator, Moses Isserles, states (*Orach Chayyim* 487:4) that "We do not have this practice, for we do not recite the *Hallel* at all in synagogue at night." Though originally practiced exclusively by Sephardim, it was subsequently borrowed by Polish *hasidim,* and is today popularized in a number of Ashkenazi conventicles in Israel and abroad. After the pattern of the morning service, it is recited immediately after the *Maariv Amidah* before the recitation of the full *Kaddish.*

**502. How did the ancient practice of reciting *Hallel* in synagogue on Passover evening originate?**

During the period of the Second Temple, *Hallel* was recited immediately after eating the Paschal lamb (See Mishnah *Pesachim* 9:3). Since not everyone knew

*Hallel* by heart (there were no written texts available in those days), people were encouraged to go and join another *chavurah* (Paschal lamb family group) where there was someone who could recite and lead the *Hallel* (see Tosefta *Pesachim* 10:8).

For a short time after the destruction of the Temple the practice continued, even though there was no longer a Paschal lamb. As the synagogue began to assume a more prominent role in the lives of communities, it became the practice for those families who had no one to lead the *Hallel* at home to repair to the synagogue during the course of the evening, to hear it recited there. As most people did not attend evening services at that early period, since it was still regarded as merely optional, they were only hearing *Hallel* recited once that night.

As the evening service gradually took on its obligatory character, the synagogue *Hallel* recitation was incorporated into the service proper. Although they had already recited *Hallel*, therefore, in their evening service, they did not feel that it should be removed from the home Seder service, where it had, after all, originated. The eighth-century *Masekhet Soferim* (20:7) states that there is obviously no requirement to recite a blessing over the repetition of the *Hallel* at the Seder. And, indeed, that provides a further explanation (see also question 384) of why we do not recite the usual blessing, *Likro et ha-Hallel*.

## ADDITIONS AND VARIATIONS IN THE *YOM TOV* EVENING SERVICES

**503. Why is the verse, *Vayedabber Mosheh* ("And Moses expounded the festivals of the Lord to the Children of Israel") recited immediately after the blessing, *Haporeis sukkat shalom* ("Who spreads the tabernacle of peace over us . . .")?**

According to Abudraham it is in order to make the latter conditional upon the former: If we observe "the festivals that Moses expounded," then we will merit the reward of peace.

**504. On Friday nights we recite the *Bameh Madlikin* (Mishnah *Shabbat*, ch. 2), which deals with the preparation of the various oils and wicks, which may and may not be used for Sabbath lights. Why is this recitation omitted on (i) a Friday night that follows a festival day, (ii) on a *Shabbat Chol Ha-Moed* (intermediate Sabbath of a major festival) or (iii) when a *Yom Tov* commences on Friday night?**

It was regarded as inappropriate to the first of those three situations above, since the *Bameh Madlikin* contains three instructions that a man should give to his household on Friday, before the onset of *Shabbat* (Mishnah *Shabbat* 2:7). One of them is *isartem*, "Have you separated the prescribed tithe?" As this act of separation is not permitted to be undertaken on *Yom Tov*, the entire recitation was suspended when Erev *Shabbat* (Friday) is a festival day. And from that situation, its nonrecitation was extended to the other two situations where *Shabbat* and *Yom Tov* are in close proximity to each other.

**505. In what way does the *Yom Tov Amidah* differ from that of weekdays and *Shabbat*?**

On weekdays, the three daily *Amidahs* (literally, "standing prayers") consist of nineteen blessings. The first three consist of praise of God, the middle thirteen are personal and national petitions, and the last three are a combination of thanksgiving and an expression of hope for the restoration of the Temple service (on the development of the *Amidah,* see J. Cohen, *Blessed Are You,* pp. 29–40).

Because it was regarded as inappropriate to emphasize our needs, and petition for them, on a *Shabbat* or festival, the middle section of the weekday *Amidah* is not recited on those occasions. We replace it with a single blessing, called *Kedushat Ha-Yom* ("Sanctification of the Day"), which deals with the theme of the Sabbath or the festival. In the latter case, it includes (in each *Amidah* except *Musaf*) the *Ya'aleh veyavo* prayer, which allows for the name of the particular festival to be inserted. Hence, every festival *Amidah* (with the exception of the extended *Musaf* of Rosh Hashanah) consists of but seven blessings.

## ADDITIONS AND VARIATIONS IN THE *YOM TOV* MORNING SERVICES

**506. In what way does the service on Pesach morning differ from that of an ordinary *Shabbat*?**

The basic structure is identical, with but a few differences: Firstly, whereas, on *Shabbat,* the Chazan commences (after *Nishmat*) with the words *Shokhein ad marom,* on the three pilgrim festivals (Pesach, Shavuot, and Sukkot), he commences with the previous verse: *Ha-Keil beta'atzumot uzekha.* Secondly, if Pesach falls on a weekday, we omit the special Sabbath insertion into the *Yotzer* blessing (the first of the two pre-*Shema* blessings). Thirdly, there is a special middle, *Yom Tov,* blessing of the *Amidah,* which replaces that of *Shabbat.* Fourthly, there is the addition of *Hallel* (on *Hallel,* see questions 382–385, 425–438). Fifthly, when Pesach occurs on a weekday, there is a special *Yom Tov* insertion, when we take out the *Sifrei Torah,* which includes the Thirteen Divine Attributes (*Ha-Shem Ha-Shem Keil Rachum Vechanun*) and a most moving and personal petition (*Ribbon Ha-Olam*). Finally, the conclusion of the last *Haftarah* blessing adds to the usual *Mekkadesh ha-shabbat* the words *veyisrael veha-zemanim.* On *Shabbat Chol Ha-Moed,* the intermediate Sabbath of the festival, we read *Shir Ha-shirim,* the Song of Songs.

**507. What differences are there in the rest of the service between Pesach and an ordinary *Shabbat*?**

On *Shabbat* we make seven *aliyot,* that is, we call seven people to the Reading of the Torah. If necessary, we may subdivide the various portions to enable us to call up more than the seven. On Pesach (Shavuot and Sukkot), however, we call up only five people, and we may not subdivide the portions to call up more. (If the festival days correspond with *Shabbat,* however, then we retain the usual seven *aliyot.*)

Secondly, each of the festival days has its own special portion of the Law and *Haftarah.* Thirdly, the *Musaf Amidah* is a special one for festivals; and, finally, on the first day, we recite the special *Tal,* the prayer for dew, in the Reader's repetition of the *Amidah.*

A major difference between Israel and the Diaspora is that, whereas in Israel they have the Priestly Blessing of the congregation (*duchaning*) in the repetition of the *Shachrit Amidah* each day, and of the *Musaf Amidah* on *Shabbat* and Rosh Chodesh, in the Diaspora we only have it on our major festivals.

### 508. Why does the Reader commence a sentence earlier, with *Ha-Keil Beta'at-zumot uzekha*, on festivals?

Because that phrase refers to "God's absolute power," which was explained to refer to the Exodus from Egypt (the common theme of the three pilgrim festivals), where it was uniquely demonstrated.

### 509. Why do we omit the recitation of the Thirteen Divine Attributes (see question 506) when *Yom Tov* falls on a *Shabbat*?

Because, although they are Divine attributes, they also imply petitions. When we hail God as "merciful, forgiving, slow to anger, abounding in lovingkindness [etc.]," we are, by implication, petitioning for Him to extend those precise attributes in our direction. As we have observed, on *Shabbat* we do not express petitions since they would impair the joy of the day by reminding us of our many needs. On *Yom Tov* we are not so worried by such indirect petitionary allusions.

### 510. Why do we not recite the accompanying *Ribbon Ha-Olam* when Pesach coincides with *Shabbat*?

Because that is a most direct petition to God. It begs for immunity from the evil inclination and for God's Presence to dwell in proximity; it petitions for wisdom, fear of God, a long and blessed life, and deliverance from evil scourges. It is therefore a most direct and multiple petition, and was, consequently, regarded as inappropriate for recitation on *Shabbat.*

## TORAH READINGS FOR THE EIGHT DAYS OF PASSOVER

### 511. Since there is a different Reading of the Torah each day of Pesach, it is difficult to remember what to read each day. Is there any mnemonic for this?

These days, with printed *Machzorim* (festival prayer books), one does not really require an aide-mémoire. In the age before printing, when few, other than the rich, could afford a handwritten festival prayer book, it was necessary that people should be able to recall such ritual data in case there was no Rabbi or learned person present at the service.

The mnemonic is an old Aramaic one, comprising the initial words of the reading for each day: *Meshokh Tura // Kaddeish bekaspa // Pesal bemidbara // Shelach bukhra.* These initial words actually do make up a sentence, which means: "Pull in the ox; sanctify by means of money; hew out in the desert; send out the firstborn."

The elucidation of the mnemonic is as follows:

*Meshokh* is a close variant of the initial word of the verse, *Mishkhu ukechu lakhem tzon,* which is the reading for the first day, from Exodus 12:21.

*Turah* is the Aramaic for the Hebrew *Shor,* and is an allusion to the phrase, *Shor o khesev,* the second day's reading, from Leviticus 22:26

*Kaddeish* is the initial word of the third day's reading, *Kaddeish liy kol bekhor,* from Exodus 13:1.

*Bekaspa* alludes to the opening of the fourth day's reading, *Im kesef talveh,* from Exodus 22:24.

*Pesal* is the opening word of the fifth day's reading, *Pesal lekha,* from Exodus 34:1.

*Bemidbara* is the equivalent of the key word of opening verse of the sixth day's reading, *Va-yedabbeir . . . bemidbar sinai,* from Numbers 9:1.

*Shelach* is an allusion to the word *beshalach,* the opening phrase of the seventh day's reading, *Vayehi beshalach Paraoh,* from Exodus 13:17.

*Bukhra* is the Aramaic of the word *bekhor,* an allusion to the opening phrase of the last day's reading, *Kol ha-bekhor,* from Deuteronomy 15:19 (though, if that day is a *Shabbat,* we commence with the previous chapter, *Aseir te'aseir,* from Deuteronomy 14:22, in order to accommodate the extra two *aliyot* that we have on *Shabbat*).

## THE FIRST DAY'S READING

### 512. What is the relevance of the Reading of the Torah for the first day of Pesach?

It is a description of the instructions given by Moses to the Israelites to set aside a Paschal lamb, to slaughter it and daub its blood on the doorposts, as a sign that theirs is an Israelite home, which will not be touched by "the destroyer."

We are told that this Paschal lamb ritual is to be "a statute for you and your children forever," and that its purpose is didactical, in order that future generations of children will ask about that strange ritual, and that it will, therefore, provide an opening for relating to them the full history of the Exodus, and of God's great act of deliverance.

The passage then goes on to describe the final plague, the death of the firstborn, of man and beast, and the effect it had of extracting permission from the stubborn Pharaoh for the Hebrews finally to leave. It gives the number of able-bodied Israelite men as 600,000, apart from children, and apart from the *Eirev rav,* the "mixed multitude" of other nationality slaves in Egypt, who also availed themselves of the opportunity to break out of the country.

It tells of the haste with which they left, and the *matzot* they were constrained to bake, and it ends with the detailed laws attending those eligible and ineligible to participate in the Paschal lamb ritual.

**513. Why did the Israelites have to daub their doorposts? Surely, God knew which houses contained Hebrews and which were Egyptian houses!**

Many explanations are found. The most plausible explanation is that it was not for God's information, but for the Egyptians. In the aftermath of that horrific plague and the Israelite escape, the latter would be leaving behind homes with their front doorposts stained with the blood they had daubed. They were leaving the Egyptians clear evidence that the Israelite God was not a God of vengeance who had determined to destroy innocent people, but a merciful and just God who had given ample warning of that plague—and all the previous ones—and ample time for the Egyptian king to repent of his obstinacy. (For notes on *Haftarah* of the first day, see question 528.)

## THE SECOND DAY'S READING

**514. What is the relevance of the Reading of the Law for the second day of Pesach?**

Bearing in mind that it was originally only the first and seventh days of Pesach that were full holy days, as is the case in Israel today, the Diaspora communities did not have sufficient biblical source material, relating exclusively to Pesach, to provide for the Reading of the Law for four holy days, and to satisfy the need to call up five people each day. Inevitably, they had to make their choice from some passages that referred, more broadly, to the general cycle of festivals and the laws governing festival days.

Thus, on the second day of Pesach, we read the *Parashat Ha-Moadim,* the portion that lists all the major days of rest, commencing with the Sabbath, and proceeding to detail all the other festivals. A section in the middle does outline the laws of the bringing of the *Omer,* which is, naturally, the main reason for its choice for the second day of Pesach, which is the first day of the counting of the *Omer.* (For notes on *Haftarah* for the second day, see question 530)

## THE THIRD DAY'S READING

**515. What is the relevance of the Reading of the Law for the third day of Pesach?**

The third day of Pesach is the first day of *Chol Ha-Moed.* On *Chol Ha-Moed* we take out two scrolls of the Torah, and call up four people. Three are called to the first scroll, and the fourth person is called to the second scroll, from which the identical section is read on each of the four days.

The third day's reading (Exodus 13:1-16) opens with a statement of the sacred status of the Israelite firstborn males, who "openeth the womb," and this theme is introduced here, as a prelude to a section of Pesach law, in order to explain the background to that special status. It was in Egypt, when God was constrained to destroy the Egyptian firstborn, and saved the Israelite firstborn even though their standards were not so superior to those of their heathen counterparts, that that relationship—rooted in God's special mercy—was cemented.

The reading continues with a description of the special regulations governing the eating of *matzah* and the removal of all *chametz*. Finally, there is a prescription that this portion "shall be for a sign upon thy hand, and as a memorial between thine eyes," in other words, that this portion be included within the *tefillin*.

For the person called up fourth each day of *Chol Ha-Moed*, we read the section (Numbers 28:19-25) dealing with the special festival sacrifices, meal-offerings, and drink-offerings. It also establishes that no work may be done on the seventh day of the festival, as on the first.

### 516. We have referred to the special sacred status enjoyed by the firstborn. Does this status still apply?

It does, and may be seen as underlying the ceremony of *Pidyon Ha-ben*, "the Redemption of the Firstborn." It was with the worship of the Golden Calf that the firstborn of all the other tribes lost that special status. It was only the tribe of Levi, that is the priests and the Levites, that did not indulge in that act of idolatry. The punishment of the firstborn of all the other tribes was that, in losing that status, they also lost the privilege that would have gone with it, namely to act as officiants in the Sanctuary and, subsequently, at the Temple (see *Talmud Yerushalmi Megillah* 1:1). Instead, that was given to the loyal tribe, whose off-spring filled that function. The Levite priests became the spiritual officiants and ministers, as well as occupying the dignified role as teachers and counselors of the community, for which they received twenty-four special tithes as their livelihood.

The ordinary Levites, likewise, had a special role to play at the central Sanctuary. They formed the Levitical choir and performed other ministrations. They were not allowed to own land and had no tribal possession, and were therefore allocated special cities to live in. In the synagogue, to this day, they are called up to the Law immediately after the priests, and they wash the hands of the priests before the administering of the Priestly blessing.

Because the original spiritual status of the firstborn is biological, not external, it means that they always retain a measure of holiness, and that their real destiny still lies within the sanctuary. The ceremony of the Redemption of the Firstborn consti-tutes the formal discharge of that status by the priest, in return for a payment of five silver shekalim, as prescribed by Torah law.

# THE FOURTH DAY'S READING

### 517. What is the relevance of the Reading of the Law for the fourth day of Pesach?

The fourth day is also the second day of *Chol Ha-Moed*. The portion chosen (Exodus 22:24–23:19) only deals towards the end with the theme of "the feast of unleaven bread," and that is contained within a single verse. But that was sufficient, for the Rabbis who chose this reading, to serve as a reminder and a point of contact with the festival.

The passage contains a collection of disparate laws, including the prohibition of usury, respect for the judiciary and the nation's leadership, prompt payment of tithes, pursuit of holiness, prohibition of cruelty to animals, of publicizing false information, and of showing partiality in the administration of justice. It describes the *Shemitah,* the seventh year of release, when the land must be allowed to lie fallow, and all private debts are cancelled. It ends with a brief survey of the three main agricultural festivals.

# THE FIFTH DAY'S READING

### 518. What is the relevance of the Reading of the Law for the fifth day of Pesach?

The fifth day of Pesach is the third day of *Chol Ha-Moed*. The Reading (Exodus 34:1–26) describes the instruction to Moses to make a second set of Tablets to replace the first set that he smashed when he caught sight of the Israelites worshiping the Golden Calf.

It also contains a reaffirmation by God of His promise to drive out the indigenous and idolatrous tribes of Canaan, and to safely settle Israel therein. Israel is warned, however, not to put herself into a compromising situation whereby she might be lured into idolatry by entering into treaties and marriage alliances with the neighboring tribes.

It is only at the end of the Reading that the theme of Pesach is introduced, again in a mere single sentence. It is accompanied by the request that all Israel's males appear three times a year at the central Sanctuary.

The passage ends with the prohibition of seething a kid in its mother's milk.

### 519. What has seething a kid in its mother's milk got to do with the context of the festivals?

We have just said that the passage does not deal exclusively with the festivals, but also contains a warning against idolatry. Maimonides states that the practice of seething a kid in its mother's milk comes from the context of just such idolatrous cults, and it was for that reason that it was prohibited to Israel.

The law of not eating or cooking milk and meat together—one of the fundamental Kashrut regulations—is derived by the Rabbis from this prohibition of seething a kid in its mother's milk. It is not easy to determine its precise rationale, though, according to Maimonides' explanation, it is simply another measure whereby Israel polarizes to the opposite extreme of the position and practices of idolatrous cults, in conformity with the law of *Velo teilkhu bechukkot ha-goy*, "not walking in their ways" (Leviticus 20:23).

## THE SIXTH DAY'S READING

### 520. What is the relevance of the Reading of the Law for the sixth day of Pesach?

The sixth day of Pesach is also the fourth day of *Chol Ha-Moed*. The Reading (Numbers 9:1–14) is devoted to the institution of Pesach *Sheni*, "The second Passover." This is the opportunity given to those who were unable to offer the Paschal lamb at the proper time, on Nisan 14, to do so one month later, on the same day of the month of Iyyar. Reasons for such inability to offer the lamb in its proper season are either impurity, through contact with the dead, or travel to a distant place, and a consequent inability to reach Jerusalem in time for Pesach.

## THE SEVENTH DAY'S READING

### 521. What is the relevance of the Reading of the Law for the seventh day of Pesach?

For the seventh day of Pesach we read the account of the crossing of the Red Sea (Exodus 13:17–15:26). This is because the actual crossing of the Red Sea took place on the seventh day after the Exodus from Egypt.

### 522. How do we know that the crossing of the Red Sea took place precisely on the seventh day?

The Midrash (*Mekhilta*) calculates this quite simply. In its comment on the verse, "And it was told to the king of Egypt that the people had fled" (Exodus 14:5), it states that the king received his information from spies that he had planted among the Israelites. Once they arrived at the third day, which represented the total number of days for which Moses had requested permission for the Israelites to "celebrate a festival to the Lord in the desert" (8:23), and it became apparent to the spies that the Israelites had no intention of returning, they hastened back to Pharaoh. They got back the next day, and reported the matter to the king. On the fifth and sixth days after the Exodus Pharaoh pursued after them, and on the evening of the seventh day the Hebrews entered into the Red Sea. The following morning they sang their song of deliverance, having witnessed the drowning and total destruction of their enemies. Hence, on the seventh day of Pesach we read the *Shirat Ha-Yam*, the Song of the Red Sea.

**523. What were the events leading up to the crossing of the Red Sea, as described in the portion of the Torah we read on the seventh day?**

We are told that God did not take them the direct route to Canaan, which would have been a mere eleven days' journey, in a north-northeast direction, since that would have brought them into proximity with the warlike Philistines. Fear of confronting the latter might have prompted the Israelites to flee in panic back to Egypt.

We are told that Moses took with him the casket of Joseph's remains, in fulfillment of the promise made by the Israelites to Joseph just before he died (see Genesis 50:25), and that God displayed His guiding presence to the Israelites by going before them in a pillar of cloud by day and in a pillar of fire by night, which lit up the way ahead for them.

Pharaoh then pursued after them with six hundred of his fastest chariots in the lead, followed by a large host of Egyptian citizens, also in chariots driven by captains of his army. When the Israelites cried out in panic at the sight of the pursuing Egyptians, Moses stilled them, saying: "Do not fear. Stand your ground and see the deliverance God will perform for you this day. For, look at the Egyptians today, for you won't see them ever again! God will fight for you—and as for you, just hold your breath!" (Exodus 14:13).

Moses was then commanded to lift up his staff, at which sign all the Israelites were to proceed into the water. No sooner did Moses raise his arm when God caused a mighty east wind to whip the waves of the Red Sea back, against their natural tidal direction, thereby creating a dry section within the sea, and a path wide enough for the Israelites to march through on a dry seabed. When the Egyptians chased into the sea after them, God dropped the wind. The waters hurtled back into their place, burying the entire Egyptian army. The next morning, as the Israelites surveyed the Red Sea from the opposite bank, they saw the surface of the water covered with corpses and with the debris of the Egyptian chariots. Moses then led the Israelite men, and Miriam the women, in a glorious Song of victory, referred to in our tradition as, simply, the *Shirah,* "The Song" (on the *Shirah,* see questions 618–635).

This portion of the Law concludes on a depressing note however, since the next few verses reveal that the great joy and faith in God was short-lasting. Within three days the Israelites were panicking at a shortage of water, and barraging Moses with complaints. (For the *Haftarah* of the seventh day, see question 532.)

## THE EIGHTH DAY'S READING

**524. What portion of the Torah do we read for the eighth day of Pesach?**

We read Deuteronomy 14:22–16:17, which is the identical portion prescribed for the last day of each of the three main festivals: Pesach, Shavuot, and Sukkot. If the last day of Pesach falls on a *Shabbat,* we are required to read that entire section because we need to accommodate the calling-up to the Torah of seven people. If it is a weekday, when we only call up five people to the festival reading, then we commence the reading from *Kol ha-bekhor* (Deuteronomy 15:19).

**525. What are the contents of the extended section that is read if the eighth day of Pesach occurs on a *Shabbat*?**

This entire section, commencing *Asseir te-asseir,* is a collection of disparate laws, all linked by a common agricultural theme. It contains the law of *Maaser Sheni,* the "Second Tithe," in the form of produce to be taken and eaten in Jerusalem, or redeemed and a corresponding amount purchased in the holy city, and eaten there. This tithe also applied to the firstborn of sheep and cattle. While this ritual was to be observed in the first, second, fourth, and fifth years of the seven-year agricultural cycle, in the third and sixth years, however, this was replaced by *Maaser Oni,* the "Poor Man's Tithe," which was given to the poor, and for which there was no requirement that it had to be eaten in Jerusalem.

It then proceeds to recount the laws of *Shemitah,* the seventh year of release, when all debts are cancelled. This was to avoid one's poor fellow Israelite debtor sliding further and further into debt. The writing-off of the debt enabled him to make a new start, and, hopefully, to build a firmer psychological and financial base for his future endeavors. The Torah strongly cautions the wealthy moneylender against refusing to lend in the final years of the seven-year cycle, out of fear that the debt will not be discharged in time for the *Shemitah,* and he will be constrained to write it off. In ringing words the Torah states: "If the poor man [unable to obtain a loan] cries out to the Lord against you, sin will attach itself to you!" (15:9).

Then there follows the law of the Hebrew slave, whose period of service may not exceed six years, after which he must be released, and laden with supplies of live-stock and produce as a farewell gift and means of immediate support. Where he refuses to leave after six years, he has to subject himself to a humiliating ceremony of having his ear pierced. This was by way of a public reprimand for choosing a life of slavery, rather than of the freedom that his people fought so hard to secure during the long, oppressive period of slavery in Egypt. According to rabbinic tradition, the piercing of the ear is symbolic. We assail that ear that heard God say at Sinai, "You are My servants," and yet chose to ignore it and become a servant to a servant (of God).

**526. What are the contents of the Reading of the Law for the eighth day if that day is a weekday?**

This section (Deuteronomy 15:19–16:17), commencing *Kol ha-bekhor,* instructs Israel to accustom herself to making material sacrifices whenever required, both personally as well as for others. This quality was engendered by the ritual of tithing, whereby every owner of produce and livestock had to offer up a gift to God, to the priests and Levites, and to the poor and less fortunate.

This section begins by detailing but one of the *Matnot Kehunah,* the twenty-four gifts specifically designated as income for the priests. This is the tithe of the unblemished firstborn of sheep and cattle. It was undoubtedly also intended to provide an emotional association with the situation of the surrender of the innocent (unblemished) firstborn of the Egyptian livestock which perished, together with the human firstborn, in the last of the Ten Plagues.

The rest of the section provides a digest of the regulations governing the three pilgrim festivals, Pesach, Shavuot, and Sukkot. It concludes with the *mitzvah* of *Re-iyah,* the obligation that devolves on all males to make the pilgrimage to Jerusalem three times a year. They were to demonstrate that national quality of generosity by "not appearing empty-handed. Each man's gift shall be in accordance with the blessing which the Lord your God has given you." (For notes on *Haftarah* of the eighth day, see question 533.)

## THE INTERMEDIATE SABBATH'S READING

### 527. What are the contents of the Reading of the Law for the intermediate *Shabbat* of Pesach?

The prescribed portion (Exodus 33:12–34:26) is an extension of that read on the fifth (the third intermediate) day of the festival. It describes the situation immediately after the Israelites had worshiped the Golden Calf, and a terrible punishment had been visited upon the prime culprits (32:35).

Moses feels desperately vulnerable. His people have demonstrated how faithless they are, and Moses is fearful that God may withdraw His grace from them at any time. He asks God for tangible proof that His presence and spirit still resides with Israel, and that he, Moses, still enjoys God's confidence as leader. He is not satisfied with any general assurance. He asks for God to give a tangible, physical demonstration of His presence. God reminds him that "no man may see me and yet live." Nevertheless, God offers to set him in the cleft of a rock, and, after passing by Moses' place, enable him to "see My back." Precisely what that abstruse phrase means we cannot know. Perhaps it was akin to the jet stream that follows the path of a supersonic aircraft, and lingers long after it has already disappeared from sight.

God then tells Moses to hew out a second set of tablets of stone, to replace those he smashed in horror at the sight of the Israelites worshiping the Golden Calf, and to prepare himself to ascend Mount Sinai for a second period of forty days and nights. God reaffirms His covenant with Israel. He tells Moses that He will indeed drive out the indigenous tribes, but that Israel should be zealous not to indulge in the practices of those tribes or be enticed into intermarriage and idolatry with them.

The section concludes with a very brief survey of the three pilgrim festivals. It opens with a single sentence providing the instruction to observe *Chag Ha-matzot,* "the festival of unleaven bread," before interposing into that theme the extraneous regulation governing the dedication of every firstborn of man and cattle to God. The ass is made an exception. In its place the owners are to donate a lamb to the priests, and can then employ that ass for their own use.

Very curiously, the Torah tacks on to the end of the last verse dealing with the latter theme (34:20) the phrase, "and they shall not appear empty-handed before My presence." This clearly belongs to the theme of the festival of unleaven bread, which was interrupted by the injection of a reference to the dedication of the firstborn. We may only conjecture that Pesach was originally so supercharged with the notion of the special relationship that Israel's firstborn entered into, as a concomitant of the death of the Egyptian firstborn, that, by association, it was deemed appropriate to insert a reference to the intrinsic law of redemption of the firstborn when dealing with the theme of Passover.

The reading concludes with the law, repeated in two other passages of the Torah, not to seethe a kid in its mother's milk. Rabbinic tradition views this as a prohibition against the general commingling of meat and milk, and it explains the necessity for three separate references as representing three separate prohibitions: against eating, cooking, and enjoying any other benefit from the admixture. (For notes on the *Haftarah* for the intermediate *Shabbat* of Pesach, see question 534.)

## *HAFTARAH* FOR THE FIRST DAY

### 528. What is the relevance of the choice of *Haftarah* (concluding reading from the Prophets) for the first day of Pesach?

The first day's *Haftarah* is taken from Joshua 5:2–6:2 and relates the wholesale circumcision of the people by Joshua. This refers to the younger generation that had been born in the desert, and had not been circumcised. Joshua called the site of that event Gilgal, from a root meaning "to roll away." The implication was that, by attending to their circumcision, he had now "rolled away" the shame that adhered to them in the form of their foreskin.

The necessity to circumcise them at that moment was occasioned by the fact that Joshua was about to celebrate the first Passover in the Promised Land. Since the Israelites did not observe Pesach during their forty years in the desert, that Gilgal Passover must have been the first celebration of its kind; and since circumcision was a prerequisite for the Paschal lamb ritual, it was necessary therefore to make the people eligible for its celebration just at that time.

### 529. Why did the Israelites in the desert not circumcise their sons?

The *Haftarah* under review suggests that their being in the desert was the cause: "For they did not circumcise them while traveling along the way" (Joshua 5:7). The Rabbis explain that the conditions of the desert, and their constant movement, would have made it a painful and uncomfortable operation. They refer specifically to the absence of a northerly wind in the desert, which would have cooled their wound and refreshed them (see Rashi on Joshua 5:2). There might also have been another reason, namely that because the parents had been doomed to die in the desert, they might have regarded it as inappropriate for them to initiate their sons into a covenant of faith with God that they themselves had so brazenly violated.

## *HAFTARAH* FOR THE SECOND DAY

**530.  What is the relevance of the choice of *Haftarah* for the second day of Pesach?**

The *Haftarah* is taken from 2 Kings chapter 23, and refers to the reforms that the righteous king Josiah (640–609 B.C.E.) introduced into the kingdom of Judah. Under the reign of his grandfather, Menasseh, the nation slid into the abyss of iniquity. Idolatry was rife in the very Temple at Jerusalem, and child sacrifice, necromancy, and grossly immoral cults were widely practiced. Worship of Baal and Astarte replaced that of the ancestral God of Israel, and the situation was so critical that all copies of the Torah had been lost or destroyed, so that no one even remembered the true Israelite traditions. The same situation continued under his son, King Amon, father of Josiah.

King Josiah broke that mold, however, through having come under the positive religious influence of the High Priest, Hilkiah. One day, when examining the Temple foundations in preparation for some major repair works, Hilkiah discovered a copy of the Torah. He had it authenticated by the royal scribe, Shafan, who then brought it to the king, and read it to him. When Josiah heard its contents, and realized how far from God his people had strayed, and how great must be God's fury with His rebellious people, he broke down and tore his robes. He then instructed Hilkiah and the true religious leaders to intercede with God on behalf of the nation, to rid the country of every trace of idolatry and to ensure that knowledge of the Torah was henceforth widely disseminated.

It is at this point that our *Haftarah* commences, and it details all those reforms introduced by Josiah, in the eighteenth year of his reign, culminating in a vast national convocation held at the Temple, and led by the king and all the leaders of Judah. The centerpiece of the occasion was the public reading of the Sefer Torah, after which the people all took an oath of allegiance to God as part of a new covenant. They then proceeded to publicly pull down and destroy all the idolatrous images, and to burn every vestige of idolatry.

This major demonstration of remorse and reconciliation was timed for the eve of Passover, so that it might be climaxed with a national celebration of that festival whose very origin, amid the idolatries of ancient Egypt, had taken the form of a similar national covenant, sealed with a meal of fellowship, to confirm Israel's loyalty to their ancestral God. As regards Josiah's Passover, we are told that, "There was not kept such a Passover from the days of the judges that judged Israel, nor in all the days of the kings of Israel, nor of the kings of Judah" (23:25).

**531.  Does it not seem incredible that not a single copy of the Torah could have been in circulation, so that just by chance Hilkiah found one?**

If we know something of the social and religious conditions of that early period, it does not seem incredible. We are dealing with a period several centuries before the period of Ezra, Nehemiah, and the Soferim, who inaugurated an unprecedented period of scribal activity, to ensure that every community had a scroll of the Torah.

We are also dealing with a period when there was only a Temple, and no localized prayer houses where a Torah scroll would have been required. Again, the synagogue had not yet developed into an institution, so that copies of the Torah were not in circulation, and indeed there were few scribes who had the skill to undertake such a task, especially on a multiple scale.

We must not forget that this was a period of total rejection of the religion of Israel in favor of the indigenous Canaanite gods. Just as Josiah's reforms destroyed every vestige of the latter, so those idolators would have done a similarly thorough job, in the previous era, of deliberately destroying every vestige of the Israelite faith. For a parallel to this we have only to recall the discovery of the so-called Dead Sea Scrolls in 1947. They were buried there hastily by a persecuted community of Essenes living at Qumran that did not wish them to fall into the hands of the Romans—and they remained hidden for nearly 2,000 years! Literary works of early antiquity with a very small circulation, and especially those that fell victim to a concerted act of destruction, had little chance of survival. They were under threat not only from the hand of human vandals, but also from the corrosive effect of natural conditions. Unless they were sealed in air-tight containers, like the scrolls, they would disintegrate in a short time. Hence, for all the reasons we have mentioned, the absence of any scrolls during the period of Josiah should not occasion any surprise.

## *HAFTARAH* FOR THE SEVENTH DAY

**532. What is the relevance of the *Haftarah* for the seventh day of Pesach?**

The *Haftarah* is taken from 2 Samuel chapter 22, and its relevance lies in its literary genre as a poetic parallel to the Song of the Red Sea. It is, likewise, a victory song, sung by King David when he had finally defeated all his enemies.

Its sentiments parallel very closely those of the Song of the Red Sea, as the following few examples demonstrate:

| **Victory Song of David** | **Song of the Red Sea** |
| --- | --- |
| The Lord is my rock and my fortress (v. 2) | He is my strength[,] . . . my salvation (v. 2) |
| my high tower (v. 2) | For He is highly exalted (v. 1) |
| my savior (v. 2) | He has become my salvation (v. 2) |
| There went up smoke from His nostrils (v. 9) | with the blast of Thy nostrils (v. 8) |
| He sent out arrows and scattered them; lightning, and discomfited them (v. 15) | Thou sendest forth Thy wrath, it consumeth them (v. 7) |
| Thou hast girded me with strength (v. 40) | Thou hast guided them in Thy strength (v. 13) |
| For who is God save the Lord (v. 32) | Who is like unto Thee, O Lord (v. 11) |

| | |
|---|---|
| I have pursued my enemies (v. 38) | I shall pursue and overtake (v. 9) |
| Then the channels of the sea appeared (v. 16) | The deeps were congealed in the heart of the sea (v. 8) |
| Then the earth shook and trembled (v. 8) | They tremble; pangs have taken hold (v. 14) |
| He teaches my hand to war (v. 35) | The Lord is a man of war (v. 3) |
| I beat them small as the dust of the earth (v. 43) | The earth swallowed them (v. 12) |

## HAFTARAH FOR THE EIGHTH DAY

**533. What is the relevance of the *Haftarah* for the eighth day of Pesach?**

The *Haftarah* for this day is Isaiah 10:32–12:6. It describes an impending deliverance of the kingdom of northern Israel from the Assyrian onslaught of Sennacherib (705–681 B.C.E.), the destruction of the latter's army and an ingathering of exiles from Egypt and other surrounding countries which had fallen to the Assyrians. The imagery employs verses again clearly reminiscent of the Song of the Red Sea in order to create the notion of a second Exodus from Egypt: "And the Lord shall utterly destroy the tongue of the Egyptian sea; and with His terrible wind shall He shake his hand over the River: and he shall smite it into seven streams, and cause men to march over dryshod. And there shall be a highway for the remnant of His people . . . like as there was for Israel in the day that he came up out of the land of Egypt."

The prophecy was fulfilled in 701 B.C.E., for, although Sennacherib laid siege to Jerusalem, he was unable to take it, and lost some 185,000 men before abandoning it and returning to Assyria (2 Kings 19:35). Since his defeat coincided with the eve of Passover, there is an additional strand of relevance in the choice of this *Haftarah* for one of the days of this festival.

## INTERMEDIATE SABBATH

**534. What is the relevance of the *Haftarah* for *Shabbat Chol Ha-Moed* (the intermediate Sabbath) of Pesach?**

The *Haftarah* for the intermediate *Shabbat* is the majestic vision of Ezekiel and the dry bones (37:1–14). It relates how God brought the prophet into a valley full of the long dried-up bones of men who had perished on the field of battle. God asks the prophet whether he thinks those bones could ever be resurrected to new life. Ezekiel is naturally reticent to make any answer. He has had no experience of such a phenomenon, and at that period the concept of resurrection was not popular or developed. On the other hand, he knows that surely nothing is too difficult for God to innovate. He answers, therefore, rather vaguely, "O Lord, God [only] You know that!"

God tells him to address those bones, and to command them to receive the spirit of life that God is about to breathe into them. Ezekiel does so, and there, before his eyes, amid a rush and thunder, the bones knit together with flesh and sinews, and, after they are infused with breath drawn from the four winds, they stand on their feet as a great army.

God then tells Ezekiel the meaning of that vision: the dried-up bones are the dispirited Jews of the Babylonian exile, who have long given up hope of deliverance. But God will, as it were, "open up their graves and bring them to the land of Israel" as a viable and prosperous nation.

The relevance to Pesach is threefold. First, it preaches the message of this festival, that of a Jewish national renascence; secondly, it promotes the doctrine of resurrection in the hereafter, which, according to rabbinic tradition, will be inaugurated in the month of Nisan, wherein Passover occurs; and, thirdly, according to rabbinic tradition, the dry bones were none other than the remains of two hundred thousand warriors from the tribe of Ephraim who had defied their leaders and broken out of Egypt some thirty years before the ordained date of the Exodus. This conveys the affirmation that Israel's destiny is not dependent upon arbitrary chance, or even human factors, but is totally the result of God's direct design and will.

## *TAL* – PRAYER FOR DEW

### 535. When is the prayer for dew recited?

It is recited during the Chazan's repetition of the *Musaf Amidah* on the first day of Pesach.

### 536. Why does the Chazan wear a kittel for the recitation of this prayer?

The *kittel* is a white garment that is also worn by the Chazan on three other occasions in the year: on the high holy days, on *Hoshanah Rabbah* (the seventh day of the festival of Sukkot), and on *Sheminiy Atzeret* (the eighth day of the festival of Sukkot) for the recitation of *Geshem* (the prayer for rain). White is a symbol of purity; and because the gift of dew in Spring is essential for the crops of Israel and for the livelihood of its citizens – as is rain during winter – the Chazan's appeal to God is especially urgent. His white dress is meant, therefore, to suggest to God that Israel is free of sin, and waiting upon His mercy and generosity.

### 537. Why do we commence referring to rain only on the eighth day of Sukkot (by including in the *Amidah* the phrase, *Mashiv ha-ruach umorid ha-gashem*, "He causes wind to blow and rain to fall"), whereas the Tal prayer, for dew, is recited already on the very first day of Pesach?

Because dew is regarded as a more blessed gift. Firstly, because all the major festivals of the Jewish year – Pesach, Shavuot, and Sukkot – occur during the period when we are praying for dew; and secondly, because dew has only beneficial effects, whereas, although rain is vital during winter, invariably we get either too much or too little of it, but never the precise amount required, in the context of a mild winter.

**538. On *Sheminiy Atzeret,* the Synagogue Warden, or *Shamash,* announces, prior to the silent *Musaph Amidah,* that the congregation should not forget to include the *Mashiv ha-ruach* line. Why, then, did tradition not prescribe an announcement, for the first day of Pesach, that we no longer recite *Mashiv ha-ruach*?**

It was deemed inappropriate to instruct the community not to recite any prayer. Furthermore, since rain is a vital divine blessing, and, according to the Talmud (*Taanit* 2a), "God keeps the key of rain in His own hand, and does not hand it over to any representative" (i.e., it is totally unpredictable and is not governed by the regular laws and rhythms of nature), hence it is not for us to make what would be tantamount to a rejection of God's personal blessing.

**539. Why were these references to rain (Geshem) and dew (Tal) inserted specifically into the second blessing of the *Amidah*?**

Because that blessing commences with the words, *Attah gibbor* ("You are mighty"), and refers to God imposing the sentence of death (*meimit*) and also bringing life into being (*umechayyeh*). Rain and dew were also considered as manifestations of God's "might," and as the instruments through which He wields His power of life and death over mankind.

## THE POETIC SETTING FOR *TAL*

**540. The proclamation, *Mashiv ha-ruach umorid ha-gashem,* is introduced by a poetic composition. Who is the author and when was it written?**

It was written by one of the pioneers of Hebrew poetry, and one of the most prolific synagogue poets of the Ashkenazi rite, Eleazar Kallir, who also wrote one of the songs recited at the end of the Seder (see question 445). Precisely when Kallir lived cannot be determined, and opinions vary widely. Some scholars place him in the fifth century; Leopold Zunz thought he lived in the eighth century, while S. D. Luzzatto placed him in the later, Geonic period (tenth century) (see L. Zunz, *Literaturgeschichte der synagogalen Poesie* [Berlin: Louis Gerschel, 1865], p. 60; S. D. Luzzatto, *Tal Orot* [Przemysl, 1881], p. 31). (On Kallir, see Cohen, *Blessed Are You,* pp. 56–57; see also Jeffrey M. Cohen, *Prayer and Penitence,* Northvale, NJ: Jason Aronson Inc., 1964, pp. 25–38, 69–71, 107–109.)

**541. What is the theme of the *Tal* poem, commencing [*Elokeinu ve-Elokey avoteinu*], *Tal tein lirtzot artzekha*?**

It is a plea for precious dew to fall and endow God's land with ample wine and corn. In the poet's imagination he perceives the dew as a gleaming crown adorning

Jerusalem. Its coming will lift the spirits of the city like a shaft of light penetrating the darkness. Kallir then includes a plea for God to deliver His people from exile so that they may enjoy the benefits of the dew at firsthand, and sing full-throated praise of God for that benefit.

In the penultimate stanza—whose sense is not too clear, and is the subject of widely differing interpretations (see Y. Jakobson, *Netiv Binah*, Tel Aviv: Sinai, 1978, pp. 78–79)—he seems to be employing dew as a metaphor for the freshness of eternal life in the hereafter, which, if bestowed upon Israel, will enable her to praise God forever.

The final stanza contains a plea for dew-blessed, rich harvests, so that God's flock, Israel, will always be enabled to flourish. The poem is followed by a confident assertion that God will send His wind and dew "for a blessing, and not for a curse; for plenty, and not for famine; for life, and not for death."

## MORID HA-TAL

**542. Whereas Ashkenazim simply omit the line *Mashiv ha-ruach umorid ha-gashem* ("He causes the wind to blow and the rain to fall") from the first day of Pesach until it is reintroduced on *Sheminiy Atzeret,* do not the Sephardim continue to add some formula at that point in the second blessing of the *Amidah*?**

Indeed. The conclusion of the *Tal* poem, to which we have just alluded, includes the phrase, *She-attah . . . mashiv ha-ruach umorid ha-tal.* It is an abbreviated form of that phrase, utilizing merely the final two words, *Morid ha-tal,* that Sephardim, and a large number of Ashkenazi congregations in Israel today, include in the second blessing of the *Amidah* between Pesach and *Sheminiy Atzeret.*

**543. What if, after Pesach, someone forgot and, out of habit, inserted into his *Amidah* the line, *Mashiv ha-ruach umorid ha-gashem*?**

The halakhah prescribes that if he remembered his error before he had concluded that second blessing then he simply returns to the beginning of the blessing again. If, however, he had already concluded the blessing, then he must return to the beginning of the *Amidah*. The reason for insisting upon this is to demonstrate that rain during the harvesting period is unwanted and harmful.

**544. What if he was in doubt whether he had actually made the mistake of reciting *Mashiv ha-ruach umorid ha-gashem* or not?**

In that case we assume that, within the first thirty days after the first day of Pesach, he most probably was influenced by the habit of the previous six months and did, therefore, recite the inappropriate formula, thereby necessitating a repetition of the *Amidah*. After thirty days, however, he may adopt the benefit of the doubt, and assume that he did not recite it.

**545. In congregations that employ the formula *Morid ha-tal* from after Pesach, in which service is it introduced?**

The Warden, or *Shamash,* announces it before the silent *Musaf Amidah* of the first day of Pesach, and the congregation introduces it, instead of *Mashiv ha-ruach umorid ha-gashem,* into that *Amidah.*

**546. What if one inadvertently omitted *Morid ha-tal* in summer?**

There is no halakhic necessity to recite this formula. Therefore omission of it requires no compensatory action.

**547. What if one inadvertently recited *Mashiv ha-ruach* after Pesach?**

There is no problem here, since he made no reference to rain and , according to the Talmud, wind is, in any case, ever present in all seasons (Taz on *Shulchan Arukh, Orach Chayyim* 114:3 [7]).

## CHOL HA-MOED AND ITS SERVICES

**548. What is the meaning of the name *Chol Ha-Moed*?**

The word *Chol* means "weekday" (literally, "profane," "nonholy"), and the word *Moed* means "festival." It refers, therefore, to the intermediate days that span the first two holy days of *Yom Tov* (in Israel, one day) and the last two holy days (in Israel, one). The days of *Chol Ha-Moed* partake of a festive spirit, and in Temple times were marked by special sacrifices and ritual, but they do not have applied to them the same halakhic restrictions as regards the prohibition of work and other activities that apply to full holy days.

## CHOL HA-MOED OBSERVANCES

**549. What, then, are the main differences between what is permitted on *Chol Ha-Moed* and forbidden on the full *Yom Tov* days?**

A full discussion of these laws is outside the scope of this book. We can only refer here, therefore, to one or two major distinctions. In talmudic times the intermediate days had a more festive spirit than today, and ordinary manual work was prohibited. A specific tractate of the Talmud, called *Moed Katan* ("The Minor Part of the Festival") is devoted to a discussion of the laws of that period, determining what type of activity, normally prohibited on the full holy days, are nevertheless permitted on *Chol Ha-Moed,* and under what circumstances.

The primary way in which the festival spirit was maintained during *Chol Ha-Moed* was in the prohibition of fasting (people used to take upon themselves a host of private fasts in earlier times, as a means of penance or to purge a bad dream) or the delivery of a funeral oration, since these are calculated to impair the festive mood. As regards work, the principle was that, as long as there was no strenuous work involved, one might indulge in any activity that would involve a person in financial loss or cause something of value to perish (*davar ha-aveid*) if it lay unattended. The classical example given in the Mishnah is that of a parched field containing many fruit-bearing trees which would all be lost if it was not watered that day.

### 550. Were there any other general principles governing what activities were declared permitted on *Chol Ha-Moed*?

Any work that had to be done as a requirement for the forthcoming festival days was also permitted as necessary work. Also, work could be done that was required in the public interest, such as digging new wells for water supply and repairing existing ones and, similarly, building and repairing roads, paths, and irrigation pipes and measuring the volume of water in the *Mikvaot* (ritual baths). It was also permitted to send representatives to conduct financial negotiations for the ransom of captured fellow Jews, and to mark out signs indicating the presence of graves, so that priests would not wander inadvertently into the area. These were all categorized as "in the public interest," and the permissibility of any similar activity could easily be gauged by inference.

### 551. What about some specific activities that were and were not permitted on *Chol Ha-Moed*?

The courts were allowed to judge civil and criminal cases on *Chol Ha-Moed*. Whereas business letter writing was prohibited as part of the general prohibition against conducting business, nevertheless, the judges were permitted to write court documents, memos, contracts, valuations, divorce documents and marriage certificates. These were all regarded as tantamount to "public interest." All preparations for burial, including the making of a coffin, were permitted.

It was declared forbidden to conduct weddings on *Chol Ha-Moed,* so that the joy of the festival does not become totally obscured by the joy of the event. An exception was made, however, in the case of someone re-marrying the wife he had previously divorced. The celebration of an engagement was permitted, but without the customary celebratory meal.

### 552. There are some people who do not shave during *Chol Ha-Moed*. What is the basis for this?

The Mishnah declares haircutting on *Chol Ha-Moed* prohibited (*Moed Katan* 3:1). The Talmud discloses that this was a measure introduced in order to ensure that men maintained a dignified and respectful attitude to the festival days proper. Permission to cut the hair on *Chol Ha-Moed* would have meant that people might not have bothered to have their hair cut before the festival, which would have involved them in taking time off their working day, in the knowledge that they would have time during

*Chol Ha-Moed* — a national holiday from work — to attend to it. They would therefore have appeared unkempt on the holy day, thus impairing its sanctity and honor. Knowing, however, that there was a prohibition on haircutting during the intermediate days meant that people would be more scrupulous before the onset of the festival to attend to it.

People who maintain the practice in our day of not having their hair cut are clearly following the talmudic prescription. As regards the shaving of one's face, however, the position is not so clear-cut, and there are many observant people — perhaps the majority — who are not particular in that regard. They argue that the Talmud was, in any case, referring to the hair of the head, and that there is no evidence that any prohibition was made concerning the hair of the beard (see question 485 above). Secondly, it may be argued, the rationale offered by the Talmud should not apply in our day for the majority of people who are accustomed, indeed scrupulous, to shave their faces on a daily basis. In our day there is a total difference in perception of, and approach to, appearance, with electric shaving being so quick and easy that it has become an essential daily routine. For those who follow that routine, therefore, no rabbinic decree, to enforce it and to punish those who are dilatory, has any purpose or relevance.

### 553. Some people do not write on *Chol Ha-Moed*. Is it truly prohibited?

It will be recalled that, in our answer to question 551 above, we referred to certain court documents that were permitted to be written on *Chol Ha-Moed*. In that list of sundry kinds of document, the Mishnah (*Moed Katan* 3:3) includes *iggrot shel reshut,* literally, "optional letters." The meaning of that term was obscure even to the classical commentators. Rashi understood it, in a totally different sense, as "state certificates" (based on a vocalization of the word as *rAshut* ("the ruling power"), whereas others (maintaining the reading *rEshut*) explain it as "personal correspondence."

Maimonides suggests that such letters were permitted because they are hurriedly written, and do not involve great precision and effort. (His one proviso would be that their contents related to the requirements of the festival itself.) For the same reason it is permitted to make financial calculations and lists of expenses, which do not involve a careful script, and which, if not committed to writing, could involve financial loss. *Raavad* adapts this rationale for permitting letter writing: since the contents could be construed as *davar ha-aveid,* something that might be lost (and forgotten), if they were not written down.

According to Joseph Karo, "It is permitted to send a personal letter to one's friend, and even a business letter on a matter where no personal loss could be incurred" (*Shulchan Arukh, Orach Chayyim* 545:5). The Ashkenazi glossator, Moses Isserles, observes: "But some forbid the writing of a personal letter [*Tur*]; and [although we permit it, nevertheless,] it is the practice to be particular to make a distinction in the shape of the script." Taz states that it was common practice to make that distinction by writing the top line in a slanting direction.

**554. So what is the situation governing doing business on *Chol Ha-Moed*?**

If we take into consideration the principles we have already referred to, we will see that since work may be done if it is to avoid financial loss, we may conclude that the maintenance of one's business and the good will of customers — especially in a highly competitive and difficult business climate — may be regarded as a "potential loss situation," fulfilling the *davar ha-aveid* criterion. Furthermore, since any work done as a requirement for the festival itself is permitted (see question 549), Isserles follows the view of Karo that if doing business enables one to lavish more on the celebration of *Yom Tov,* then the entire business activity may be construed as serving that end, and permitted accordingly. It is obviously preferable if one can afford to observe *Chol Ha-Moed* as a holiday, or to reduce the amount of work done on these days.

## *TEFILLIN* ON *CHOL HA-MOED*

**555. Why do most worshipers in synagogues in Israel not put on *tefillin* on *Chol Ha-Moed*, whereas in the Diaspora they do put them on?**

Since the intermediate days of a festival are also called *mo'ed* (festival), and consequently represent a "sign" in themselves of the God-Israel covenant, thereby rendering the additional "sign" of the *tefillin* unnecessary, Joseph Karo declared it forbidden to wear *tefillin* on those days (*Shulchan Arukh, Orach Chayyim* 31:2). The Ashkenazi authorities, on the other hand, recommended that they should be worn, since these days had acquired the character of ordinary working days. Moses Isserles states that "nevertheless, in synagogue one should not recite the blessing over them in a loud voice, as is customary throughout the rest of the year" (31:2). There are some authorities (see *Taz,* ad loc.) who recommend wearing the *tefillin* but without reciting the blessings!

The *hasidim* of Poland adopted the Sephardi practice of not wearing them, and adherents of Hasidism — even those living in other countries — have retained this practice. Both those influences — the Sephardic and the hasidic — have become predominant in the State of Israel, especially through the dissemination of the Lurianic *Nusach Ari* prayer rite, and hence the almost universal practice of not wearing *tefillin* on *Chol Ha-Moed.* The unadulterated Ashkenazi and *Mitnagged* (nonhasidic) tradition is becoming something of a rarity, so that even in synagogues of that ilk it is not uncommon to find some worshipers present on *Chol Ha-Moed* and not wearing *tefillin.*

**556. At what stage should the *tefillin* be removed on *Chol Ha-Moed*?**

Taking account of Karo's view that *Chol Ha-Moed* also represents the "sign" of the God–Israel covenant, *Taz* advizes that they be removed "before *Hallel* and certainly before the Reading of the Torah, both of which are specific to the festival itself and underscore its role as 'a sign' " (ad loc.). It would therefore be wholly inappropriate to be wearing *tefillin* when we should rather be highlighting the more comprehensive "sign" that the festival represents. Some have the custom to leave the *tefillin* on for the Reading from the Torah on the first day of *Chol Ha-Moed* (only), since on that day we read, *Kaddesh liy kol bekhor,* which is one of the four portions included in the *tefillin.*

### 557. What other differences are there between the morning service of *Chol Ha-Moed* and that of ordinary days?

We omit *Mizmor Le-todah* (Psalm 100) and we omit the *Tachanun* petitionary prayers after the repetition of the *Amidah* by the Chazan. The ordinary weekday silent *Amidah* is recited, but with the addition of *Ya'aleh Veyavo.* After the Chazan's repetition of the *Amidah* we recite the shortened form of *Hallel,* followed by full *Kaddish* (including the line commencing, *Titkabbel tzelot'hon*). The two Torah scroll are then taken out, and we call up four people to the appropriate passages for each day of *Chol Ha-Moed* (see questions 515–520). From the second scroll we read *Vehikravtem* (Numbers 28:19–25.) On *Chol Ha-Moed* (and on the days of *Yom Tov*) we do not recite *Hazkarot* or *Hashkavot* (memorial prayers for the departed). After the Torah reading we recite half-*Kaddish,* and while dressing the scrolls we do not recite the petitions commencing, *Yehiy ratzon milifnei avinu shebashamayim,* which are usually recited on Monday and Thursday mornings at that point. Instead, we proceed straight to *Ashrei* and *Uva Letzion,* omitting *Lamenatzei'ach* (Psalm 20). After returning the scrolls to the Ark, the Chazan recites half-*Kaddish,* and the *Musaf Amidah* for festivals is recited silently by the congregation and then repeated by the Chazan. The difference between its recitation on *Yom Tov* and on *Chol Ha-Moed* is that on the latter days the ordinary weekday *Shacharit Kedushah* (which, for Ashkenazim outside Israel, commences *Nekaddesh et shimkha,* and for Sephardim and Israelis commences *Nakdishakh*) is recited, instead of the *Musaf Kedushah.*

### 558. Are there any differences in any of the other services on *Chol Ha-Moed*?

The ordinary prayers are followed for *Minchah* and *Ma'ariv* services, with the exception that *Ya'aleh Veyavo* is again inserted into each of the *Amidah* prayers of those services, as well as into the *Birkat Ha-Mazon* (Grace after Meals). Also, no *Tachanun* petitions are recited after the repetition of the *Minchah Amidah.* Indeed, there is a custom not to recite *Tachanun* for the entire month of Nisan.

### 559. Why do some not recite Tachanun for the entire month of Nisan?

The reason is that since the majority of the month has a festive character, we regard the entire month as festive. The installation into office of the twelve princes of the tribes of Israel took place on the twelve consecutive days commencing on the first of Nisan, on which day the *Mishkan* (desert Sanctuary) was erected (see Numbers 7:10–88 and Rashi on Leviticus 9:1), and they each offered their special sacrifice on their appointed day. Thus, those twelve days have a happy and festive association. The day before Pesach, when the Paschal lamb was offered, and the entire festival, together with *Isru chag* (the day afterwards), add a further ten days (nine in Israel) of festivity. Hence, because most of the month is historically festive, we give the entire month that attribution. The sentiments of *Tachanun* – which partake rather of a spirit of national lament – are therefore deemed inappropriate for this month.

### 560. Why is *Mizmor Le-todah* (Psalm 100) omitted on *Chol Ha-Moed Pesach*?

That psalm, whose title means, "A psalm of thanksgiving," was sung in the Temple as an accompaniment to the Thanksgiving Offering (*Korban Todah*). That particular offering could not be brought on Pesach, since it had to be offered together with loaves of bread which were, naturally, impossible to offer on this festival.

### 561. Why, when dressing the Torah scrolls, do we omit recitation of the Yehiy ratzon petitions?

These petitions are popularly classified as belonging to the *Tachanun* genre, and were introduced for recitation on Mondays and Thursdays in order to provide an accompaniment to the dressing of the Torah scroll, rather than have a period of nonprayerful silence. Their omission on *Chol Ha-Moed* is on two counts: firstly, since *Tachanun* is omitted on *Chol Ha-Moed,* these were also omitted. Secondly, for a very practical reason of time constraint. Unlike Mondays and Thursdays, the *Chol Ha-Moed* service is extended greatly, by *Hallel* and *Musaf.* Proceeding immediately with *Ashrei,* while the scroll is being dressed, helps to save a little time.

### 562. Why do we omit Lamenatzei'ach (Psalm 20) on *Chol Ha-Moed*?

That psalm begins with the words "May God answer you in the day of trouble," a description hardly appropriate to a day which partakes of the joyful spirit of a (semi-)festival.

## YA'ALEH VEYAVO

### 563. What if someone inadvertently omitted to say Ya'aleh veyavo in any of his *Chol Ha-Moed Amidahs*?

If he remembers his omission almost immediately, and before he has concluded the *Retzeh* blessing, then he stops and recites it then, and finishes with the concluding sentence of the *Retzeh* blessing: *Vetechezenah eyneynu.* If he has proceeded further with his silent *Amidah,* he again returns to the beginning of the *Retzeh* blessing. If, however, he has gone beyond the sentence commencing, *Yiheyu leratzon imrei fiy* (just before *Oseh shalom*), then he must go back again and recite the entire *Amidah.*

**564. Why was the Ya'aleh Veyavo insertion for the three main festivals and Rosh Chodesh (New Moon) placed inside the Avodah (Retzeh) blessing, whereas the Al Ha-Nisim insertion for Chanukah and Purim was inserted into the following, Modim (thanksgiving) blessing?**

*Tosafot* (see on Talmud *Shabbat* 24a, D. H. *Bevoneh*) explains that the *Retzeh* blessing, with its plea to God to "restore the Temple service to the habitation of Your House" (*Vehashev et ha-avodah lidvir beitekha*) is far more suited as a context for a reference to a pilgrim festival at the Temple (Pesach, Shavuot, and Sukkot) and for occasions when special festival sacrifices are biblically prescribed (which includes Rosh Chodesh). Chanukah and Purim are historical festivals, with no biblically prescribed extra sacrifices, so they were placed in a separate blessing which deals specifically with thanksgiving for "miracles that are daily dispensed" (*Al nisekha shebkhol yom immanu*).

The Palestinian Talmud (*Talmud Yerushalmi, Berakhot* 4:3) establishes the principle that "Any subject that refers to the future [such as a plea for a request to be fulfilled] is inserted into the *Retzeh* blessing; and any reference to the past [that is, a historical reminiscence or thanksgiving] is placed in the *Modim* [Thanksgiving] prayer."

**565. When else is Ya'aleh Veyavo recited during Pesach?**

It is also recited in the Grace after Meals (*Birkat Ha-Mazon*), where it is inserted into the third blessing (*Rachem*). This blessing asks God to "Have mercy upon . . . Jerusalem Your city, on Zion the abode of Your glory." Also, its conclusion refers specifically to "the Lord who, in His mercy, will rebuild Jerusalem [*Boneh berachamav Yerushalayim*]." For that reason this blessing was selected as most appropriate for *Ya'aleh Veyavo* with its specific reference to the pilgrim festival to which, in Temple times, Jerusalem played host.

**566. Is the festive nature of *Chol Ha-Moed* restricted then to the domain of the synagogue service?**

While for most Diaspora Jews this is unfortunately so, in the State of Israel the whole week of Pesach is largely taken as holiday from work, especially in the public sector. There is no prescribed home ritual, as for the full holy days, but it is traditional to have more formal and festive family meals, especially at night, and some have a tradition to have candles on the table each evening.

## *YIZKOR* – MEMORIAL PRAYERS FOR THE DEPARTED

**567. When is the *Yizkor* memorial prayer for the departed recited?**

It is recited on the last day of Pesach. In the case of the other main festivals it is also reserved for the last day, because on the final day of each festival we recite the same portion of the Torah (Deuteronomy 15:19–16:17), which refers to "each man contributing [charity] in accordance with his ability" (16:17). This was viewed as a most appropriate reference, reinforcing thereby the need to mark the memorial to the departed through a charitable donation in their memory.

Because some might consider that an emotionally nostalgic recollection of the departed conflicts somewhat with the joyful spirit that we are supposed to foster on a festival, its recitation on the very last day of festivals is most appropriate, since that day, in various halakhic respects, does not possess the same festive aura as the previous days.

### 568. For which relatives does one recite *Yizkor*?

*Yizkor* is recited for any relative for whom one had an obligation to mourn and sit *shivah,* namely, parents, sister, brother, son, daughter, or spouse. There is no objection to reciting it also for grandparents, aunts, uncles, or any other relative, or even for people to whom one is not related but who have not left behind any relatives to recite the prayer.

By the same token, a communal *Yizkor* memorial prayer is recited for the victims of the Holocaust.

## HISTORY OF *YIZKOR* MEMORIAL PRAYERS

### 569. What is the origin of memorial prayers for the departed?

Eulogies for the dead go back to early biblical times. When Abraham returned from the *Akedah* (the binding of Isaac), we are told that, "Abraham came to mourn [*lispod*] for Sarah and to weep for her" (Genesis 23:2). The two forms of mourning detailed here suggest that the former took the form of a eulogy and, possibly, also a prayer for her repose. Because the notion of the hereafter was undeveloped at that early period, however, we cannot be sure what sentiments might have invested such a prayer. The common noun *hesped,* "eulogy," is derived from that verb, *lispod.*

We also have in the Bible the most moving memorial tribute uttered by David for Jonathan and Saul after they were killed in battle against the Philistines (2 Samuel 1:17–27). These eulogies and prayers were uttered at the time of burial. There is no evidence, however, that in biblical times there was any subsequent commemoration of the dead, such as we have on a *Yahrzeit.*

It was in the Maccabean period (165 B.C.E.) that we find a reference to Judah the Maccabee and his men praying for the souls of their fallen comrades, and bringing sacrifices to the rededicated Temple as an atonement for the sins of the dead (2 Maccabees 22:39–45). This was clearly a one-time national commemoration, and there was no thought at that time to introduce the practice at community or family level on a regular basis.

### 570. When were memorial prayers popularized?

The custom probably first arose in Franco-German, Ashkenazi communities in the wake of the Crusades and the countless thousands of martyrs who perished as victims of the misguided religious fervor of medieval Christianity. The Christian armies, marching to Palestine to liberate the holy land from the hands of the Muslim infidel, began by purging themselves of the Jewish infidel within their midst. They showed no mercy, to young or old, men or women, as they decimated countless great and vibrant centers of Jewish religious life.

The endless lists of martyrs were carefully recorded and preserved in the *Memor-buch* or *Yizkor-buch* of the various communities, and they were read out at certain times, together with a special *Yizkor* or *Hazkarah* ("memorial") prayer for their repose in paradise.

### 571. On what occasions were these *Yizkor* prayers recited?

They were recited at first exclusively on Yom Kippur, the Day of Atonement. The *Shulchan Arukh* merely states that "it was a custom to contribute charity on Yom Kippur on behalf of the departed" (*Orach Chayyim,* 621). Moses Isserles, quoting the *Mordechai* (a thirteenth-century German halakhic authority), adds the comment, "And we make mention of the names of the departed souls, since they also obtain forgiveness on the Day of Atonement." This idea inspired another German authority, Rabbi Jacob Weil (fifteenth century), to explain the plural form Yom Kippurim (literally, "Day of Atonements") in that it atoned for both the living and the dead.

During the sixteenth century, the recitation of *Yizkor* was extended to include memorial prayers not only for the martyred but for all departed relatives; and their recitation was extended to all the other major festivals, with the exception of Rosh Hashanah.

### 572. Does not the recitation of memorial prayers impair the joy of the festival?

The authorities who permitted their recitation clearly did not view the recitation of *Yizkor* in that light. They believed that even if its recitation drew a silent tear, it actually had a beneficial and therapeutic effect, helping, by releasing the emotions, to dispell one's residual grief. For this reason—totally in consonance with the modern views on the psychology of bereavement—they did not see any conflict between the recitation of *Yizkor* and the joyous experience of a festival day.

### 573. Why should such memorial prayers be required? Surely, close relatives never forget their precious loved ones whose absence has left such a void in their lives?

The truth is that nature cushions us from morose preoccupation with thoughts about the dead, however precious they were to us. Thus, although visions of our loved ones, and recollections of their actions and words, do periodically flit through our minds, yet those thoughts generally have to jostle with competing impressions and experiences while we are being distracted with other activities or conversations. Not so during *Yizkor.* At such a time, the departed are given our complete attention—a consecrated attention—as befits their immortal spirit.

Then again, how infinitely more meaningful and symbolic it is to remember the departed in synagogue, on a *Yom Tov,* in the context of a sacred prayer, making mention of their personal Hebrew names. And all in an atmosphere of whispered reverence.

### 574. What is the Jewish view of life after death?

We do believe that there is a world beyond the grave, that death is, indeed, a starlit strip between the companionship of yesterday and the reunions of tomorrow, and that, just as we sometimes breathe a sigh of relief when awakening out of a nightmare, so it will be the moment after death.

We believe that there is a final day of judgment, and a granting of reward to the righteous and punishment for the wicked. We also believe that the reward is an eternal bliss, whereas for most, the punishment is but transitory, and that, once it has been undergone, the soul is restored to grace.

## *YIZKOR* LAWS AND PRACTICES

### 575. May *Yizkor* be recited only in the presence of a *minyan*?

It is, naturally, preferable that it should be recited in that context. However, one who is sick, and cannot get to synagogue, is permitted to recite it at home. Similarly, if a synagogue cannot muster a *minyan,* it may still be recited.

### 576. Since suicide is a heinous sin in Judaism, may one recite *Yizkor* for a departed person who died by his own hand?

According to the *Duda'ei Ha-Sadeh* (quoted in Y. Greenwald, *Kol Bo Al Aveilut,* New York: Moriah, 1947, p. 403), one may do so. We may infer that his view would be identical as regards reciting *Yizkor* for people who had been cremated.

### 577. Does one recite *Yizkor* during the first year of mourning for a departed relative?

Yes one does. Just as one recites *Kaddish* during that period, which, although technically not a specific prayer *for* the departed, yet recalls them to mind every time it is recited, so, especially during the first year, is a memorial prayer particularly appropriate. Many authorities strongly denounce "the erroneous view" that it should not be recited during the first year (see Greenwald, *Kol Bo Al Aveilut,* p. 404).

### 578. If one's spouse has died and one has remarried, is it appropriate to continue to recite a *Yizkor* prayer for the first spouse?

While authorities regard the continued observance of the *Yahrzeit,* with its requirement to light a memorial candle in the home, and the attendant public recitation of *Kaddish* and synagogue memorial prayer, as inappropriate, since it might upset, and create barriers with, the present spouse, they did not, however, feel that the inclusion of a departed spouse's name in the silently intoned *Yizkor* prayer created any such problems. If the person felt a strong wish to recite the prayer, as for example in a situation where there were no children or other relatives to recite it for the departed former spouse, then it is certainly permissible (see Greenwald, *Kol Bo Al Aveilut*).

### 579. What is the origin of the custom that those whose parents are living are made to leave the synagogue for the duration of the *Yizkor*?

While this is a custom hallowed by time, for which reason many modern-day Rabbis are still wholly committed to it, yet it has to be admitted that it is rooted in the grossly superstitious belief in the evil eye and in "not giving Satan an opening." The latter fear is that, if the people with parents demonstrate eagerness to remain in synagogue together with those reciting prayers for departed relatives, then Satan will seize the pretext to grant that wish in its absolute entirety, and place them in the category of the bereaved so that they will have cause to recite it as an obligatory memorial!

A distinguished English rabbi, the late Dr. S. M. Lehrman, makes the following apposite observation:

> The custom of sending out of the synagogue, during the recital, those who have parents, causes much upheaval, is disturbing to the prayerful mood prevailing then, and ought to be discouraged. Religious decorum is a thing of great value, and children will have more regard for their parents when they see how they recall their own dear parents since called to their eternal rest (S. M. Lehrman, *Jewish Customs and Folklore* [London: Shapiro, Vallentine and Co., 1964], p. 200).

From a halakhic perspective, there are many illustrious authorities (see *Chatam Sofer* on *Yoreh De'ah* 346) who have declared it permissible for those who are unperturbed by superstitions (*man delo kapid*) to disregard customs and practices that arose purely as evasive measures. Hence, Moses Isserles states categorically that if a man loses his wife and, through irrational and superstitious fear, seeks to prevent his son saying *Kaddish* for his mother, the son must disregard his father's sensibilities and proceed with his filial obligation (*Remah* on *Shulchan Arukh, Yoreh De'ah* 376:4). The *Bet Lechem Yehudah* (ad loc.) goes further and states that where the deceased left no sons and a grandson wishes to say *Kaddish,* he may disregard his mother's superstition-based objections!

We may assume that most sophisticated Jews of the modern era would feel no unease at their children standing by them during *Yizkor.* Where the children knew and loved their grandparents, is it not truly appropriate, therefore, for the grandchildren to stand in reverent and fond recollection at that sacred time while their parents are reciting the memorial prayer?

Another consideration for recommending that children remain in synagogue is that of *kallut rosh,* the noisy behavior and unseemly levity of the younger generation massing in the synagogue foyer, which frequently creates a distraction and disturbance to those solemnly intoning their *Yizkor* prayers inside. Halakhic authorities are far more concerned with *kallut rosh* than they are by patently superstitious considerations.

**580. So if those with parents remain in synagogue, what should they do while the rest of the congregation is reciting *Yizkor*?**

In his *Yizkor: A Memorial Booklet* (London: Gnesia Publications, 1994, p. 23) the present writer has compiled a special Hebrew and English "Prayer of Thanksgiving for the Health and Wellbeing of One's Family" for those of his congregants who, fortunately, do not have to recite *Yizkor.* The English translation reads as follows:

Father in heaven, I stand on this holy day amid the congregation of Israel who pour out their hearts before You, and who are remembering their parents and family who have gone to their eternal rest. As for me, I offer You my most profound gratitude, for, in Your great loving-kindness and abundant favor, there is no grief in my heart nor tear on my cheek. For my father and mother [husband/wife; brother(s)/sister(s); son(s)/daughter(s)] are with me. None is missing. They ask life of You; You give it to them.

Therefore my heart rejoices, in the knowledge that my near family has been spared anxiety. May the Lord preserve them from evil. May He watch over their every movement. May He prolong their days in happiness, that they may behold children and grandchildren occupying themselves with religious practice and the study of the Torah.

I have entreated Your favor with my whole heart. Be gracious unto me according to Your promise.

## THE PRIESTLY BLESSING

**581. What is the meaning of the term "*dukhaning*," which is popularly applied to the Priestly Blessing?**

It derives from the fact that the priests in the Temple stood on a *dukhan,* that is, a platform, to bless the people each day.

## *DUKHANING* PRACTICES

**582. If it was a daily ritual, why is it not continued on a daily basis in our synagogues today?**

In Israel it is. In the Diaspora, however, another consideration militated against allowing its recitation other than on festivals. Since one has to have a totally happy frame of mind and a tranquil spirit to confer a blessing, it was felt that the pressing problems of earning a livelihood and the need to get to work quickly meant that people, including the priests, were *terudin bimelakhtam* ("preoccupied with business"), and would not be able to concentrate properly upon giving—or receiving—that blessing in the proper frame of mind. The Rabbis felt that even on *Shabbat* people might well be preoccupied by problems of the previous week, to which they had to return very shortly. In Israel, however, that was no excuse. Living in Zion brought with it a special joy and tranquillity that enabled one to concentrate on the blessing notwithstanding one's problems. Secondly, Zion being the source of all blessing ("For there the Lord bestows His blessing," Psalm 133:3), it was regarded as singularly inappropriate not to take full advantage of drawing forth from that perennial source for even a day.

### 583. So, do we *dukhan* every day of Pesach?

No. Since the intermediate days of *Chol Ha-Moed* are not full festival days, and for most people they are actually ordinary working days, bringing with them the business anxieties we have alluded to, for that reason Diaspora communities do not include the Priestly Blessing on those days.

### 584. What about *dukhaning* on a day of *Yom Tov* proper that coincides with *Shabbat*?

There has been much halakhic debate on this point. Some authorities were against *dukhaning* on *Shabbat*, since, in premodern times, when water had to be carried into buildings from an outside source, the fear was that one might go out into the public domain to bring water for the priests to wash their hands, forgetting completely that it is not merely *Yom Tov* (when carrying is permitted), but also *Shabbat*, when it is prohibited to carry. They made an exception, however, on Yom Kippur, when it was felt inconceivable that anyone could forget the sanctity of that day.

Other authorities see no reason to suspend *dukhaning* on *Shabbat* for such a fear, especially in the modern period when every building has its own water system. And this seems to be the majority view.

### 585. Where is the source for the Priestly Blessing?

It is expressly stated in Numbers 6:23–27:

And the Lord spoke to Moses, saying: "Speak to Aaron and unto his sons, saying: In this way shall you bless the children of Israel; you shall say unto them: May the Lord bless you and keep you; The Lord make His face to shine upon you and be gracious unto you; The Lord lift up His countenance upon you, and give you peace. So shall they put My name upon the children of Israel, and I will bless them."

## PRIESTLY PREPARATIONS

### 586. What preparations do the priests have to make before performing their blessing?

They have to remove their shoes and wash their hands. They have to ensure that they are wearing, or are provided with, a *tallit* (prayer shawl) large enough to cover their back and to hang down, at the front, sufficiently to cover entirely their faces and their hands outstretched in front of them. They also have to be sure that they know the proper blessing by heart, that they are in the proper frame of mind, and that they have a benign attitude toward the congregation they are being called upon to bless.

### 587. Why do the priests have to remove their shoes?

The removal of the shoes is popularly explained with reference to Moses, who, at the Burning Bush, was told to remove his shoes "because the ground upon which you stand is holy" (Exodus 3:5). This is not the reason, however. If it was, then the Chazan when taking out the scrolls and members standing before the Ark to perform the honor of *petichah,* would also have to remove their shoes!

Surprisingly, the reason for their removal is a very practical one, though it may appear rather unreasonable to our modern thinking. The fear was that if one of the priest's shoe laces came undone, people noticing him bending down to tie it might misconstrue his action, and conclude that he was a disqualified priest (see questions 589–590) and was not joining in therefore with the prescribed ritual, but merely standing there with fellow priests so that the community would not learn of his disqualification.

Although the problem is obviated if priests are wearing slip-on shoes, yet, for consistency, it became the practice to forbid all shoes. There are some synagogues, however, where special, cloth foot-warmers are provided for the priests to wear!

### 588. Why do priests have to wash their hands?

It is in conformity with the verse "Lift up your hands in holiness [i.e., in cleanliness] to bless the Lord" (Psalm 134:2). The washing of the priests' hands, by means of a vessel, is performed by Levites, members of their own ancestral tribe. This is by way of privilege, to give them some participatory role in the ritual.

## PRIESTLY QUALIFICATIONS AND DISQUALIFICATIONS

### 589. What qualifications and disqualifications apply to priests blessing the congregation?

Perhaps it should first be emphasized that the priests are not actually "blessing" the people, in the sense in which we normally understand that term, namely, conferring their own blessing. They are merely acting as conduits for the divine blessing by reciting the biblically prescribed formulae (see question 585). This is made abundantly clear in the final phrase: "And I [God] will bless them" (Numbers 6:27).

It is thus not a question of the priest's personal piety or commitment. Every priest, whether he is observant or not, has the duty of reciting the biblical formulae that call down blessing upon his congregation. And the nonobservant should not feel uneasy about doing so, just as they presumably do not feel uneasy about accepting the honor of being called up to the Torah. In the latter context they may be said to be doing an equally audacious religious act in calling upon the rest of the congregation to recite a blessing of God. For that is what the recitation of the phrase, *Borakhu et Ha-Shem ha-mevorakh* ("Bless the Lord . . .") means, and hence, the congregation's immediate response with the blessing, *Barukh Ha-Shem ha-mevorakh le'olam va'ed* ("Blessed be the Lord . . .").

That having been said, there are certain basic requirements that have to be satisfied. The priest must have attained the age of *Bar Mitzvah*. He must be a person who has warm feelings for his congregation, which, in turn, is well-disposed towards him. One cannot confer, or, more precisely, invoke, a blessing upon another—and it is highly unlikely that the latter would himself be prepared to be party to it—unless it reflected mutual feelings of love and regard. It is for this reason that the *berakhah* over the Priestly Blessing is the only one that includes the word *be'ahavah,* "in love" ("who has commanded us to bless His people in *love*").

A priest who has willingly compromised his special status is, naturally, debarred from exercising its privileges. Hence, if a priest enters into a prohibited marital relationship, he renders himself thereby a *challal,* "profane priest," who may not, therefore, participate in this blessing of the congregation. Included in this category are a priest who marries (i) out of the faith, (ii) a divorcee, (iii) a woman who has not received a *get* (Bill of Divorcement) from her previous husband, (iv) a convert, (v) a widow who had undergone the ceremony of *Chalitzah* (release from the family tie) by her deceased husband's brother, and (vi) the daughter of a woman who had contracted any forbidden marriage with a priest.

### 590. Are there any other situations that might prevent a priest from *dukhaning*?

Because the priest has to be in a happy mood to invoke a blessing, it was declared forbidden for a mourner during the first thirty days of mourning for relatives other than parents, and for the entire year of mourning for parents, to participate in this ceremony. It is also forbidden for a priest who has a serious physical blemish or deformity, to the extent that the curiosity of people seeing him going up to bless will be aroused, and they will comment on him and be distracted, instead of concentrating on being recipients of the blessing. The classical example is of a tanner whose hands are impregnated with dye. However, if such people are well known in their community, to the extent that no one would comment or take a second glance in their direction, then they may participate.

If a priest feels unwell, and unable to stand for the duration of the ritual or concentrate properly on it, or if he is unable to walk properly and ascend the *Bimah,* there is no obligation for him to perform the *dukhaning.*

A priest who was the accidental cause of someone's death may not *dukhan;* neither may a priest who has drunk a glass of wine.

**591. What do disqualified or unwell priests do while their colleagues are performing their priestly duty?**

They should leave the synagogue before the Chazan commences the *Retzeh* blessing, and remain in the vestibule until after the Priestly Blessing is concluded, before rejoining the service.

## FACING TOWARD OR AWAY FROM THE PRIESTS?

**592. There are some congregants who turn away while the priests are blessing them, believing that it is forbidden to look in the direction of the priests. Is this correct?**

No it is not. One should not look directly *at the priests,* but it is equally forbidden to turn one's back to them. This is tantamount to a rejection of the blessing they are offering. One must face the priests but keep one's eyes lowered, so that one is not looking directly at them, which would be a source of distraction from the formula of the blessing they are uttering.

**593. We have mentioned that one should really face in the direction of the priests. What about the people whose seats are at the side of the Ark, and who find themselves either on a level with or even behind the priests?**

Those on a level are included in the blessing. There is a tradition—not universally observed—for the priests to turn to their right and their left, to include also all those on a level with them. Those behind the priests are not, however, included in the Priests' Blessing, and should accordingly move forward.

**594. Why do the priests face the Ark for the first half of their introductory blessing, and only on reaching the word *vetzivanu* turn around to face the congregation?**

It is simply a compromise between two authoritative halakhic opinions, one of which required the entire blessing to be recited with back to congregation, and the other requiring the entire blessing to be recited facing the congregation.

The rationale of the first opinion is to maintain the usual requirement of reciting a blessing *before* performing the *mitzvah*. By facing away from the congregation, we follow the custom of candle lighting on the eve of *Shabbat,* where the eyes are covered with our hands after lighting so that the blessing may be recited and so that, when removing the hands, it is tantamount to creating the light at that moment (one could not light the match after reciting the blessing, since the act of reciting the blessing automatically inaugurates the Sabbath day, after which point lighting a match is, naturally, forbidden. The first opinion quoted above believes, therefore, that merely facing the congregation in a mode of blessing already activates the blessing, and may be construed, therefore, as the beginning of the performance of the *mitzvah*. The second authority was not troubled by such considerations and, regarding the *berakhah* as an essential component of the formula of blessing, preferred that it should be recited while in the proper position for blessing.

## PERFORMING THE PRIESTLY BLESSING

### 595. Why do the priests have their *tallit* hanging down low over their hands?

Again, it is in order not to distract the congregation, whose gaze would inevitably be drawn to the strange finger formation that the priests have to make. Also, it is so that the priests themselves do not become distracted by the congregation.

### 596. What is the finger formation that the priests have to make?

Based upon a phrase in Song of Songs (2:9), which speaks of the "beloved" — understood as a metaphor for God—"peeping out through the lattice" (2:9), the mystics believed that Israel's Beloved directs His blessing through the fingers of the priests, which are consequently made into a lattice formation. This is achieved by placing the right hand adjacent, but slightly above, the left, and spacing out the middle of the four fingers of each hand. A further space is created by stretching the thumbs of either hand inward, and towards each other.

### 597. What if there is only one person who can lead the *Musaf* service for the congregation, and he happens to be a priest. Does he leave the *Bimah*, and join his fellow priests before the Ark?

No. He must remain in his place, and someone else takes over and recites the blessing formula for the priests.

### 598. What if there is only one priest in the synagogue?

He may then ascend the *Bimah* and bless the congregation, before returning to resume the service. In the pre-fifteenth-century period, halakhists were concerned that, without the benefit of a written prayer book, the priest-Chazan, on returning from *dukhaning*, might become confused as to how to continue. They therefore made permission for him to bless the congregation conditional upon his being sure that he would not become confused. Nowadays, that we have benefit of printed prayer books, there is no such fear (*Magen Avraham* on *Shulchan Arukh*, *Orach Chayyim* 128:20 [31]).

## THE MEANING AND STRUCTURE OF THE BLESSING

**599. What are the precise blessings that are being conveyed by the biblical formulae used by the priests?**

Rashi explains it as follows:

*May God bless you* — "May you be endowed with material prosperity."

*And keep you* — "And keep your possessions safe from thieves."

*May the Lord cause His face to shine upon you* — "May He always appear kindly and generous to you."

*And be gracious unto you* — "May He endow you with grace."

*The Lord turn His countenance towards you* — "May He suppress any anger He might feel towards you."

*And grant you peace* — Rashi does not comment on this last phrase, assuming that Jews know precisely what peace means. Indeed, it is the most cherished objective of Jewish life, and the most frequently prayed-for blessing. The *Kaddish* prayer, the *Amidah,* and the Grace after Meals all conclude with the line, *Oseh shalom bimromav hu ya'aseh shalom aleinu . . .* , He who makes peace in His celestial regions, may He bestow peace upon us and upon all Israel."

*Shalom* (peace) is our age-old traditional greeting. We employ it in Modern Hebrew to mean both "Hello" and "good-bye." It is the special greeting for the Sabbath: *Shabbat Shalom.* According to our mystic tradition, it is even one of the names of God.

**600. Is there anything significant about the structure of the Priestly Blessing?**

It is interesting to note that the number of words in the three lines of the blessing proceeds from three in the first line, to five in the second, and seven in the final line. All three numbers are, of course, significant numbers in Jewish tradition. Also, the divine name occurs as the second word of each line.

## TO BLESS OR NOT TO BLESS?

**601. If a priest arrives late in synagogue, and has not yet said his prayers, may he *dukhan*?**

He may.

**602. If a priest has already blessed his own congregation, and after the service he enters another service which has not yet reached the stage of *dukhaning*, may he, or ought he to, join with the priests once again?**

He may do so, but, having already fulfilled his duty, it is entirely optional.

### 603. Have Reform congregations retained the Priestly Blessing ritual?

No. They have abandoned the traditionally privileged positions of both Priests and Levites. At the end of the service, the Rabbi generally recites it as a closing benediction.

### 604. Have Conservative congregations retained the Priestly Blessing ritual?

No universal decision has been taken to abandon the ritual, but it is left to the discretion of the Rabbi and the individual congregation. A small number of more traditional congregations still retain it, but the majority have abandoned it.

## HAVDALAH

### 605. What is *Havdalah*?

*Havdalah* means "separation," and it is a formal ceremony of officially "separating off" the ordinary days to come from the sacred *Shabbat* or festival days.

### 606. What is the purpose of such a separation?

It was inferred by the Rabbis from the biblical command to "remember the Sabbath day, to keep it holy" (Exodus 20:8). They understood "remembering" in the sense of "making mention" of its holiness; and to this end they introduced the *Kiddush* ceremony at the inauguration of the holy days and the *Havdalah* at their termination.

The idea of demarcating nature's separate categories looms large in Judaism. The verb *lehavdil* ("to separate") occurs as one of the earliest acts of Creation, when, on the first day, "God separated [*va-yavdel*] the primordial light from the darkness" (Genesis 1:4). The same verb is used when, on the second day of Creation, "God separated [*va-yavdel*] the waters that were beneath the firmament from those above the firmament" (1:7). And it is used yet again to describe the creation of the heavenly luminaries, on the fourth day, which were "to separate between the light and the darkness" (1:18).

The verb *lehavdil* is also employed in order to demarcate the holy from the less holy, as in the case of the veil of the Sanctuary which separated off the innermost, most holy, enclosure from the outer, less holy section: "And the veil shall separate [*vehivdilah*] between the holy place and the holy of holies" (Exodus 26:33).

The same verb is employed to set apart a holy nation, Israel, from the surrounding ungodly peoples: "I am the Lord your God who has separated you [*hivdaltiy*] from the nations" (Leviticus 20:24; see also 20:26). And the verb is used again (*Vehivdalta et ha-Leviim*) to describe the separation of the Levites from the rest of the tribes as a most holy fraternity (Numbers 8:14).

To such an extent does Judaism like to affirm the unique characteristics of nature's species, by maintaining their separate and distinct features inviolate, that it prohibited the sowing of divers seeds, and the grafting of different species of fruit and vegetation, the crossing of different species of animals and, indeed, the wearing of *shaatnez,* clothes containing the admixture of wool and linen (Leviticus 19:19; Deuteronomy 22:11).

The rationale of the separation of milk and meat may well lie within this same broad concept. Meat lies in the category of dead food; milk, which is secreted by nature as a life-nurturing fluid, lies within a totally separate, and diametrically opposite category.

Hence the ceremony of *Havdalah.* We cannot just merge the holy Sabbath or festival day into a secular working day. They are opposing entities – like the light and darkness of Creation – and a demarcation-line has to be drawn between them in the form of an official ceremony of "separation."

### 607. When is *Havdalah* performed?

It is recited in the form of a prayer, inserted into the blessing for knowledge (*Attah Chonen*) of the *Maariv Amidah,* and it is then enacted as a ritual at the end of the *Maariv* service in synagogue. That ritual is also prescribed as a home ceremony for all the family.

### 608. Why was the *Havdalah* prayer inserted into the blessing for knowledge in the *Amidah*?

The Talmud (*Berakhot* 33b) views the connection conceptually, asking rhetorically, "If one has no knowledge, how can he make any *Havdalah* distinctions?" In other words, our understanding of the concept of Sabbath sanctity, of the "distinctions" between things permitted and prohibited, and the manifold laws and practices that nurture that sanctity, require the application of intelligence, knowledge and sensibility: hence the blessing for knowledge was chosen as the context for the *Havdalah.*

Another reason offered is that, because the middle thirteen blessings of the weekday *Amidah* take the form of petitions, and it is forbidden to petition for personal needs on the Sabbath, we have to terminate the Sabbath, through the recitation of that *Havdalah* prayer, before we can proceed to the recitation of the petitionary blessings of the *Maariv Amidah.* Hence *Havdalah* is inserted into the very first of the weekday blessings, the *Attah Chonen* petition for knowledge.

### 609. Why is there a necessity for a *Havdalah* prayer in the *Amidah* as well as a ceremony at the end of the service?

The Talmud (*Berakhot* 33a) states that the duplication arose as a result of economic necessity: "When the Men of the Great Assembly first introduced *Havdalah,* it was in the form of a prayer. When the Judaean community became more prosperous, they made it part of a ceremony, accompanied by wine. They subsequently suffered an economic setback, so they reverted to merely marking it by a prayer." It was in order not to demean *Havdalah,* by constantly having to change its form, that they determined that even when times were prosperous, and wine cheap and plentiful, the *Havdalah* prayer should be retained in the *Amidah:* hence the duplication.

## *HAVDALAH* REQUIREMENTS

### 610. What is required for the *Havdalah* ceremony?

We require a goblet of wine, which is filled to overflowing as an augury for a bountiful week. We also require a multiwicked candle. A single wick provides merely a flame, whereas the blessing praises God as *Borei me-orei ha-esh,* "The Creator of the light*s* of the fire." To convey the appearance of such "lights of the fire" we require several wicks. We also require a spice box with spices, the most common choice being cloves.

### 611. We have referred above (see question 261) to the spices that we use for *Havdalah*. What is the origin of our ornamental spice boxes?

In medieval Europe the myrtle was the preferred choice for the *Havdalah* spices, probably on account of its sacred use as a symbol of rain, fruitfulness, and prosperity on Sukkot. Hence the spice box itself attracted, by association, the name *hadas,* the Hebrew word for the myrtle branch.

The earliest mention of a special glass spice box is found in the writings of Rabbi Ephraim of Regensburg (twelfth century). Exquisitely wrought silver spice boxes were produced in Germany in the mid-sixteenth century, and a fine example of one of the earliest of those is housed in the Jewish Museum of New York, having been originally commissioned as a gift to the Synagogue at Friedberg in Germany (see *Encyclopaedia Judaica,* 7:1482; illustration, p. 1486). In the State of Israel a wide variety of spice boxes are manufactured, reflecting the traditional art of the many communities from which the immigrant artists and craftsmen originate.

### 612. Why were the traditional Ashkenazi spice boxes invariably shaped like a tower?

Some scholars have suggested that this reflects the contemporary reality of the locations in which the more exotic spices were kept. As they were imported from the Orient and were very expensive, there was a need to keep them stored in the most secure of places. One of the city fortification towers was the popular choice.

Another theory has it that the gentile siversmiths who executed the boxes for their Jewish patrons were mainly engaged in the production of ecclesiastical appurtenances. They therefore designed them on the pattern of church towers or steeples.

### 613. Why was wine prescribed for *Havdalah*?

It has been suggested that this also has to do with the withdrawal of the *Neshamah Yeteirah* we referred to above (see question 261). The wine is intended to fortify us at the withdrawal of that extra soul, and to restore a little of the joy of the festival that has suddenly vanished.

### 614. What if one has no wine?

One may use grape juice, tea, or coffee (and, during the rest of the year, even beer. On Pesach beer is, of course, forbidden, as it is made of fermenting grain). The principle is that any drink that one might serve to an honored guest is acceptable in the absence of wine.

### 615. We have referred above (questions 259–260) to the reason for making a blessing over fire. Is there any significance in the order of the *Havdalah* blessings?

Joseph Karo (*Shulchan Arukh, Orach Chayyim* 296:1) points out that the acronym Yabneh indicates the proper order of blessings: *Y-ayin* (wine), *B-esamim* (spices), *N-er* (light) and *H-avdalah* (blessing over separation of *Shabbat* from working week).

The order has also been explained as reflecting, in ascending order, the bodily senses that are employed in the *Havdalah* ceremony. The sense of taste comes into play with the blessing and subsequent drinking of the wine. This is followed by the sense of smell as the nose inhales the spices. The eyes see the light of the fire and, finally, the brain makes the distinction (*Havdalah*) between the holy *Shabbat* and the ordinary working days.

### 616. Is there any difference in the *Havdalah* for *Motzei Shabbat* and that for the termination of *Yom Tov*?

There is. We make a blessing over the candlelight on *Motzei Shabbat* because that indicates that we may now strike a match and use fire in whatever way we wish, since the *Shabbat* restrictions are over. We do not light a candle in the *Havdalah* at the termination of *Yom Tov*, however, since during *Yom Tov* we have been permitted to have benefit from fire, and to use it for cooking, heating, and so forth.

We also omit the spices, since the additional soul we referred to above (see question 261) is not required on *Yom Tov*, since the pleasure of the festival provides its own joy and refreshment of the soul. There is, therefore, no requirement for any spices to help revive us at the sudden removal of any additional soul.

### 617. Why is it that, after the Chazan has made *Kiddush* in shul on a Sabbath or festival eve, he does not drink from the wine himself, but gives it to a child under *Bar Mitzvah* to drink, while at *Havdalah* he drinks it himself?

It goes back to a basic distinction between *Kiddush* and *Havdalah*. The *Kiddush* is meant to be recited at table. In earlier times, meals were provided in an adjoining room of the synagogue for travelers, as well as for the poor. Hence, *Kiddush* was recited in the synagogue on their behalf, and it was justified as being an extension of their table next door. It was recited in synagogue so that the worshipers could hear that important testimony to God as Creator, even though they would be repeating it for their families when they arrived home.

Because the Chazan's intention is to make *Kiddush* exclusively for others—not for himself, since he will be making it at home—he excludes himself by refraining from drinking from the wine. At *Havdalah,* on the other hand, his intention is to make it for himself and for all present in synagogue—to terminate the Sabbath for all—and hence he drinks from the wine to fulfill an immediate personal, as well as congregational, religious duty.

# XVII

# Festival of Songs: The *Shirah* and *Shir Ha-Shirim*

## THE *SHIRAH* IN TEMPLE AND SYNAGOGUE

**618. Why is the *Shirah*, the Song of the Red Sea (Exodus 14:30–15:18), so important that it is not only read from the Torah on the seventh day of Pesach but also forms part of the weekday and *Shabbat* morning service throughout the year?**

Abraham ben Nathan Ha-Yarchi (thirteenth century), in his *Sefer Ha-Manhig* (see *Sefer Ha-Manhig* [Jerusalem: Levin-Epstein, 1961]), states that it is in order to conform to the biblical duty to "remember the day when you came forth out of the land of Egypt *all the days of your life*" (Deuteronomy 16:3).

**619. How far back can we trace the custom of reciting the *Shirah* as part of the liturgy?**

As far as the development of the synagogue liturgy is concerned, the inclusion of the *Shirah* may also be explained in the light of the guiding principle that any biblical sections that were regarded as sufficiently significant to merit regular recitation in the Temple were also considered as worthy of being recited in the synagogue. The *Shirah* was sung every *Shabbat* in the Temple, as an accompaniment to the late afternoon sacrifice (Talmud *Rosh Hashanah* 31a), and hence its position of honor in the synagogue liturgy.

**620. But if it was recited only once a week in Temple times, then why has the synagogue accorded it even greater significance by making its recitation a daily exercise?**

Its introduction into the synagogue liturgy was not so straightforward, and just as, after the destruction of the Temple, Babylon and Palestine differed in many areas of law and ritual, so did their attitude towards the place of the *Shirah* in the daily liturgy.

In Babylon they were reticent at first to introduce it on a daily basis, since it had not been so recited in the Temple. They preserved the Temple practice, therefore, of reciting it only on *Shabbat.* They did see fit, however, to allude to it on a daily basis, by including, into the *Ge'ulah* blessing, which follows the *Shema,* the verse from the *Shirah* beginning, *Miy khamokha ba-eylim* (Exodus 15:11). It was retained there even when later Babylonian authorities prescribed the daily recitation of the *Shirah.*

233

Its elevation to a daily act of thanksgiving owes its origin to the lead given by the Palestinian authorities after the destruction of the Temple. We may conjecture that this vigorous victory song, with its fighting spirit and its affirmation that "God's right hand would dash the enemy in pieces" (v. 6) served as a contemporary rallying cry for a Jewry and a homeland recently decimated by the merciless Roman armies. They would have viewed the daily recitation of the *Shirah* as a most useful psychological release for all their pent-up national tensions.

**621. We have referred above to the verse from the *Shirah* (Exodus 15:6) that is inserted into the concluding blessing over the *Shema* (ending, *Ga'al Yisrael*), just before the commencement of the *Amidah*. Are there any other references to the crossing of the Red Sea in our daily prayers?**

Indeed. Immediately before that verse, there is a long passage, commencing, *Ezrat avoteinu attah hu me'olam*. That passage refers to God's great acts of deliverance to His people in every generation. It makes specific reference to the fact that God redeemed us from Egypt, slew their firstborn, "split the Red Sea and drowned the proud, bringing Your beloved ones across safely." It proceeds to allude specifically to the Song of the Red Sea: "For this, the beloved ones praised [*Al zot shibechu ahuvim*] and exalted God . . . offering psalms, songs and praises, blessings and thanksgivings to the King."

Again, towards the end of the *Ge'ulah* blessing there is a further reference to the crossing of the Red Sea, beginning with the words, *Shirah chadashah shibechu ge'ulim*. It states: "With a new song the redeemed people offered praise to Your name at the sea shore. All of them together gave thanks, proclaimed Your sovereignty, and declared: 'The Lord shall reign for ever and ever' " (Exodus 15:18). We see clearly, therefore, that this *Ge'ulah* (redemption) blessing links up thematically with the *Shirah,* recited a little earlier in the service. The *Shirah* commemorates an incomparable past redemption; the *Ge'ulah* blessing pleads for that redemption to be speedily repeated.

If we glance at the same formulation of the *Ge'ulah* blessing in the evening service (commencing *Emet ve-emunah*), we find the identical theme, though couched in slightly different phraseology. One main difference, in the paragraph commencing, *Malkhutekha ra'u vanekha,* is the addition of an extra quotation from the *Shirah* — "Your children beheld your sovereign power as You parted the sea before Moses. They exclaimed, 'This is my God!' [15:2], and added, 'The Lord shall reign for ever and ever.' " The verse, "This is my God" is not in the version of this *Ge'ulah* blessing found in the morning service.

**622. In the *Sefer Torah,* and in our Chumashim, the *Shirah* is set out in a strange form, with broken half-lines and spaces. What is the point of this?**

This is prescribed in the Talmud (*Megillah* 16b; *Rabbeinu Nissim Megillah* 16b; *Talmud Yerushalmi, Megillah* 74b; *Soferim* 12:10). Its shape, a half-line above, spanning the point of meeting of two other half-lines below, is suggestive of a wall of bricks. This underscores the reference to the waters of the Red Sea "serving as a wall on their right side and their left" as the Israelites walked safely through.

## PHRASEOLOGY OF THE *SHIRAH*

**623. Why does the opening phrase (Az yashir) have the verbal form in the future tense, meaning, literally, "Then Moses will sing," instead of employing, as expected, the past tense: *Az shar Mosheh*?**

First, it has to be realized that this is poetry, not prose; and in biblical poetry the tenses tend to be far less circumscribed, with the future often being employed to denote a continuous or drawn-out activity, as was the case with this Song of Praise.

Rashi has a different explanation, understanding it as a description of Israel's response-process. He states: "*Az*—'Then'—namely, when they saw the great miracle that had been wrought on their behalf, the idea immediately suggested itself *that they might sing* [*yashir*] a song of thanksgiving." Thus, since they were, as yet, still contemplating a future activity, the form of the verb is logically that of the future tense.

**624. Two verses seem to be unnecessarily repetitive, and also contradictory. Verse 1 reads, "Horse and rider he hurled high into the sea [*ramah va-yam*], while a few verses later (v. 4), we have, "The chariots of Pharaoh and his host He cast down into the Sea [*yarah va-yam*]."**

Rashi draws our attention to this, and informs us that it comes to teach us that God did, in fact, inflict both terrors on the Egyptian cavalry. He tossed them high up into the air, and then hurled them into the very depths of the sea.

**625. How do we explain the rather irreverent way of referring to God in the phrase, "This is my God" (v. 2)?**

It is, indeed, irreverent—at least by our standards of detachment and remoteness from God. The Midrash states, however, that it reflects the unique intimacy and clarity of spiritual vision experienced by the Israelites at that moment of incomparable revelation.

The comment of the *Targum Yonatan* on that phrase captures its mystical audacity:

From their mothers' breasts the babes pointed [God] out with their fingers, saying: That is the One who gave us honey to suck from the rock, and provided oil from a flinty rock, when our mothers went out to the fields to give birth, leaving us on our own. He is the One who sent an angel to wash and swathe us. Now, therefore, let us praise the God of our fathers and exalt Him.

**626. But is this not a rather gross portrayal of God?**

It is quite true that *Targum* makes no attempt here to soften the directness of the biblical phrase. Quite the contrary: it is heightened by the additional reference to a finger gesticulation accompanying the excited "vision" of God that had been vouch-safed. Our shock at such a daring tradition is somewhat relieved by the fact that it invests the innocent and pure babes with the unique spiritual privilege of sensing and "seeing" God, rather than granting that gift to their parents.

It has to be said that rabbinic tradition did not apologize for, and neither was it embarrassed by, the belief that the crossing of the Red Sea was indeed accompanied by a revelation of God that surpassed, in clarity and intensity, even that of the later Sinaitic revelation. In the words of the Sages, "An ordinary maidservant, at the Red Sea, was granted an even clearer vision and insight than that experienced by the prophets themselves" (see Rashi on v. 2).

**627. What is the meaning of the rather complex Hebrew word, *ve'anveihu*, which follows the phrase, "This is my God"? Although normally translated "And I shall glorify Him," the Hebrew lexicons tell us that the root of the verb is *navah*, which means "to beautify," "to adorn." But how is it at all possible to "beautify" or "adorn" God?**

This is precisely the question which exercised the minds of the talmudic Sages. They concluded that it has to be understood in the sense of, "I shall beautify *myself* before Him." And they explained that by purchasing the very best and most aesthetic sacred objects, to garland our ritual and our performance of *mitzvot* with beauty, we, in turn, make ourselves more beautiful and worthy in the sight of God. Hence the Rabbis state: "Beautify yourselves with a splendid *sukkah,* a beautiful *etrog,* a fine *shofar,* a lovely *tallit;* write a *Sefer Torah* in the most elegant script, with the best materials, employing the most skilled scribe, and dressing it in the finest mantles" (*Mekhilta* on v. 2).

**628. Is not this verse, "This is my God . . . my father's God . . ." in the wrong chronological order? Surely one's father's religious dialogue precedes one's own, and one's own is inherited from that of one's parents!**

According to Malbim, this is precisely the point the Israelites wished to make by reversing the order here, namely, that their own spiritual insights had been obtained independently of what their ancestors had bequeathed to them. The "God of their fathers" was merely a God of tradition, a God to whom they were committed exclusively on account of the goodness He had dispensed to previous generations. It was an inherited debt of gratitude which, by its very nature, lost much of its urgency with every passing generation.

The Israelites who came out of Egypt, on the other hand, had experienced directly the immediacy of God's intervention on their behalf. So dramatic had this been that He had even set aside the laws of nature in order inflict the ten miraculous plagues upon the Egyptians. Their own God was consequently far more of a reality, and far more an object of love and awe, than "their father's God," whom they had to learn about indirectly through tradition.

**629. How is it possible to speak of God as a "man of war"? Surely, on both counts, it demeans Him; for He is neither "a man" nor "warlike," in the sense that we understand it!**

This is a very old problem, which occupied the minds of all our medieval Jewish philosophers: the problem of biblical anthropomorphisms, that is, the frequent description of God in human terms.

The answer of the Rabbis is, simply, "Scripture speaks in the language of men," which is another way of saying that if the Torah was going to be able to talk about God in any way at all, then it had to employ the simplest and most primitive form of "God-speak." It had to reduce His "Being" to terms which were intelligible to ordinary folk, and—more important—which were within the parameters of their own experience.

Imagine if the Torah had really told us how God created the world! We would have had to be given volumes of chemical equations instead of a Bible, and it would have meant that only scientists would have had access to the Bible! That would have created an interesting state of affairs, to be sure! Whether it would have resulted in a reduction in the high proportion of atheists and agnostics traditionally found in their ranks is a matter of speculation.

The Genesis account is merely for popular consumption. It does little more than commit us to the acceptance of Creation by Almighty God. It certainly does not further our understanding, even by one iota, of how God went about His majestic and uniquely creative task.

God set aside His own honor when He referred in His Torah to such concepts as His "strong hand," "outstretched arm" "His own image and likeness," and "the work of His fingers." In His desire for humans to seek Him out, and to feel that His existence is meaningful and significant for their lives and for the destiny of the universe, God had to provide an "operating vocabulary" to serve as a religious medium and vehicle of spiritual emotion.

The medieval philosophers insisted that these terms were not to be taken literally. Indeed, Maimonides asserts that the only positive statement that we can make about God is what He is *not*. In other words, we may well succeed in refining our gross perceptions of Him, but we cannot arrive at any positive or tangible understanding of anything approximating His attributes or real nature. Maimonides explained the biblical anthropomorphisms, therefore, in purely allegorical terms.

Regarding the phrase "man of war" (*ish milchamah*), Rashi explains that the Hebrew word *ish* is also employed synonymously in the Bible with the word *ba'al,* "master" or "supreme architect." There is thus no anthropomorphic difficulty here, since the phrase is merely an allusion to God's devastatingly effective way of neutralizing the violence of all Israel's enemies.

**630. What is the sense of the continuation of the phrase we have just discussed, namely, *Ha-Shem shemo,* "Lord is His Name"?**

*Seforno* explains that, although we have just alluded to His retributive nature, yet the ultimate objective of removing the evildoers is to enable those committed to truth, justice and mercy to enjoy freedom and happiness. That merciful objective is expressed through the use of the name *Ha-Shem*, which indicates the God of mercy (as opposed to *Elokim,* God in pursuit of strict justice).

**631. How could Moses and the Israelites possibly say, *Miy khamokha ba'elim Ha-Shem* — "Who is like You among the gods, O Lord?" How could they even breathe a hint of the existence of other gods?**

Although *Elim* is probably the plural of *El,* which usually refers to a god, or, indeed, to God Himself, yet in the *Shirah* it is used to denote, simply, "the mighty." Hence, in verse 15 we have a reference to *elei moav,* "mighty men of Moab." While the very comparison between God and other mighty forces remains strange, it is still not quite as problematic as a comparison between God and idolatrous counterparts.

Perhaps the simplest solution is offered by Rabbi Z. Sorotzkin, in his *Oznayim La-Torah.* He states that the author of this query ("Who is like You among the other gods?") is actually the idolatrous Pharaoh. The previous verse refers to the words of the enemy ("I shall pursue, I shall overtake . . ."). This verse, therefore, proceeds to quote from the words of the arch-enemy, Pharaoh, when, totally humiliated and defeated, he acknowledges God's supremacy. He can be forgiven, therefore, for employing the reference to the gods he believed in; and his praise is accepted as sincere, if unfortunate! Tradition has it that he alone was saved from the watery grave because of his remorse and praise of God.

**632. What is the sense of the apparently unnecessary repetition, *Ad ya'avor amkha Ha-Shem* ("Until Your people had passed over, O Lord") — *Ad ya'avor am zu kanita* ("Until the people You had acquired had passed over")?**

The Talmud (*Berakhot* 4a) explains that the first phrase refers to the first return of the Israelites to their land, while the second phrase refers to the subsequent return from exile in Babylon.

Rav I. Kuk (see *Olat Reiyah,* vol. 1, Jerusalem: Mosad HaRav Kuk, 1989, p. 236) expands upon this, and explains the repetition in this verse on the basis of the talmudic observation (*Yoma* 21a) that the pervading spirituality of the first Temple period (tenth–sixth centuries B.C.E.) was far more intense, and the divine Presence far more accessible, than that of the second Temple period (sixth century B.C.E.–70 C.E.)

Rav Kuk states that the Jews of the second Commonwealth compensated for the greater remoteness of the divine Presence by the greater intensity of their religious life. That was the period which gave rise to the Men of the Great Assembly who added so many extra *mitzvot* and rituals to the Jewish way of life, and the age of the *Soferim* (Scribes) who disseminated Torah scrolls and Torah learning among the masses.

In this way he elucidates the above talmudic attribution of each half of that verse to the first and second "return" to Israel, respectively. "Until *Your people* had passed over, O Lord" refers to the Jews who constituted the citizens of the first Commonwealth. They were "God's people," recipients of holiness that was dispensed at His initiative. "Until the people You had acquired" refers to the citizens of the second Commonwealth who were not originally in such close proximity to God's Presence until He voluntarily "acquired" them, and brought them into a close relationship purely as a reward for their own spiritual exertions.

**633. Why do we repeat the verse, *Ha-Shem yimlokh le'olam va'ed,* when it is not repeated in the Torah itself?**

It is done simply to indicate at precisely which verse the *Shirah* ends (Abudraham). A similar device is the addition of the word *Amen* at the end of the third blessing of the Grace after Meals (*Boneh verachaman yerushalayim—Amen*) to indicate the ending of the original grace, to which the rest was appended at a later time.

The reason why such an indication is required at the end of our verse in the *Shirah* is because it is followed in the Torah by another verse—*Kiy va sus paraoh* (v. 19)—which may easily be construed as a continuation of the Shirah's verses of praise. Indeed, there are some commentators who construe it as such, and some editions of the Siddur, on that basis, append it to the end of the *Shirah,* together with three other extraneous verses (*Kiy la-Shem hamelukhah . . ., Ve'alu moshiyim . . ., Vehayah Ha-Shem lemelekh*).

**634. On the seventh day of Pesach, when we read the *Shirah,* we include the reference to Miriam taking all the women and dancing with them. She is referred to as a "prophetess" (Exodus 15:20). What is the basis of that title?**

The Talmud (*Sotah* 12a) attributes it merely to the fact that before her younger brother, Moses, was born, she prophesied one day that her mother would give birth to a boy who would become the savior of Israel.

## MIRIAM AND THE ISRAELITE WOMEN

**635. Why is Miriam described there as "sister of Aaron," and not also as sister of Moses?**

Rashi explains that it reflects the special relationship which Miriam and Aaron had, and which Moses did not share. Whether it was caused by the fact that they did not get on with Moses' Midianite wife, Zipporah, we can but speculate. We do know that they did not flinch from talking disparagingly about Moses on that account (see Numbers 12:1), with the result that Miriam was struck down with leprosy. It was Aaron, at that sad time, who remonstrated with Moses to plead with God to heal their sister.

Moses Nachmanides (see his commentary to Exodus 15:20) accounts for her description as "sister of Aaron" somewhat differently. He believes that it was simply a device to show respect to Aaron by including mention of his name, since both Moses and Miriam figured prominently in the song of praise, and, otherwise, Aaron would have been the only one not mentioned at all.

### 636. Were the women organized subsequently into any religious collective?

We have little evidence of that. However, according to Moses Nachmanides (commentary to Exodus 38:8), there may well be an allusion to a guild of religious women who congregated at the entrance of the tent of meeting.

On the verse "And he made the laver of brass, and the base thereof of brass, of the mirrors of the women who thronged [*ha-tzov'ot*] at the entrance of the tent of meeting," Nachmanides quotes *Targum* who renders the word *ha-tzov'ot* as "who came to pray." He also quotes Abraham ibn Ezra, who writes of those women that, "they were God-fearing people who turned away from worldy desires, surrendering their mirrors because they had no more need to appear beautiful. They preferred to spend their day praying and receiving religious instruction at the tent of meeting." Do we have here the first example of a women's prayer group?

## A DISPUTED LOCATION

### 637. Do we know exactly where it was that the Egyptian army caught up with the Israelites?

Not precisely. Martin Buber sums up the diversity of scholarly opinion when he states, "We do not know where the pursuers caught up with the fugitives; whether in the neighborhood of the present Suez or, if the Gulf of Suez was then differently shaped from its contemporary form, further north at one of the bitter lakes—or even, as some suppose, only at the Gulf of Akaba (though in that case it is hard to understand why the pursuing chariots should not have caught up with them sooner" (M. Buber, *Moses* ([Oxford: East and West Library, 1947], p. 75).

The *Encyclopaedia Judaica* (6:1050) enumerates three main theories regarding the journey. The first is the "Northern Route Theory," which has it that the Israelites marched in a northerly direction, towards the Mediterranean coast. The Red Sea, or, as a more accurate translation of *Yam Suf,* the Sea of Reeds, is then either Lake Manzala, west of Port Said, or Lake Sirbonis. This identification is boosted by the abundant presence of reeds, by the strong east winds (see Exodus 14:21) and by the identification of Baal-Zephon (Exodus 14:2) with the Temple of Zeus Casius, which sits atop a tongue of land jutting into Lake Sirbonis.

A differing reconstruction assumes the "Central Route Theory," namely, that from Goshen the Israelites traveled in an easterly direction. According to this view, the Red Sea has to be identified with the Bitter Lakes between the Gulf of Suez in the south and the Delta estuary in the north.

A third view adopts "The Southern Route Theory," which postulates that the Israelites turned south to reach the Red Sea, which is to be identified with the Gulf of Suez. Baal-Zephon, on this view, is Jebel 'Ataqa, just northeast of the top of the Gulf of Suez.

## *SHIR HA-SHIRIM:* THE SONG AND ITS AUTHOR

### 638. When is *Shir Ha-Shirim* read in synagogue?

On the intermediate *Shabbat* of Pesach, before taking out the scrolls of the Law. When the first day of Pesach falls on a *Shabbat,* the custom in the State of Israel is to recite it then. In the Diaspora, however, it would then be read on the eighth day.

### 639. Where is *Shir Ha-Shirim* found in the Bible?

It is in the third section of the Bible, called in Hebrew, *Ketuvim,* "Sacred Writings," or by its Greek name, *Hagiographa.* After Psalms, Proverbs, and Job, there follow, in the order of the festivals of the year with which they are associated, the five "scrolls." These are *Shir Ha-Shirim* (recited on Passover), Ruth (Shavuot), *Eikhah* (or Lamentations, recited on the Fast of Av), *Kohelet* (or Ecclesiastes, recited on Sukkot) and Esther (on Purim).

### 640. Song of Songs suggests that this is the most important in a list of other biblical songs. Do we know with which other songs it is being compared?

Indeed, the Midrash (*Mekhilta Shirah*) enumerates ten biblical songs, of which *Shir Ha-Shirim* is, chronologically, the second. They are: (i) the song—alas, not preserved—that the Israelites sang on the eve of their departure from Egypt; (ii) The Song of the Red Sea; (iii) the song of joy sung when the well sprung up in the desert; (iv) the *Ha-azinu* song, recited by Moses just before his death; (v) Joshua's song on his victory over the five Amorite kings; (vi) Deborah and Baraks's song of victory over Sisera and his army; (vii) David's psalm of victory when he had triumphed over all his enemies; (viii) Solomon's song (Psalm 30) at the dedication of the Temple; (ix) Jehoshafat's song of faith and trust in God as he went into battle against the Ammonites and Moabites; and (x) the song of triumph that Israel will sing in the future at her final release.

### 641. The title—*Shir Ha-Shirim asher li-Shelomo*—attributes its authorship to King Solomon. Is there any other evidence, either within the song itself or elsewhere, to support this attribution?

In 1 Kings 5:12 it speaks of Solomon having composed 1,005 songs, in addition to which his name occurs several times within the poem (1:5; 3:7, 9, 11; 8:11). In light of the vast number of songs that Solomon composed, "The Song of Songs" may well refer to the most sublime song of them all.

The Talmud attributes the love song of *Shir Ha-Shirim* to Solomon's youth, the mature wisdom of the book of Proverbs to his middle age, and the skepticism of Kohelet to his old age (*Shir Ha-Shirim Rabbah,* ch. 1).

**642. Are there any variant traditions in the Talmud relating to the authorship of** *Shir Ha-Shirim*?

There were, indeed, many talmudic Sages who realized that the work was of a later date than the Solomonic period. Hence the view (*Bava Batra* 15a) that "King Hezekiah and his circle wrote the Song of Songs." This would bring its authorship down to about 700 B.C.E. — some three centuries after Solomon! It is important for us to note this equally authoritative talmudic view that it was not actually written by Solomon, though attributed to him.

**643. But how do we equate this particular view with the actual opening verse which states, unambiguously, "The song of songs of** *Solomon*?

The Hebrew phrase may just as readily be rendered "A song of songs *relating to* [*asher li* . . .] Solomon." This may be a reference, therefore, not to the historical Solomon as author of the song, but rather to the fictional Solomon who is portrayed within it as wooing the shepherdess, who spurns his advances. It contains his most intense song of love—his *Shir Ha-Shirim*. There is thus no conflict between the opening line and the theory that it is of a much later date.

In the light of the two conflicting talmudic traditions, it is clear that the Sages were themselves not too sure of its origins, and the views expressed were mere conjecture. Below (see on Q. 667) we shall quote the current scholarly view as regards its date of composition.

## ITS LITERARY ORIGIN AND TRANSMISSION

**644. Are there any other talmudic traditions regarding the literary transmission of** *Shir Ha-Shirim*?

There is a view, recorded in *Avot D'Rabbi Natan* (ch. 1), that *Shir Ha-Shirim* (together with Proverbs and *Kohelet*) was banned, and that all copies were stored away from the public gaze. It was the men of the Great Assembly who expounded and rehabilitated it.

**645. A cursory reading of the song suggests that it is somewhat disjointed, and that the plot is difficult to follow. Is that, indeed, the case?**

It does seem to be so, and for that reason some scholars have viewed it as a loosely assembled collection of independent love poems. This view is contested by others, who have argued strongly that it is, indeed, a unified lyrical poem. Just as the individual psalms were kept strictly separate, and not lumped together, so it is difficult to imagine that an early editor would have taken independent love poems and merged them into one.

**646. A song is normally composed for a particular occasion. Do we have any idea what the background of its composition might have been?**

Rashi repeats so often in the course of all his commentaries that "Scripture can never lose its literal sense." This is very important when considering the later allegorical interpretations that the talmudic Sages—and the early Church Fathers—read into this song.

While we cannot be sure, therefore, of its original setting, yet parallels with Syrian marriage practices, demonstrated in the middle of the nineteenth century by J. G. Wetzstein, have prompted scholars to view our book as having been originally composed for wedding festivities (see "Die syrische Dreschtafel," in *Zeitschrift fur Ethnologie* 5 [1873]: 270–302).

In the Syrian context, the bride and groom were feted as king and queen, and a lengthy poem, called a *wasf,* was recited each day during the week of their wedding celebrations. This gave expression to the majesty and beauty of the bride, as well as the love her groom, the king, had for her, and she for him.

It is well known that Jewish tradition still accords royal status to bride and groom; and, on the Syrian parallel, this may well go back to a similar enactment of their status, in song and dance, throughout the week of celebration, which is still observed through the ritual of *Shevah Berakhot.* The Jewish bridegroom may well have been hailed by the name Solomon, after the most romantic of Israel's kings, and the bride as (Avishag) the Shunammite who, although she did not become queen, was nevertheless the fairest maiden in all Israel, and nurse of King David in his last years (see 1 Kings 1–2).

We learn from the Mishnah (*Sotah* 9:14) that brides and bridegrooms were actually crowned as monarchs in ancient Israel, until the practice was curtailed by the Romans. It seems very probable, therefore, that at those "royal weddings" songs of the genre of *Shir Ha-Shirim* were sung.

## LOVE AND SEX IN THE BIBLE

**647. Was the inclusion of this somewhat erotic poem into the Bible just an editorial quirk, or are there other examples of human passion being employed as a spiritual metaphor?**

It is not an editorial quirk. The Bible is not the least bit prudish in its references to sex. In the very first book of the Bible we find references to aphrodisiacs (the mandrakes with which Leah "hired" Jacob on the night he was to visit Rachel), to the seizure, by Reuben, of his father's concubine, Bilhah; and to rape (Dinah), seduction (Joseph by the wife of Potiphar), and prostitution (Tamar).

The prophet Hoseah employs the imagery of a faithless harlot, in the person of his wife, Gomer, to draw an analogy to the faithlessness of Israel towards God.

Love and marriage are found in Jeremiah as a metaphor for the developing relationship and coming together (at Sinai) of God and Israel: "I remember for thee the affection of thy youth, the love of thine espousals; how thou wentest after Me in the wilderness, in a land that was not sown" (2:2). In the same chapter, Jeremiah employs the imagery of a harlot reclining to receive her customer as a metaphor for Israel's faithlessness and idolatry: "Upon every high hill, and under every leafy tree thou didst recline, playing the harlot" (2:20). It should not surprise us, therefore, against such a background, that the beautiful and innocent love depicted in *Shir Ha-Shirim* should have found its place among the biblical books.

**648. Following on from the point just made, might not *Shir Ha-Shirim* have been included in the Bible specifically in order to promote the Jewish attitude to sex and love?**

This is indeed suggested by Benjamin J. Segal, who states:

One might well consider that the inclusion of the Song of Songs in the Canon might derive not from the later allegorical interpretation given to the Song, but from the fact that it presents what is a particular approach to sex and love, one which differed markedly from that of the neighboring pagan cultures. As such, it would share this distinction with such aspects of biblical literature as the creation and flood stories, the law codes and a number of Psalms, each type of literature sharing some qualities with non-Hebrew literature and revealing at the same time, through the differences, the unique qualities of biblical culture. (Benjamin J. Segal, "The Theme of the Song of Songs," *Dor Le-Dor* 15:2 (Winter 1986–1987): 113 n. 22).

## ITS STATUS AS A BIBLICAL BOOK

**649. So was *Shir Ha-Shirim's* place among the Canon of biblical books accepted without reservation by all the talmudic Sages of the period (end of first century C.E.) that saw the Canon finalized?**

No, it was not accepted; and, according to Rabbi Yosi, there was considerable doubt among the early talmudists as to whether it was to be construed as a biblical book and handled with special care (*metam'in et ha-yadayim;* see Mishnah *Yadayim* 3:5). By that time, attitudes to sex were not quite as healthy and open, due in no small measure to the immorality of the Graeco-Roman heritage which left a negative influence on the Jewish way of life. It is clear that there were many Sages who were opposed to its inclusion, on account of its eroticism, and the effect it might have upon those who were not initiated into the mysteries of its symbolic and allegorical interpretation.

**650. So how did it succeed in winning its place in the face of such understandable fears?**

It was due to the towering prestige of Rabbi Akivah, who countered all his colleagues' arguments and allayed their fears, claiming: "There was no day in the whole of history as worthy as that day when *Shir Ha-Shirim* was given to Israel. For if all the other biblical books are holy, then *Shir Ha-Shirim* is holy of holies" (*Midrash Tanchuma, Tetzaveh,* ch. 5; Mishnah *Yadayim* 3:5).

### 651. How do we explain Akivah's obviously strong attachment to the book?

Akivah was the premier figure in the mystical movement of his period, the only one of four colleagues to immerse himself into its mysteries and emerge sound in body, faith and mind. As a mystical allegory, *Shir Ha-Shirim* must have provided him with unlimited ideas and stimuli.

As a romantic, Akivah would also have warmed to that poem. One of the most well-loved stories in the Talmud (*Ketubot* 62b–63a) is that of his early youth as an ignorant farmhand on the great estate of Kalba Savua. There he met his master's daughter, Rachel, and they fell in love. She agreed to marry him only if he went away to study Torah. Her father would in no way countenance the marriage, and cut his daughter out of his will when she ran away with Akivah.

Akivah enrolled in the talmudic academy for twelve years, while Rachel lived far away, on her own, in a shack, in direst poverty. She received no visit from her husband throughout that time, as they both knew that if he came home, his resolve to gain a mastery in Torah might be broken.

After twelve years he decided to return and break off his full-time studies. Approaching the door of Rachel's shack, he heard a neighbor inside, telling Rachel to forget about her husband, since it was obvious he would never return to her. "You don't understand the demands of Torah," Rachel chided her; "If he asked me for another twelve years' grace, I would readily grant it." Akivah never entered his home, but instead returned to the academy and became the greatest rabbi of his age.

Finally, after some twenty-four years, he returned to his wife's place, surrounded by an entourage of 24,000 students, augmented by a Judaean populace from all the surrounding towns. Rachel pushed her way through the crowds, falling down and embracing his feet. His disciples immediately moved to push the woman away, but Akivah stopped them, saying, "Leave her; what is mine and what is yours is hers! All the Torah we have together acquired is only through her unique merit."

It is not surprising then, that the love poem of *Shir Ha-Shirim,* which chronicles the trials and tribulations that are strewn in the path of true love, should have found a special place in the heart of Akivah, who knew from firsthand the power and sanctity of love, and the sacrifices that are so often demanded in its pursuit, and who discerned in the story of the poem the saga of his and Rachel's own love story.

### 652. Are there any other reasons why Rabbi Akivah should have fought for the inclusion of this book in the biblical Canon?

Bearing in mind the traumatic conditions of Jewish life under the Roman occupation, especially in the aftermath of the destruction of the Temple, and the widespread loss of faith among so many of the survivors, the allegorical message of *Shir Ha-Shirim* would have been viewed by Akivah as a most powerful medium for demonstrating, through the Bible, that the traumas suffered by Israel did not mean that her Lover had abandoned her, but that, quite the contrary, it would have the effect of making His love even stronger still.

### 653. How would such a message have been inferred?

This would depend upon precisely how the events of the poem were interpreted, for there was no one, single "authoritative" way of understanding and identifying the allegorical strands.

Akivah may well have made this point by making an analogy between the suffering of the Jews of his day at the hands of the Romans and the suffering of the shepherdess (Israel) at the hands of the watchmen. The splendor of Solomon's court, and that of the daughters of Jerusalem—both spurned by the shepherdess—would have been interpreted as representing the superficial allure of the Graeco-Roman civilization, rejected by Israel in favor of a life of Torah study and the performance of *mitzvot*.

## THE ALLEGORICAL METHOD

### 654. Do we have any evidence of precisely when the allegorical method was applied to *Shir Ha-Shirim*?

If we examine the Greek translation of the Septuagint (third century B.C.E.), we do not find any hint of the allegorical method, which we would have expected within the Greek philosophical orientation. The only slight departure from literalness is in its rendering of the phrase, *meirosh amanah* ("from the top of Mount Amanah," 4:8), which it translates as "from the beginning of faith." We cannot read anything into this, however, as the Septuagint frequently confuses proper and common nouns.

There is no evidence that it was allegorically interpreted within Jewish tradition before the first century C.E.. Had it been a well-known, traditional view, it would certainly have appeared in some of the writings of the Apocrypha, or in the works of Philo of Alexandria, an arch-allegorist. This fact also substantiates the view that this interpretation of the song was created not only to "purify" it of its literal excesses, but, primarily, as a profound stimulus to the flagging faith of a Jewry that felt that it had been forsaken by its "Beloved."

### 655. What is the first reference we have in Jewish writings to *Shir Ha-Shirim*?

It is not referred to or quoted in the early postbiblical books (third to first century B.C.E.), such as Ben-Sira or the other books just quoted. The first reference to it is in the Mishnah (*Taanit* 4:8) where a verse from it is reported as having been recited at an ancient courtship ceremony when the daughters of Jerusalem would go out into the vineyards and parade themselves before the eligible young men. The girls were given a formula to recite, which included the verse from Song of Songs: "Go out, O daughters of Zion, and look upon King Solomon in the crown with which his mother crowned him on the day of his marriage and the rejoicing of his heart" (3:11).

This verse appears to be employed here by the girls as a kind of tribute to the dignity and beauty of their would-be suitors, describing them as veritable "King Solomons." This is particularly significant in the context of the theory of the origin of *Shir Ha-Shirim* as a marriage poem, wherein bride and groom are hailed as monarchs, with the groom being specifically designated as King Solomon (see question 691).

### 656. What prompted Akivah and his school to emphasize the allegorical method?

It was clearly their wish to provide a biblical basis and framework for their theology of comfort and hope to a Judaean community being ground into the dust by the heels of the Roman occupiers. The ordinary Jews of those days could not possibly make sense of what they perceived as God's rejection of His people, His Temple and His land, in favor of an impious and cruel enemy. Many, unable to resolve their religious perplexity, were abandoning their faith or being attracted to the new cults which were springing up in the country, not the least Christianity, and which were offering a variant interpretation of God's covenant and a more comprehensive theology to replace that of the Chosen People.

It was vital for the Sages of Israel to address the Jewish existential problem; and our poem, a paradigm for strained love relationships, alternative lovers, and the doctrine of ultimate reconciliation, provided an ideal framework and metaphor for an ancient "guide for the perplexed."

### 657. What was the subsequent history of the allegorical interpretation of *Shir Ha-Shirim*?

The method was not developed in talmudic times; and it was only in the eighth century that a *Targum* (Aramaic translation and commentary) was produced on it, as well as on Ruth, Lamentations, Esther, and Ecclesiastes. The allegory is presented as a figurative representation of the history of Israel from the time of the Exodus until the ultimate messianic salvation.

We then have a break of several centuries, until the period of the illustrious medieval commentators, such as Rashi (1040–1105), David Kimchi (1190–1250), Abraham ibn Ezra (d. 1167), and Moses Maimonides (1135–1204), all of whom refer to the targumic allegories, regarding them as history and prophecy.

### 658. Besides utilizing the allegory to chronicle Jewish history, were there any other major emphases in this particular approach?

In the period of the Hadrianic persecutions (138–135 c.e.), when basic observances of *Shabbat, Kashrut,* and circumcision were outlawed and many Jews suffered martyrdom for their faith, interpretations of the book were given which sought to reveal allusions to Jewish martyrology and the uniqueness of Israel among the nations.

**659. How would such an interpretation be read into the text?**

One dominant approach is to employ phrases from the poem as part of a supposed Jewish–heathen dialogue, wherein the latter question Israel as to the benefit of her continued faith in the light of her having been clearly abandoned by God, and left to the mercy of violent enemies. The following Midrash (see *Mekhilta D'Rabbi Ishmael, Beshalach,* ch. 3; see also *Shir Ha-Shirim Rabbah* 5:9, 6:1) is a good example of the martyrological genre:

> Rabbi Akivah expounded thus: I shall speak of the glory and praise of the Holy One in the presence of all the nations of the world. For they ask Israel, saying, *"What is thy Beloved more than another Beloved, that thou dost so adjure us* [Song of Songs 5:9], and suffer such martyrdom for Him? Do not the maidens *love you* [1:3] – For you are beautiful and strong? Come, then, and intermarry with us." But Israel replies to them, saying, "Clearly you do not know Him. Let us declare then but a little of His praise: *Our beloved is pure and ruddy, preeminent above ten thousand"* (5:10).
>
> When they hear God's praise declared in that way, they say to Israel: "We will follow in your faith," as it states: *Whither is thy beloved gone, O thou fairest among women? Whither hath thy beloved turned, that we may seek Him with thee?"* (6:1).
>
> But Israel responds: "You have no share in Him – *for my beloved is mine, and I am His"* (2:16).

## MYSTICAL INTERPRETATION

**660. Do any other methods of interpreting *Shir Ha-Shirim* exist?**

There is also a mystical interpretation of the poem which also stretches back to Rabbi Akivah, the leading mystic of his age. There is a midrashic tradition that Rabban Gamaliel wept when Rabbi Akivah moved on in his exposition from the first verse to the second, believing that it was on account of his own unworthiness to receive from Akivah its full store of secrets.

**661. What form did the mystical method take?**

*Shir Ha-Shirim* was employed in the context of the most esoteric of mystical traditions, called by the name *Shi'ur Komah,* "the measure of the [divine] body." In the words of Gershom Scholem, "When the mystic attained the vision of the supernal world and found himself standing before the throne, he was vouchsafed a vision of the *Shi'ur Komah* as the figure in the form of a man which Ezekiel had seen on the throne in his first vision of the *Merkabah* [Ezekiel 1:26]" ("Shi'ur Komah," *Encyclopaedia Judaica* 14:1417).

This daring form of meditation on the Body of God utilized the description of the lover in *Shir Ha-Shirim* (5:11–16) as its basic revelatory source, one which was also a primary reservoir of mystic inspiration for the entire kabbalistic tradition.

### 662. Did the Church have any view on *Shir Ha-Shirim*?

This question is best answered by a Christian scholar, R. A. Redford, who writes: "Not only did they [Christian commentators], almost without exception, treat the book as an allegory, but they strained the interpretation beyond all limits of common sense and Scripture analogy" (*The Pulpit Commentary,* London: Kegan, Paul, Trench, Truebner and Co., 1897, p. xi). The Church naturally used the allegorical method to read a host of Christological teachings into every verse, and viewed the story as chronicling the love of their savior for the Church.

An example of one of its interpretations that goes "beyond all limits of common sense" is that of the fourth-century Bishop Ambrose, who suggested, in a sermon on the perpetual virginity of Mary, that there are allusions to her in such expressions as the "locked garden" and the "sealed fountain" (4:12)!

## TALMUDIC ATTITUDES

### 663. Once *Shir Ha-Shirim* had been accepted as an official biblical book (circa 90 C.E.), are any rabbinic attitudes towards it recorded in the Talmud?

The Talmud (*Sanhedrin* 101a) states, "*Our Rabbis have taught* that whoever sings a verse from *Shir Ha-Shirim* as an ordinary [secular] song or who declaims it in a place of revelry rather than when it is prescribed to be read, brings evil into the world."

The introductory phrase, "Our Rabbis have taught," already suggests a rabbinic consensus regarding the work. It was clearly regarded as a sacred work by those Sages who must already have assumed its primary meaning to be an allegorical account of the relationship, through Torah, between God and Israel. They clearly also realized its erotic potential, particularly when recited by common folk inebriated through drink, and they therefore made strenuous attempts to counter such a situation.

### 664. In their emphasis on the allegorical meaning of the poem, did the Rabbis deny then its literal meaning and significance?

Certainly not; talmudic Sages who were prepared to discuss openly and unashamedly such topics as the breasts of a woman, and what may be regarded as a normal, abnormal, beautiful, or blemished shape (see Talmud *Ketubot* 75a) were certainly on the wavelength of literalness as regards the themes of *Shir Ha-Shirim*.

### 665. But do any interpretations of the book provided in the Talmud actually prove that they inferred the applicability of a literal meaning of the text?

Indeed, to quote but one example; the Talmud (*Ketubot* 75a) asserts, "A deep voice is a blemish in a woman, since, it states, 'For your voice is sweet and your appearance beautiful' " (Song of Songs 2:14). The Rabbis were clearly looking to our poem, in its literal sense, as a paradigm of beautiful feminine characteristics.

## THE STORY

**666. What is the basic story of *Shir Ha-Shirim,* to the extent that it can be discerned within the poem?**

It is a story of a beautiful shepherdess from Shunem who had pledged her love to a shepherd from her village, a union that her family refused to countenance. In order to curtail the lovers' meetings, her family put her to work closer to home in the vineyards. One day she is noticed by some passing servants of King Solomon, and, at her refusal to accompany them to his court, she is taken away forcibly and led as a captive to his chamber.

Solomon falls for her at first sight, and strenuously attempts to woo her by serenading her with tributes to her beauty and charm, and the promise of the finest jewelry and apparel. He enlists the help of the "daughters of Jerusalem," ladies of the court, who try to persuade her to submit to Solomon's advances by taunting her that, in any case, her beloved shepherd boy will, by now, have rejected her.

Sorely tormented, she dreams at night that her lover has come to rescue her and take her back to their village. Awakening from her dream, she escapes from the palace. Outside at such an hour, she is mistaken for a harlot, and is pursued and assaulted by the watchmen of the city.

Brought back to the palace, the king is finally convinced of the futility of his efforts, and of the constancy of her love for her shepherd boy. He releases her, and she makes a triumphant return to Shunem, entering on the arm of her beloved. She recounts all that has happened to her, and asserts that true and pure love is far more precious than all the hollow luxuries of the king's court.

## ITS DATE AND PLACE OF COMPOSITION

**667. Can we ascertain the date when this poem was written?**

Linguistic usages, particularly the many Aramaisms, point to a late period of authorship. The earlier books of the Bible employ the word *asher* to denote the relative pronoun. Through the evolution of the language, by the third century B.C.E., this had become contracted to *sheh,* which has remained the relative particle ever since.

Among the Aramaisms we may note *natar* (1:6; 8:11, 12) for the Hebrew *natzar; berot* (1:17) for the Hebrew form, *berosh,* as well as the word *setav,* "Winter" (2:11). To these may be added such Persian loan-words as *pardes,* "park" (4:13); and even Greek words such as *apiryon,* "a palanquin" or royal coach (3:9). We are thus brought into at least the early Greek period, around 300 B.C.E..

Those who affirm King Solomon as the author of the work must assume, in the light of the above, that it went through several later editorial revisions—hence the accretion of the late and loan words—before it entered the Bible in the present form.

### 668. Can we ascertain precisely where it was composed?

No, we cannot. However, the Greek influence suggests that it must have been composed where the bulk of the Jewish community would have resided at that period, namely Jerusalem and its environs. The fact that the story seems to portray the rural life of Shunem as the preferred choice of the heroine, rather than the sophisticated court of Solomon at Jerusalem, is no proof that the author was a country dweller. He is merely setting his poem within the conditions of a much earlier period when Shunem, in the far north of Israel (near present-day Haifa), was a well-known city.

### 669. Can we conjecture why a third-century B.C.E. author should have chosen to portray just the city of Shunem as the home of his heroine, when that city had long ceased to be a place of significant Jewish domicile centuries earlier?

Clearly he had in mind the well-known Israelite tradition regarding the beautiful maiden, Avishag, nurse of David in his old age, who was born at Shunem (1 Kings 1:3, 15). We may conjecture that a tradition had survived concerning Solomon's unrequited love for Avishag, and that it was that which provided the muse for this poem.

## SHUNEM AND THE SHUNAMMITE

### 670. Is there any basis in the Bible for assuming that Solomon desired Avishag the Shunammite?

We believe there is. We are told (1 Kings 2:13–25) that after Adonijah, brother of Solomon, was passed over as successor to King David, in favor of his younger brother Solomon, he requested his mother, Bathsheba, to ask Solomon, as a consolation, to grant that Avishag be given to him in marriage:

> A throne was set for the king's mother, and she sat at his right hand. Then she said, "I have one small request to make of you; do not refuse me." "What is it, mother?" he replied. "I will not refuse you." "It is this, that Avishag, the Shunammite, should be given to your brother, Adonijah, in marriage." At that Solomon answered his mother, "Why do you ask for Avishag, the Shunammite, as wife for Adonijah? you might as well ask for the throne, for he is my elder brother. . . ." Then King Solomon swore by the Lord: "So help me God, Adonijah shall pay for this with his life. . . . [T]his very day Adonijah shall be put to death!" Thereupon King Solomon gave Benaiah son of Jehoiadah his orders, and he struck him down and he died.

Solomon's response to that harmless request was so irrational and uncharacteristically violent that we must suspect that his own feelings for Avishag were intense, and that he was consumed by jealousy at the very thought of his brother having her when he, himself, was rejected. If this was, indeed, the tradition that survived regarding Solomon's tragic love affair with the Shunammite, then we understand precisely from where the setting, the story, and the origin of the heroine and the poor royal victim have been culled.


## FLEXIBLE ORDER OF BIBLICAL BOOKS

**671. We have already referred to the final decision on which particular books were to be considered "biblical" as having been taken towards the end of the first century, in the period of Rabbi Akivah. Was the present order of those biblical books established at the outset?**

No. It is clear that the order of the books was rather flexible at first. Hence, surprisingly, the order given in the Talmud does not conform with our accepted Masoretic tradition.

The Talmud prescribes the following order for the books of the *Ketuvim* (Sacred Writings): Ruth, Psalms, Job, Proverbs, Ecclesiastes, Song of Songs, and so on (*Bava Batra* 14b), whereas our order is: Psalms, Proverbs, Job, Song of Songs, Ruth, Lamentations, Ecclesiastes.


**672. Do any other traditions exist with further variations in the order of those biblical books?**

Yes, we possess biblical manuscripts, from both Leningrad and Aleppo, wherein Song of Songs precedes Ecclesiastes.


**673. But if we open a Christian Bible, do we not find a further difference in the order?**

We do. Based on the order of the early Greek translation, the Septuagint, the Bibles produced by the Church list the Solomonic books in the order given in the Talmud (*Bava Batra* 14b) — Proverbs, Ecclesiastes, Song of Songs — after which they place the books of the Later Prophets. The logic of that order is that it follows the chronological order of their authors, since King Solomon lived before the later prophets (Isaiah, Jeremiah, Ezekiel, and the twelve minor prophets).

Our order, as we have stated, places the five *Megillot* in the chronological order of the succeeding festivals of the year to which they are allotted.


## CHARACTERISTICS OF HEBREW POETRY

**674. We have observed that the *Shir Ha-Shirim* is a poem. What are the main characteristics of Hebrew poetry, and how does it differ from Hebrew prose?**

Biblical Hebrew poetry is characterized by a metric rhythm, generally created by having a more or less equal number of words or stresses in each line. Each line is generally broken up into two half-lines (hemistiches), with the second half-line paralleling the first. Indeed, the device of parallelism is the primary characteristic of Hebrew poetry.

### 675. What is the nature of poetic parallelism?

Three main types of parallelism are employed in biblical Hebrew poetry:

(i) *Synonymous parallelism:* where the second line repeats, paraphrases, or expands upon the first, though pursuing the same poetic concept. Deuteronomy 32:1 is an example of this:

> *Ha'azinu ha-shamayim va-adabeira — vetishma ha-aretz imrei fiy*

> Let the heavens give ear while I speak, and let the earth
> hear the words of my mouth.

(ii) *Antithetical parallelism:* where the second line forms a contrast to the first. Isaiah 1:3 is a good example of this:

> *Yada shor koneihu, vachamor eivus be'alav*
> *Yisra'el lo yada, ammiy lo hitbonan*

> The ox knoweth its owner, and the ass its master's crib;
> But Israel doth not know, my people do not consider.

(iii) *Synthetic parallelism:* where the parallelism is apparent, but where the second line is only a loose counterpart to the first in construction and imagery. These lines, from the well-loved Twenty-Third Psalm, conform to this system of parallelism:

> *Ta'arokh lefanay shulchan, neged tzorerai*
> *Dishanta bashemen roshiy, kosiy revayah*

> Thou spreadest before me a table, in the presence
> of mine enemies;
> Thou hast anointed my head with oil; my cup runneth over.

There are also other forms of parallelisms that have been observed, within the psalms in particular, but the above three are the most common categories.

### 676. What about the imagery of biblical poetry?

Naturally, the usual differences between poetry and prose — in the richer quality of the imagery employed when expressing oneself in poetry — apply in biblical Hebrew poetry. The lyricism and deep emotional outpouring of the psalmists and prophets have continued to inspire successive generations, and particularly those who have set their words to music, and proclaimed or sung those sacred sentiments in Temple, synagogue, and church, as a vehicle for their own feelings, moods, prayers, and praises.

### 677. What about the language and style of biblical poetry?

Hebrew poetry, though economic in its use of words, yet succeeded in sustaining a flowing, rhythmic style. Occasionally it made use of archaic words and grammatical forms that had long been discarded within prose style, and certainly within the popular conversational Hebrew of the contemporary biblical age.

There are also some special stylistic devices that are used to enhance the poetic quality. The first is *assonance:* where the sound of the words employed serve to heighten the meaning and atmosphere of the emotion being expressed. An interesting example of this is the famous passage from Isaiah where he speaks of the messianic age when nations "will beat their swords into ploughshares and their spears into pruning-hooks" (2:4). If we read the Hebrew line aloud we can almost hear—through its regular repetition of the hard *t*-sound—the weapons being beaten into a new form: *Vekhitetu charvotam le'itim, vachanitoteihem lemazmeirot.*

Other devices are rhyme, alliteration, onomatopoeia, and paronomasia (for examples of these, the reader is referred to the *Encyclopaedia Judaica,* 13: 679–681).

## TYPES OF PARALLELISM IN *SHIR HA-SHIRIM*

### 678. How is this parallelism employed in *Shir Ha-Shirim*?

Occasionally, the parallelism is employed within a single line, with the second half-line merely repeating part of the first, for added emphasis. Thus:

> *Hinnakh yafah ra'yatiy—Hinnakh yafah*

> You are beautiful, my beloved—You are truly beautiful (4:1).

More commonly, the second line, while paralleling the first, yet carries the description a stage further. Thus:

> *Sa'reikh ke'eider ha-izzim, shegalshu meihar Gil'ad*
> *Shinnayikh ke'eider ha-ketzuvot, she'alu min ha-rachtzah.*

> Your hair like a flock of goats, streaming down Mount Gilead,
> Your teeth are like a flock of ewes just shorn,
> which have come up fresh from the dipping.

As regards the number of words in each half-line, the most popular scheme employed here is to have three words in the first half-line, and three in the parallel half-line (as in the immediate above example), though sometimes this is varied to four words followed by three, or four and four.

### 679. Are there examples of synonymous parallelism in *Shir Ha-Shirim*?

There are. We quote 6:1 as but one example of this:

> *Annah halakh dodeikh, ha-yafah be-nashim;*
> *Annah panah dodeikh, unvakshennu immakh.*

> Where has your beloved gone, O fairest of women?
> Which way did your beloved go, that we may help you seek him?

### 680. Are there examples of antithetical parallelism?

There are. Note 1:6:

> *Samuniy noteirah et ha-kramim;*
> *Karmiy sheliy lo natartiy*

> They made me a guard of the vineyards;
> But my own vineyard I could not protect.

Another example occurs in 3:1, repeated almost verbatim in verse 2:

> *Bikkashtiy eit she'ahavah nafshi;*
> *Bikkashtiy velo metzativ.*

> I have sought my true love;
> I have sought him but not found him.

### 681. Are there examples of synthetic parallelism in *Shir Ha-Shirim*?

It is very common indeed. The following verse (7:3) provides a typical example:

> *Shorereikh aggan ha-sahar, al yechsar ha-mazeg*
> *Bitneikh areimat chittim, sugah ba-shoshanim.*

> Your navel is a rounded goblet that never lacks spiced wine;
> Your belly is a heap of wheat fenced in by lilies.

### 682. Are there examples of alliteration?

One of the most prominent features of the style of this poem is its employment of alliteration. It especially seeks to emphasize the sh-sound, and its focus on just this consonant is clearly inspired by the title of the poem, *Shir Ha-Shirim*.

The clearest example is, quite obviously, the opening line:

> *Shir Ha-Shirim asher liShelomo*

It is employed again in the lines:

> *Shuviy shuviy ha-shulamit,*
> *Shuviy shuviy venechezeh bakh.*

> Return, return, O Shulamit,
> Return, return, and let us behold you. (7:1)

And, to give but one further example:

> *Al tir'uni she'ani shecharchoret*
> *Sheshzafatniy ha-shamesh*

> Do not look down on me because I am dark;
> It is the sun that has bleached me. (1:6)

# THE SHEPHERD BOY, THE SHUNAMMITE, AND THE PURITY OF THEIR LOVE

**683. Can we construct, from the text, any picture of the physical characteristics of the shepherd boy, so beloved of the Shunammite?**

Allowing for poetic licence, we may discern certain physical characteristics as they are praised in the respective descriptions of the hero and heroine. At the same time, we must also allow for the fact that, being shepherds, their imagery is drawn almost exclusively from their own narrow, unsophisticated, even earthy, experience and perspective. The result of this is that the similes they employ may hardly appear complimentary to those outside their fraternity!

Hence, the Shunammite describes her lover as a gazelle or a young wild goat who comes "bounding over the mountains and leaping over the hills" (2:8–9) — presumably a tribute to his fleet-footedness. His body is depicted as "ivory work overlaid with sapphires" (5:14), that is, possessing the smoothness and symmetry as of a beautiful ivory statue, the work of the highest artistic excellence. He is of exceptional height: "lofty above tens of thousands" (5:10). His complexion is described as "fair and ruddy" (5:10), and his cheeks as "beds of spices or banks of sweet herbs" (5:13), which might be a reference to a luxuriant beard. His hair is "curly and black as a raven" (5:11), and his eyes are "like doves beside the water-brooks, splashed by the milky water" (5:12), suggestive of the clear, moist, steady and strong look of fine eyes.

**684. Does it not appear rather unseemly for an innocent shepherdess to be giving such a brazen description of her beloved's body?**

To regard it as such is to impute unworthy thoughts to a girl whose whole demeanor and attributes exude chastity and purity of thought. The author of *Shir Ha-Shirim* is truly worlds apart from the writers of modern, popular love songs, with their suggestive — and often openly erotic — lyrics. The descriptions of her lover's physical characteristics are so abstractly poetic, and so detached from any sexual association or connotation, as to convince us that she had never seen the parts of the body in question. "To the pure, all is pure." And our Shulamit is uniquely pure. As such, she is a model of Jewish maidenhood, and a most appropriate symbol of Israel's higher love of God.

**685. What evidence do we have from the text of the pure quality of her love relationship?**

Apart from there being not the slightest hint of sexual impropriety, there is the express statement that the shepherdess brings her beloved "to my mother's home and my parents' chamber." In other words, their relationship is conducted openly, with the blessing of their families and in conformity with the accepted norms of contact between young people.

True, the shepherdess does not hide the fact that "she is love-sick." She owns up to those strong feelings. There is no pretense or pretentiousness. She looks forward to the moment of union; but she is aware that it has to be in the context of marriage. Indeed, she is outraged by the "daughters of Jerusalem," who were clearly trying to convince her to succumb to the king's desires. She tells them three times that love is not to be confused with sexual arousal, and that its proper, and only, context is within marriage: "I charge you, daughters of Jerusalem . . . not to awaken or stir up love until it is ready" (2:7, 3:5, 8:4).

### 686. Are there any other ways of explaining the propriety of those intimate references?

Indeed. Some commentators regard a few of the passages in the poem as reflecting the situation at the ultimate marriage of the young lovers, or even immediately following it.

Now, if, as has been suggested, *Shir Ha-Shirim* was originally written as a marriage song, intended to be sung also throughout the week of festivities following the marriage (see question 691), then the rather intimate references may be explained, simply, as an expression of rapture uttered by the shepherdess once their union had been consummated, and in full knowledge of the body of her beloved.

### 687. Is there any real evidence, from within the text, to support the theory that the intimate descriptions reflect the love of a new husband and wife, rather than that of two unmarried people?

While the precise attribution of all the changing scenes and descriptions to specific moments and events is not possible, yet one of the most amorous passages (4:1-5:1), spoken in the main by the shepherd—with but one interjection (4:15-16) by his bride—does appear to reflect his rapturous response to the initial marital union.

His description of his beloved as "a sealed garden" and "a spring shut up" (4:12) appears to be a celebration of her virginity, a tribute to her previous chasteness and an expression of his delight in the sense of absolute and sole possession.

It is important to note that chronology and order is totally absent from this poem, so that we have verses that reflect their single-person situation cheek-by-jowl with verses descriptive of their procession to the bridal canopy, juxtaposed to verses descriptive of the bride inviting her husband into the bridal chamber (4:16), coupled with lengthy descriptions of their respective rapture following on from the consummation of their marriage. The intimate description of her body (chs. 4:1-14; 5:1; 7:1-10) is, more than likely, to be placed within the marital context.

The shepherd's reference to his "beloved's veil" (4:3) may refer to the veil that Israelite married women would wear at all times outside their home, and does not necessarily imply an exclusively bridal situation. Thus, the accompanying references to intimate parts of her body may well be the tribute of a husband, rather than of merely a lover, and may reflect his excitement and awe at the new disclosure that marriage has brought him, of the physical and spiritual beauty of love.

### 688. Can we construct, from the text, any picture of the beauty of the Shunammite?

Like her beloved, she is also exceedingly tall and stately; hence the description of her as "just like a palm tree" (7:8). She walks with superb grace (7:2). Her face is sunburnt from working in the fields and vineyards (1:5); and against that dark background the milky whiteness of her perfectly shaped teeth is greatly accentuated (4:2). She has a long, slender neck, reminiscent of the Tower of David (4:4), with lustrous black hair, trailing down her back "like a flock of goats streaming down the mountainside of Gilead" (6:5). Her body is firm (7:8–9), in perfect proportion (4:5), and as shapely as if it had been "sculpted by a skilled craftsman" (7:2).

### 689. Do we know anything of her social status?

The reference to her as "a prince's daughter" (7:2) suggests that she was born into an upper-class family with estates around Jerusalem. David Kimchi (1160–1235. His commentary to the Books of the Prophets and the Sacred Writings was first published in the Venice 1548 edition of the standard Rabbinic Bible and in most subsequent editions.) actually understands the etymology of her title "Shulamite" as being derived from *Shalem* (Salem), the early name for Jerusalem (see Radak's comment on 7:1).

Her upper-class status is confirmed by the fact that she wears the finest perfumes (1:12–14; 4:10). In her younger years she suffered from being the only daughter in a family of boys (6:9). The reference to "her mother's only child" (1:6) suggests either that she was a stepsister, or that their father had died and their mother felt a stronger bond with her daughter than she did with her sons.

Either way, her (step-) brothers disliked her, took advantage of her, and made her work out-of-doors on the family estates. It was while working on the land that she met and fell in love with the shepherd boy.

## THE ROLE OF KING SOLOMON

### 690. Is there not a touch of confusion in the poem as regards the persona of King Solomon, who seems to appear at the outset of the poem (1:4) as the noble and desired lover of the shepherdess, and at the end of the poem (8:11–12) in the guise of the rejected suitor?

It is true that the references to King Solomon do not make it clear precisely how he is being portrayed. In the opening chapter the shepherdess cries out, "Take me with you, and we will run together; the king has brought me into his chambers; we will be glad and rejoice in thee, finding thy love more fragrant than wine." This suggests that she glories in her royal suitor, a relationship reinforced a little later in the same chapter, where she sings, "While the king reclines on his couch, my spikenard gives forth its scent" (v. 12). Indeed, as the poem develops, so does her relationship with the king: "The hair of your head is like purple; the king is held captive in its tresses" (7:6).

However, at the end of the poem, there is a totally unexpected expression of disdain for all the luxuries that Solomon possesses and longs to confer upon the shepherdess! "Solomon can keep his vineyard, she exclaims. My vineyard, which is all my own, is for my beloved and me to share" (8:11–12). Indeed, the poem ends with the Shunammite crying out for her beloved to hurry to her.

### 691. How do we resolve the problem?

The present writer believes that it can only be adequately resolved within the context of the theory that *Shir Ha-Shirim* belongs to the genre of ancient Near Eastern wedding poems that we have referred to above (see questions 655, 686), wherein the bride and groom enacted the roles of a king and queen during the week-long wedding festivities. The Rabbis (*Pirkei D'Rabbi Eliezer*, ch. 16) also inherited a tradition that accords a bride and groom the status of monarchs (*chatan domeh lemelekh*); and we believe that this motif is foreshadowed in the image of King Solomon in our poem.

What we have here, then, is our young couple (whose true identity literary history never preserved for us) being feted as royalty. But not just any royalty. They are encouraged to act out, in their vivid fantasies, and with vocal and musical stimuli, the role of the greatest Israelite monarch, King Solomon. We have referred above (see question 655) to the ancient ceremony of courtship, whereby the girls hailed their would-be bridegrooms as "King Solomons." This provides clear support for our theory that it is merely a designation of the lover, not of the real Solomon, that our heroine desires as her bridegroom-king.

Such an identification is fine for the shepherd bridegroom. The problem comes, however, for the Shulamite; for there is no single wife of Solomon of such fame and distinction as to enable her name and identity to be borrowed with pride by our bride. The way around this problem was, simply, to turn the situation to the advantage of our bride-queen. She is given speeches to recite, wherein she chides Solomon, telling him, among other things, to "keep his thousand" (8:12). This would have been readily understood as a reference to his one thousand wives (1 Kings 11:3). Thus, the bride is able to lord it over Solomon, who, for all his wealth, was unable to find a single true love. This poetic speech would be calculated to warm the heart of her own bridegroom, and to remind him of his particular good fortune in having found an ideal and true partner.

Hence, the bride is acting out her royal role at two levels. On the one hand, her new husband becomes the personification of King Solomon, so that she is now being wooed by the most romantic figure in ancient Israel, with her husband's marital chamber, where the marriage is consummated, becoming transformed into a veritable royal boudoire. At the second level—and the contradiction was not one that would have troubled the ancients in such a fictional dramatic context—her vanity is enabled to be flattered by her being made to imagine that there were two suitors, the second being the love-sick King Solomon, and that she, the shepherdess, rejects the monarch, and all he has to offer, in favor of her true love.

**692. According to the simple interpretation of the opening words of the poem, which attribute this Song of Songs to Solomon, is there any hint in the text that might connect its authorship to him?**

There is one phrase in our poem which constitutes an actual paraphrase of a verse in the famous *Eishet Chayil* ("Woman of worth") passage from the book of Proverbs (ch. 31), traditionally attributed to King Solomon. We provide here a comparison of the two verses:

| Proverbs 31:28 | Song of Songs 6:9 |
|---|---|
| *Kamu vaneha vaye'ashruha* | *Ra'uha vanot vaye'ashruha* |
| *Ba'lah vayehallelah.* | *Melakhot ufilagshim vayehalleluha.* |
| Her children rise up and declare her happy. | Daughters see her and declare her happy |
| Her husband also, and he praises her. | Queens and concubines, and they praise her. |

## NO DIVINE NAME

**693. Why does the divine name not occur at all in *Shir Ha-Shirim*?**

We must assume that the Rabbis who accepted this poem into the Canon of biblical books did not regard the presence or otherwise of divine names as constituting the criterion for holiness. It has been wisely said that holiness can exist in a laboratory or a hospital, as much as in a synagogue. It is less a matter of the holy words declaimed than of the holy thoughts and intentions engendered, and holy works initiated.

It has also been suggested that, since this poem contains many passages that would inevitably have been quoted in ancient Israel, by bridegrooms and brides and husbands and wives, as endearments and preludes to arousal, it was felt inappropriate to include any lines containing the divine name which should only be uttered in a state of purity and in the context of prayer.

Some believe that the name of God does actually occur in the poem, in the word, *shalhevetyah* (8:6), which may be broken up into two words and translated, "flame of God." But most commentators understand the final syllable as merely denoting "might," and they render the word, "mighty flame."

This usage of the divine name to denote "power" is referred to by *Metzudat Tziyon*: "For this is the way of Scripture, if it wishes to convey a superlative sense, it attaches the divine name to it, as in the phrase *eretz ma'pelyah*, "a land of dense darkness [Jeremiah 2:31]" (see *Metzudat Tziyyon* on *Shir Ha-Shirim* 8:6).

## RABBINIC EXPOSITIONS

**694. How do the Rabbis explain the verse, "I am black and beautiful, O daughters of Jerusalem. Like the tents of Kedar, like the curtains of Solomon" (1:5)?**

The rabbinic translators of the Prophetic books of the Bible into Aramaic, whose work is known as *Targum* (according to the Talmud *Megillah* 3b it was the work of one author, Yonatan ben Uzziel), explain our poem in accordance with the principles of their own exegetical (midrashic) style of interpretation. This views each phrase as alluding to some facet of the agonies and ecstasies of Israel's religious history, and her relationship with the God who presides over her historic destiny.

Thus, the subject of the verse "I am black" is Israel; and the blackness suggests being in disgrace as a result of having made the Golden Calf. *Targum* interprets our verse to mean that as soon as they made the calf, the faces of the Israelites grew as dark as those of Ethiopians who live "in the tents of Kedar." Their radiance was only restored when they did penitence; and it was even augmented when they made "the curtains of Solomon," that is, when they created the Sanctuary to God's greater glory.

### 695. Are there any alternative rabbinical interpretations?

The Midrash (*Shir Ha-Shirim Rabbah* 1:35) suggests various interpretations to explain what it perceives as a contrast between Israel's "blackness" and her "beauty." Among such explanations are that Israel was "black" and depressed through her oppression in Egypt, but, nevertheless, "beautiful" through the Passover and circumcision laws that she observed there. She was "black" and unworthy when she committed immorality at Shittim (Numbers 25:1), but "beautiful" when that sin was purged through the prompt action of the zealous Phinehas (25:7–26:15). Israel is "black" and burdened with business preoccupations throughout the week, but "beautiful" on the Sabbath day. Israel is "black" in this world, but "beautiful" and radiant when she receives in the hereafter the reward for all her earthly suffering.

### 696. What is the precise sense of the analogy with the "tents of Kedar"?

The midrashic explanation (*Shir Ha-Shirim Rabbah* 1:38) is that, just as those tents are black on the outside, having been made from the skins of the black goats of the region, and yet, within those tents are stored great and magnificent treasures, so are Israel's Sages reviled and mocked for their unprepossessing external appearance, yet inside they are "beautiful" through the spiritual and intellectual gems that they store in their minds, and reflect in their souls.

### 697. How does the Midrash expound the verse, "My mother's sons [benei immiy] were incensed with me [nicharu biy]. They made me keeper of the vineyards; but my own vineyard have I not kept" (1:6)?

Midrashic interpretations frequently depart radically from the literal sense, though there is invariably some justifiable philological or semantic association with the wording of the text. This verse yields a classical illustration of this.

The Midrash on this verse (*Shir Ha-Shirim Rabbah* 1:43) interprets the words, *benei immiy,* not as "sons of my mother" but, more widely, as "sons of my people" (equating *benei immiy* with *benei ammiy*). It also understands the difficult phrase, *nicharu biy,* not in the sense of "to be incensed," but "to harm" (which is quite justifiable, as derived from the literal sense of the verb *nachar,* "to pierce.") So, so far we have the midrashic meaning of "my own people had done me harm."

The Midrash further understands "vineyards" as the common idiom for *mitzvot* — the luscious spiritual fruits of the service of God; and it proceeds to render the rest of the verse in a most surprising way, emphasizing the contrast between the plural form, "vineyards," that they made him "keep," and his own *single* "vineyard" that he could not. In the hands of the midrashic interpreters this suggested a complaint that, through the sons of his people's iniquity, in failing to observe even the biblically-prescribed, one, holy (first and seventh) day of each of the main festivals, "they made me keep two vineyards," that is, I was penalized by having to observe, outside Israel, two holy days (the *Yom Tov Sheni shel Galuyyot,* second day's festivals of the Diaspora). The result of this exile from our land (inflicted upon me by the iniquity of "the sons of my people"), was that "my own vineyard" — but one single festival day, "I could not keep," — I was not privileged to observe.

For the many Diaspora-based religious Zionists who are riled at having to observe the two days of *Yom Tov,* this Midrash provides a sympathetic echo of their frustration.

### 698. How did the Sages expound the verse, "Tell me, O thou whom my soul loveth, where thou feedest, where thou makest thy flock to rest at noon. For why should I be as one that veileth herself beside the flocks of thy companions" (1:7)?

The *Targum* expounds the verse in relation to Moses. When the moment of his death approached, he said to God: "It has been revealed before me that this people is destined to sin, and to be driven into exile. Please, God, tell me how they will be provided for when they dwell among nations whose decrees are as unbearable as the noonday sun in the summer solstice? Tell me why they should be driven among the flocks of the children of Esau and Ishmael who place their idols as equal companions to You" (*Targum Yonatan* ad loc.).

### 699. How do the Sages expound the verse, "As a rose among thorns, so is my beloved among the daughters" (2:2)?

The *Targum* explains it with reference to Israel: when she departs from God's ways, and is sent into exile, she resembles a rose among thorns. Just as the thorns pierce and tear the skin of the rose, so do the other nations tear Israel in pieces.

### 700. Are there any other interpretations?

The Midrash (*Shir Ha-Shirim Rabbah* 2:7) interprets it in a manner that reflects the religious ignorance of the masses in talmudic times. Not surprisingly, the talmudic term for "the masses," *ammei ha-aretz,* became the accepted term for "ignoramuses." The midrashic interpretation runs thus: "It frequently occurs that ten people enter a synagogue, and not one of them can lead the congregation in the recitation of *Shema* or *Amidah.* If one person among them is able to do so, to what may he be compared? To a rose among thorns!" Compared with that situation in talmudic times, perhaps our own day's prophets of doom should not so quickly despair!

**701. How did the Sages expound the verse, "My beloved is unto me as a bag of myrrh that lieth betwixt my breasts" (1:13)?**

The Sages refer this to the fragrance of the Torah, which is located (in the form of the two Tablets of the Law) inside the Ark of Sanctuary.

The reference to "breasts" in this context has to be understood in relation to the fact that the Holy of Holies, wherein the Ark was housed, was fractionally too small to accommodate it, with the result that the two carrying staves, attached to either side of the Ark, just protruded, like two breasts, against the *parochet,* the veil or curtain that partitioned off the Holy of Holies area of the Sanctuary from the main officiating area.

Since Israel's "Beloved" resided in the inner sanctum together with the Ark, and since *mor* ("myrrh") is also associated with the word *Torah,* "instruction" (cf. *moreh,* "teacher"), the verse was construed as a reference to the fragrance of God's Torah which wafted forth from the "breasts" of the Ark.

**702. How did the Sages understand the verse, "Behold it is the litter of Solomon; threescore mighty men surround it, of the mighty men of Israel" (3:7)?**

The *Targum* views Solomon's "litter" as the Temple, and the sixty warriors as representing the sixty letters that are contained in the Priestly Blessing, recited daily in the Temple and employing the secret divine name used only in that formula of blessing:

> When Solomon built the Temple in Jerusalem, God said: "How magnificent is this Temple, built for Me by Solomon, son of David, and how beautiful are the priests at the time when they stand on the dais and spread their hands to bless Israel with the sixty letters which were revealed to Moses their master. That blessing surrounds them like a high and strong wall, and, through it, all the valiant [in faith] of Israel are strengthened and prosper."

**703. How does *Targum* understand the continuation of that verse: "All handlers of the sword and expert in war; every one with his sword upon his thigh because of the dread in the night" (3:8)?**

It understands this verse in the light of the well-known and frequently repeated talmudic imagery of their own academies of learning as fields of battle, and the sharp, penetrative debates as acts of gladiatorial contest. Hence *Targum* uses the reference to "the sword" as a metaphor for the Torah, and the "experts in war" as its exponents. The second reference to the "sword upon his thigh" *Targum* interprets as the sign of circumcision which serves as an extra defense against "the dread in the night."

**704. How does the Midrash understand the phrase** *benot tziyyon*, **"daughters of Zion" (3:11)?**

The Midrash was aware that this is an unusual term that occurs nowhere else in the entire Bible, though there are several occurrences of the singular form *bat tziyyon*, "daughter of Zion," as a personification of Jerusalem. Again, the term, "sons of Zion" (*benei tziyyon*) is also found in Lamentations 4:2.

In typical midrashic fashion, even the slightest unusual textual form or occurrence calls for exegetical treatment. Hence, the Midrash treats the plural phrase *benot tziyyon* as an attribute, connecting *tziyyon* with the word *metzuyyanim*, "distinguished." Hence, in employing this phrase, God is believed to be paying tribute to an Israel that is "distinguished" from the heathen nations in three ways: through its distinctive hairstyle (in not shaving the corners of the head; see Leviticus 19:27), through circumcision, and through the wearing of *tzitzit* (fringes on the corners of garments; see Numbers 15:38).

**705. Is there any midrashic identification of the King Solomon that is alluded to in** *Shir Ha-Shirim*?

The Midrash (*Shir Ha-Shirim Rabbah* 3:19, 20) understands the references to Solomon, or, simply, to "the king," as synonyms for God, taking the phrase, *ha-melekh Shelomo* as "the king to whom all peace belongs" (*sheha-shalom shelo*). This rather bold identification is probably derived from the fact that the Bible speaks of Solomon "sitting on the throne *of God*" (1 Chronicles 29:23).

The notion of God as supreme dispenser of peace is derived from the verse, *Oseh shalom bimromav*, "He creates peace in his celestial regions" (Job 25:2) – which has become perhaps one of the most well-known verses through its frequent repetition in the liturgy.

**706. But if the actual poem makes the Shunammite reject King Solomon, how, then, can the Rabbis identify him with God?**

We have to understand the midrashic method in order to make sense of this apparently perplexing situation. Midrash is not in any way a consistent and integrated scheme of interpreting a text. The midrashic method can lift a verse totally out of its literal context in order to expound it "midrashically," along the lines we have just been exemplifying. It can also, at the very same time, follow the plain, textual sense. Every interpretation, though set cheek-by-jowl with the next, is by a different Sage, a product of another age, and inspired from an independent creative perspective.

The Midrash on any particular book is an amalgam of varied interpretations, created by Sages of varying propensities: some veering towards plain, textual interpretations, others towards the mystical, others towards the philosophical, others towards the historical, others towards the martyrological, and so on. When they originally wove the verses from *Shir Ha-Shirim* into their sermons and addresses, they were not necessarily speaking on the theme of this poem. It was simply that a verse from it lent itself, through the way they were able to interpret it, to being adduced in that context. Such interpretations—on a host of topics—were later collected together, because they had the common denominator of containing interpretations of verses from *Shir Ha-Shirim*. And that diverse collection became the Midrash on that particular book of the Bible.

Hence, we should not be perplexed as to how, within the same Midrash, King Solomon may appear, exegetically, as a designation of God, or, in other passages of the same Midrash, as the historical personage, or as an ideal messianic type, or as a thwarted suitor of the Shunammite.

# XVIII

## Bereavement at Pesach Time— A Selection of Regulations

### OBSERVANCE OF *SHIVAH* AND *SHELOSHIM*

**707. If a near relative passes away a few days before Pesach, what is the law regarding observance of mourning during the festival?**

There is a principle that a festival cancels the specific period of mourning that is currently being observed. Thus, if a mourner has already commenced observing *shivah* (the first seven days of home-based mourning), then the festival interrupts and cancels out the obligation to complete the remainder of the seven days. This applies even if the burial takes place late afternoon on the eve of Pesach, as long as the mourner has had time to take his seat and receive a greeting of consolation.

**708. What if Pesach arrived after the mourner had already completed *shivah*, and while he is in the middle of the next period of modified mourning, the *Sheloshim*?**

Again, if Pesach occurs at any time during those subsequent weeks of *Sheloshim* (that is, from the termination of *shivah* until the morning of the thirtieth day after burial), then its effect is to cancel the regulations governing the *Sheloshim*.

**709. What practical effect would that have?**

It would mean that for those in mourning for relatives other than for parents—and who only observe the thirty-day *Sheloshim* period—their mourning restrictions come to an end with the commencement of the festival.

**710. Can they then have a haircut and shave in honor of that festival, even though they will not have completed the full thirty days of mourning restrictions?**

They may, and it should be taken before noon on Erev Pesach. We stress that this does not apply to those in mourning for parents. Only when they have completed their *Sheloshim* may they get a haircut or shave in honor of a festival.

**711. If there is no post-*Sheloshim* festival, when may a mourner for parents have his haircut and shave?**

When he experiences "social reproach." This means, in effect, when friends tell him that he is looking unacceptably unkempt, particularly to go about his business or

266

profession among gentiles. While this originally applied in a beard-wearing society, in our modern society, and for clean-shaven people who normally shave daily, it is generally accepted that "social reproach" follows very closely after the *Sheloshim* have terminated. Customs vary, and one would need to consult one's Rabbi for specific guidance as to the practice of one's community in this respect.

## BURIAL ON *CHOL HA-MOED*

### 712. What if one's near relative passes away, and/or is buried during *Chol Ha-Moed*?

Since no mourning had been initiated before the incidence of the festival, it is not cancelled by *Chol Ha-Moed* or the remaining days of *Yom Tov*.

### 713. So does that mean that one must commence *shivah* during *Chol Ha-Moed*?

No, that is not permitted. One may not inject a spirit of sadness and mourning into the community, by their having to visit a *shivah*-house, during a festival week. *Shivah* commences, in this difficult situation, immediately after the festival has terminated.

### 714. Does Kaddish also commence, then, at the termination of the festival?

No. Once the burial has taken place the obligation of reciting *Kaddish* comes into effect, even though the *shivah* is postponed.

### 715. Are there no adjustments at all then, as a result of the festival?

Account is taken of the lesser significance of the last (Diaspora) day of a major festival, and, although *shivah* has not yet begun on that day, it nevertheless counts as the first day of *shivah*, thereby shortening its observance by one day.

### 716. What is the status of the mourner in that situation where one is waiting for the end of Pesach in order to commence sitting *shivah*?

He is in an unfortunate state of religious limbo. He cannot resume his ordinary business or professional life which, strictly speaking, ought to be restricted anyway by the laws of *Chol Ha-Moed*. (Where considerable financial loss would be involved, one should consult with one's Rabbi.) He is not obliged, however, to stay at home, as in the case of someone sitting *shivah*, but should naturally conduct himself and his activities as befits one who has just buried his dead. He attends synagogue, and performs normal religious duties. Marital relations are not permitted until the termination of *shivah*.

**717. What if one's near relative was buried just before Pesach, or even on *Chol Ha-Moed,* but the mourner did not receive notice of it until after *Yom Tov* had begun?**

Then full *shivah* and *Sheloshim* must be observed in the usual way after Pesach is over.

**718. Does one make the *keri'ah* (tearing of the garment) if the funeral takes place on *Chol Ha-Moed*?**

Customs vary. Some authorities draw a distinction between the tearing for a parent and for other near relatives. In the former case they insist that it should be made, whereas for other relatives it is delayed until after the festival. One should consult one's own rabbi.

**719. Do we light a *Yahrzeit* candle on *Chol Ha-Moed*?**

Even though *shivah* does not commence until the termination of *Yom Tov,* the *Yahrzeit* candle should be lit on returning from the funeral, and kept burning throughout the remainder of the festival and until the end of the duration of the *shivah.* It is customary not to place it in the main dining room in order to reduce the prominence of that symbol of grief on what is, after all, a festive period for the rest of the Jewish community.

**720. When the burial takes place on *Chol Ha-Moed,* and *shivah* is delayed until after the termination of the festival, does the mourner wear *tefillin* (for those who normally have the custom to wear them on *Chol Ha-Moed*)?**

Yes, he does.

## THE MEAL OF CONDOLENCE

**721. Is the special meal of condolence *(Se'udat Havra'ah)* served if one returns from the burial on the late afternoon of Erev Pesach?**

It is not served, since that is a time when there is no public observance of mourning, since the mourner would normally be permitted at that time to attend to his or her preparation for the approaching holy day.

**722. Is the meal served if the burial takes place on *Chol Ha-Moed*?**

It is. However, since there is no formal mourning on *Chol Ha-Moed,* the mourner's meal should be eaten while seated at one's ordinary dining room table.

**723. What does the mourner's meal consist of?**

Normally it consists of rolls, but, naturally, on *Chol Ha-Moed* Pesach we have to substitute with *matzot* instead. We also serve hardboiled eggs, and some have the custom of serving lentils. Though not prescribed, it is common practice to eat salted herring at that first meal.

### 724. Who provides that first meal, and what is its purpose?

It should be provided by friends or nonmourning relatives. Its original purpose is unclear. Rabbi Maurice Lamm, in his excellent book, *The Jewish Way in Death and Mourning* (New York: Jonathan David Publishers, 1969, p. 99), suggests that it is an opportunity for a demonstration of warmth, consideration, sympathy, and solidarity by close friends to those who, devastated by their loss and desperate to join their departed as part of a "death wish," might well be driven to deprive themselves of food and to sink into total despair.

### 725. When the festival of Pesach cancels the *shivah,* how do we calculate the numbers of days outstanding towards the *Sheloshim*?

It is rather complicated. The partial *shivah* mourning period, however short, which was interrupted by Pesach counts as a full seven days of *shivah*. To that we add the eight days of the festival, making a total of fifteen days. An additional *fifteen* days of *Sheloshim* require to be observed, therefore, on the completion of the *shivah*.

## THE *ONEN*

### 726. What is the situation regarding the obligation of making a Seder for someone who is an *Onen,* namely, who has had no opportunity of burying his dead before the festival commenced?

The basic halakhic principle is that one who is occupied with the performance of one *mitzvah* is absolved at that time from performing others. Therefore, since the *Onen* is preoccupied with the arrangements for the *mitzvah* of burying his dead, he is not obliged to pay attention to prayer and other positive *mitzvot*. However, since there are no funeral arrangements that he can make once the festival has commenced (and there is also a view that the status of *Aninut* does not apply on *Yom Tov* nights; see *Shakh* on *Yoreh De'ah* 341:1 [9]), it is recommended, therefore, that he observe the main *mitzvot* of the Seder. However, as regards the reading of the Haggadah, which contains midrashic expositions that come under the category of Torah study, which is forbidden to the *Onen,* many authorities take the view that he should not read them (see *Magen Avraham* on *Orach Chayyim* 558:8). One should be guided by one's Rabbi.

### 727. Does an *Onen* make the search for *chametz* in his home?

If possible, someone else should do this for him. He, himself, may recite the *Kol chamirah* declaration.

**728. Does the *Onen* have to count the *Omer*?**

He is not required to count the *Omer,* unless he is eager not to lose the opportunity of reciting it on subsequent days with the blessing. In the latter case, even if the burial is delayed, and his period of *Aninut* is consequently extended for a few days, he counts the *Omer* without a blessing, and after the burial he may resume with a blessing.

# XIX

# The Second-Day Diaspora *Yom Tov*

**729. What is the origin of the second-day Diaspora *Yom Tov*?**

During Temple times, Rosh Chodesh (first day of the new month) and, consequently, any festival occurring during that month, was determined exclusively on the basis of witnesses coming to the *Bet Din* and testifying that they had seen the first appearance of the new moon in the skies the previous night. This information would then be transmitted all over Palestine, as well as signaled to the Babylonian Diaspora, by means of fire beacons; and, when that method was found to be unreliable, by means of messengers sent out to inform those far-flung communities.

Alas, the latter method was also found to be unreliable, primarily because the messengers were frequently delayed, and did not arrive in time to inform those communities of the precise day declared by Jerusalem to be Rosh Chodesh. Thus, when a festival occurred during the coming month they could not be sure which of two days had been fixed as the festival day by the court at Jerusalem. This depended upon whether the previous month had been declared "defective" (i.e., of twenty-nine days) or "full" (i.e., of thirty days).

Thus, to be on the safe side, and to avoid observing as an ordinary working day, out of ignorance, the actual day designated as a biblical *Yom Tov* according to the Jerusalem court's pronouncement, the Diaspora communities were constrained, in the case of Pesach, Shavuot and Sukkot, to observe *two* days as holy days, to cover either eventuality *(mi-shum sfeika deyoma)*. The second day, in each case, is known as *Yom Tov Sheni shel Galuyyot* ("The Diaspora's second day").

This became standard practice after the destruction of the Temple and with Babylon assuming the position of spiritual ascendency in the Jewish world, notwithstanding the fact that the Jerusalem authorities possessed the astronomic and mathematical data and know-how to enable them to determine the precise day of each new month, and to publish a fixed calendar. This knowledge was zealously guarded, however, by the Jerusalem authorities, and made subsidiary to the more primitive method of cross-examining witnesses in Jerusalem, because by the latter method Jerusalem was able to retain its calendrical and spiritual hold over the Diaspora.

When the turbulent conditions of the Jewish world motivated Hillel II finally to release the secret of the fixed calendar to the Diaspora communities, he issued a decree that their prerogative to use the fixed calendar, rather than be tied to a Jerusalem pronouncement, was conditional upon their solemn agreement to be forever bound by their centuries-old Diaspora practice of observing two days to avoid any doubt.

We have noted above (see question 697) that a midrashic comment of the Rabbis suggests that they perceived the second day as an imposition upon Israel for past lax observance of the one festival day. The fact that it was only the Diaspora communities that had to bear the brunt of that punishment suggests that they bear the additional guilt of forsaking the Holy Land to live in impure countries and away from the source of our spiritual vitality and national cohesion.

And this is still regarded as a justifiable rationale by many Orthodox Jews to the present day, notwithstanding the fact that others do, nevertheless, carp at it. We must not lose sight of the fact that our brethren in Israel are making daily sacrifices so that Jews the world over may have that unprecedented degree of confidence, protection, and national pride.

Israelis are entitled to some privilege for the many hardships entailed in their day-to-day life there, one of which, for observant Jews at least, is the surrender of their one day off each week through their observance of the Sabbath. It is fair, therefore, that they should be granted some compensation by way of having to observe but one holy day when the rest of us are observing two. Perhaps the totality of the religious experience and intensity of life in Israel, by comparison with that of the Diaspora, is also a justification for their shorter holy day observances. And those of us in the Diaspora who, for whatever reason, refrain from making ourselves a part of that great enterprise in Jewish national and spiritual cohesiveness deserve to have that brought to our attention every few months when the pilgrim festivals show up our less than total loyalty.

### 730. Apart from Israelis living permanently in Israel, are there any other categories of people who are absolved from the obligation of keeping the second Diaspora day?

People who arrive in Israel with the intention of settling there permanently are regarded as full citizens from day one, even if they arrive on Israeli soil on the eve of the festival.

People who are merely holidaying in Israel, or those who arrive there for a protracted stay, but whose intention is eventually to return to their own country (da'atan lachzor), and not to remain in Israel, must continue, according to most authorities, to observe the second day. It has to be said that the distinguished Rabbi Shmuel Salant, who served as Chief Rabbi of Jerusalem in the nineteenth century, took the opposite view, maintaining that even visitors to Israel could regard themselves as subject to the calendrical influence of the Holy Land, and therefore only subject to the one day observance. Rabbi Tzvi Ashkenazi, known as the *Chakham Tzvi* (1660–1718), had even declared that visitors are positively prohibited from observing the second Diaspora day! (See J. David Bleich, *Contemporary Halakhic Problems,* vol. 1, New York: Ktav Publishing House, 1977, p. 54.)

Given Rabbi Salant and Rabbi Ashkenazi's lenient stance, those who own property in Israel, and live there for some time each year, may well be able to make out a case for having satisfied the requirement of *yeshivah,* domicile. Given the general mobility of people in our day, especially businessmen subject to international jetting, residence even for a short period each year may well qualify under the category of *yeshivah*. Obviously, one would require to be guided by one's own Rabbi on such a matter.

While most authorities might not entertain the latter plea, yet in the case of students taking a year off to take courses in Israel, there are many authorities who rule that, from day one, they may also be regarded as Israelis in this regard. The principle is that an uninterrupted twelve-month stay is regarded, halakhicaly, as establishing residence (see Rabbi Yechiel Michal Epstein, *Arukh Ha-Shulchan* 496:5). Secondly, there is an assumption that, being as yet undecided as regards their future, the pull of Israel might well motivate them to decide to settle there permanently. They are regarded, therefore, as "citizens-in-waiting."

As regards Israelis who leave Israel to work in another country, if their intention is to settle permanently in the new country, then, from the moment they arrive at a Jewish community there, they are regarded as subject to the Diaspora's holy day regulations. Temporary *Shelichim* (Jewish Agency emissaries), and others whose intention is to return to Israel on completion of their limited contract, are regarded as subject to Israel's holyday regulations. However, from the moment of their arrival at a Jewish community, they are not permitted, on the second Diaspora days, to publicly violate the sanctity of that day. They don their *tefillin* and recite the weekday prayers in the privacy of their homes.

# XX

# Jewish Life in Egypt down the Ages

## A BIBLICAL PROHIBITION?

**731. Is there any biblical directive regarding the permissibility or otherwise of Jews returning to live in Egypt?**

There is, indeed. In three passages the Torah implies that, because of Israel's terrible experiences in Egypt, she must totally sever all association with that land forever.

The first passage is Exodus 14:13, "For whereas you have seen the Egyptians today, you shall see them again no more for ever." The second passage is Deuteronomy 17:16, "For the Lord has said unto you: 'You shall henceforth return no more that way.' " The third is an indirect reference, and occurs in the context of the fearful *Tokhechah* (Deuteronomy 28:15–68), the threat of dire punishment if Israel defects from God's ways. One of the threatened punishments is that, "The Lord will bring you back to Egypt in ships, by the way whereof I said unto you: 'You shall see it no more again' " (v. 68).

**732. Was this prohibition observed?**

Middle Eastern international political and economic circumstances, even in biblical times, made it almost impossible for Jews to live in a vacuum and abide by such a ban. Solomon already entered into alliances with Egypt, cemented by his marriage to an Egyptian princess. In order to build up his army, we are told (1 Kings 10:28) that his merchants imported horses and chariots from Egypt, and even acted as agents for sales to all the kings of the Hittites and Aram. Undoubtedly such trade links involved Israelite emissaries settling in Egypt, as well as military personnel being trained there in the handling of such chariots and their weaponry. The same biblical source describes a splendidly furnished palace for his Egyptian wife, erected adjacent to the Temple. Her own lines of communication with her home must also have involved her Jewish courtiers and servants in travel to Egypt.

## EARLIEST JEWISH SETTLEMENT

**733. What specific reasons prompted Jews to abandon their homeland and settle in Egypt?**

There is no doubt that, just as the Patriarchs sought refuge in Egypt from conditions of famine in Canaan, so, in subsequent centuries, did Jews flee there, in

274

substantial numbers, from before such natural disasters, as well as in trepidation before the advance of invading armies. We know, for example, that after the assassination of Gedaliah, puppet ruler of Judea, in 587–586 B.C.E., Jeremiah was carried to Egypt against his will by a large party of pro-Egyptian refugees who had previously counseled an alliance with Egypt against the Babylonian invaders. Other Jews, who had served in the armies of the kings of Judah, would have found their way to Egypt, offering their professional services as mercenaries.

### 734. Where did those early refugees settle?

Jeremiah's company settled at Tachpanches (Daphnae), just within the frontier (see Jeremiah 43:7), and we may conjecture that their descendants remained there throughout the Persian period (see Isaiah 19:18ff.), to be joined by a successive flow of immigrants, which increased dramatically in the third century B.C.E., when Judea itself came under the domination of the Egyptian Ptolemaic kings, making Egypt a veritable center of world Jewry.

### 735. We have just referred to Jewish mercenaries in Egypt. What evidence do we have of their existence, and where was their base?

We have archaeological evidence, in the form of documents and inscriptions that have come to light this century, and which have provided an enormously rich source of background knowledge to further our understanding of the history of the peoples of the biblical world.

These documents were originally published by the distinguished scholar, James B. Pritchard in his *Ancient Near Eastern Texts Relating to the Old Testament* (2nd ed.; Princeton, NJ: Princeton University Press, 1955). They tell of a Jewish military colony that existed through the fifth century at Elephantine, by the first cataract of the Nile, and that developed into a thriving and settled community.

### 736. What do we learn from these documents about the religious practices of the Elephantine Jewish community?

We learn that they practiced a rather strange form of Judaism, establishing their own Temple — wherein they offered animal sacrifices in defiance of biblical law which restricted that to the Jerusalem Temple — and practicing a form of mixed worship that was basically Jewish, but which also contained elements of worship from heathen cults: hence their invocation of other gods, such as *Eshem-bethel, Herem-bethel,* and *Anat-bethel.*

### 737. Do we have any evidence that they observed Passover?

We do, indeed. One of the documents Pritchard calls "The Passover Papyrus." It dates from 419 B.C.E., and takes the form of a letter from Arsames, the Satrap of Egypt, to Yedoniah, the head of the military colony, informing him that King Darius had authorized the observance of a festival of unleavened bread for the Jewish garrison, and instructing them, by order of the king, to ensure that it is observed meticulously: "Be ritually clean; do no work; drink no beer nor anything in which there is leaven" (Pritchard, *Ancient Near Eastern Texts*, p. 278).

### 738.  What was the state of relations between the community at Elephantine and the native Egyptian population?

As we have seen from the royal instruction just quoted, the Persian monarchy sought to encourage Jews in the western part of their empire to regularize their worship according to the law as promulgated by Ezra, its supreme adviser on Jewish affairs (see Ezra 7:25ff). A unified Jewish observance helped reduce religious tensions and promote stability among a major minority people.

However, we learn from the texts that a riot broke out during the absence of the Satrap from the country. This was led by the priests of Khnum, and in the course of it the Jewish Temple was destroyed. This suggests that local Egyptian feeling was not favorable to the Jews. They must have resented the privileged position accorded to the Jews by the Persian conquerors, as well as the offering of animal sacrifices, which was anathema to the Egyptians. The Temple was eventually rebuilt, as a result of the intervention on their behalf of the governors of Judah and Samaria, but not until the Elephantine Jews had compromised on the sacrifice of animals, restricting their offerings to meal and drink offerings and incense. It is probable that it was at that point that the heterodox elements were removed from Elephantine worship, enabling Egyptian Jewry to be regarded as an official Jewish Diaspora.

### 739.  For how long did the Elephantine colony survive?

We have no clear evidence to answer that, as documentation does not go beyond the beginning of the fourth century B.C.E. We must assume that its favored position in the eyes of the Persians left it vulnerable to resurgent Egyptian nationalism. Some of its members, who had survived by the time of the arrival of Alexander the Great (332 B.C.E.), must ultimately have been scattered over the empire; others would have moved north to Alexandria to join the growing Egyptian Jewish Diaspora, founded by Jeremiah and the exiles from Judea at the time of the Babylonian invasion in 586 B.C.E.

## THE DEVELOPMENT OF THE EGYPTIAN JEWISH COMMUNITY

### 740.  How did Egyptian Jewry develop into such a vast and influential Diaspora?

When Alexander the Great died, in the year 323 B.C.E., his vast empire was divided between his two generals, Ptolemy and Seleucus. Ptolemy seized Egypt, and made Alexandria his capital (see question 356). This soon became one of the greatest cities in the world, a center of Hellenistic culture and opportunity, attracting a vast influx of traders, craftsmen, and artisans. When Ptolemy won control of Palestine, at the battle of Ipsos in 301 B.C.E., this effectively linked Egyptian and Palestinian Jewry, making travel between the two countries much easier, and attracting a further Jewish influx, from Palestine and the surrounding areas of Jewish domicile, into the more attractive and vital new center at Alexandria.

### 741. Were there any other factors that encouraged the development of Egyptian Jewry?

It must not be forgotten that the Ptolemies were Greek invaders. Their relationship with the Jews within their Empire, especially in the East, was most cordial. On the other hand, they did not trust the native Egyptians who, naturally, resented their presence as invaders. The Ptolemies therefore encouraged the Jews to enter the sensitive and responsible areas of the military, the police force and the tax in-gathering and inspectorate. Jews rose to the highest ranks, while also prospering as merchants and farmers. This prosperity in turn generated a high rate of Jewish immigration.

### 742. Do we know the size of the Alexandrian Jewish community?

We have no precise details, as, naturally, Jews were averse to taking censuses. The *Letter of Aristeas,* written around the end of the second century B.C.E. (Moses Hadas, *Aristeas to Philocrates* [New York: Harper & Brothers, 1951], p. 13), relates that Ptolemy brought back 100,000 Jewish captives from one of his campaigns to conquer Palestine; that must have constituted a significant expansion of the already large community. Scholars assess that the community must have numbered about one million by the first century C.E. The Talmud corroborates this in its reference to the cavernous synagogue at Alexandria, which alone could accommodate over one million worshipers—"double the number of Israelite men who came out of Egypt" (on the Alexandrian synagogue, see Cohen, *Blessed Are You,* p. 167).

### 743. What language did the Jews of Egypt speak?

At first the newcomers would have preserved their native Aramaic language. We have a large number of commercial documents dating from this period which are all written in Aramaic. Hebrew was also preserved by the more educated classes, though probably only reserved for synagogue use and more formal communal occasions. Before long, however, the total Hellenization of the country enabled Greek to achieve predominance as the lingua franca, and Hebrew was rapidly forgotten.

## RELIGIOUS LIFE IN EGYPT

### 744. What was the nature of religious life in Alexandria?

As we have indicated, the Jews of Alexandria soon became sophisticated city dwellers, taking on the dress, language, customs, and culture of their environment.

This was the heyday of Hellenism, by which is meant the fruits of novel Greek thinking on the total reorganization of society's main structures, covering such spheres as religion, politics, commerce and finance, law, education, language, literature, poetry, philosophy, science, mathematics, art and architecture, and, most important, physical exercise and prowess.

The effect of all this on the Jews, especially on the upper classes and the youth, who are always the first to assimmilate, was quite dramatic. Whereas Judaism emphasized the beauty of holiness, Hellenism preferred the holiness of beauty. In Palestine, where Jews were geographically and emotionally close to their roots and traditions, a head-on clash was inevitable; and it came in the form of the Maccabean revolt of 167–165 B.C.E. Alexandrian life, on the other hand, made it easier for the already sophisticated Jews to find a comfortable synthesis between the best of Hellenistic and Judaic values. This reached its apogee in the works of Philo Judaeus, who wrote a major commentary on the Bible, in Greek, interpreting it allegorically and apologetically, in order to demonstrate that its teachings were in total accord with the axiom's of Greek philosophical thought. Significantly, although his was a monumental commentary, it was never referred to by subsequent rabbinic scholars of the succeeding centuries in their own voluminous talmudic and midrashic literature. By contrast, the early Church Fathers drew heavily on his interpretations and concepts.

The attraction of the gymnasia was stronger than that of the synagogue, and the authority of the Greek courts was preferred—even for matters of marriage and divorce—to that of their own Jewish courts which were licensed to preside over such domestic matters. Jews abandoned Hebrew names in favor of Greek and, sometimes, Egyptian ones, and the upper classes were rather lax in Sabbath and dietary law observance. The reference to the great synagogue of Alexandria suggests that they remained loyal to their monotheistic tradition, and that synagogue attendance was their main way of expressing their religious identity. The requirement of a Greek translation of the Bible—called the *Septuagint,* after the seventy Jewish scholars who are credited with having produced it—suggests that reading of the Torah in synagogue, as well as of most of the prayers, was conducted in Greek. Any study circles that were held were probably conducted in either Greek or Aramaic.

While the picture of middle and upper class Alexandrian Jewry is largely that of an acculturating community, yet the lower class, farming and artisan stratum, who lived in the *chora,* the provincial districts around the metropolis, maintained a much higher level of observance.


## A HISTORY OF PAIN AND PERSECUTION

### 745. How did Egyptian Jewry fare in the Roman period?

Not too well: because of growing anti-Semitism on the part of the Greek authorities in Egypt, as well as worsening relations with the native Egyptians, the Jews welcomed and gave much support to the Roman conquerors. Julius Caesar and

Augustus I expressed their appreciation of Jewish support by reaffirming their citizenship of Alexandria in 47 B.C.E.

In the course of time, the Romans came to regard the Greeks of Alexandria as their more natural allies, and relations deteriorated. Jews were excluded from the army and lost their right to serve as tax gatherers. When Augustus revised the constitution of Egypt, Jews found themselves relegated to the lowest class, excluded from the gymnasia and liable to an offensive poll tax. Even the post of Ethnarch of Alexandria, the supreme Jewish leader, was abolished around 10 B.C.E., and was replaced by a *gerusia,* or Council of Elders.

During the reign of the rabidly anti-Semitic emperor, Caius Caligula (37–41 C.E.), the Greeks of Alexandria made a concerted attack on all the synagogues, polluting them and setting up statues of the emperor inside them. Anti-Semitic writings made their appearance, and were popularized during the subsequent centuries of the Roman period. The murder of three Jews by the Egyptian Alexandrians, on suspicion that they had infiltrated a meeting to discuss the sending of a delegation to the emperor Nero, prompted a widespread Jewish uprising, which was mercilessly supressed.

It was the general Jewish uprising against the emperor Trajan in the year 117 C.E. that resulted in the decimation of the great Jewish community of Alexandria. The revolt was prompted by the anti-Semitism of the local Greeks, as well as the desperate condition of Jews throughout the Roman Empire. Taking advantage of Trajan's preoccupation with his battle against the Parthians, the uprising began in Cyrenaica, and soon spread to Egypt, Cyprus, and Mesopotamia.

The revolt was soon crushed with unparalleled brutality. A large part of the beautiful city of Alexandria was razed to the ground, including the great synagogue, and the great majority of Egypt's entire Jewish population was put to the sword.

## 746. Did that mark the end of Jewish life in Egypt?

Certainly, for another two centuries we hear nothing of any significance regarding any fluttering of Jewish life in that country.

In papyri from the early fourth century, however, there is mention of Jewish names, and even reference to a hierarchical communal structure of leadership. It seems, therefore, that Jews were returning to Egypt, perhaps in flight from places of intense Christian anti-Semitism as Christianity assumed the position at this time of official religion of the Roman Empire. Jewish communal life was renewed, though we know little about the community from 640, when Egypt was conquered by the Muslims, until the tenth century, when the Fatimids, a Shi'ite Muslim sect, took control. Under the Fatimids, as well as under their successors, the Mamelukes, Jews and Jewish culture prospered, and many Jews, among them many who had been expelled from Spain in 1492, settled in Egypt.

When the Ottoman Turks conquered the country, in 1517, they adopted a liberal attitude towards the Jews, many of whom were elevated to the highest offices of state, particularly in the realm of public finance. With the decline of the Turkish empire, and its wars against Russia, the fortunes of the Jewish community also went into decline, and many of the frustrations of the Turkish governors found release in jealousy and persecution of the Jews.

At the beginning of the twentieth century, there were about 30,000 Jews living in Egypt. Those who had lived there for centuries inhabited an area of Cairo referred to as *Haret el Yahoud,* the Jewish Quarter. They spoke Arabic, and were acculturated to the general population. By far the most prosperous and entrepreneurial group were the European Sephardic Jews, including many who hailed from Italy, North Africa, and the Levant. They spoke Ladino among themselves but conducted their business of manufacturing, banking, and real estate in French. They were joined by a community of Ashkenazi Jews, most of whom had fled from the Russian pogroms, the remainder consisting of those forced to leave Palestine during World War I by the Turkish allies of the Germans. (For an outline of the history of the Jews of Egypt during the medieval and modern periods, see *Encyclopaedia Judaica* 6:491–502; see also V. D. Sanua, "The Vanished World of Egyptian Jewry," *Judaism* 43:2 [Spring 1994]: 212–219.)

## JEWISH RESIDENCE IN EGYPT: A HALAKHIC PERSPECTIVE

**747. Bearing in mind a clear biblical prohibition against taking up residence in Egypt (see question 731), how did later rabbinic law codify this prohibition?**

Maimonides states the law thus:

It is permitted to live anywhere in the world except Egypt.
In three passages the Torah warns us not to return there.
It is permitted to return there, however, for business purposes or en route to conquer other places. The only prohibition is against permanent domicile.
                    (Maimonides, *Mishneh Torah, Hilkhot Melakhim* 5:7)

## JUSTIFYING MAIMONIDES

**748. How then do we explain the fact that Maimonides himself lived in Egypt from 1165 until his death in 1204?**

The distinguished sixteenth-century halakhic authority, Rabbi David ibn Abi Zimra (Radbaz, *Responsa* 4, no. 73), states that Maimonides simply had no choice. His father had to flee his native Spain as a result of the fall of Cordova to the fanatical Muslim fundamentalist sect of Almohads in 1148, and the religious persecution they initiated. He wandered with his family from place to place in Spain, then to Fez in Morocco. The family then made a brief visit to Palestine before taking up domicile in Egypt.

His intention, states Radbaz, was not to settle permanently in Egypt—which would be forbidden by biblical law—but only to bide his time there until conditions enabled him to return to his native country. However, he was soon pressed into the service of the Sultan, to serve as permanent physician to him and his court, and he could find no way of extricating himself from that situation or, indeed, of finding any other country that would welcome him and provide him with livelihood.

### 749. Was there any other compelling reason that might have justified Maimonides' setting aside of the law opposing Jewish residence in Egypt?

We know that the influence of the Karaite heresy in Cairo prior to Maimonides' arrival was growing dramatically. The Karaites were numerically more populous and more prosperous and influential than the Rabbanite community, and it thus constituted a great danger to the survival of mainstream Orthodox Judaism. On his arrival, Maimonides mustered all his energies to countering their influence.

A seventeenth-century Egyptian authority, Rabbi Jacob Faraji, suggests that it was in order to undertake that pressing mission that Maimonides was drawn to Egypt, against his natural wishes and halakhic conscience, in conformity with the overriding principle that where the very existence of the religion is at stake one may set aside certain individual prohibitions.

### 750. But how did the other great rabbinic figures and religious people who lived in Egypt throughout the ages justify the flouting of the biblical law prohibiting residence in that land?

Again Radbaz helps us resolve this problem. He states (*Responsa* 4:73): "Some say that the Torah only prohibits returning to Egypt 'by that way' [Deuteronomy 17:16], namely, if it involves leaving the Holy Land in order to descend [geographically and spiritually] to Egypt. To move there from other lands, however, is permitted."

Radbaz then proceeds to demolish that particular method of resolving the difficulty, pointing out that it still leaves the problem of the other two biblical verses (Exodus 14:13, Deuteronomy 28:68) which prohibit residence without any mention of the phrase "by that way." The phrase, "You shall never ever see them again" particularly cannot be overlooked in this context.

Radbaz concludes that the overriding consideration must have always been one's mental attitude when taking up residence in that country. If the intention is that one's stay should be temporary, and that one's ultimate wish is to find one's way back to the land of Israel—surely the traditional wish of every Jew—then this would not be prohibited by biblical law. The prohibition was only ever intended to cover permanent settlement.

We may find some support for Radbaz's interpretation from the Midrash quoted in the Pesach Haggadah. On the phrase, *Va-yagar sham,* the Midrash states that "this teaches us that Jacob our father never went down to 'settle' in Egypt, but only to 'dwell' there [temporarily]." Interestingly, the Midrash wishes to present Jacob (and the other patriarchs) as fulfilling the laws of the Torah long before they were given at Sinai. Hence, it had to justify his domicile in Egypt in the light of that particular biblical prohibition.

### 751. What is the precise rationale behind that prohibition of living in Egypt?

The *Sefer Ha-Chinukh* (*Mitzvah* 500) states: "The rationale of this prohibition is that the Egyptians were inately sinful and evil. Hence God brought us out from there, and redeemed us in His great mercy, in order to guide us in the true and righteous way, so that we should never again become defiled by their proximity and learn from their sinful ways."

### 752. Are we meant to be committed to that derogatory assessment of the Egyptians to the present day?

The seventeenth-century exegete Rabbeinu Bachya ben Asher writes (Commentary on *Parashat Shoftim*), "The prohibition of living in Egypt was not intended in perpetuity." His view is based on the fact that such an assessment of Egyptian morality can no longer be justified. Support for this is forthcoming from a clear statement in Maimonides' *Mishneh Torah:* "Nowadays, the Egyptian nation has been diluted, and the present-day citizens are not descendants of those original evil-doers. Hence there is no longer any prohibition against living among them" (*Hilkhot Issurei Biah,* ch. 12, end).

### 753. On what basis does Maimonides conclude that the Egyptian population "has become diluted"?

It is on the basis of the talmudic axiom that "Sennacherib came and intermingled all the world's population" (*Tosefta Kiddushin* 5:4; *Talmud Yerushalmi, Kiddushin* 4:3, 66a). Sennacherib was king of Assyria and Babylonia (705–681 B.C.E.), and it was during his victorious campaign of 701 that he inflicted a major defeat upon Egypt and many other countries and tribes throughout Asia Minor. His wholesale removal of captive populations convinced the talmudic Sages that it was no longer safe to assume that the citizens of any country could be regarded as its original indigenous population. It was on the basis of this same principle that the Talmud also relaxed the biblical prohibition against marriage with Ammonite and Moabite proselytes (Deuteronomy 23:3).

# XXI

# Pesach Customs from around the World

## THE PASCHAL LAMB RITUAL LIVES ON

**754. One frequently hears mention of a sect that continues to practice the slaughtering and eating of the Paschal lamb. Who are they?**

They are the Samaritans, who take their name from the area of Samaria, in Israel, where they have lived for about three thousand years. Their community still survives, though numbering a mere 400 souls.

**755. Are they Jews?**

This has always been a bone of contention between them and the mainstream Jewish community. The Samaritans lay claim to having been an intrinsic part of the ethnic Israelite people, tracing their geneology to the tribes of Ephraim and Manasseh, sons of Joseph.

They claim that it was their particular tribal land, around their "holy mountain" of Gerizim and encompassing the city of Shechem, that was the original center of Israelite settlement, forming the base for the launching of Joshua's invasion of the rest of the land. Indeed, it has to be admitted that it was in Samaritan country, on Mount Ebal, that Joshua established his first central altar, and it was there that he proceeded to write the first copy of the Torah (Joshua 8:30–35) on the twelve stones that they had raised from the River Jordan (see Joshua 4:20). Similarly, it was to Shechem that Joshua summoned all the tribes in order to ratify a solemn national and spiritual covenant prior to his death (see Joshua, ch. 24).

The Samaritans claim that it was the rest of the Israelite tribes who were the defectors. They blame Eli for having caused the first major schism when he left Shechem to found a new spiritual and national center at Shiloh, and for initiating novel religious practices that formed the basis of an independent cult. The Israelite iniquity was compacted, as far as the Samaritans were concerned, when a monarchy was established against the true desire of God, and with the creation of an alternate spiritual center and national capital at Jerusalem.

It is for that reason that the Samaritans only accept the Five Books of Moses and the book of Joshua. The history of Israel after Joshua is, as far as they were concerned, that of a renegade, sectarian community. Only they remain the faithful "Israel."

### 756. What is the official Jewish answer to that claim?

The Jewish claim is contained in the biblical account of Samaritan origins, as described in 2 Kings 17:24. This effectively rejects as a fabrication the Samaritan story of their Israelite tribal origins, and describes them as having originally been foreign heathen tribes, imported into Judaea by the Assyrian conqueror (probably Sargon) around 721 B.C.E. He brought them from various places around his empire in order not to leave the land depopulated and unproductive after the Jews had been removed into captivity. The imported settlers were primarily from Cuthah in Babylonia—hence the name *Cuthim,* applied to the Samaritans in talmudic literature.

### 757. Do the Samaritans observe Pesach on the same day as the Jewish community?

They do not follow the same calendrical system as the Jews. According to our system, Pesach can never fall on the second, fourth or sixth days of the week. (The popular mnemonic for this is *Lo badu* Pesach, "Pesach cannot fall on *badu.*") The letters *b, d,* and *v* (dotted to give the *u*-sound) have respective numerical values of two, four, and six.

Since they do not adjust their calendar to create that limitation, inevitably they will celebrate Pesach most years on different days of the month. Since their system of leap years also does not accord with ours, it follows that on some years they will be celebrating Pesach in the middle of the Jewish second month of Iyyar.

### 758. Why did they continue to perform the act of slaughtering of the Paschal lamb when the Jews abandoned it?

The reason the Jews abandoned it was that the Torah restricts the bringing of sacrifices to "the place which the Lord shall choose to cause His name to reside" (Deuteronomy 16:6), namely, the Temple at Jerusalem. Hence, with the destruction of the Temple by the Romans, in the year 70 C.E., the sacrificial system came to an abrupt end.

As far as the Samaritans were concerned, they identify that "place where God causes His Name to reside" with their own holy mountain of Gerizim. Since they did not participate in any revolts against the Romans, and suffer any consequential loss of their sacred mountain, which has always remained in their possession, they were not religiously precluded, therefore, from offering sacrifices on it.

### 759. What preparations do they make for the Paschal lamb ceremony?

A few days before 14 Nisan, according to their calendar, a proclamation is made, and the entire community repairs to Mount Gerizim. Originally they would pitch their tents around the mountain; today they are accommodated in the houses of members of the community living close to the holy site.

In accordance with the biblical prescription, they select "a lamb without blemish, a male of the first year, from the sheep or from the goats" (Exodus 12:5), and they "keep it until the fourteenth day of the same month" (v. 6). The size of the animal is determined by the number of people within the family group (v. 3), and if there is an insufficient number of people to eat a lamb, then they follow the biblical prescription to "take one together with one's neighbour that is close to one's house" (v. 4).

### 760. What equipment is required for the slaughtering of the lamb?

A large deep pit, serving as a furnace, is heated up from midday, and the youngsters of the community, dressed in white tunics and belts, stand around the perimeter and keep it fueled by throwing in bundles of wood and branches. A large cauldren of water is suspended over the furnace, to provide the boiling water required for scalding and cleaning the animal after it has been slaughtered.

To hand, at the side of the furnace, are long, blackened wooden skewers, as well as large wooden blocks onto which the lambs are placed after slaughter, and upon which they are quartered and salted. An altar also stands in the vicinity, upon which the entrails of the lambs are offered.

### 761. How is the ritual conducted?

At sundown all the male participants are in their places; the women and children remaining closeted in their tents. The shepherd–suppliers of the lambs appear, bringing with them the requisite number of unblemished yearling lambs ordered by each family group. At that point the High Priest leads the community in a monotonic chanting of special prayers, including all the biblical passages referring to Pesach, and this liturgical prelude concludes with a succession of prostrations.

Towards dusk, all eyes are fixed upon the High Priest, who, standing a rocky pedestal, will give the signal to commence the slaughtering when he is truly satisfied that the sun has sunk below the western horizon. At that moment he raises his arm and recites aloud the biblical verse, "And all the assembly of the congregation of Israel shall slaughter it towards evening" (Exodus 12:6).

After the slaughter of the lambs has been completed a delegated priest goes around each group examining the entrails of the lambs to ensure that there is no disease or other disqualification. The animals are then flayed, and the stomach, kidneys, the lobe above the liver and other entrails, as well as any dung, are all removed and thrown into the fire of the altar. All the blood is drained off, and salt is liberally sprinkled over and inside the animals to bring out the rest of the blood within the veins and organs. Incisions are then made on each side of the carcass to facilitate the removal of the sciatic nerve, in accordance with biblical law (see Genesis 32:33).

The long skewers are then driven into the body of the lambs, which are then carefully lowered into the furnace. When all the lambs of the participating family groups (about twenty for a current community of about 400 souls) have been placed inside, the furnace is covered with a wooden trellis. Upon this are stuffed as many branches and other vegetation as it will hold. It is finally sealed with mud, so that no smoke or smell escapes.

The lambs remain in the roasting for about four hours, until midnight. This time is spent in the recitation of prayers and psalms, sung primarily in Arabic intermixed with Aramaic, and with a reading from the Torah. Just before midnight they all assemble around the furnace, carrying special containers in which to place their roasted lambs. They break open the mud seal of the furnace, and each family head lifts out his own lamb by grabbing hold of its skewers. They place them inside the containers, and carry them back to their tents.

### 762. Are there any special regulations governing how the lamb is to be eaten?

Indeed. The Samaritans follow the biblical prescription to the letter. They eat it with "loins girded, sandals upon the feet, staff in hand, and with great haste" (Exodus 12:11), to symbolize the haste that characterized the first Passover, as the Israelites made ready to flee from Egypt. It is eaten together with unleaven bread and bitter herbs, as prescribed in the same verse.

The men and women eat apart. After the men have eaten, what remains is divided and taken to the women and children. No one from outside the community is permitted to eat of the lamb, again in accordance with the biblical verse (Exodus 12:43).

### 763. What do they do with any meat left over uneaten?

They collect it up, and take it to be burnt in the furnace, to ensure compliance with the biblical verse, "And you shall let nothing of it remain until the morning; but that which remaineth of it until the morning ye shall burn with fire" (Exodus 12:11).

### 764. Are outsiders permitted to attend and witness the ceremony of the Paschal lamb?

The Samaritans have no qualms about performing their historic rite in front of spectators, providing they remain at a distance. A former president of the State of Israel, Yitzchak ben Zvi (1884–1963), who was an authority on the Samaritans, reported that, although before World War I only a handful of Jews would attend the ceremony, it nevertheless attracted a vast throng of local Arab inhabitants of Shechem, as well as a number of Englishmen and other Europeans tourists. Since the establishment of the State of Israel the event has attracted greater interest among Jews, and continues to draw vast numbers of spectators, notably European visitors coming to witness an ancient biblical ritual (See I. Ben-Zvi, *Sefer Ha-Shomronim,* Jerusalem: Yitzchak Ben-Zvi Foundation, 1976, pp. 144–147).

### 765. Is there any situation where a member of the Samaritan community might be excluded from participation in the ritual?

No one who is in a state of uncleanliness may participate in the ritual or eat of the meat. This applies to anyone who has come into recent contact with a corpse, a man who has had a seminal discharge or a woman during the week of her menstrual impurity.

Yitzchak Ben-Zvi records another situation which occasioned some discord during one of his Passover visits. It seems that a member of the community had married a Jewess, and he was pressing for permission to enable her to partake of the lamb. The Samaritan priests declared it prohibited, much to the chagrin of the man concerned.

The problem was compounded by the fact that his wife had a son, from her first, Jewish, husband. The Samaritan also expressed a desire that his Jewish stepson be permitted to partake of the lamb, and a fierce row broke out on the propriety or otherwise of this. The priests declared that in no way could the child enjoy a privilege reserved exclusively for those bearing Samaritan status, whereas the stepfather countered that, because the child was a minor, he had to be considered as under Samaritan stewardship. The petitioner stood his ground, and won his application!

## PASSOVER AND THE EARLY CHURCH

### 766. How did the early Church relate to the festival of Pesach?

The early Church observed all the Jewish festivals. Pesach took on the added significance as representing also the Easter, the anniversary of the death and resurrection of the founder of the Christian faith. The Christians of Asia Minor observed the day before Pesach as a fast day, in memory of their Lord's suffering, and at nightfall they would sit down to the traditional Seder, whose significance they reinterpreted in terms of the Last Supper. Indeed, the wafers and wine of the Eucharist are clearly derived from the Seder practice of unleavened bread and wine.

It was a constant source of embarrassment to the Church that its religious calendar was dependent upon that of Judaism, and many attempts were made during the first few centuries to cut that religious umbilical cord. The first international Church Council (which met at Nicaea, in Asia Minor, in 325 C.E.) decided that Easter was henceforth to fall only on a Sunday, the day upon which their Lord was alleged to have arisen from the dead. It was no longer to coincide with the Jewish Passover or to be determined by its date. Today, Easter falls on the Sunday following the first full moon after the twenty-first of March.

### 767. Were there any discriminatory measures brought in by the Church in order to restrict the Jewish observance of Pesach?

Indeed. Not long after that decision of the Council of Nicaea, in the reign of the Emperor Constantius (337–361), the Roman authorities, pressured by the increasingly influential Christian religious leaders, adopted measures calculated to disrupt the ordered observance of Jewish festivals and to make it impossible for Christian traditionalists to continue observing Easter on the first day of the Jewish Passover.

They therefore prevented the Rabbis from meeting as a court to proclaim new moons and to intercalate leap years, or from sending messengers to the Diaspora communities in order to communicate their decisions, so as to enable those communities to observe the festivals on the appropriate days.

**768. So did those measures sow chaos within Jewry as regards the celebration of the festival?**

Quite the contrary: as with so many other attempts by our enemies, throughout history, to curtail our religious observances, the effect of such measures was to create a veritable strengthening of our national resolve. The crisis they thought to plunge us into was viewed by our resilient religious tradition as an inspired challenge to apply our halakhic principles to the resolution of the problem.

In this particular case, the restrictions imposed by the Romans on the meeting of a Jewish court to regulate the calendar prompted the patriarch Hillel II to abandon the old system of determining the first day of a new moon on the basis of the visual testimony of witnesses that they had seen its appearance in the skies the previous evening. In the year 358 C.E., Hillel disclosed the mathematical equations and astronomical principles traditionally employed by the Sanhedrin to calculate the precise occurrence of a new moon. These calculations had hitherto only been permitted to be used as a subsidiary control. Now, by putting them in the hands of the community, he created a "fixed calendar." It meant that, henceforth, the Diaspora communities were no longer tied to Jerusalem's apron-strings, having no longer to rely upon the authority of Jerusalem to hand down the directive regarding when to observe the various festivals. It was, therefore, a major concession of the Palestinian patriarch, clearly not lightly made, but necessary in the face of the Roman threat to sow chaos within the Jewish world.

Ironically, just at the time when Palestine was entering into decline as a religious center, the fixed calendar proved a boon to the authority of the religious authorities of Babylon who were about to take over the leadership of the Jewish world through their incomparable mastery of the talmudic system.

**769. Do we have any examples, from that period of antiquity, of Jewish Passover requirements being respected by gentile authorities?**

During the reign of King Kabad I of Persia (488–531 C.E.), many Jews served in the Persian army. It is recorded that, during a battle against the Byzantine general, Belisarius, the Persian commander, arranged with his adversary a cease-fire during Passover, for the sake of his Jewish soldiers!

## PASSOVER OBSERVANCE AMONG THE MARRANOS

**770. Were the Marranos of Medieval Christian Spain able to observe Pesach?**

It was certainly not easy for those Jews, who, under the threat of death, had been forced into the Catholic faith, to maintain any vestige of Jewish identity. The Inquisition was most thorough and most brutal, and its instruments and methods of torture were sufficient to deter even the most courageous from attempting to live the double life of a Christian in public and a Jew in secret. That many continued to practice some basic Jewish traditions in the privacy of their basements and garrets is a great tribute to their indomitable faith, courage and commitment to their ancestral heritage.

Many observed the Seder in secret, making their own wine, baking their own *matzot* and gathering in their stocks of extra food in good time before the festival so as not to arouse any suspicion among their Catholic neighbors that they were preparing for the Jewish festival.

### 771. How were they able to calculate when to celebrate it?

Having no Jewish calendars or contacts with other Jews, it was not possible for them to be sure to celebrate it on the proper day according to the traditional Jewish calendrical regulations. They therefore resorted to observing Pesach at the full moon of the civil month of March. At a later period this date had to be abandoned because the Church authorities discovered its significance. Instead, the Seder was observed sixteen days after the new moon of March (some two days later).

### 772. What is the significance of the name "Marranos"?

Its precise etymology is not clear, and various suggestions have been offered. It is generally regarded as a derogatory term, though the late Dr. H. J. Zimmels was of the opinion that it derived from a contraction of the two Hebrew words, *mumar anus*, "forced apostate." Others connect it with the Arabic term *mura'in*, "a hypocrite," though the most favored view is that it derives from the medieval Spanish word for a swine, indicative of the fact that those crypto-Jews refrained, whenever possible, from eating of that animal.

### 773. Do we know of any exclusively Marrano custom relating to Pesach?

They had the practice of taking willow branches and beating the waters of a stream or river, apparently in commemoration of the separation of the waters of the Red Sea. Since the Jews of Morocco also visit a stream on the last day of Pesach, where they recite various prayers and blessing, it is conceivable that both traditions hark back to a pre-expulsion Spanish custom.

The Marranos might have absorbed it into their Passover practice, viewing it as a compensation for their inability to take the willow branch at its proper time during the Sukkot festival.

### 774. Do we have reports from medieval travelers regarding any novel Passover traditions?

Around 1238, one Rabbi Jacob was sent on a mission to the Holy Land on behalf of his mentor, the distinguished Rabbi Yechiel of Paris. He kept a diary of his visit, and, referring to the Pesach practices of the Jews of Meron, he notes that the burial places of Hillel and Shammai and thirty-two of their disciples are to be found there.

He states: "The Israelites meet there on the second day of Passover, and pray and recite hymns. If they find water in the cave they all rejoice, for it is a sure sign that the year will be blessed. However, many times they find no water, but when they pray the water comes in a twinkling" (quoted in *Jewish Travellers,* ed. Elkan Nathan Adler, London: George Routledge and Sons, 1930, p. 122). The State of Israel could do with such miracle-working "Israelites" at the present time!

## PASSOVER OBSERVANCE AMONG THE KARAITES

**775. We have referred above to the Samaritan sect. We know that, from the eighth century c.e., there was another significant sect of Karaites. What was their origin and theology?**

The sect was founded by one Anan ben David, and its name derives from the fact that it rejected the rabbinic-talmudic tradition and followed a strictly literal interpretation of Scripture. Hence their name *Bnei Mikra* ("followers of the Scriptural text) or "Karaites."

The mainstream Jewish rationale of the Karaite schism attributes it to Anan's pique at having been passed over for the position of Exilarch, leader of babylonian Jewry, at the death of the previous incumbent, his uncle, around the year 760 c.e. His uncle died without offspring, and Anan, though older and better qualified, was passed over in favor of his younger brother, Josiah. He therefore promptly went and founded his own movement.

Historians provide a number of other conditions and circumstances to account for the rise of the movement, taking account of economic and sociological factors, including a strong heterodox tendency that grew up in the wake of the Arab conquests and the collision of Islam with Judaism, and, indeed, with other faiths.

Professor Naftali Wieder has demonstrated that there are many strong points of contact between Karaism and the theology of the Essenes of the Dead Sea Scrolls, and he suggests that Karaism was, doctrinally, a reincarnation of that earlier religious tendency (see N. Wieder, *The Judean Scrolls and Karaism* [London: East and West, 1962]).

**776. How do the Karaites calculate the date of Pesach?**

Their founder, Anan, was bitterly critical of the fixed calendar as computed by Rabbanite (Orthodox Jewish) tradition from the period of Hillel II (fourth century c.e.) onwards. He regarded that as repugnant to the spirit and letter of Scripture, which he interpreted (with original Jewish tradition) as insisting upon actual observation by witnesses of the first light of the new moon. His criterion for adding an extra leap year (Adar II) coincided with that of Orthodox Judaism, namely, the delayed ripening of the barley crop, since the latter had to coincide with Pesach.

Nevertheless, by the fourteenth century, the Karaite method of fixing Rosh Chodesh (the first day of the new month), by waiting for witnesses to declare that they had observed the new moon, was abandoned, and the Karaites succumbed to acceptance of the rabbinic fixed calendar, based upon the nineteen-year cycle of intercalation.

### 777. Do we know of any unique Karaite Passover practices?

The great medieval Bible commentator, Abraham ibn Ezra (1098–1164), derides the Karaite practice of a certain place, called, variously, Argelon or, in the Paris Mss. of his commentary, Wargelan (possibly in Algeria), whereby, on the first day of Pesach, the entire Karaite community picks itself up and travels a distance from their town, in commemoration of the journeying forth of the Israelites out of Egypt (see comment of Ibn Ezra to Exodus 12:10).

There is a problem, however, regarding this tradition, namely that it is not mentioned by a single other Karaite or Rabbanite authority as being practiced either in that or any other Karaite locale!

A solution to this enigma is suggested by Chaim Leshem (see *Shabbat Umoadei Yisrael,* vol. 2, Tel Aviv: Niv, 1969, p. 435), who believed that the community of that particular place must have been subjected to particular persecution by a local Muslim fanatical group, and felt constrained, therefore, to leave their town in order to be enabled to celebrate Pesach unhindered in some isolated desert location. Ibn Ezra, on being told of their practice, probably misconstrued it as an empty symbolic custom, devoid of any traditional basis, and accordingly wrote disparagingly about it.

### 778. Do the Karaites observe the ceremony of the slaughtering and eating of the Paschal Lamb?

No, they do not. This may appear somewhat inconsistent, since, after all, they are committed to the literal sense of Scripture. Nevertheless, they accepted that, with the destruction of the Temple, the Paschal Lamb ritual was suspended. The Karaites maintained that there was a biblical distinction between the "Feast of Unleavened Bread," on the one hand, and the "Festival of Passover" on the other. The former remained operative, while the latter—and with it the ritual of the lamb—was inextricably interconnected to the Temple ritualism.

Consequently, in the Karaite liturgy the only references to the Paschal Lamb are in the context of the biblical verses that are recited in the Eve of Passover Service (only). No later compositions refer to the Korban Pesach in the way that rabbanite liturgical poets do.

### 779. Are there any major differences between the spirit of our festival of Pesach and that of the Karaite "Feast of Unleavened Bread"?

Although the Karaites follow, in large measure, the same laws governing *chametz* and *matzah* as characterize rabbinic Judaism, yet in spirit the two methods of celebration are poles apart. Whereas, for us, Passover has always been a festival permeated by a spirit of joy and festivity, for Karaites it is a serious, almost somber, observance.

And their Passover liturgy partakes of that same somber spirit. Indeed, they made Passover the occasion for numerous confessional and petitionary compositions— "types of prayers unthinkable in a Rabbanite Festival Prayer Book" (M. Turetsky, *A Critical Edition and Translation of the Karaite Liturgy for Passover,* thesis, University of Leeds, England, 1963, p. 123). Indeed, the Karaites believed that "true piety demanded self-imposed denial of the legally permitted festival pleasures. Only by converting the festivals, of one's own volition and zeal, into days of sadness and fasts did one truly invest exilic mourning with its deepest and most intense meaning" (Turetsky, *Karaite Liturgy*, p. 124).

It was in this spirit that Karaite authorities declared marital relations prohibited on festivals, and that the Byzantine Karaites used to observe the "Fast of Daniel" from the 13th to the 24th of Nisan, which takes in the entire festival of Pesach, including its intermediate Sabbath!

### 780. What form does their Seder take?

Because the Karaites rejected rabbinic traditions and interpretations, it meant that they did not accept the authority of the Talmud nor the validity of any of the rabbinic modes of midrashic interpretation. Not surprisingly, therefore, their Haggadah does not contain any of the midrashic interpretations of biblical verses or any of the other rabbinic compositions that form the lion's share of our Haggadah.

### 781. What was the rabbinic view of the Karaite's abbreviated Haggadah?

They maintained the traditional disdain that they had for the rest of the Karaite "heresy." What perturbed them more was the attraction of such an abbreviated Seder for some members of the Orthodox fraternity who, aping the Karaites, arbitrarily abbreviated the traditional Haggadah. This is reflected in a passage from the *Seder Rav Amram* (ninth century):

> Thus said Rav Natronai: "Whoever recites the Karaite Pesach *Kiddush* of *Asher kiddesh et Yisrael*, and, at the conclusion of *Mah Nishtanah*, does not recite *Avadim Hayyinu*, omitting *Mitchilah ovdei avodah zarah*, and reciting instead . . . [various biblical verses are then listed], and omitting the Midrashic expositions of the biblical verses: . . . Whoever adopts this practice, not only does he not fulfill his religious duty, but he is also a heretic, sowing discord, denying the authority of the Rabbis and despising the words of the Mishnah and Talmud. The community is obliged to excommunicate such a person. (*Seder Rav Amram*, ed. D. Goldschmidt, Jerusalem: Mosad HaRav Kuk, 1972, pp. 111–112)

## PASSOVER AND CHRISTIAN PERSECUTION

### 782. Are there any other examples of medieval Jewish communities suffering violence at Pesach time?

We have clear evidence from Christian sources that Jews were particularly vulnerable to assault at Pesach time due to the recurring exercise of the blood libel. The twelfth-century bishop, Bishop Vincent, states that "Jews are pelted with stones on Palm Sunday in return for their having stoned Jesus" (see L. Poliakov, *The History of*

*Antisemitism,* vol. 1 [London: Routledge & Kegan Paul, 1974], p. 145; see also H. H. Ben Sasson, *A History of the Jewish People* [Cambridge, MA: Harvard University Press, 1976], p. 482; see Y. T. Levinsky, *Sefer Ha-Moadim* vol. 2 (Tel Aviv: Devir, 1960], p. 265). The clergy would preach fiery anti-Semitic sermons at that time, and urge Christians to go straight from church on to the rampage against the Jews. When the practice was stopped, it was replaced by a fine imposed upon every Jew, to be paid before Easter, the proceeds of which were employed to the refurbishing of churches.

Two centuries later we hear of Jews in southern Italy being subjected to the same violent stoning. It became customary in many towns for the Jews to shore up their doors and windows and not to dare to leave their homes for the entire week preceding Easter – the week of Jesus' chastisement and crucifixion.

In Toulouse it was replaced by a humiliating and often violent cheek slapping of the head of the Jewish community. This was formally and publicly administered on the Friday before Easter; and often it was done with such force that the recipient suffered heart failure and died on the spot. The Jews of Toulouse were also required to provide annually, at that period, thirty liters of wax for the Church celebration of Easter (see Leshem, *Shabbat Umoadei Yisrael,* pp. 428–430).

### 783. What was the origin of the blood libel?

Its origin is not necessarily to be identified with the first recorded example of the libel charge being ventilated. Its antecedents lie centuries earlier in the traditional Christian antipathy towards Jews and Judaism, going back to the charge of Jewish complicity in, and responsibility for, the crucifixion of Jesus. Centuries of hostility followed from that event, and, when the Emperor Constantine declared Christianity the official religion of the Roman empire in the fourth century, Jews were hounded and discriminated against, and were used as the emotional scapegoat for all the economic ills, military setbacks and superstitions of any and every Christian country. They were painted as the anti-Christ, the embodiment of all evil, people deprived of heavenly grace, in league with the devil, with no possibility of salvation in the hereafter; people who were, consequently, without rights, without faith, without dignity. In short, people whose continued existence was of no benefit to the world. Hence the straight line, of cause and effect, from Magdelene to Maidanek, from Christianity to crematoria!

### 784. What were the circumstances and precise allegations of the first blood libels?

In 1144, shortly before Passover, a Christian child was discovered murdered in the fields around the English city of Norwich. The cry went round that the Jews had perpetrated the murder in order to obtain blood required to mix with their *matzot.* In 1171, the false blood libel was the cause of the massacre of the entire community of Blois, France, and in 1255 the Jews of Lincoln were subjected to a similar charge of having crucified a Christian child and then having removed his intestines for use in witchcraft rites. Towards the end of the thirteenth century the baseless charge was made every year, and countless thousands of Jews lost their lives in the Christian orgy of murder and rapine.

**785. Were there any Christian voices raised in defense of the Jews?**

When the charge was leveled against the Jews of Fulda in 1235, the Emperor Frederick initiated a thorough enquiry into the charges, interviewing, among others, Jewish converts to Christianity. When he received unanimous confirmation that Jews could not, and did not, indulge in such gross acts of murder, and not only did not require Christian blood for their rituals, but, indeed, were strictly prohibited from drinking even the minutest amount of animal, let alone human, blood, the emperor openly publicized the results of his findings and totally exonerated the Jews.

Although Pope Innocent IV followed suit in denouncing the falseness of the charges, yet they failed to convince a Christian world whose hatred of the Jew ran so deep that it refused to be deflected from its murderous purpose by such irrelevancies as facts! Anyone reading Geoffrey Chaucer's *Canterbury Tales* will be made aware of the depth of anti-Jewish feeling in fourteenth-century England; and *The Prioress's Tale,* in particular, resurrects the myth of the blood libel.

**786. Were there any other Jewish communities who, like the Samaritans, observed a Paschal lamb ritual?**

It was the practice of the *Benei Israel* of India to slaughter a lamb on the eve of Passover, and to daub its blood upon the doorposts and lintel of their homes, in commemoration of the biblical prescription for the first Passover in Egypt. They did not, however, have any Seder-night ritual observances.

Their ignorance of the Haggadah and the later rabbinic rituals is on account of the fact that they lived, for over two thousand years, away from the mainstream of Jewish life. Though their origins and the date of their arrival in India is shrouded in legend, their claim is that they fled there from Galilee in the wake of the persecutions of Antiochus Epiphanes (175–163 B.C.E.).

## MOROCCAN PASSOVER PRACTICES

**787. Does Moroccan tradition observe the practice of hiding the ten pieces of bread before the search for *chametz* on the night before Pesach?**

Not only do Moroccans observe the custom, but they actually embellish it by hiding slices of grilled liver with the bread. The reason for this is uncertain, though it may constitute a wish to demonstrate that they have removed from their homes not only the pure *chametz* contained in their bread, but even any trace of indirect *chametz* absorbed within the meat of their animals.

**788. Are there any pre-Seder practices observed by the Jews of Morocco?**

It is the custom that, after the synagogue service and before the commencement of the Seder at their own homes, people make a detour to visit senior and elderly members of their family who will not be present at their Seder. This enables the visitors to bless, and be blessed by, each and every member of their family. The blessing is administered by raising the Seder plate above the head of the one being blessed, and reciting two formulae. The first subtly converts this brief and hasty visit into a kind of representation of the haste of the ancient Israelites, hence, *Bibehilu yatzanu mimitzrayim; ha lachma anya benei chorin* ("In haste we had to leave Egypt; this is the bread of affliction; may we speedily be free people"). The second invokes the traditional blessing for redemption, *Leshanah haba-ah biYerushalayim.*

The identical blessing of the family is repeated at the Seder table, before the commencement of the Seder.

### 789.  Are there any other unique Moroccan Seder practices?

The men dress in long, white robes in honor of the Seder and as a symbol of freedom. After the *Mah Nishtanah,* the father leaves the table, and returns holding a stick in his hand and with the *Afikoman* wrapped in a napkin over his shoulder. Everyone questions him excitedly as to where he has come from. He tells them all the story of the oppression and the Exodus as if he had been a redeemed Israelite. He spices his account with quotations from the Book of Exodus and then explains the significance of the broken piece of *Afikoman* on his shoulder. Every biblical verse that he employs is taken up and repeated as a kind of refrain by all around the table.

The Moroccan custom is to read or chant the Haggadah, rather than, as with the Ashkenazim, to make it as choral as possible. They do not leave the reading of the Haggadah primarily to the person leading the Seder. Instead, the men present take it in turns reading each paragraph. The rest join in with the chanting of the last verse of each paragraph. Some translate passages of the Haggadah into their vernacular: Arabic, French, or Ladino.

### 790.  Are there any other special culinary traditions of Moroccan Jewry?

It is their custom, unlike that of Ashkenazim, to eat lamb, accompanied by sweetened vegetables.

During *Chol Ha-Moed* (the intermediate days), eggs and potatoes are eaten to breakfast, after the morning service in synagogue. In the villages of Morocco, they bake fresh, unleavened bread in clay ovens during *Chol Ha-Moed.* It resembles pita bread, and is known by the name *tanurt* ("oven baked").

### 791.  Is anything special provided for the children in Moroccan communities?

There is a special "third Seder," called by the Arabic name *mindara,* which is provided during *Chol Ha-Moed* for the young children. The children help to prepare all the dishes themselves, and would eat their food in tiny dishes at low tables.

**792. The Jews of North Africa have a custom of kissing the *matzot*, *maror*, and *charoset*. What is the object of this?**

It is not confined to North Africa, but it is also observed by the Jews of Aleppo and elsewhere. They also kiss the *sukkah* when they enter and leave; they also kiss the Four Species used on Sukkot, and some even kiss the *shofar*. The reason is, simply, to demonstrate *chibuv mitzvah*, their love for the *mitzvot*, just as we kiss the *Sefer Torah* as it passes, to demonstrate our love for it.

**793. Do they reserve any special rituals for the seventh day of Pesach?**

The Jews of Morocco pray *Minchah* (Afternoon Service) earlier than usual. After that, they load themselves up with fruit, nuts, and a variety of other goodies, and make their way beyond the city limits. There, in some forest or gardens they sit under the trees and have a family picnic. The men rush back just in time for *Maariv*, but the women linger behind until dark.

## MAIMUNA

**794. The Jews of North Africa have a unique festival of their own, called *Maimuna*, at the termination of Pesach. What is the meaning of the name?**

The precise etymology of the term is unclear. Some regard it as a variation of *shemonah* ("eight"), namely, "the festivity of the eighth day" of Passover. The fact that others pronounce it as *emunah*, which means "faith," has suggested a link with the well-known talmudic statement, "In the month of Nisan the Israelites were redeemed from Egypt, and in the same month they will be granted their ultimate redemption" (Talmud *Rosh Hashanah* 11b). Thus, this extra celebration is to express their joyous expectation of an imminent messianic redemption.

A more popular explanation links *Maimuna* with the name *Maimon*, since it was on the day after Pesach that Maimon, the father of Moses Maimonides died in Fez, Morocco (around 1170). He was one of the most distinguished rabbinic scholars of his day, and he sought refuge in Fez from the fanatical Muslim Almohads, who had forced him to leave his home city of Cordova where he served as *dayyan*, judge and leading religious authority.

The community of Fez regarded him as having raised their prestige to dizzy heights by his presence among them, and there was wholesale sorrow and lament at his death. Now it is suggested that, since the usual *Hillula*, public mourning demonstration, is not permitted to be observed during the joyous month of Nisan, they initiated, instead, a novel form of commemoration, the *Maimuna*, which was more a festivity and celebration of his life than a mourning ritual. (For the present writer's explanation of the name *Maimuna*, see question 800).

**795. Moroccan Jews have the custom of offering each other special greetings for good fortune on the termination of Passover, which is also the inauguration of the *Maimuna*. What is the origin of this custom?**

They use an Arabic form of greeting, *Tarbekhu utisa'adu*, "May you be successful and have many festivities." There is a tradition that links this to the fact that the ancient Israelites took with them much booty out of Egypt that they had obtained from the Egyptians. Since they had been subjected to such haste from the time they seized that wealth until the festival was over, it was only at the conclusion of the festival that they were able to unpack and examine their prize: hence the greeting, which wishes them "success" in having seized a valuable collection.

**796. Are there any festive additions to the eve of *Maimuna Ma'ariv* (evening service)?**

As it is also the termination of Pesach, they could not convert the prescribed, ordinary weekday *Ma'ariv* into a festival service. Instead, they added special readings to the end of the service. Thus, they recite the entire *Pirkei Avot* (Ethics of the Fathers), which other traditions reserve for *Shabbat Minchah* (afternoon service), commencing its reading in synagogue only on the *Shabbat* after Pesach. They also read the opening verses from the book of Proverbs, the first of the special *Azharot* (poetic formulations of the biblical *mitzvot*) prescribed for recitation on *Shavuot*, and, in some congregations of Fez, a Ladino translation of the prayer, *Kavvei el Ha-Shem* ("Wait for the Lord"), which in some Sephardic prayer rites is recited before *Ein Keiloheinu* each day. In Marrakech, they sang the *Ein Keiloheinu* at the end of the service, in both Hebrew and Arabic.

**797. Did they proceed straight home from synagogue immediately after the evening service?**

No. It was their custom to visit the house of their Rabbi, where they were greeted to the accompaniment of musical instruments. The Rabbi's wife would have a table ready-laid, with a white cloth. On it there would be placed a glass of milk, a jar of honey, a plate of dates, and a plate of flour, into which was stuck a green bean. There would also be a bowl of swimming fish and a vase of mint.

The Rabbi would bless every individual in turn, a procedure that could take over an hour. It mattered not, because the Rabbi's blessing is taken very seriously in Moroccan tradition. After the blessings are completed, everyone is served with sweet tea, a beverage that is not drunk during the whole of Pesach for fear that it might contain *chametz*.

**798. What form did the home celebration take on the eve of *Maimuna*?**

Immediately after the termination of Pesach and the recitation of *Ma'ariv*, and while the menfolk are being entertained at the house of their Rabbi, the firstborn is sent to the grocer's store to buy flour. On his return, the mother and other female members of the family set-to, baking delicious pancakes called *muflitas*. This thin, doughy fritter is fried in oil and then dipped into butter and honey.

Meanwhile, a large festive table, festooned with flowers and green stalks of wheat, is laid in each house. In the center of the table is placed a jug of buttermilk and a bowl of flour topped with five dates, five bean stalks, and five eggs. The white tablecloth is barely visible between the countless platters and bowls, containing a variety of delicious fresh and crystallized fruits, cakes, nuts, petit fours, and wines.

After the women have finished their hasty preparations, they would wash and dress in their best clothing. Many don magnificently embroidered kaftans especially for this occasion. The custom is to go from home to home, visiting family and friends, sampling the delicious refreshments and offering each other the special Arabic blessing: *Allah maimuna ambarkha massauda*, "May God bless you with a successful *Maimuna*."

### 799. Are there any other practices associated with *Maimuna* evening?

It is regarded by many families as the most propitious time for arranging marriages. In Libya it used to be the custom for marriageable girls to don their most beautiful dresses, and stand, with faces uncovered, at the doors of their homes, giving the young men a rare opportunity of talking to them unchaperoned, and of deciding whether any particular young lady was pleasing to him.

If the young man returned home satisfied with his choice, he would send by return special gifts for his intended. Acceptance of these meant that the girl's parents gave their blessing to the match. He would then visit her home, bearing a basket full of lettuce and flowers. That visit was accordingly called *Khass Wa-nuwwar*, "Lettuce and flowers" (see Issachar Ben-Ami, *Yahadut Marokko*, Jerusalem: Reuven, Mass, 1975, p. 144).

### 800. How was the day of *Maimuna* celebrated?

It was the custom to rise very early on this day. A popular belief had it that anyone who rose late on that morning would be sluggish (and miss opportunities) the rest of the year. In many communities of Morocco, the young men would participate in races on horseback, the object being to see who could arrive first at a given river, and immerse in it. The origin of this practice is unclear, but, taken together with some other customs of *Maimuna* day, wherein water figures quite prominently, it would seem that it was to recall the horses of Pharaoh which were drowned in the Red Sea.

The centrality of water in the day's rituals suggests that the primary objective of this entire festival was to celebrate the crossing of the Red Sea. Hence, on *Maimuna*, they go to every well in the area and draw water, which they then proceed to pour out over their feet, as well as over the threshhold of their homes.

The Jews of the Tafilalet area of Morocco positively drench their homes in water, accompanying the drenching with the recitation of a formula for warding off evil. In other places, they draw water from the rivers, and pour it out all the way back to their homes. One authority (see Ben-Ami, *Yahadut Marokko*) interprets these water rituals as reminiscent of the Temple water libation on the festival of Tabernacles. Why they should have been transferred to Pesach he does not make clear. It might, of course, be a symbolic way of demonstrating and celebrating the end of the rainy season, parallel to the prayers for dew (*Tal*) recited on Pesach.

In Marrakech, early in the morning, the Jews make their way to the well called *Sakis el mazodi*, where the women beat the water seven times, and the men dip their feet in it for over an hour, and wash their faces and bodies. (For the significance of that particular well, see Ben-Ami, *Yahadut Marokko*, p. 145.)

These multiple water rituals suggest to the present writer another, simple explanation of the term *Maimuna*, namely, that it is a mixed-form, derived from a combination the Hebrew word for water, *mayim*, with the Arabic (nominative) noun ending *un*.

A modern-day application of the water motif is for families to go for a picnic to the seaside on *Maimuna*. In Larache it was the custom to go to the gardens on this day, and to recite the *Birkat ha-ilanot* over the early-blossoming trees.

It is traditional to eat only dairy foods on *Maimuna*. This was possibly in order to break the monotony of a strictly meat and vegetable diet over the whole of Passover, because of the difficulties of getting supervized milk from the dairies.

*Maimuna* is still joyously observed by Jews in Morocco, as well as by the large ex-patriot communities in Israel, America, and France. In Israel, it is a national holiday.

### 801. Are any special candles lit at the *Maimuna*?

In Fez it was the custom at the *chupah* to present the young couple with a memorial glass. At the *Maimuna* they would fill it with water and oil, place in it rings and other jewelery, and light the wicks. It is suggested that the point of the jewelery was in order to commemorate the booty the Israelites carried away with them from their Egyptian neighbors.

### 802. As we shall see, Morocco is not the only country to observe the day after Pesach as a special occasion. Is there any talmudic basis for the significance of that day?

Indeed. The day following each of the major festivals is known as *Isru chag*, a term borrowed from the psalm verse: *Isru chag ba-avotim ad karnot ha-mizbe'ach*—"With myrtle branches in their hands, *they form a festal procession* up to the horns of the altar" (Psalm 118:27). The particular reason for the designation of that particular day as *Isru chag* is unclear. It may also mean, "release the festival [obligations]," and may refer to the residual excitement of the festival days that is carried over into the following day when, in Temple times, people were leaving Jerusalem to wend their way home.

The Talmud (*Sukkah* 45b) wished us to preserve the sacred festive spirit of *Isru chag*, hence the statement, "Whomsoever makes a party, with eating and drinking on the day after the festival, is regarded as if he had built the Temple altar and offered a sacrifice upon it, since it states: *Isru chag ba'avotim ad karnot ha-mizbe'ach*" (which the Talmud expounds exegetically to mean:) "If you celebrate *Isru* [the day of release] as a *chag*, then it is like [officiating at] the horns of the altar."

### 803. Are there any customs from that part of the world that are clearly unacceptable from a halakhic point of view?

Professor Daniel Sperber, in a chapter of his book, *Minhagei Yisrael* (Jerusalem: Mosad Ha-Rav Kuk, 1990, 1:36–37), records details of the community of Souk-Ahras, in Eastern Algeria, who have a custom to repair, on the last day of Pesach, to the ruins of a Roman theater outside the town, where they proceed to eat *chametz*, even though the festival has not yet terminated!

A visiting Rabbi, curious to know the origin of that ludicrous and forbidden practice, learnt that it arose several generations ago, when the community was visited by an emissary from Palestine. On the last day of Pesach he was observed leaving the town and making for that ruin, where he proceeded to eat bread. Obviously, that emissary was eager to eat bread now that, for him, Pesach (only a seven-day festival for inhabitants of the Holy Land) was over. The townspeople, ignorant of his situation, assumed that if such a pious and learned man, immersed in the sacred atmosphere of the Holy Land, allowed himself to eat on the last day of the festival, as long as it was done outside the town, then it must certainly be an authoritative practice, worthy of observing!

## LIBYAN PASSOVER PRACTICES

### 804. Did the Jews of Libya have any distinctive Pesach practices?

Weeks before Pesach, the women of Yefren would begin their onerous and physically exhausting task of grinding sufficient flour for fifteen days. This was to supply their families' entire requirement for the week before Pesach (when everything in the house was being given its final cleaning, and no grains of flour that could become *chametz* were wanted in the house), and the eight days of Pesach itself. So strict were they to avoid any fermentation, that the women would cover their mouths with a scarf, to avoid any inadvertent escape of saliva if they sneezed, and they would avoid talking or singing while preparing the *matzot*.

During the Ottoman period, at least until the end of the nineteenth century, Pesach was a time for courtship, as we have mentioned (see question 799). The afternoon of the last day of Pesach was known, by the Jews of Libya, as *Chag Ha-Shoshanim*, "Festival of Roses." This derived from the custom for the boys of marriageable age to throw roses to the girls of their choice. The adults would follow suit, and throw roses in front of the newly engaged couple.

On the last day of Pesach (and the last day of Sukkot) it was the custom in Tripoli for the community to prepare a special festive meal in honor of the members of the *Chevra Kadisha* (Burial Society).

## SYRIAN PASSOVER PRACTICES

**805. Do we have any traditions regarding how Syrian Jewry, now almost completely removed to Israel, prepare for Pesach?**

In the main, their preparations do not differ markedly from those of other communities of the Middle East and North Africa. In synagogue, from the beginning of Nisan, they read each day from the Torah the section (Numbers, ch. 7) dealing with the gifts presented by the princes of the tribes of Israel to the desert sanctuary that was consecrated on the first day of Nisan.

We know that rice used to be their staple food throughout Pesach, though in their new places of domicile this will, naturally, have changed. It used to be the task of the women to examine the rice scrupulously, to ensure that no wheat had found its way in among the rice grains. They would spread out a white tablecloth to examine the rice grains minutely.

The members of the community always sold their *chametz* to their Rabbi, and, following the strict letter of the halakhah, would deliver to him the keys of the rooms or containers in which their *chametz* was being stored away over Pesach, which he would, in turn, deliver to the non-Jew to whom he sold the *chametz* of the entire community.

In Syria, they took the Fast of the Firstborn very seriously, and those living in outlying villages would travel far in order to attend the *siyyum,* in order to be freed of their obligation to fast. They would take back from the reception pieces of cake which they would distribute to their firstborn wives, daughters, infants, and to those firstborn too sick or old to attend the *siyyum.* It was generally believed that partaking of food brought from the *siyyum,* was, in itself, sufficient to absolve them of their responsibility to fast that day.

**806. Do they have any special tradition regarding the baking of *matzot*?**

It was their practice to keep all their *lulavim* (palms) from Sukkot, and to use them for fueling the ovens in which they baked the *matzot.* This served the dual purpose of ensuring that they did not have to discard their *lulavim,* which had, after all, been used for a holy ritual purpose (*tashmishei mitzvah*), in a disrespectful way. Secondly, it enabled them to use one *mitzvah* for the launch of another.

**807. Do Syrian Jewry have any special Seder practices?**

Before the Seder, it is the custom to mix all the wine with water—a relic of the ancient practice in talmudic times, when the wine was so potent that it required *mezigah,* diluting.

Syrian Jewry was influenced by the mysticism of Isaac Luria. They therefore set out the Seder Plate according to Luria's formation (see question 203), and they break the two pieces of the middle *matzah* for *Yachatz* into the shapes of the letters *dalet* and *vav,* which have a combined numerical value of *ten,* corresponding to the ten *Sefirot,* or primordial "emanations"—the process of self-extension employed by the God who is All-Spirit in order to create the physical world. The Seder Plate is removed from the room, and then immediately returned, just before the recitation of *Mah Nishtanah,* in order to stimulate the curiosity of the children so that they start asking about all the weird and wonderful things going on around them, which is, of course, a cue to the parents to relate the story of the Exodus for them (and at their level).

Syrian Jewry also has that familiar charade of acting out the Exodus. The *Afikoman,* wrapped in a napkin, is first placed upon the shoulder of each participant, when they recite the Hebrew biblical verse, *Mish'arotam tzerurot besimlotam al shikhmam—*"their kneading-troughs were bound up in their clothes upon their shoulders" (Exodus 15:34).

This is then followed by the charade, conducted in Arabic. One of the children enters the room, and is asked where he or she has come from, to which the answer "From Egypt!" is given. "And where are you heading for?" everyone asks. "To Jerusalem," is the response.

The Syrian practice is to eat the roasted shank bone and the roasted egg at the beginning of the meal. They do not normally eat any other roasted meat at the seder.

### 808.  What is their special ritual for the seventh day of the festival?

They have what is called *Tikkun Leil Shevii Shel Pesach,* "The special order for the eve of the seventh day of Passover," which is very similar in concept to the more widely observed *Tikkun,* (which we are familiar with) on the first night of Shavuot, and the less widely observed *Tikkun* on the night of *Hosha'na Rabbah,* the seventh night of Sukkot.

The *Tikkun* commences a few hours before dawn and comprises the reading and study of passages, primarily on the theme of redemption and faith, from the three sections of the *Tanakh* (the Bible), and appropriate selections from Talmud and from the *Zohar,* the central work of our mystical heritage. These are followed by some petitions for "an era of divine mercy and of attention to our people's needs." There then follows the recitation of the ten biblical *Shirot* (songs), sundry psalms, and the entire book of *Shir Ha-Shirim* (Song of Songs). The *Tikkun* concludes with the beautiful poem, *Yom LeYabashah,* by Yehudah Ha-Levi.

### 809.  How do they mark the termination of Pesach?

Immediately after the service for the conclusion of the festival, they take stalks of wheat and tap each other with them on the shoulder, while uttering the greeting, *Santak Khadra* ("Here's to a fruitful year!"). The employment of the wheat is presumably to indicate the moment of transition from *matzah* to *chametz,* and symbolizes the fact that new flour may now be procured for the baking of *chametz* bread.

## BALKANS PASSOVER PRACTICES

### 810.  How do Jews living in the Balkans (Greece, Turkey, and the former Yugoslavia) prepare for Pesach?

The baking of *Matzot* was regulated, and in some communities the licence was granted exclusively to the bakery that offered the keenest price. (Perhaps our Ecclesiastical Courts should take a leaf out of their book!)

An interesting and quaint practice, in Salonika and some other communities, was to reserve *Shabbat Ha-Gadol* for providing children—especially those in orphanages or from families supported by the community—with their new clothes. This event was even given the name, *Chag Ha-Halbashah,* "Festival of the New Clothing." It is suggested that this was to mark the spring season. (See H. C. Dobrinsky, *A Treasury of Sephardic Laws and Customs,* New York: Ktav Publishing House, Yeshivah University Press, 1988, p. 273. I am indebted to this work, which has ably supplemented and confirmed the detailed information I have obtained from personal interviews with friends and congregants who hail from the various countries referred to in this book.)

Turkish Jewry did not have the tradition to sell their *chametz* to a non-Jew, though many of those who have migrated to Israel, America and Britain have now adopted the practice.

### 811. What type of *matzah* do they bake?

They bake *matzot* of two types of consistency: a thick *matzah,* which they call *boyo,* and a thin variety, called *maniuo.* The latter is used for cooking, especially for the midday meal preceeding the festival when it is customary to cook deep-fried *matzah* (*buermelos*), accompanied by eggs and vegetables. They eat exclusively *Matzah Shemurah* during the two *Sedarim,* and they drink a special liquor called *Raki,* made from raisins. They invest *matzah* with protective powers, and keep some of it on them when undertaking any potentially hazardous adventure, such as when going on a long journey abroad.

### 812. Do they have any distinctive Seder customs?

Again we encounter the custom of holding the Seder Plate over the heads of all the gathering, and again we find the influence of the *Ari* (Isaac Luria) in the arrangement of the Seder Plate, with the ten symbolic foods highlighting the significance of the ten *Sefirot* or emanations. They also explain the three *matzot* in similar vein, as representing the first three of the ten *Sefirot* (divine emanations), those of *Keter* (crown), *Chokhmah* (wisdom), and *Binah* (intelligence).

On reaching the verse, *Kol dikhfin yeisei veyeikhol,* "Let all who are hungry come and eat," in the *Ha lachma Anya* composition, they have the tradition to open their front doors, and to step outside to see if there are any poor to welcome in.

The Spanish tradition has left its imprint with the custom of reciting the Seder in a mixture of Hebrew and Ladino. The *Mah Nishtanah* was originally chanted by the entire gathering, rather than being the exclusive preserve of the child, though the dominant practice has nowadays infiltrated the ex-patriot communities.

The charade of the enacting of the Exodus is also found in this tradition, with the head of the family leaving the room and then returning with staff in hand, a belt tied around his cloak, to recall the reference to the Israelites having *motneikhem cha-gurim,* their "loins girded" (Exodus 12:11), and the *Afikoman* wrapped in a napkin over his shoulders. The traditional dialogue, as found in other Mediterranean traditions, is followed, and every participant would take it in turn to hold the *Afikoman* on their shoulder. They would keep a piece of the *Afikoman* as a good luck charm for the entire year—a belief shared also by Persian Jewry (see question 819).

They do not have any Cup of Elijah, nor do most Balkan communities open the door at *Shefokh Chamatekha.* It was the custom in Istanbul and Salonika to sing *Chad Gadyah* in Ladino. There was also a custom to throw pieces of *maror* onto the floor, to indicate that our bitterness should now be cast away, and be replaced by pure joy.

### 813. Do any communities of the region have any distinctive ritual associated with the *Afikoman*?

They do not have the custom of hiding the *Afikoman*. However, Rabbi Shemtob Gaguine relates (*Keter Shem Tov,* p. 173) that in Salonika the one leading the Seder, on handing out the *Afikoman,* announces to all: *Esto comemos zekher lekorban Pesach kelo comeamos sovre arto—*"This that we are eating is in commemoration of the Paschal lamb, which they used to eat on a full stomach." This explanatory declaration is parallel to the one recited before eating of Hillel's sandwich. Gaguine cannot explain, however, the origin or rationale of this particular declaration (see Gaguine, *Keter Shem Tov,* p. 169).

Gaguine relates that some communities (which he does not identify) had the custom of making a hole in the *Afikoman,* and suspending it, as a good luck charm, on a wall in one of the rooms of the house. He also reports that the Spanish Jews of Palestine would declare in Spanish, after eating of the *Afikoman, Salvo agua asta la manyana—*"Only water until tomorrow!" (Gaguine, *Keter Shem Tov,* pp. 175, 174).

### 814. Do Balkan Jewry have any distinctive post-Seder practices?

It is their custom, once the Seder is over, to drink Turkish coffee in order to keep themselves awake for the recitation of the book of *Shir Ha-Shirim.*

### 815. What of their customs during the last days of Pesach?

They also observe the *Tikkun Leil Shevii Shel Pesach,* which we have described in relation to Syrian Jewry (see question 808), and they also share with the latter a ritual for the termination of the festival. Instead of wheat, they go out and collect fresh grass, which they proceed to throw, together with money and sweets, onto the floor, to be eagerly grabbed by the children.

Dobrinsky (*Treasury of Sephardic Laws and Customs,* p. 278) quotes a source that records the practice of Bulgarian Jewish husbands to hold the grass over their wives and recite, in Hebrew, the verse, "Like the growth of the field I caused thee to increase. And thou didst increase and grow up" (Ezekiel 16:7). This suggests that its origin may well lie in some primitive fertility ritual associated with the onset of spring. It also suggests that the entire practice of throwing the grass, money, and sweets on the ground may also have its roots in a primitive superstition, and may represent a propitiatory gift to the demons in order to win protection for their wives that they should not miscarry (hence the relevance of that particular biblical verse), and, in general, for their families, throughout the coming year.

## PERSIAN AND MESHEDI PASSOVER PRACTICES

### 816. Were the Jews of Persia (modern Iran) able to observe Pesach, bearing in mind their subjection to Islam?

It is true that they were "subjected" to Islam, to the extent that all Jews were officially registered as Muslims, the community having been forcibly converted under Shah Abbas II (1642–1646). In Isfahan, the synagogues were closed down and all the Jews were led to the mosque, where they were made to proclaim a public confession of the Muslim faith. The Jews lived a double life, as courageously as the Marranos before them, and, in due course, successfully petitioned to have their synagogues reopened and Jewish practices restored. However, with the arrival of the Kajar dynasty (1794–1925), the Shi'ite concept of the impurity of nonbelievers made Jewish life intolerable. The entire Jewish community of Meshed—a holy city for Muslims—was forced into the Islamic faith in 1839 by Mohammed Shah. Again, they adhered secretly to their tradition, under the most difficult of conditions. An expatriot Persian Jew, now living in London, reported that his grandfather even made the pilgrimage to Mecca in order to maintain the pretense of being a committed Muslim!

Unlike the Jews of Teheran, who were more assimilated, the Jews of Meshed were determined to observe their Judaism scrupulously. With no Rabbis, Jewish schools, or organized Jewish life, they went to great pains to pass on their traditions from father to son; and their great pride was that there was hardly any intermarriage. This they achieved by marrying off their daughters at a very young age—as young as eleven or twelve years.

Hence, it is no surprise that they observed Pesach to the very best of their ability, commencing their preparations some three months in advance, in order not to betray to their "fellow Muslim neighbors" signs of any special activity as the festival approached.

Conditions improved under Shah Muzaffar-ed-Din (1896–1907), with establishment of a constitutional parliament, aided by strong international pressure for the relaxation of discrimination against the Jewish community. The result was the opening of the first Jewish school of the Alliance Israelite Universelle in 1898.

### 817. What form did the preparations for Pesach take prior to the departure of the Jews subsequent to the deposition of the last Shah?

To answer this question we quote from an eye-witness account, provided by Mrs. Parry Faigenblum of Stanmore, N.W. London, writing in the Emunah magazine *At,* of March 1984 ("Pesach as a Child in Iran," p. 5):

Everything for this festival had to be prepared by hand, and in those days this meant that it had to be done at home to assure the *Kashrut*. Even basic commodities, such as salt, pepper and other spices had to be specially ground and then stored. Weeks beforehand the large cellar was scrubbed and cleared of *chametz*. This was where all the preparations took place, and it also acted as the warehouse. Nuts were very necessary for our enjoyment, and many varieties were bought, washed, salted, ground or roasted. Similarly, fruit was prepared in many different ways, as were the wines and juices.

Nearer the time the baker came to make the *matzot*. This gave the opportunity to taste. We had egg *matzot*, thick ones, thin ones, big ones and small ones, but the ones used for the Seder were made thick, and were about three feet in diameter!

The *shochet* also had to visit the house, and slaughter several lambs, chickens and turkeys. The lamb was deep fried, to preserve the meat, or smoked. Nothing was wasted; the fat was collected and kept for cooking.

We did not eat any dairy produce during the whole eight days, and many Iranian Jews to this day feel uncomfortable eating milk and cheese, notwithstanding the most impeccable *hechsherim* (Certification [of rabbinical supervision]).

### 818. How was the Seder table laid out?

Again, we can do no better than allow Mrs. Faigenblum to explain:

A large white tablecloth was laid on the floor, surrounded by about forty cushions. In the center was placed the Seder Plate, *matzot* and vinegar. For the children the focus of attraction on that cloth were the spring onions which were to be used during *Dayyeinu*. At the end of the first verse, we took hold of an onion and beat the person next to us. For a while chaos would reign, until father regained control ("Pesach as a Child in Iran," p. 5).

We may conjecture that the beating of the onions upon one's neighbor is to symbolize the beatings that the Israelites received at the hands of the Egyptian taskmasters.

### 819. What other distinctive Seder customs were observed?

Mr. Nicky Cohanim is our informant for this aspect of Meshed Jewry's Seder customs (interview, December 1994). He tells us that, for *Urechatz*, it is the youngest member of the family that brings in the bowl of water, and, instead of only the Seder-leader washing his hands, all present wash, including the women. For *maror*, a lettuce leaf is always used and the *maror* is placed within it. For Hillel's sandwich, again a lettuce leaf is used with the *matzah*. Their custom is also to add *charoset* within Hillel's sandwich.

As in many traditions, a piece of the *Afikoman* is kept throughout the year as a *segulah*, an augury for wealth and happiness. After each of the four cups, everyone's cup is washed in a communal bowl by the mistress of the house. They do not throw that water away in their own home, believing it to have an evil potency. If they have a hostile neighbor, they would secretly pour it away on his property! The last of the four cups is diluted with water.

### 820. Are there any other culinary aspects of their Pesach celebration?

Nearly all their cakes are made from ground rice. For weeks before the festival one could hear the sound of pestle and mortar emanating from every house. It was the task of the women to grind the rice; and by the time Pesach arrived, they were generally totally exhausted, from that, as well as from having to cook and make every single item of food and drink by hand. They ground their own pepper and salt. They had large dombs of sugar, and if they required sugar lumps, they would cut off a piece; if they required ground sugar, they would grind it as required.

They made their own drinks. A special favourite was *Sharbat al Balu,* made from Morello cherries. Their juice was cooked in sugar until its consistency was like syrup. It was then mixed with water and ice. Another drink was called *Sakanjabin.* This was made with vinegar, fresh mint, and sugar. It was also mixed with water and ice to provide a most refreshing drink.

Because they could not supervize the dairies, they did not eat any dairy foods, but consumed lots of meat and fish. Even for breakfast they would eat a meat cutlet called *Ghormeh,* which was deep fried in onions and then smoked so that it was able to last for weeks. This would be eaten with boiled potatoes and eggs.

Throughout the year they had a dish called "*Shabbat* eggs," which was also eaten on festivals. For a few hours they would boil eggs in water, together with the skin of apples and oranges. The white skin of the eggs goes brown, as does the inside, and this is eaten as an accompaniment to the main course.

In every home there was a buffet table, groaning with food, which stood at the ready for the daily arrival of countless visitors. Their custom, throughout the year, was to put rosewater in many foods, so that their houses always smelt of fragrant roses.

As nothing was obtainable for Pesach in any shop, it was common practice for a family who had emigrated from Iran to Europe to send back special Pesach food parcels.

### 821. Was there any part for the children to play in the proceedings of the Seder?

Mrs. Faigenblum's answer will assuredly come as no surprise to those who have read our account of the Seder as observed in a number of other Middle Eastern countries:

Before the eggs were distributed, at the commencement of the meal, the children left the room. They returned dressed as weary travelers, saying that they had dropped in on their way from Egypt, and that they were bound for Jerusalem. Father asked them if they had eaten, and the answer was that they had partaken of nothing but unleavened bread. At that, they were formally invited to join in the festive meal ("Pesach as a Child in Iran," p. 5).

### 822. Were there any distinctive practices for when Pesach was over?

Mrs. Faigenblum tells us that they would keep the shells from the eggs eaten at the Seder, and, after the termination of Pesach, they were put into a bowl of water together with some silver coins. The contents of the bowl were then hurled into a nearby stream, to ward off the "evil eye." We have already referred to post-festival superstitions, and it is interesting to see how universal these practices are.

We will avail ourselves once again of Mrs. Faigenblum's nostalgic reminiscences on the transition from Pesach to *chametz:*

At the conclusion of Pesach the family gathered once again, this time to feast upon all the foods that they had been denied during those eight days. As the shops were open until late, we were able to buy pita, cheese, butter and milk. Dairy dishes were prepared, as well as pancakes. The first piece of bread was spread with butter and honey, and a special prayer was recited over it, wishing us all a happy and successful year ahead ("Pesach as a Child in Iran," p. 5).

## AFGHANISTANI PASSOVER PRACTICES

### 823. What do we know about the Jews of Afghanistan and their preparations of *matzot* for Pesach?

Again I have the benefit of the firsthand information of one of my congregants, Mr. David Moradoff, who lived in Herat, one of the larger cities of Afghanistan, from 1931 until 1957.

Herat was quite primitive, with no cars, telephones, or electricity in houses until the 1940s. The Jewish community had no contact, therefore, with the outside world. There were no Jewish organizations or kosher shops to provide food for Pesach, and each family had to do everything for itself. Soon after *Tu Bishvat* — that is, some two months before Pesach — every family started their preparations by buying wheat for the *matzot*. The wealthy members of the community would distribute wheat to the poor families, in accordance with their requirements.

The women would examine and clean every single grain of wheat, throwing away any that were broken or damaged. It would then be subjected to two further examinations before being declared suitable for Pesach use. It was then placed into white cloth sacks which were marked with the family name.

Two weeks later, at the beginning of the month of Adar, the community hired a millstone to grind the wheat. It was thoroughly cleaned, and soon after Purim each family brought their sack of cleaned wheat to the synagogue courtyard, and handed it over to the organizers appointed to this task. The sacks were then taken to the millstone, and each family's wheat was ground separately. The *Shomer* (supervisor) watched over the entire process, and once the milling had been completed, each family would collect their flour. From two weeks before Pesach the baking of the *matzot* commenced, at specially designated centers where, each day, a few families would join together to form a rota.

The *Mayim shelanu,* the water that was drawn the evening before the baking, and that had to remain overnight to get very cold, was placed inside a new clay jug, the top of which was covered with a piece of thin cloth. A metallic object, usually a needle, knife, or skewer, was placed upon the jug in order to keep away the evil spirits. The water was then filtered before being used to make the dough.

On the day of the baking, each family brought their flour, water, and firewood to the center. Young, fit men did the kneading, which had to be performed with great speed and care. The women helped with the rolling and shaping of the *matzot.* They were made round in shape, and were approximately 40 centimeters (15 inches) in diameter. They were baked in a new, wood-burning clay oven, and during the kneading and baking verses from *Hallel* were recited.

### 824. Were there any alternative methods of baking *matzah*?

Some families had a quite different tradition as to how their *matzot* should be prepared. On Erev Pesach they would bake them on a Saj, a big frying pan, with its convex side up, and placed over an earthen or brick oven. The dough was spread over the outside of the pan, and turned over frequently until baked. The result was a fresh, soft and tasty *matzah.* They would bake the same during *Chol Ha-Moed.*

After the establishment of the State of Israel, and the opening up of contacts with the outside world, most families received their *matzot* from Israel, America, or England. Sadly, this spelt the demise of a unique tradition of *matzah* baking.

### 825. How did they make their utensils "kasher" for Pesach?

The majority of people did not own an extra set of utensils for Pesach, and therefore had to resort to "kashering" all their vessels, which were mostly made of copper and brass.

About a week before Pesach, every Jewish quarter would engage the services of a professional Muslim tinsmith. One particular courtyard was designated for as the center for the Pesach kashering. Each family would bring him their utensils, which he would burn inside and out. He would then whiten them by plating them with a layer of pewter or tin. They were then cleaned and made ready for *Hag'alah,* the immersion into boiling water. This was also done in that same courtyard center of operations, with each utensil being immersed in the continuously boiling water, and then dipped into cold water.

### 826. What unique Seder traditions did the Jews of Afghanistan observe?

Before the washing of the hands for *karpas,* and, indeed, before each of the other ritual acts, verses from the Psalms are sung. The *Afikoman* is placed inside a small scarf and tied around the arm of the youngest child present. It was the duty of that child to ensure that none of the other children seized the *Afikoman* during the meal. This was another way of keeping the children awake and interested for the whole of the Seder.

They also dramatized the story of the Exodus, as we have noted in many other traditions. *Mah Nishtanah* was recited by the father, and the children were expected to ask him questions about the Exodus and the Seder. During the recitation of the Ten Plagues they would cover all the cups of wine with lettuce leaves, and during the recitation of *Dayyeinu* they had the custom we have already described of taking a spring onion and striking each other on the back and shoulders, at each verse, which they explain as recalling the flogging the Israelites received from their taskmasters.

The shank bone for the Seder Plate was roasted together with its adjoining meat. While the meat was eaten as part of the meal, the bone was kept in that same dining room throughout the year as a *segulah* (omen of good luck).

### 827. Did the Jews of Afghanistan have any special Seder and festival foods?

There was a special dish before the main course, reserved for all festivals, called *pishkhurd.* This consisted of some fried minced meat called *gontaveh* or *katlet;* fried mashed potato mixed with egg and shaped either round or flat, called *koku kartufi;* and fried spinach or leek mixed with egg, called *koku sabzi.* This is followed by the main course, which was fried chicken with potatoes or goulash.

For the eight days of Pesach, they relied greatly on rice dishes. Most popular were rice mixed with meat, called *pellau;* rice with meat balls, called *gondi;* and vegetable soup called *chellow.* For breakfast, fried egg on *matzah* was the norm.

### 828. What practices did they observe during the remaining days of Pesach?

*Chol Ha-Moed* was observed strictly as a holiday. No shops were open and no one went to work. Most families went on picnics during these days, eating, drinking, and generally enjoying themselves.

On the seventh night, after the evening service, they celebrated the *Seder Shevii Shel Pesach* in a manner very similar to that of the Jews of the Balkans and Syria (see questions 808 and 815). In the morning they would rise early to recite the biblical passage relating to the crossing of the Red Sea, together with selections from the commentary of the *Zohar* (central book of the mystical literature) on that theme. These would be read with intense devotion and emotion as if to recreate the actual experience and miracle of crossing the sea.

At the end of the festival they had a similar ritual to that which we have already described (see question 815), wherein the youngsters go out to the fields to cut green ears of corn, wheat, and barley. They would take these to the synagogue, and after the *Maariv* service the Rabbi would hold these in his hands to bless the congregation with the words, *Tizku leshanim rabbot un'imot*—"May you be blessed with many and sweet years!"

At home they would find a specially laid table, on which was placed a large bowl of water. Gold and silver coins were placed in it, as well as jewelery and precious stones. Next to the bowl they placed a mirror. It was believed that it was an augury of good luck to see oneself through the water in the mirror, and at the same time to touch the gold. Everyone would then bless each other with a happy and prosperous year.

After *Havdalah* and dinner, people would pay a visit to the home of their Rabbi, as well as to the homes of the elders and leading members of the community, and ² nally to the homes of their relatives, to give and receive blessings. Nearly the entire night was spent visiting, eating, and drinking.

The day after Pesach, *Isru Chag,* was also an important day – a time to bid farewell to the festival. Again, no one went to work, but spent the day eating, drinking and socializing within their family groups.

## SUDANI PASSOVER PRACTICES

829. What do we know about the Jews of Sudan and their preparations for Pesach?

Again, I have the benefit of a friend and member of my synagogue, Mrs. Ruth Synett, for ² rsthand family information regarding the Jews of that region (interview, December 1994).

The Jews of the Sudan hailed mainly from Iraq, Syria, and Egypt, and only came there at the turn of the century. By World War I there were about one hundred families living there.

There was only one synagogue, in Khartoum, and the community was closely knit, though not particularly observant. Kosher meat was available at the meat market, but the *shochet* would have to make a special visit to one's home to slaughter chickens.

The staple diet during Pesach was, and still is, rice, which is usually served with every meal. No kosher foods were obtainable locally, so they had to do without butter, jams and cheeses. Everything had to be made at home using fresh ingredients, and only *matzah* was imported, generally from Egypt or England. Hence Pesach was a busy and di⊬cult, though joyous, time, and the housewife needed to be very imaginative if she wanted to provide any degree of culinary variety.

A popular dish for Pesach is *minena,* a sort of meat lasagne, containing layers of *matzah* dipped in a strong beef stock with minced beef.

## 830. Did the Jews of the Sudan have any distinctive Seder practices?

Their customs were principally those of the countries from which they hailed, and their Seder did not di⁴ er greatly from the Ashkenazi Seder.

They used vinegar for the dipping, instead of saltwater. They used celery for *Karpas* and lettuce for *maror.* The *charoset* was made from dates stewed in *Kiddush* wine, with ground almonds and chopped walnuts, and it was eaten, as a sweet desert, throughout the week of Pesach.

The *Afikoman* was placed in a bag, which was passed around the table. Each person would place it, in turn, upon his or her shoulders to remind themselves of how their ancestors left Egypt. The rest would address the same question, in Arabic, each time to the person holding the *Afikoman:* "Where are you coming from?" On receiving the answer, "From Mitzrayim," the follow-up question would be asked, "And where are you going?" The person would reply, "To Yerushalayim!"

One practice we have noted previously: the wine from the Ten Plagues is regarded as bad luck. It would be poured into a bowl, taken into the street, and thrown away.

Before the meal is served each guest will eat a hard-boiled egg. This is traditionally followed by a piece of roast lamb. When the *Afikoman* is distributed, half is eaten and the other half kept for the entire year as a token of good luck.

## YEMENITE PASSOVER PRACTICES

### 831. Do we have any traditions regarding the way the Jews of Yemen prepared their *matzot*?

They had a special method of softening the wheat before milling it, utilizing a special plant called *chermal* which, to be effective, had to be cut at noon on a clear day. They would spread the wheat in between two layers of those *chermal* leaves, and leave until the required consistency was achieved. This method can supposedly be traced back to Palestinian practice in talmudic times, since there is a reference in the Palestinian Talmud (*Yerushalmi, Pesachim* 3:1) to two alternative methods of softening the wheat: either utilizing a special plant or leaving it in a moist atmosphere. The former method is permitted; the latter method is not.

In Yemen it was the custom that teams of three women would work together in the making of *matzah,* in conformity with the tradition in talmudic times, when one woman would knead the dough, one would mold it into the required shape, and the third would bake it (see Mishnah *Pesachim* 3:4).

They had a special name for the *mayim shelanu* (see question 131), namely, *meshumar,* "supervised." Before the kneading of the dough the women would make a special declaration: "Whatever [water] is inadvertently spilt, and whatever [dough] is inadvertently scattered around, should be regarded as the dust of the earth." This unique formula is, of course, based on the wording of the *Kol chamirah* (see questions 149, 151).

### 832. Do we know of any distinct Seder practices of Yemenite Jewry?

As we have observed among some other communities, their *charoset* was not made exclusively for use at the Seder, but was prepared in large quantities for eating throughout Pesach. Its ingredients were: pomegranates, apples, dates, almonds, raisins, walnuts, ginger, wine, and sesame seeds that had been roasted and seasoned with cinnamon. They called the *charoset* by the name *dukeh,* which is the original name as used by the Jews Palestine some two thousand years ago, as preserved in the Palestinian Talmud (*Talmud Yerushalmi, Pesachim* 10:3).

It is their custom to decorate the Seder table with all kinds of vegetables, probably to commemorate the season of *Aviv* (Spring). They do not use a Seder plate, but arrange the specific Seder vegetables in a circle in the center of the table, and the food to be eaten as their meal is set in front of each person's place. All the dippings are made exclusively into *charoset.*

## INDIAN PASSOVER PRACTICES

### 833. What do we know about Indian Jewry?

Between the thirteenth and the eighteenth centuries, Jews settled in Cochin from various places, including Egypt, Syria, Turkey, Iraq and Iran, Palestine, and Spain. Most emigrated to Israel in the 1950s.

Of more recent vintage are the Baghdadi Jews who came from Middle Eastern countries of the Ottoman empire, settling in Bombay and Calcutta. They were joined by Jewish refugees from Central Europe, fleeing Nazi persecution in the 1930s.

### 834. What was Pesach like for the Jews of the Raj?

To answer this question, I can do no better than quote from a firsthand, authoritative source, namely, Mrs. Mavis Hyman, who, in a private correspondence (November 28, 1994), observes:

Pesach was a festival associated with relative deprivation so far as food was concerned. We did not use oil, tea or sugar, because of the uncertainty of being contaminated with *chametz*. Instead, we relied on chicken fat as a cooking medium, drank coffee, and sweetened our food with *Halek* (see below). Spices were not used because the seeds and powder could not be supervised, but there appeared to be no objection to using roots, such as tumeric and ginger, which were dried, pounded and stored for the festival. We bought rock salt, which was also ground at home. There were no cakes, confectionery or sweets, and we offered our guests roasted almonds and nuts.

We also celebrated *Santak Khadra* night, just after Pesach goes out. It is the Arabic for "Green Year," and symbolizes fertility and fruitfulness. We would tap each and every member of the family with soft branches, wishing them success in whatever their interests happened to be.

The community would bake its *matzot* communally, in makeshift kitchens in the compounds of the synagogues. These would be collected and stored in large baskets, lined with cloth, and suspended from the ceilings of houses in order to be protected from vermin (see Mavis Hyman, *Indian–Jewish Cooking,* London: Hyman Publishers, 1992, pp. 179–181).

The Baghdadian Jews of Bombay maintained the practices and traditions of their country of origin, the *Minhag Bavel*. In a private correspondence, Mr. Percy Gourgey, M.B.E., writes (December 18, 1994) that it was their custom to eat a kind of pancake, called in Hindustani, *chawal-ka-roti*, a mixture of rice flour and coconut milk. They also ate *Halek;* and, in the absence of sugar, consumed a great deal of marzipan, which they referred to by its Judeo-Arabic name, *moussafan*.

Mr. Gourgey writes:

Paragraphs of the Haggadah are read in Hebrew and then translated into Judeo-Arabic. A Seder custom which we, as young children, enjoyed was to leave the house with a bag of *matzot* on our backs, knock on the door, and, on being invited to enter, asked, in Arabic, *"Mein jeet* [Where are you coming from]?" We made answer: *"Mi-Mitzrayim* [From Egypt]." We were then asked, *"Wein catruh* [Where are you going to]?" to which we would reply, *"Li-Yerushalayim* [To Jerusalem]." The next question put to us was, *"O-ven izhak lidmun* [What is your purpose]?" to which we would reply: *"Mah Nishtanah ha-laylah ha-zeh. . . ."*

### 835.  What is *Halek?*

*Halek* is the dual-purpose *charoset* which served Indian Jewry not only for the Seder ritual but also as a general sweetener in the absence of sugar.

I am grateful to Mavis Hyman for allowing me to quote this description of its preparation from her excellent book, *Indian–Jewish Cooking* (pp. 185–186):

> *Halek* is cooked date juice. It is a delicious preparation, and, although it does take time and effort to make it, some people do so on a commercial basis, while others prefer to make it themselves.
>
> Soak 12 lbs. of stoned dates in a large container, with just enough water to cover them, for 36 hours. The softened dates should be broken up in a food processor in cupfuls at a time, and left to stand overnight.
>
> Place the softened dates in a stout linen bag, a little at a time, and squeeze them dry. Alternately, a small manual press may be used—such as that used for home-made wines. Even with the aid of a press, it could take a few hours to complete this stage of the preparation.
>
> Use a large container or preserving pan to cook the juice, to which a cup of cold water should be added. Begin cooking over a high flame until it comes to the boil, and then lower to moderate heat. From time to time it will be necessary to remove the froth from the surface and stir the liquid. Keep the date juice on the boil for about five hours, or until the consistency is of a heavy syrup. At this stage the froth may become tinged with an orange hue.
>
> Cool and leave to stand overnight, and then decant into cold bottles. This quantity should fill between 4 and 4½ wine bottles.
>
> Many people find it convenient to make *Halek* during Passover and generally keep in store for the following year. It has an indefinite shelf life if it is airtight and stored in a cool place. Ground walnuts or almonds are added to the individual portions of the date syrup to complete the *charoset.*

## SPANISH AND PORTUGUESE PASSOVER PRACTICES

### 836.  Do Spanish and Portuguese Jews celebrate a Siyyum on the Fast of the Firstborn?

The Spanish and Portuguese Jews who found their way to Amsterdam after 1492 did not observe the custom of having their firstborn participate in a *Siyyum* on the morning of Erev Pesach in order to free themselves of the obligation of fasting.

Instead, they observed the day as a full-blown fast, with a special service for the firstborn, at which they read the prescribed fast-day Torah portion of *Va-yechal*.

My friend, Rabbi Dr. Abraham Levy, Senior Rabbi of the Sephardi communities of Great Britain, tells me that in Syria the community would arrange (and pay for) the celebration of the marriage of a poor boy and girl to take place on that day of the Fast of the Firstborn, so that it became transformed into a communal *Seudat Mitzvah* (religious festivity), thereby enabling everyone to eat and drink in order to make the couple rejoice.

### 837. Do the Spanish and Portuguese Jews have any unique pre-Seder practices?

They recite the complete *Hallel* at the conclusion of the evening service in synagogue on the two first nights of Pesach, and recite over it the blessing, *Ligmor et Ha-Hallel*, "to complete the *Hallel*." This explains why it is unnecessary to repeat the blessing over the *Hallel* recited within the Haggadah. The Ashkenazim, who do not recite it in synagogue, explain the absence of the blessing somewhat differently (see questions 384, 502).

In many communities they follow the talmudic practice of distributing almonds and other goodies to the children before the Seder, in an attempt to keep them awake so that they will ask questions.

The Sephardi authorities of England recommend to their communities that the Seder leader should take a bundle of *matzot* in a bag on his shoulders before the commencement of the Seder, and walk up and down with it, in recollection of the biblical verse.

### 838. Do they have any practices relating to the *Afikoman*?

It is not the original tradition, as practised by the Spanish Jews of Holland, to hide the *Afikoman* for the children to find, although Dobrinsky reports (*Treasury of Sephardic Laws and Customs*, p. 283) that more and more Spanish and Portuguese Jews have adopted that custom in recent years, probably from their Ashkenazi neighbors.

Some Gibraltarian Sephardim retain the custom of tying the *Afikoman* around their neck, in commemoration of the Israelites of the Exodus who went out, "with their kneading-troughs bound up within their garments upon their shoulders" (Exodus 12:34).

### 839. Do they have any distinctive way of pouring out the wine for the Ten Plagues?

It is not their custom to dip their fingers into the wine at each plague and drip it onto a plate, as do the Ashkenazim, but rather to pour out a drop of wine from their goblet at the mention of each plague. It is also their custom to pour out a drop of water simultaneously with the wine. According to Dayan P. Toledano, this practice has its roots in the Kabbalah, which tells us that, "When the merciful God punishes a nation, He mingles His quality of justice with that of mercy. And so, to the present day, most

Sephardim mix wine with water to show that the punishment of the Egyptians was mingled with mercy" (Dayan P. Toledano, "The Halakhot of Pesach," *Spanish and Portuguese Synagogue Bulletin,* March 1992, 8).

### 840. What do the Sephardim use for *maror*?

While Ashkenazim have a preference for horseradish, the Spanish and Portuguese custom is to use only lettuce. This was the preferred choice of the kabbalists, and was based upon their particular interpretation of the mishnaic words for lettuce, *chasa* and *chazeret.* They point out that the former is suggestive of God's "mercy" (*chas*), and the latter denotes "returning" (*chazar*), suggestive of our hopes for a return to our land. In Spain they used artichokes, as is apparent from the illustration in *The Sarajevo Haggadah,* text and introduction by Cecil Roth (facsimile edition; Bergrad, 1970).

Rabbi Levy reports that the Gibraltarians grind some brick dust into the *maror,* to recall the bricks made by the hapless Israelites.

### 841. Do they have any special practices associated with the eating of *maror*?

Some English Sephardim preserve the practice we have referred to earlier (see question 812) of throwing a small portion of *maror* on the floor, "signifying that the bitterness should depart from them" (Toledano, "The Halakhot of Pesach").

Those who are well-versed in Jewish superstitious practices, however, might well view this particular practice as an attempt to feed bitterness to the demons (in which people universally believed), and who, they feared, might be tempted, in their jealousy of human celebration on this evening, to do some harm to those present.

Many superstitious practices are rooted in such attempts to deflect the assaults of demons; and it is in consonance with the various methods employed of dealing with such malevolent spirits that they should share with them their bitter food in order to convince them that they have no reason to be jealous since it is not a celebration, but rather a bitter commemoration, that is taking place.

### 842. Do they recite the songs at the end of the Haggadah?

Again, those are not native to the Spanish and Portuguese tradition which concludes the Haggadah with *Nirtzah,* that is, with the recitation of *Chasal siddur Pesach* and *Leshanah ha-ba'ah biYerushalayim.* Once again, Ashkenazi influence has penetrated the bastion of Sephardic tradition, with many families finding that those concluding songs bring the Seder to a more joyful climax.

## HASIDIC PASSOVER PRACTICES

### 843. Does the hasidic movement have any special customs as regards the baking of *matzot*?

*Hasidim* only eat hand-baked *Matzah Shemurah* for the duration of the festival. In many hasidic dynasties the baking is a festive event, for which they dress up in their

Sabbath attire. This includes the drawing of *mayim shelanu*, the water that has to stand overnight. The Late Rebbe of Lubavitch would draw this water in a small ceremony in the presence of his intimates.

The baking is accompanied by the recitation of the phrase, *Leshem mitzvat matzah* ("This baking is for the sake of fulfilling the *mitzvah* of eating *matzah*"), and some *hasidim* would also sing *Hallel* while baking, in commemoration of the *Hallel* sung, in Temple times, to the accompaniment of the slaughtering and the preparation of the Paschal Lamb. For that reason, some are particular to delay the baking until the afternoon of Erev Pesach, the time when the Paschal Lamb was prepared.

It was the practice of the late Lubavitcher Rebbe that, after *Minchah* on the afternoon of Erev Pesach, he would stand outside his home and distribute pieces of *Matzah Shemurah* to all by-passers, and wish them a *Chag Kasher vesame'ach*.

### 844. Do *hasidim* have any special customs with regard to the preparation of the Seder table?

The table is adorned with the most beautiful silver and gold vessels the family possess, to fulfill the recommendation of *hiddur mitzvah*, performing a religious duty in as beautiful a way as possible, but also to commemorate the fulfillment of the divine promise that, "after that they shall go out with many possessions" (Genesis 15:14). In some hasidic communities they also place a bowl of live fish on the table, to recall the crossing of the Red Sea.

The arrangement of the Seder plate follows that of the *Ari,* with the ten items symbolizing the ten *Sefirot* (see on question 203).

### 845. Is there any difference in the order of the questions of the Mah Nishtanah?

The Haggadah as used by *Chabad hasidim* (see Rabbi M. M. Schneersohn, *Haggadah Shel Pesach im Likutei Taamim, Minhagim Ubiurim,* New York: Kehot Publication Society, 1976, p. 13) interchanges the first two questions, so that its first blessing refers to dipping, and its second to the eating of *chametz* and *matzah*. This interchange is found in many, nonhasidic traditions, and is based upon the version found in the Mishnah version of the Palestinian Talmud, and followed by the Rif, Rosh, Rambam, Tur, and many other early authorities.

### 846. Do *Chabad hasidim* read any particular significance into the opening of the doors for Shefokh chamatekha?

Based upon the midrashic statement (Midrash *Shemot Rabbah* 30:9) that God only demands of Israel what He Himself does, *Chabad* believes that if Israel is commanded to open their doors at this time, then God must also do likewise on the night of Pesach, and He must therefore open all the doors and gates of mercy to all Israel. Thus, anyone, irrespective of his actions throughout the past year, can leap to the highest spiritual rung, aided by the force of the word Pesach, which means to "leap over" (all the intermediary rungs) (Rabbi M. M. Schneersohn, *Likkutei Sichot,* vol. 4 [New York: Kehot Publication Society, 1962], p. 1298).

### 847.  What are the main differences between the Ashkenazi Haggadah and that used by the *hasidim*?

The *hasidim* do not recite any of the poems and songs that are found in our Ashkenazi Haggadah. The *Chabad hasidim* do not recite *Chasal Siddur Pesach* ("Completed is the order of Passover") because, in the words of the *Alter* (Lubavitcher) *Rebbe*, "For *Chabad*, Pesach never has an ending. It [the redemption] is an on-going process" (see *Haggadah Shel Pesach*, p. 50).

### 848.  Are there any unique Seder customs practiced by *hasidim*?

*Hasidim* have the custom of translating the *Mah Nishtanah* into Yiddish. When some wine is poured out at the recitation of the words, *Dam Va-eish Vetimrot ashan,* the *Chabad* Haggadah prescribes that the wine be poured out into a broken cup. This conforms to Kabbalistic theory, with the cup of wine and the wine itself representing the higher grades of the *Sefirot,* and the broken cup representing the *Kelipot* ("shells"), or impure residue, of the physical world. It is also their custom to top up the cup with more wine after pouring out the wine for the Ten Plagues.

They generally follow the view of the Vilna Gaon, as opposed to that of the *Shulchan Arukh* (*Orach Chayyim* 475:6), that there is a positive biblical *mitzvah* to eat *matzah* not only on the first (and second) night, but also during the rest of Pesach. Some *hasidim* (not *Chabad*) even recite the blessing, *Al akhilat matzah,* after *Ha-Motziy,* although this is fiercely condemned by many authorities as a *berakhah levatalah* (a blessing in vain) as well as constituting an unacceptable interruption between the *Ha-Motziy* and the eating of the bread.

### 849.  Are there any special stringencies or precautions observed by *Chabad hasidim* over Pesach?

In their great zeal to avoid eating anything that they themselves have not personally supervised, most *Chabad hasidim* will not buy anything mass produced for Pesach. Wine, produced under their own movement's supervision, is the exception. Hence, they cook all their own food, and do not eat supervised sweets or chocolates. An exception is made by some families in the case of children.

They are scrupulous to avoid any remote possibility of contact with the minutest trace of leaven. Hence, all *matzah* is eaten out of bags, so that no moisture or liquid might come into contact with it. Some are so particular that if an item of crockery or cutlery falls to the floor, they will put it aside and not use it until after Pesach. They are also particular to clear away immediately any *matzah* crumbs that may have fallen onto the table, for fear of liquid spilling onto the crumbs and creating *chametz*. All sugar, tea, and coffee are boiled in advance of Pesach, to totally remove even the minutest trace of grain.

An extra stringency observed by *hasidim* is the prohibition of eating, throughout Pesach, *matzah sheruyah, matzah* immersed in water or fruit juice. An exception is made, however, on the final (Diaspora) day of *Yom Tov.*

Although the *Shulchan Arukh* permits it (see *Orach Chayyim* 461:4), the *Chabad hasidim* attribute this stringency to the founder of their sect, Rabbi Shneor Zalman of Liadi (1747–1812). The stringency has been shown, however, to be centuries older, and reflects the practice of individual pietists, such as Rabbi Eliezer bar Nathan (*Raavan*), who lived in the twelfth century (see Daniel Sperber, *Minhagei Yisrael* 2:143–146).

### 850. On the last day of Pesach, *Chabad hasidim* celebrate the *Seudat Moshi'ach*. What is its significance and how is it celebrated?

It is related that the Baal Shem Tov, the seventeenth-century miracle-working founder of the hasidic movement, would eat three meals on the last day of Pesach, and the final meal, taken towards evening, was called *Seudat Moshi'ach,* "The Meal of the Messiah," because of his belief that at that point in the festival, the messianic illumination was at its brightest.

This concept was derived from the idea that, at the Exodus, not only was the present redemption activated, but there was also released the energy for the future messianic redemption. Hence, each year, at this particular time, when the Egyptian redemption reached its climax, so is that source of messianic energy and light released and transmitted in its most potent form (see *Likkutei Sichot,* vol. 7 [New York: Kehot Publication Society, 1975, p. 272]).

Some *hasidim* refer to this meal by the name *Seudat Ha-Baal Shem Tov* because he revealed its special messianic significance.

### 851. How is this celebration observed?

The late Lubavitcher Rebbe would hand to members of his close circle four cups of wine, or other drink, announcing, *Dos is Seudat Moshi'ach.* His followers would then follow by pouring out four cups. These constitute a toast to the future (messianic) redemption, and the four cups of comfort that, according to the Midrash (*Bereishit Rabbah* 88:5), God will give Israel to drink when He gives the cup of retribution to her enemies. The drinking of these four cups by the *hasidim* is meant to arouse within God the urge to bring about the redemption and to hand Israel her cups of salvation.

May that salvation, and the blessing of everlasting peace to our people and our land, be achieved speedily in our days.

# XXII

# Seder Quiz Questions and Activities for the Younger Generations

## ESPECIALLY FOR YOUNGER CHILDREN

*How the Israelites Came to Live in Egypt*

**852. Who was sold into Egypt by his brothers?**

Joseph.

**853. Why did they sell him?**

Because they were jealous of him and hated him.

**854. What was the name of their father?**

Jacob.

**855. What country did Joseph and his brothers grow up in?**

Canaan.

**856. What new name was this country called by, when, much later, the Jewish people made it a land of their own?**

Israel.

**857. What happened to Joseph when he was first sold into Egypt?**

He was put in charge of the large household of Potiphar, one of the King of Egypt's most important ministers, and his master was very pleased with his work.

**858. What terrible thing then happened to Joseph?**

He was thrown into prison?

**859. What had he done to deserve that?**

Nothing at all. His master's wife wanted Joseph to run away with her and marry her. When Joseph refused to do such a terrible thing, the wicked lady made up a lie and told her husband that Joseph was trying to take her away from him. Her husband was, naturally, very annoyed, and he threw Joseph into jail.

**860. Whom did Joseph meet in jail?**

The king's butler and baker.

**861. How did Joseph help them both?**

He interpreted the dreams that they kept dreaming, and that were troubling them a great deal.

**862. Which one of them did Joseph say would be given back his job as Pharaoh's minister, and which one did he say would be put to death?**

Joseph correctly said that the butler would be given back his job and that the baker would be hanged.

**863. What favor did Joseph ask the butler?**

To speak up for him to Pharaoh and to tell the king that he was wrongly put in jail, since he had never done anything wrong.

**864. Did the butler immediately tell Pharaoh about Joseph?**

No. He forgot all about him for two whole years.

**865. What reminded the butler about his promise to Joseph?**

King Pharaoh was himself troubled by dreams, which no one could explain. It was then that he remembered the young man to whom God had given the amazing ability of explaining the meaning of all dreams.

**866. What was Pharaoh's first dream about?**

He dreamt that there were seven fat cows and seven thin cows, and that the seven thin cows gobbled up the fat cows, and yet no one could even notice that they had put on any weight at all.

**867. What was Pharaoh's second dream about?**

He dreamt that there were seven thick ears of corn and seven thin ears of corn, and that the seven thin ears of corn gobbled up the fat ears, and yet there was no change in their appearance.

### 868. How did Joseph explain these dreams?

He told the king that the dreams were to let him know that there would be seven years of "fatness," when there would be wonderful harvests and lots of food in Egypt, after which there would be seven "thin" years, when there would be no rain and nothing would grow, and the people of Egypt would be starving for food.

### 869. What did Joseph tell the king to do in order to save everybody from dying for lack of food during the seven thin years?

He told him to build big cities, which would not have any houses in them, only vast, covered places for storing corn and barley. He told Pharaoh that during the seven "fat" years, when the fields of Egypt produced much more food than the people needed, they should store as much as possible, ready for use during the seven "thin" years when nothing grew. He told the king to appoint a man who could be trusted to organize all that and to make sure that the food was given out properly to all the citizens during the "thin" years, so that no one would take more than he needed and no one would go without.

### 870. Whom did Pharaoh decide to appoint?

Joseph.

### 871. Why did Joseph's brothers decide to come down to Egypt?

Because there was no food in Canaan, and they had heard that Egypt had stored up plenty of corn during the previous seven "fat" years. They came down, therefore, in order to buy corn for their family.

### 872. When his brothers saw Joseph, standing there in charge of the selling of corn to people who had come from other countries, did they immediately recognize him?

No, they did not. When they had sold him, twenty-two years before, he had been only seventeen years old. Now he was a man, with a beard. When they were children together he used to dress in the many-colored coat that his father had made for him. Now he was dressed in a rich royal robe, made by the king's own tailor. They could never have guessed that the man in charge there was their own brother, Joseph. Nor would they ever have dreamt that he could have become such a great man, after having been sold a slave.

### 873. Did Joseph immediately throw his arms around them, kiss them and tell them that he was their long-lost brother?

No, he did not. He preferred to find out first whether they were truly sorry for their great sin in having sold him as a slave to Egypt.

### 874. How did Joseph test his brothers?

At first he spoke harshly to them, and told them that he believed they were spies who had entered Egypt in order to learn secrets about it for an enemy country. They denied it, telling him that they were simply all members of a family, with one other younger brother, Benjamin, still remaining back home, looking after their old father.

### 875. What did Joseph then demand?

That, to prove that they were telling the truth, they go back and bring Benjamin down to Egypt.

### 876. What did Joseph do to ensure that they had to come back again to Egypt and bring Benjamin with them?

He took Shimon and imprisoned him, offering to release him only when they returned with their youngest brother.

### 877. What did they discover, to their horror, when they opened their sacks on the journey home?

That the money they had paid for their corn had been put back, without their knowing, into their sacks. They were scared that they would be falsely charged with having stolen back their money when no one was looking.

### 878. When they came back to Egypt with Benjamin, what bitter trick did Joseph play on them?

They obviously needed to stock up with more corn. After selling it to them, Joseph secretly commanded his servant to hide his own silver cup in the sack of Benjamin. When they had gone a little way on their journey home, he sent his men after them to bring them back. When Joseph told them that one of them had stolen his cup, they all said that no son of Jacob would ever do such a terrible thing. They were so sure about that, that they suggested that if it was, indeed, discovered with any one of them, then that person should die and the rest would readily remain in Egypt as slaves to Joseph. Imagine their horror when the cup was "discovered" in Benjamin's sack.

Joseph became convinced that his brothers were sorry for what they had done to him when he overheard them saying that all this evil had come upon them as a punishment for having ignored their brother Joseph's cries, all those years before, when they threw him into a pit and then sold him. He then realized how the brothers had changed for the better.

### 879. When Joseph finally told them who he was and they all made friends again, what did he ask them to do as soon as possible?

To return home, tell their father about his greatness in Egypt, and ask him and all the family to return to live in Egypt for the rest of their lives. He promised to look after them, so that they would never again be short of food, and life would be good for them as members of the family of the one who was second-in-charge after Pharaoh.

### 880. Did Jacob agree to that plan?

He did. He and all his sons, and their wives and the grandchildren—seventy people in all—went down to Egypt to begin a new life. There they grew into a great people, with the result that the Egyptians became worried about their strength, thinking that they might one day take over the land. It was for that reason that they started to enslave the Israelites. It is at this point that the story of our festival of Pesach commences.

## The Festival

### 881. What season does Pesach fall in?

Spring.

### 882. What do we begin doing at home a long time before Pesach?

Cleaning it to make it ready for the festival.

### 883. What do we call the foods that we must not have, eat, or see on Pesach?

*Chametz.*

### 884. What do we do on the night before Pesach to make sure that we have no *chametz* in our home?

We search the home from room to room.

### 885. How many pieces of bread do we put out in all our rooms before starting the search?

Ten.

### 886. Why do we put out pieces of bread?

Because we recite a blessing that speaks of our being commanded "concerning the removal of *chametz,*" we want to ensure that it is not recited unnecessarily. By putting out the bread, we ensure that there is indeed some *chametz* to remove.

### 887. During our search for *chametz,* what do we hold in our hands?

A candle and a feather.

**888. In the morning of Pesach, what do we do with any last pieces of *chametz*, that we have to remove?**

We burn them.

**889. How many Seder nights do we have?**

Two, but only one in Israel.

**890. What should children do in the afternoon before Seder night so that they will be able to stay up late?**

Take a nap.

**891. What did the king, Pharaoh, do to the newborn boys?**

Drown them in the river.

**892. What did he do to the baby girls?**

Allowed them to stay alive.

**893. Who did God choose to be the leader of the Jewish people?**

Moses.

**894. When Moses was hidden from the King's soldiers, where was he kept?**

In a basket, which was placed by the rushes along the River Nile.

**895. Who watched over Moses?**

His sister, Miriam.

**896. Why did God punish the Egyptians?**

Because they did not let the Jewish people leave Egypt.

**897. How many plagues did God punish the people of Egypt with?**

Ten.

**898. Who went with Moses each time to warn Pharaoh that a new plague would be sent if he didn't let the Israelites go?**

Aaron.

**899. What happened to the waters of Egypt?**

They turned into blood.

**900. What do we call the special book that we read on Seder night?**

A Haggadah.

**901. Before dinner on Seder night, various foods are dipped and eaten. What are these foods at our table placed on?**

A special Seder plate.

**902. What is the prayer that is said over wine on *Shabbat* and *Yom Tov*?**

*Kiddush.*

**903. How many cups of wine do we drink on Seder night?**

Four cups.

**904. What do we do while we eat on Seder night?**

Lean.

**905. What do we eat on Pesach instead of bread?**

*Matzah.*

**906. What is *matzah*?**

A cracker made from dough that has not baked long enough to rise.

**907. How many pieces of *matzah* do we have with our Seder plate?**

Three pieces.

**908. What unusual thing is done with half of one of the *matzot*?**

It gets hidden.

**909. Who finds the hidden *matzah*?**

The children.

**910. What does the saltwater remind us of?**

Tears of sadness.

**911. How many questions do we ask in *"Mah Nishtanah"*?**

Four questions.

**912. How many Seder nights do people in Israel have?**

Only one.

## QUESTIONS FOR OLDER JUNIORS

**913. What do we celebrate on Pesach?**

We celebrate the fact that God "passed over" the Israelite homes and freed us from Egypt.

**914. What is the Hebrew date of Pesach?**

The fifteenth of Nisan.

**915. For how many days does Pesach last?**

Eight days (only seven in Israel).

**916. Before Pesach we buy lots of food. What do we look for on the label of every packet or tin of food?**

The words "Kasher for Passover."

**917. What do some firstborn people do the day before Passover?**

Fast.

**918. Pharaoh, the wicked king of Egypt, disliked the Jews. What particular harsh task did he make them do?**

He treated them as slaves and made them build store-cities for his kingdom. (Later, he drowned all the newborn baby boys.)

**919. Who was the sister of Moses?**

Miriam.

**920. Who was the brother of Moses?**

Aaron.

**921. Who saved baby Moses from the river?**

The daughter of King Pharaoh.

**922. Who said to whom, "Let my people go"?**

Moses and Aaron to Pharaoh.

**923. When God asked Moses to go to Pharaoh and plead with him to let the Jewish people out of Egypt, Moses at first refused. What was his excuse?**

That he could not speak very clearly.

**924. Try to name as many of the Ten Plagues as you can.**

Blood, frogs, lice, wild animals, animal disease, boils, hail, locusts, darkness, death of the firstborn.

**925. What do we do at the Seder table while we recite the names of the Ten Plagues?**

We spill out a little wine from our glasses.

**926. What did God do to save the Jewish people at the Red Sea?**

He split it to allow the Jews to cross, but when the Egyptian army entered, he closed it up again and drowned them all.

**927. When the Jewish people left Egypt, how many years did they spend in the desert?**

Forty years.

**928. What is the Hebrew date when *Bedikat Chametz,* the Searching for *Chametz,* is performed?**

The night of the fourteenth of Nissan.

**929. Until what time in the morning, on the day before Pesach, may we still eat *chametz*?**

About 10 A.M.

**930. What is often referred to as "Poor man's bread"?**

*Matzah.*

**931. Why do we eat *matzah* on Pesach?**

There are two reasons for this: (1) this is the bread they ate in Egypt and (2) the Jewish people left Egypt in such a hurry that their bread didn't have enough time to rise, so they ate *matzah* instead.

**932. On which side do we lean at the Seder table?**

The left.

**933. Some leaders of the Seder wear a "kittel." What is this?**

A white gown.

**934. When else do we wear a "kittel"?**

On Rosh Hashanah and Yom Kippur, and on the first day of Pesach (for reciting the *Tal* prayer of dew) and on *Sheminiy Atzeret* (for reciting the *Geshem* prayer for rain).

**935. How many sons do we speak of in the Haggadah?**

Four sons.

**936. What do children look for after the Seder meal?** *(Give its proper name.)*

The *Afikoman*.

**937. Whom do we welcome to our Seder table during the course of the evening?**

Elijah the prophet.

**938. Complete the sentence: "Pesach is described in our siddur as *Zeman* _____."**

*Cheiruteinu.*

**939. How do we show Elijah that he is welcome?**

By filling a special cup of wine in his honor.

**940. What do we start doing from the second night of Pesach until Shavuot?**

Counting the *Omer.*

**941. How many weeks are there of the *Omer*?**

Seven.

## QUESTIONS FOR YOUNG ADULTS

**942. What do we call the *Shabbat* before Pesach?**

*Shabbat Hagadol.*

**943. What was the "Pesach"?**

A lamb that was sacrificed and eaten.

**944. What does the Hebrew word *Pesach* mean?**

Pass over.

**945. Who passed over what? And when did that happen?**

God passed over the Jewish homes during the final plague, when he killed the Egyptian firstborn.

**946. To be protected from the final plague, the Jewish people were required to do something in return. What were they required to do?**

Sprinkle blood on the doorposts of their homes and stay inside.

**947. What date was the lamb sacrificed?**

The 14th of Nisan.

**948. A Jew must not own any *chametz* during the whole of Pesach. What does one do with the *chametz* one cannot eat or remove before Pesach?**

One sells it to a gentile. Most Rabbis will sell the *chametz* on one's behalf.

**949. What was the name of the place in Egypt where the Jews lived?**

Goshen.

**950. Who were the mother and father of Moses?**

Yocheved and Amram.

**951. Moses was living like a prince in the comfort of the palace. Why did he run away to Midian?**

He killed an Egyptian whom he saw beating a Jew.

**952. How did God appear to Moses for the very first time?**

God appeared to Moses in a Burning Bush.

**953. On our Seder plate we have *maror*. What is this and why do we eat it?**

*Maror* are the bitter herbs, usually horseradish or an alternative bitter vegetable. We taste this bitterness to remind ourselves of the suffering of our forefathers.

**954. What is *charoset*? Why do we eat it and what is it made from?**

It is a brown mixture that resembles the cement that our forefathers used for building cities for the wicked Pharaoh. It is made from apples, almonds, wine and cinnamon.

**955. Why do we have a shank bone on the Seder plate?**

To remind us of the *Pesach* offering, the Paschal lamb.

**956. Name four things that are connected with the Seder and that come in units of four.**

Four questions, four sons, four cups of wine, four specimen foods (*matzah, maror, charoset, and karpas*).

**957. What are the four "Mah Nishtanah" questions about?**

(1) Eating *matzah* instead of bread; (2) eating bitter herbs; (3) dipping vegetables twice; (4) leaning at the table.

**958. In which town were the five Sages celebrating the Seder?**

Bnei Berak.

**959. How many of the five Sages can you name?**

Rabbis Eliezer, Joshua, Eleazar ben Azariah, Akivah, and Tarfon.

**960. There are a number of reasons why we have three *matzot* at the Seder table. How many do you know?**

To represent the three categories of Jews who all left Egypt: Kohen, Levi, and Yisrael. Another reason is to represent our three forefathers, Abraham, Isaac, and Jacob. Finally, because we require two for the usual two *challot* we eat every *Shabbat* and *Yom Tov*, and a third for the special *mitzvah* of bread of affliction and *Afikoman*.

### 961. What is *"Matzah Shmurah"*?

Special hand-baked *matzah* that has been watched at every stage of the process of preparation.

### 962. Who are the Four Sons?

The wise son, wicked son, the simple son, and the son who cannot ask.

### 963. When we recite the Ten Plagues during the Seder, we spill out a little wine from our glasses. Why?

Out of sadness that God had to punish the Egyptians. We don't rejoice over our enemy's downfall.

### 964. Pesach is one of the *Shalosh Regalim* when the Israelites were commanded to walk up to Jerusalem. What are the other two of the *Shalosh Regalim*?

Shavuot and Sukkot.

### 965. What do we call the intermediate days of Pesach and Sukkot?

*Chol Ha-Moed.*

### 966. Instead of baking with flour over Pesach, what do we use?

*Matzah* meal.

### 967. What may we not do during the *Omer* period?

Celebrate weddings, have a haircut, or listen to music.

### 968. Which modern-day festivals occur during the *Omer*?

*Yom Ha-Atzmaut* (Israel's Independence Day) and *Yom Yerushalayim* (Day of the Reunification of Jerusalem).

### 969. What day of the *Omer* is *Lag Ba'Omer*?

The thirty-third day.

### 970. What was the name of the great Rabbi whose pupils were killed between Pesach and Shavuot?

Rabbi Akivah.

**971. What are the theories as to how the pupils of Rabbi Akivah were killed?**

(1) In a horrific plague, (2) in battle, helping Bar Kochba with his revolt against Rome.

## IS IT TRUE THAT . . . ?
**(Watch out for any deliberate mistakes.)**

**972. . . . Moses' wife, Yocheved, bore three children to him?**

No. His wife's name was Tzipporah.

**973. . . . from Moses' tribe, Dan, came the future judges of Israel?**

No. Moses' tribe was Levi.

**974. . . . all the 300,000 men who left Egypt were armed?**

No. There were 600,000 men who left Egypt.

**975. . . . Moses' "right-hand man," Korach, later took the Israelites into the Promised Land?**

No. It was Joshua who achieved that.

**976. . . . Moses' brother, Nachshon, became the first High Priest?**

No. His brother's name was Aaron.

**977. . . . as they traveled through the desert, the Israelites were guided by a pillar of fire by night and a company of angels by day?**

No. By day they were protected by a pillar of cloud.

**978. . . . as they stood by the Red Sea, God told Moses to lift up the hem of his garment and the waters would part?**

No. He was told to lift up his rod.

**979. . . . the victory song that all the Israelites sang is called the Shirah?**

Correct.

**980. . . . Moses remained the leader of Israel throughout the thirty years of wandering?**

No. They wandered for forty years.

**981. . . . Moses personally carried with him the coffin of Joseph?**

Correct.

**982. . . . the Israelites all carried their prayer books in a sack upon their backs?**

No. They carried their utensils for kneading and baking.

**983. . . . the festival is called Pesach (Passover) because the Israelites "passed over" the corpses of the Egyptian firstborn on their way out of Egypt?**

No. It was because God "passed over" the Israelites' homes when He slew the Egyptian firstborn.

**984. . . . the Israelites were commanded to smear blood on their doorposts and foreheads?**

No. Not on their foreheads, but on the lintels (top horizontal beams) of their doors.

**985. . . . if the Paschal lamb was too big for a family to eat, they were allowed to eat chicken instead?**

No. They were to invite their neighbors to join with them.

**986. . . . when they ate the lamb, the Israelites were to be dressed and ready for the journey, with their flowing robes hitched up by a belt and carrying their walking sticks?**

Correct.

**987. . . . Moses sent out ten spies to bring back a full report about the Promised Land?**

No. He sent twelve spies.

**988. . . . one man was punished for publicly desecrating the Sabbath by gathering fruit?**

No. He gathered sticks.

**989.** . . . one day, when Moses and his family were staying at an hotel on the way to Egypt, God confronted him and threatened to kill him for having failed to circumcise his son?

Correct.

**990.** . . . his wife, Tzipporah, took a flint stone and carried out the operation herself?

Correct.

**991.** . . . the land of Canaan, which God gave to the Israelites, was inhabited by such tribes as the Hittites, Amorites, Yeshurites, and Perizzites?

Not the Yeshurites.

**992.** . . . Moses' first request to Pharaoh was simply for the Israelites to be permitted to go into the desert to celebrate a two-day festival?

No. It was for a three-day festival.

**993.** . . . when Moses first saw the Burning Bush, his reaction was curiosity to understand why it did not burn out?

Correct.

**994.** . . . God told him to remove his turban because the place where he was standing was holy ground?

No. He was told to remove his shoes.

**995.** . . . Moses smashed the two clay Tablets on which the Ten Commandments were engraved because of his shock at seeing the Israelites worship the Golden Calf?

No. They were two tablets of stone.

**996.** . . . when the Israelites fought the Amalekites, the battle went Israel's way as long as Moses' hands were raised in prayer to God, but when he lowered his hands, Amalek gained the upper hand?

Correct.

**997.** . . . to ensure that the Israelites continued to gain the upper hand until victory was secured, a stone was placed under Moses' arms to support them in a raised position?

Correct.

**998.  . . . when God spoke the Ten Commandments at Sinai, the people were so excited at hearing His voice that they broke out into spontaneous songs of praise?**

No. They were so frightened that they asked Moses to relay to them what God was saying.

**999.  . . . before Moses was buried, by his brother, Aaron, and his two children, he was allowed a glimpse of the Promised Land?**

No. No one was present at his death and burial. However, he was allowed that glimpse.

**1,000.  . . . the journey of the Israelites through the desert is commemorated by the festival of Shavuot?**

No. The festival of Sukkot.

**1,001.  Can you recommend some other activities to keep the interest of children (and adults) during the Seder?**

We present below some ideas, but we stress that, just like any successful event involving more than one person, there is no substitute for advanced planning. The "religious Seder entertainment" needs to be carefully thought out in relation to the number and ages of your children and guests. Some of the suggestions below require collecting or making certain items before the Seder. So don't leave it to the last minute! Here's to a memorable Seder which will leave a lasting and warm impression on all your guests, young and old.

## FROM FIVE YEARS

1. Tell them in good time before Pesach to prepare acting out the Ten Plagues. They might do it in a different order, and see if the adults can guess which plague they are presenting.
2. Tell them in good time before Pesach to prepare "faces" of the Four Sons. These can be made by using round paper plates, with wool for hair, buttons for eyes, and so on. Two apertures should be punched, and strung through to enable the "faces" to be tied around the head. Children should hide the faces around the living room(s) before the Seder starts, and, when the time for the game arrives, the adults must look for the faces, and guess which "Son" they have found. Any adult who guesses wrong has to wear that face for five minutes!
3. Dress the children up in flowing robes (sheets may be used), with a sack over their shoulder, containing *matzah* "for the journey." Act out with them the going out of Egypt, the fear of seeing the Egyptian army approaching, the jumping into the Red Sea and arriving on the other side, and the witnessing of the Egyptians pursuing them into the sea and then drowning. End with a circle dance of thanksgiving to God, using any jolly Hebrew song they know (such as, *Am Yisrael Chay* or *David Melekh Yisrael*).

## FROM SEVEN YEARS

1. The adults act out or mime part of the story of Joseph, and of the Children of Israel in Egypt and the Exodus, and the children have to guess which particular episodes they are depicting.
2. Discuss with the children what life might have been like for the Israelites as slaves. Ask them to list particular things they like to do and then to consider, item by item, whether they think the Israelite children of their age, being slaves, would have been able to enjoy those things.
3. Select one of the children to be Moses. Dress him or her in a flowing robe (sheet) and seat him or her at the top of the Seder table. Each guest asks Moses a question about his life and leadership, and why he acted as he did at different times.

## FROM TEN YEARS TO ADULTS

1. You have just seen the Red Sea split. Give an interview to a reporter from the Egyptian newspaper, The *Raamses Times*, describing everything you witnessed and your feelings about what happened to the Egyptian army.
2. The Yes–No Game: One child is chosen to be Moses, and each person around the table, in rapid succession, asks him or her questions about Moses' life and leadership. The questions should be phrased to elicit the answer "yes" or "no," but Moses must not use either of those words in his response—which also, must not be delayed. If the child says either "yes" or "no," he or she can no longer be leader, and the one who tricked him or her into that reply takes over the hot seat as Moses.
3. "When the Israelites left Egypt they took . . ." This is a memory game. The Seder leader starts by using the above formula and adding *one* item that the Israelites might have taken with them when they left Egypt (e.g., *matzah*, a tent, a sack, a staff, robes, baking tins, etc.). The person next to him repeats the formula, adding the item his next-door neighbor has just added, and then adding to it his own item, and so on, around the table. The list will soon get so long that people will inevitably be knocked out as they fail to get the list right. We need not insist upon the perfect order of items, providing no item was omitted.
4. The "Immediate Response" Game: Go around the table, firing off statements from the list below. You might wish to supplement this with your own statements (humorous or serious). The answer must be given instantaneously. Any fumbled or irrelevant or patently silly answers, puts the respondent out of the game.

A Jewish hero I admire is . . .

A general I admire is . . .

Intermarriage is . . .

I'm a Jew because . . .

When I see a *hasid* . . .

As far as I am concerned, Arabs . . .

Seder night is . . .

I feel proud to be Jewish when . . .

I am the ideal Jew because . . .

One fault I have is . . .

I'd be ready to lose my freedom for . . .

In one hundred years' time I'd like to see . . .

Judaism is the easiest religion because . . .

Judaism is the hardest religion because . . .

Chopped liver is . . .

I'd never be a vegetarian because . . .

I'd never eat meat because . . .

The three things I can't stand are . . .

If I had unlimited money, I'd . . .

I just have to live in Israel because . . .

5. The "Find the Seder Champion Public Speaker" Game ("Just a Half-Minute"). Starting with the person on the left of the one leading the Seder, each person has to speak for a half-minute without deviation, hesitation or repetition of a key word. The one leading the Seder, or a volunteer, acts as chairman and time-keeper.

A successful challenge from anyone around the table enables that person to continue speaking on that subject for as much time as remains from the allocated half-minute. If, at the end of that period, they are still speaking uninterruptedly, they are awarded one point. Anyone who interrupts with a challenge that is rejected by the chairman forfeits his participation in the game.

Below are ten numbered subject headings. The person whose turn it is to speak chooses a number, and speaks on the corresponding subject.

1. *Maror*.

2. How my ancestors prepared for the Exodus from Egypt.

3. Which of the "Four Sons" I think I am.

4. Why I like Pesach best of all the festivals.

5. The Ten Plagues.

6. If the Temple were rebuilt today.

7. That we eat too much on Pesach.

8. What I mean by "Next Year in Jerusalem."

9. If Elijah allowed me the fulfillment of one wish.

10. What Judaism means to me.

# References

This reference list is restricted to major works actually referred to or quoted in the body of the text or notes to the text. Where no publisher is listed, a private publication—usually that of the author himself—may be assumed.

Adler, E. N., ed. *Jewish Travellers*. London: George Routledge and Sons, 1930.

Amram bar Sheshna Gaon. See *Seder Rav Amram* (next section).

Ben-Ami, I. *Yahadut Marokko*. Jerusalem: Reuven Mass, 1975.

Ben-Sasson, H. H. *A History of the Jewish People*. Cambridge, MA: Harvard University Press, 1976.

Ben-Zvi, I. *Sefer Ha-Shomronim*. Jerusalem: Yitzchak Ben-Zvi Foundation, 1976.

Bleich, J. D. *Contemporary Halakhic Problems*. 3 vols. New York: Ktav Publishing House, 1977.

Buber, M. *Moses*. Oxford: East and West Library, 1947.

Cohen, J. M. *Moments of Insight*. London: Vallentine, Mitchell and Co., 1989.

——. *Blessed Are You*. Northvale, NJ: Jason Aronson Inc., 1993.

——. *Prayer and Penitence*. Northvale, NJ: Jason Aronson Inc., 1994.

——. *Yizkor: A Memorial Booklet*. London: Gnesia Publications, 1994.

Dimont, M. *Jews, God and History*. London: W. H. Allen, 1964.

Dobrinsky, H. C. *A Treasury of Sephardic Laws and Customs*. New York: Yeshivah University Press, 1988.

*Encyclopaedia Judaica*. Jerusalem: Keter Publication House, 1972.

*Encyclopaedia Talmudit*. Jerusalem: Talmudic Encyclopaedia Publications, Ltd., 1955.

Epstein, Rabbi Yechiel Michael. See *Arukh Ha-Shulchan* (next section).

Feinstein, Rabbi Mosheh. See *Iggrot Mosheh* (next section).

Ferber, Z. H. *Kerem Ha-Zevi*. London: Jonathan Winegarten, 1983.

Finkelstein, L. "The Oldest Midrash: Pre-Rabbinic Ideals and Teachings in the Passover Haggadah." *Harvard Theological Review* 31 (1938): p. 291.

——. "The Origin of the Hallel." *Hebrew Union College Annual* 23 (1950–1951): 324.

Gaguine, S. *Keter Shem Tov*. London: author, 1948.

Goldschmidt, D. *The Passover Haggadah: Its Sources and History*. Jerusalem: Bialik Institute, 1960.

Grant, M. *The Jews in the Roman World*. London: Weidenfeld and Nicolson, 1973.

Greenburg, W. H. *The Haggadah According to the Rite of Yemen.* London: David Nutt, 1896.

Greenwald, Y. *Kol Bo Al Aveilut.* New York: Moriah, 1947.

Honig, L., ed. *Haggadah Shel Pesach LeMaharal.* London: L. Honig and Sons, 1960.

Hyman, M. *Indian–Jewish Cooking.* London: Hyman Publishers, 1992.

Isserles, R. Moses, See *Remah* (next section).

Jakobson, Y. *Netiv Binah.* Vol. 4. Tel Aviv: Sinai, 1978.

Josephus, Flavius. *Jewish War (Bellum Judaicum).* London: Loeb Classical Library, 1926-1963.

Kuk, I. *Olat Re'iyah.* Jerusalem: Mosad HaRav Kuk, 1989.

Lamm, M. *The Jewish Way in Death and Mourning.* New York: Jonathan David, 1969.

Lehrman, S. *Jewish Customs and Folklore.* London: Shapiro, Vallentine and Co., 1964.

Leshem, C. *Shabbat Umoadei Yisrael.* Tel Aviv: Niv, 1969.

Levinsky, Y. T. *Sefer Ha-Moadim.* 9 vols. Tel Aviv: Devir, 1960.

Luzzatto, S. D. *Tal Orot.* 1881.

Neuwirth, Y. Y. *Shemirath Shabbat Ke-hilkhatah.* Jerusalem and New York: Feldheim, 1984.

Pichenik, A. H. "Tisporet ha-zakan biyemei ha-sefirah." In *Shanah BeShanah* Yearbook. Jerusalem: Heikhal Shelomo, 1974, pp. 220-223.

Polakov, L. *The History of Antisemitism.* 4 vols. London: Routledge & Kegan Paul, 1974.

Pritchard, J. B. *Ancient Near Eastern Texts Relating to the Old Testament.* (2nd ed.) Princeton, NJ: Princeton University Press, 1955.

Redford, R. A. *The Pulpit Commentary.* London: Kegan Paul, Trench, Truebner and Co., 1897.

Sanua, V. D. "The Vanished World of Egyptian Jewry." *Judaism* 43:2 (Spring 1994): 212-219.

Sarna, N. *Understanding Genesis.* New York: Schocken Books, 1970.

Segal, B. J. "The Theme of the Song of Songs." *Dor Le-Dor,* 15:2 (Winter 1986–87): 106-113.

Silbermann, A. M. *The Children's Haggadah.* 1st ed. London: Shapiro Vallentine, 1933.

Sperber, D. *Minhagei Yisrael.* Jerusalem: Mosad Ha-Rav Kuk, 1990.

Stein, S. "The Influence of Symposia Literature on the Literary Form of the Pesach Haggadah." *Journal of Jewish Studies* 8 (1956): 13-45.

Szyk, A. *The Haggadah.* Ed. C. Roth. Jerusalem and Tel Aviv: Massadah and Alumoth, 1960.

Ta-Shema, Y. *Minhag Ashkenaz Ha-Kadmon.* Jerusalem: Magnes Press, Hebrew University, 1992.

Toledano, P. "The Halakot of Pesach." *Spanish and Portuguese Synagogue Bulletin.* March 1992.

Turetsky, M. *A Critical Edition and Translation of the Karaite Liturgy for Passover.* Unpublished Ph.D. thesis, University of Leeds, 1963.

Turnowsky, W. ed. *Four Haggadot.* Facsimile ed. Tel Aviv: W. Turnowsky, n.d.

Wetzstein, J. G. "Die syrische Dreschtafel." *Zeitschrift fur Ethnologie* 5 (1873): 270-302.

Wieder, N. *The Judean Scrolls and Karaism.* Oxford, U.K.: Oxford University Press, 1962.

Yaari, A. *Bibliography of the Passover Haggadah.* Jerusalem: Bamberger and Wahrman, 1960.

Yahudah, A. S. *The Language of the Pentateuch in Its Relation to Egyptian.* Oxford, U.K.: Oxford University Press, 1933.

Yerushalmi, Y. H. *Haggadah and History.* Philadelphia: Jewish Publication Society of America, 1975.

Zeitlin, S. "The Liturgy of the First Night of Passover." *Jewish Quarterly Review* (n.s.) 38 (1948): 455.

Zunz, L. *Literaturgeschichte der synagogalen Poesie.* Berlin, 1865.

## PRIMARY RABBINIC SOURCES
## (INCLUDING BACKGROUND INFORMATION)

*Abudraham Ha-Shalem.* Halakhic commentary on the liturgy and rules of prayer by fourteenth-century Spanish authority, R. David Abudraham. First published, Lisbon, 1490. Frequently republished; critical edition, ed. S. A. Wertheimer, Jerusalem, 1959.

*Arukh Ha-Shulchan.* 8 vols. Novellae and halakhic rulings on the four parts of the *Shulchan Arukh,* by Rabbi Yechiel Michael Epstein (1829–1908). Tel Aviv: Yetzu Sifrei Kodesh, n.d.

*Avot D'Rabbi Natan.* Midrashic treatment and amplification of Mishnah *Avot.* Critical edition, ed. S. Z. Schechter. Vienna: M. Knoepfelmocher, 1887.

*Ba'er Heitev.* Commentary on the *Shulchan Arukh* by R. Judah b. Simeon Ashkenazi, eighteenth-century German codifier. Amsterdam, 1742.

*Bet Ha-Levi.* 2 vols. of novellae on the Talmud by R. Joseph Baer Soloveitchik, also incorporating 102 responsa and sermons. Vilna: Reuven Romm, 1863.

*Bet Yoseph.* Commentary on the *Tur* by Joseph Karo. First published 1555. Appended to most editions of the *Tur.*

*Biur Halakhah.* Supplementary glosses, added by R. Yisrael Meir Ha-Cohen to his *Mishnah Berurah,* and printed in all editions.

*Chatam Sofer.* Extensive writings of talmudic novellae and 7 vols. of responsa, by R. Moses Sofer (1762–1839). Pressburg, 1855–1912.

*Chayyei Adam.* Popular halakhic work based upon *Orach Chayyim,* by R. Abraham ben Yechiel Michal Danzig (1748–1820). Zolkiev: S. D. M. Hoffer, 1837.

*Chazon Ish.* Talmudic novellae and responsa of R. Avraham Yeshaya Karelitz (1878–1958). Vilna, 1911.

*Chazon Ovadiah.* Commentary on the Haggadah with lengthy introduction covering many aspects of Pesach, by R. Ovadiah Yoseph. Jerusalem: Yeshivat Porat Yoseph, 1979.

*Choshen Mishpat.* Third section of Karo's *Shulchan Arukh.* Treats Jewish civil law (see *Shulchan Arukh*). Also name of third section of Yechiel b. Asher's Code (see *Tur*), on whose four-part division Karo based the structure of his own code.

*Da'at Zekeinim Mi-Ba'alei Ha-Tosafot*. Eclectic commentary on Pentateuch attributed to the twelfth–fourteenth-century Franco-German school of the Tosaphists (see *Tosafot*).

*Darkei Mosheh*. See *Remah*.

*Entziklopedia Talmudit*. Monumental talmudic encyclopedia. 22 vols. Published to date. Founding eds., R. Meir Berlin and R. S. Y. Zevin. Jerusalem, 1946. See *Encyclopaedia Talmudit* (in first section).

*Etz Chayyim*. Twelfth-century liturgical work of Jacob b. Judah, reflecting the traditions of pre-expulsion England and northern France. 3 vols. Ed. I. Brodie. Jerusalem: Mosad HaRav Kuk. 1962-1967.

*Hagahot Maharsham*. Seven volumes of responsa by R. Shalom Mordechai ben Moses Shvadron, distinguished Galician Rabbi (1835-1911). Stomaru, 1932.

*Haggadah Shel Pesach im Likutei Taamim Minhagim Ubiurim*. Ed. R. M. M. Schneersohn. New York: Kehot Publication Society, 1976.

*Haggadah Shel Pesach LeMaharal*. London: L. Honig and Sons, 1960.

*Ha-Torah VeHa-Mitzvot*. Commentary on Bible by R. Meir Leibusch Malbim. New York: Torath Israel Publishing Co., 1950.

*Iggrot Mosheh*. Collected responsa of R. Mosheh Feinstein, grouped according to chronological order of four sections of *Shulchan Arukh*. New York: Moriah Press, 1959.

*Kanfei Yonah*. Commentary to the Haggadah by R. Jonah Eddlesohn. Published in *Haggadah Shel Pesach Migdal Eder HeChadash*. New York: Netzach Yisrael Publishers, 1955. First edition included in commentary section on *Midrash Shir Hashirim Rabbah*. Warsaw, 1875.

*Kerem Ha-Zevi*. See under Z. H. Ferber (in first section).

*Keter Shem Tov*. See under S. Gaguine (in first section).

*Ketav Sofer*. Responsa of R. Abraham Samuel Sofer (1815-1871). Pressburg, 1879.

*Kitzur Shulchan Arukh*. Popular digest of laws of *Shulchan Arukh* (taking account of Ashkenazi glosses of Moses Isserles; see *Remah*), compiled by R. Solomon Ganzfried (1804-1886). Ungvar, 1864.

*Kol Bo Al Aveilut*. Y. Greenwald. New York: Moriah, 1947.

*Likkutei Sichos*. Published lectures of Rabbi M. M. Schneersohn of Lubavitch. New York: Kehot Publication Society, 1985; 1989.

*Machzor Vitri*. Prayer book and commentary (including Laws of Prayer), by R. Simcha b. Samuel (d. 1105) of Vitri (disciple of Rashi), and reflecting halakhic traditions of Franco-Germany.

*Magen Avraham*. Commentary on the *Shulchan Arukh* by R. Avraham Abeli Gombiner (1637-1683). Appended to most editions.

*Masekhet Soferim*. Late minor talmudic tractate. Published with standard editions of Babylonian Talmud (see below, *Talmud Bavli*.)

*Meiri*. Rabbi Menachem ben Solomon (1249-1316). Author of *Bet Ha-Bechirah* commentary on all tractates of the Talmud. Modern editions all based upon one complete (Parma) manuscript. Tractate *Yevamot* (cited) first published in Salonika (Abulafia) 1794.

*Mekhilta.* Tanaitic Midrash on book of Exodus. I. H. Weiss. Vienna: J. Schlossberg, 1865. Many other editions.

*Mekhilta deRabbi Shimon bar Yochai.* Critical edition, based upon *Midrash Ha-Gadol* and fragments discovered in Cairo Geniza. Ed. J. N. Epstein and E. Z. Melamed. Jerusalem: Mekitzei Nirdamim, 1955.

*Metzudat Tziyyon.* Popular commentary, offering simple explanations of textual meanings of the books of Prophets and Hagiographa, by R. David Altschuler, eighteenth-century Bible exegete. Formed part of his main work, *Binyan Ha-Bayit.* 5 vols. Leghorn, 1780–1782.

*Midrash Rabbah.* Various editions, including Jerusalem, Rome, Vilna.

*Midrash Tanchuma.* Various editions. With commentaries "Etz Yoseph" and "Anaph Yoseph" by R. Chanokh Zundel b. Yoseph. New York and Berlin: Horeb, 1924.

*Mishnah.* Various editions. Trans. H. Danby. London: Oxford University Press, 1933. *Art Scroll* (with commentary), ed. N. Scherman and M. Zlotowitz; New York, 1982. Commentaries: P. Blackman, 7 vols., Oxford, 1951–1956; P. Kehati, 12 vols., Jerusalem, 1963.

*Mishnah Berurah.* Halakhic Code and commentary on *Shulchan Arukh Orach Chayyim* by R. Yisrael Meir Ha-Cohen (*Chafetz Chayyim;* 1838–1933).

*Mishneh Torah.* See *Rambam.*

*Netiv Binah.* See under Y. Jakobson (in first section).

*Nimmukei Yoseph.* Talmudic and halakhic novellae on commentary of Isaac Alfasi (Rif), covering seven tractates by R. Yoseph ibn Chaviva (fifteenth century). Mantua, 1550.

*Nodah BiYehudah.* Responsa of R. Yechezkiel Landau (1713–1793). Prague: J. L. Rubenstein, 1776.

*Olat Re'iyah.* See under I. Kuk (in first section).

*Orach Chayyim.* Title of one of the four main sections into which the *Shulchan Arukh* is divided. This section deals with the subjects of prayer, blessings and daily rituals, Sabbath, and various festivals and fasts.

*Otzar Ha-Geonim.* 12 vols. Ed. B. M. Levin. Haifa–Jerusalem: Otzar Ha-Geonim Publications, 1928–1942.

*Oznayim La-Torah.* Commentary to the Pentateuch by R. Zalman Sorotzkin. First published 1951–1960. 7th ed. 5 vols. Jerusalem: Ha-Vaad Lehotza'at Sifrei Ha-Gaon Rav Zalman Sorotzkin, 1990.

*Pri Chadash.* Commentary on *Shulchan Arukh, Orach Chayyim, Yoreh De'ah* and laws of divorce. R. Hezekiah ben David daSilva. Amsterdam, 1730.

*Pri Megadim.* R. Joseph ben Meir Teomim (1727–1792). Commentary to the *Shulchan Arukh.* Frankfort on the Oder, 1771–1772.

*Radak.* Acronym of Rabbi David Kimchi. Author of standard biblical commentary to Prophets and Sacred Writings, 1160–1235. First published in Venice edition of the *Rabbinic Bible* (1548) and in most subsequent editions.

*Radbaz.* Responsa of R. David ibn Abi Zimra (1479–1573), distinguished halakhist and kabbalist who published three thousand responsa over a forty-year period as Chief Rabbi of Cairo. Warsaw ed., 1862.

*Rambam.* Moses Maimonides, halakhist and philosopher (1135–1204). Author of many works, including major Code of Jewish Law (*Mishneh Torah*), commentary on the *Mishnah* (*Peirush Ha-Mishnayot Le-Ha-Rambam*), philosophical work (*Guide to the Perplexed*), epistles to communities, and so forth.

*Ramban.* Moses Nachmanides (1194–1270), talmudist and Bible commentator. Commentary published in most editions of rabbinic Pentateuchs. A critical edition, based upon manuscripts and early printing, was issued by C. D. Chavel. Jerusalem: Mosad Ha-Rav Kuk, 1959–1960.

*Ran.* Commentator on Talmud and Halakhot of Isaac Alfasi (Rif) by R. Nissim b. Reuven of Gerondi. Constantinople, 1711.

*Rashba.* Talmudic novellae (*Chiddushei Ha-Rashba*) by R. Shelomo b. Avraham Adret (1235–1310). Various editions. Venice, 1523.

*Rashbam.* R. Shmuel b. Meir (1080–1158). Grandson of Rashi, talmudic commentator and author of commentary on Pentateuch.

*Remah.* Acronym for R. Moses Isserles, author of standard Glosses to all four sections of Karo's *Shulchan Arukh,* codifying divergent Ashkenazi practices. Separately titled *Mapah,* though work was incorporated into the main body of the text in all standard editions and distinguished by the employment of a special ("Rashi-type") script. Also wrote *Darkei Mosheh* and commentary on all four sections of the *Tur,* as well as numerous responsa.

*Rosh.* Comprehensive halakhic compendium on entire Talmud (*Tosafot Ha-Rosh*) by R. Asher b. Yechiel (1250–1327). Fiorda, 1745.

*Seder Rav Amram.* First attempt to produce a systematic text of the prayers, by Amram Gaon (858–870). Quoted extensively by Rashi, Tosafot, Karo, and others, though only in 1865 was complete manuscript of the work discovered. Ed. D. Goldschmidt. Jerusalem: Mosad HaRav Kuk, 1972.

*Seder Tephillot Kol Ha-Shanah.* Superscription of Maimonides' (1135–1204) "Order of Prayer," incorporated as section of the Laws of Prayer in his *Mishneh Torah.*

*Sefer Ha-Chinukh.* Anonymous work on 613 biblical *mitzvot,* popularly attributed to Aaron b. Joseph Ha-Levi of Barcelona (1235–1300). 1st edition, Venice, 1523. Critical edition, C. B. Chavel. Jerusalem: Mosad HaRav Kuk, 1962.

*Sefer Ha-Manhig.* Liturgical work of R. Abraham b. Nathan Ha-Yarchi (1155–1215). First published, Constantinople, 1519. Rep., Berlin: J. M. Goldberg, 1855. Critical edition based on various manuscripts, Jerusalem: Levin-Epstein, 1961.

*Sefer Ha-Sichos.* Writings of R. Menachem Mendel Schneersohn of Lubavitch. New York: Kehot Publication Society, 1989.

*Sforno.* Ovadiah ben Yaakov, Italian Bible commentator (1470–1550). Wrote commentary on Pentateuch, Song of Songs, and Ecclesiastes (Venice, 1567), and on Jonah, Habakkuk, and Zechariah (Amsterdam, 1724–1728). See *Biur Ha-Seforno al Ha-Torah,* Jerusalem: Mosad HaRav Kuk, 1984.

*Sha'ar Efrayim.* Responsa on the *Shulchan Arukh* by R. Ephraim bar Jacob Ha-Kohen (1616–1678). Sulzbach: R. Aryeh Loeb Ha-Kohen, 1689.

*Shearim Metzuyanim Behalakhah.* Edition of *Kitzur Shulchan Arukh,* R. S. Z. Braun. New York: Feldheim, 1978. With halakhic commentary, embodying modern problems and rulings of later and contemporary authorities.

*Shemirat Shabbat Ke-hilkhatah.* See under Y. Y. Neuwirth (first section).

*Shibbolei Ha-Leket.* By Zedekiah ben Avraham Anav (thirteenth century). Popular halakhic compendium. Abridged editions published; Venice, 1546; Vilna, 1886. Full version only discovered in recent times, and published by S. Buber as *Shibbolei Ha-Leket Ha-Shalem.* 1886.

*Shulchan Arukh.* Authoritative Code of Jewish Law, compiled by R. Joseph Karo (1488–1575), though not taking account of divergent Ashkenazi practices (but see *Remah*).

*Siddur Saadiah.* The *Siddur* was compiled in Sura, Babylonia, in 985, but only one manuscript survived, from which an edition by I. Davidson, S. Assaf, and B. I. Joel was published. New York: Mekitzei Nirdamim, 1941.

*Talmud Bavli.* Babylonian Talmud. Various editions; Jerusalem, Rome, Vienna, Vilna. English-language edition, ed. I. Epstein. London: Soncino, 1948–1957. Hebrew annotated edition, A. Steinsaltz (several tractates issued to date). Jerusalem: Institute for Talmudic Publications, 1967. ArtScroll series, New York: Mesorah Publications, 1991.

*Talmud Yerushalmi.* Palestinian Talmud. Krotoschin, 1886.

*Talmud Yerushalmi Ha-Gadol.* 6 vols. Vilna: Romm Press, 1922.

*Targum.* Aramaic versions of Bible; Onkelos, Pseudo-Jonathan (*Targum Yonatan*), fragmentary *Targum* (*Yerushalmi,* etc.), as printed in various editions of the rabbinic Bible.

*Taz.* See *Turei Zahav.*

*Tosafot.* Collection of comments on the Talmud and earlier authorities (especially Rashi). Printed together with Rashi in all standard editions of the Talmud.

*Tur.* Major halakhic code of Jacob b. Asher (full title, *Arbaah Turim*). 1st complete edition, Piove di Sacco, 1455. Warsaw, 1882; Jerusalem: Feldheim, 1969.

*Turei Zahav (Taz).* Halakhic commentary to *Shulchan Arukh,* by R. David b. Shemuel Ha-Levi. 1st edition, on *Yoreh Deah,* Lublin, 1646. Now published in most editions.

*Vilna Gaon Haggadah.* Ed. N. Scherman and M. Zlotowitz. New York: Mesorah Publications, 1993.

*Yalkut Me'am Lo'ez.* Expositional Ladino Bible commentary by Rabbi Jacob Culi (1685–1732). Jerusalem: Ohr Chadash Publications, 1967.

*Yalkut Shim'oni.* Jerusalem: Levin-Epstein, 1967.

# Index

Note that the numbers correspond to questions, not pages.

## About the Author

Rabbi Jeffrey M. Cohen has distinguished himself in the field of religious affairs as a broadcaster, lecturer, writer, and reviewer. A graduate of the Yeshivot of Manchester and Gateshead, Rabbi Cohen received a master's degree in philosophy from London University and a Ph.D. from Glasgow University. He is the author of several books, including *Understanding the Synagogue Service, Understanding the High Holyday Services, A Samaritan Chronicle, Horizons of Jewish Prayer, Moments of Insight, Blessed Are You: A Comprehensive Guide to Jewish Prayer,* and *Prayer and Penitence: A Commentary on the High Holy Day Machzor,* as well as over 200 articles. He is a member of the cabinet of the chief rabbi of Great Britain. He currently serves as the rabbi of Stanmore and Canons Park Synagogue, the largest Orthodox congregation in Great Britain. He and his wife, Gloria, reside in London. They have four children and five grandchildren.